American Indian Rock Art

Volume 46

Dinétah, New Mexico • Richard Jenkinson

With Contributions By

Peter Anick

Evelyn Billo

Amanda M. Castañeda

Jon Harman

Janine Hernbrode

Richard Jenkinson

David A. Kaiser

James D. Keyser

Charles W. Koenig

Chester R. Liwosz

Lawrence Loendorf

Robert Mark

David L. Minick

César A. Quijada

Jerod L. Roberts

Victoria L. Roberts

Richard A. Rogers

Karen L. Steelman

Cynthia Sturm

Mark Willis

American Indian Rock Art
Volume 46

Edited by Richard A. Rogers, Evelyn Billo, and Robert Mark

American Rock Art Research Association

Cupertino, California
2020

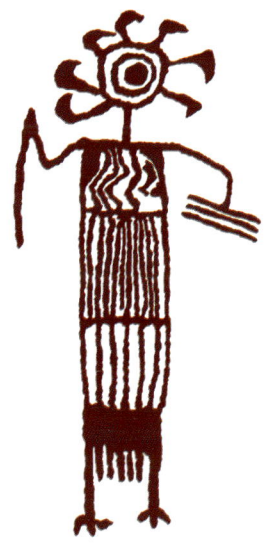

Compilation Copyright © 2020
American Rock Art Research Association

c/o Jack Wedgwood
20137 Las Ondas Way
Cupertino, California 95014-3132

This volume is published as a compilation of papers submitted by independent researchers. All rights to the content of individual papers remain with their respective authors.

ISBN 978-0-9888730-7-0

The American Rock Art Research Association is a 501(c)(3) non-profit organization.

Printed and bound in the United States of America.

Editors: *Richard A. Rogers, Evelyn Billo, and Robert Mark*
Copy Editing, Layout, and Design: *Ken Hedges and Anne McConnell*
Cover Layout: *Ken Hedges*
Cover Photograph: *Robert Mark (see page ix)*
Title Page Photograph: *Shumla Archaeological Research and Education Center (see page 65)*
Flyleaf Photograph: *Richard Jenkinson (see page 1)*

About the cover:

This year's cover highlights the iconic petroglyph panel from the Picture Canyon Natural and Cultural Preserve featured on the conference program cover and on the conference logo for the 46th Annual Meeting of the American Rock Art Research Association in Flagstaff, Arizona, June 14–17, 2019. For background on this panel and Sinagua rock art, see the essay by Evelyn Billo on page ix.

Printed by Jostens Commercial Printing,
Clarksville, Tennessee

Table of Contents

Preface vii

About the Cover—Contemplations on the Sinagua: History, Styles, and Interpretation
    Evelyn Billo. ix

Rock Art of Dinétah: Stories of Heroes and Healing
    Richard Jenkinson. 1

Hoofprints and Footprints—The Grammar of Biographic Rock Art
    David A. Kaiser and James D. Keyser. 23

Where are the Hohokam Leaders? An Examination of Complexity of Rock Art
    Anthropomorphs at Cocoraque Butte, Arizona
    Janine Hernbrode. 47

Portable X-ray Fluorescence Analyses at the Meyers Spring Pictograph Site
    Karen L. Steelman, Charles W. Koenig, Amanda M. Castañeda, Jerod L. Roberts,
    and Victoria L. Roberts 65

Re-Imagining Fremont: A Color Palette for the Ages
    James D. Keyser and David L. Minick 79

A Leviathan in the Desert
    Jon Harman 97

The Paintings of the Red Rock Shelter: An Example of Rock Graphics in the
    Central Coast of Sonora
    César A. Quijada 107
        Versión en Español 113

Contextualizing the Pictographs of Southwest Maine
    Peter Anick. 117

Samsal: A Bison-form Petroglyph Boulder Near the Sweet Grass Hills, Montana
    Cynthia Sturm and James D. Keyser 135

A Cryptic Carved Stone Head in the Santa Cruz Mountains: Implications of
    ICP-MS Results
    Chester R. Liwosz. 157

Tool Grooves and Drill Holes at the Robert's Indian Caves Site, New Mexico
    Lawrence Loendorf and Mark Willis 163

"Your Guess is as Good as Any": Rock Art, Public Interpretation, and Ownership
    Richard A. Rogers. 173

Picture Canyon • Robert Mark

Interpretive signage at the Waterbird panel, Picture Canyon Natural and Cultural Preserve.

Preface

The 46th annual conference of the American Rock Art Research Association (ARARA) was held on the campus of Northern Arizona University in Flagstaff, Arizona, June 14–17, 2019. Flagstaff sits at the base of the San Francisco Peaks on homelands sacred to Native Americans throughout the region. We therefore begin our introduction of this volume with a recognition and acknowledgment of the tribes on whose traditional lands we met, conversed, slept, ate, and walked. We give thanks for the opportunity to experience the images placed on rock by indigenous peoples during the millennia they have inhabited the region.

The conference included 24 research presentations and site reports along with five posters, and featured presentations by Hopi musician and storyteller Ed Kabotie, Diné archaeologist Jason Nez, Flagstaff-based writer and explorer Scott Thybony, and Coconino National Forest archaeologist Peter Pilles. From the conference's base at 7000 feet, field trips took participants in every cardinal direction, not to mention up and (mostly) down: from the Hopi mesas to Chevelon Canyon, Anderson Mesa to the Little Colorado River Valley, the San Francisco Peaks to the Verde Valley.

This volume of *American Indian Rock Art* contains 12 of the papers presented at the 2019 ARARA conference. Their subjects range geographically from Maine to coastal California, Baja California to the Great Plains, and the Colorado Plateau to the Sonoran and Chihuahuan deserts.

The first three papers in the volume present in-depth research into the rock art of particular times and places. Richard Jenkinson's highly accessible and informative paper, "Rock Art of Dinétah: Stories of Heroes and Healing," links traditional Navajo (Diné) stories directly to specific rock art images in the traditional Navajo homeland in northwest New Mexico. David Kaiser and James Keyser's "Hoofprints and Footprints—The Grammar of Biographic Rock Art" presents an analysis and identification of the "grammar" of this Plains rock art tradition, including the types of perspective used and how narratives are organized. Their paper demonstrates the value of combining careful formal analysis of the imagery with an informed approach rooted in the cultures that produced the imagery in order to identify the conventions that guided their creation and interpretation. Janine Hernbrode's "Where are the Hohokam Leaders? An Examination of Complexity of Rock Art Anthropomorphs at Cocoraque Butte, Arizona" is an ambitious analysis of over one thousand anthropomorphs in southern Arizona that not only details the types and frequency of various embellishments to the basic anthropomorphic form, but also works to correlate such embellishments with three periods of ancestral O'odham use of the area.

The next five papers each report on the rock art of a particular site or set of related sites, and each uses specific technologies to make sense of those marks on rock. "Portable X-ray Fluorescence Analyses at the Meyers Spring Pictograph Site" by Karen Steelman, Charles Koenig, Amanda Castañeda, Jerod Roberts, and Victoria Roberts reports on the use of pXRF for the non-destructive, in situ analysis of the elemental composition of the paint used to produce pictographs. This can aid in distinguishing pre-contact, post-contact, and modern rock paintings, all of which are present at the Meyers Spring site.

The four remaining papers in this group use DStretch to aid in the identification of imagery, but for somewhat different purposes. In "Re-Imagining Fremont: A Color Palette for the Ages," James Keyser and David Minick analyze "shorthand" Fremont anthropomorphs in the Uinta region of Utah and Wyoming, using DStretch to assist in identifying colors in the imagery other than the commonly visible red and white. Keyser and Minick then present digital reconstructions of what some Fremont panels may have looked like when all of the colors used were still visible. In "A Leviathan in the Desert," Jon Harman uses DStretch to identify a variety of figures at a Great Mural pictograph site in Baja California Sur, including a life-size orca. Harman's approach, involving not only digital enhancement but also an examination of traditional orca imagery in other rock art traditions and in other media, allows for a convincing identification of the image as an orca and furthers the identification of other images and superpositioning sequences on the panel. In "The Paintings of the Red Rock Shelter: An Example of Rock Graphics in the Central Coast of Sonora," César

Quijada reports on a recently identified site on the Sonoran coast of Mexico and utilizes DStretch to clearly identify the images as well as instances of superimpositioning (the original Spanish version of Quijada's paper follows the English version).

In "Contextualizing the Pictographs of Southwest Maine," Peter Anick also uses DStretch to identify faded indigenous imagery at two sites, which he then interprets in the context of the Canadian Shield pictograph tradition and Algonkian culture. One of the sites he examines, "Frye's Leap," has been a Euro-American tourist attraction for at least 200 years, and it is here that Anick's research merges into the next group of papers, which are focused in some way on rock art "oddities." In Anick's case, the "oddity" is that while this site evidences indigenous imagery, it is also described historically as having had several large images painted on it for tourists to view from passing steamboats. Anick's engaging historical research determines that Euro-Americans did indeed paint the rock with fake "Indian" images to promote tourism, but no trace of those images remains today.

The next three papers also explore rock art "oddities" of some kind. Perhaps the least "odd" of these is examined by Cynthia Sturm and James Keyser in "Samsal: A Bison-form Petroglyph Boulder Near the Sweet Grass Hills, Montana." This petroglyph boulder's shape has been modified with carvings to enhance the resemblance to a reclining bison, much like other, similar petroglyph boulders. However, it is also unique among known Plains petroglyph boulders in having a Biographic tradition fight scene in addition to marks consistent with the Hoofprint tradition. Significantly, Sturm and Keyser also document contemporary indigenous offerings at the site, which are consistent with those left at many other Great Plains rock art sites and evidences these sites' ongoing cultural significance to indigenous peoples.

While Sturm and Keyser worked to resolve inaccuracies in previous interpretations of the petroglyph boulder, in the next paper, "A Cryptic Carved Stone Head in the Santa Cruz Mountains: Implications of ICP-MS Results," Chester Liwosz attempts to decrypt the origins of a large carved and painted human head through the use of inductively coupled plasma mass spectrometry, a 3-D digital model to examine tool marks and tailings, and consultation with the local Ohlone Band of Native Americans. While few of the results are definitive as to time period or cultural affiliation, Liwosz concludes the head is likely the product of a "local folk art tradition" in Santa Cruz (aka "hippies"). As rock art sites are increasingly marked with contemporary images that mimic traditional imagery, unraveling this kind of mystery may become less of an oddity.

The final paper focused on rock art "oddities" is Lawrence Loendorf and Mark Willis's "Tool Grooves and Drill Holes at the Robert's Indian Caves Site, New Mexico." Grooves in particular are a phenomenon often encountered at rock art sites in the western U.S. and clearly have a utilitarian role in manufacturing and sharpening tools. Drill holes, while less common, are found at several other rock art sites in the Pecos region. In this case, Loendorf and Willis argue that the evidence points to both the grooves and holes as part of the process of manufacturing arrows. They also suggest that some painted designs associated with the grooves and holes could be the same as painted designs found on arrows, thereby linking some of the site's paintings to these types of utilitarian marks.

The final paper of the volume presents another kind of "oddity"—a paper not about rock art itself, but instead about how we "talk" about rock art. Richard Rogers's "'Your Guess is as Good as Any': Rock Art, Public Interpretation, and Ownership" examines how rock art is interpreted for the public, such as through interpretive signs and brochures. Focusing on how these materials characterize the relationship between indigenous images, contemporary Native communities, and contemporary (non-Native) visitors, Rogers assesses different approaches to public interpretation in terms of the ethical and political dimensions of cultural heritage management in an effort to identify "best" and "worst" practices.

This introduction of the papers that follow would be incomplete without a hearty "thank you!" to the authors and anonymous reviewers who directly contributed to the content of this volume, as well as the ARARA publications team, ARARA officers, and the conference planners and programmers, all of whom contribute to the ongoing success of *American Indian Rock Art*, the principal publication in North American rock art studies.

—Richard Rogers, Evelyn Billo, and Robert Mark

About the Cover
Contemplations on the Sinagua: History, Styles, and Interpretation

Evelyn Billo

This year's cover highlights one of the first petroglyph panels documented within the Picture Canyon Natural and Cultural Preserve (PCNCP) in Flagstaff, Arizona. Rock art plays a role in the history of the ancient peoples who thrived in the region that is southeast of their sacred San Francisco Peaks. The Hopi term for these regional indigenous people, "those who lived long ago," is *Hisat'sinom*, the descendants of the ancient *Motisinom* or "first people" (Downum 2012:2). Interpretive signs at PCNCP identify seven modern Native American groups with cultural ties to Picture Canyon, the Rio de Flag, and the plant, animal, and soil resources found there. These groups almost certainly have their own names for the ancient people who left their images on the ancient lava flow. Archaeologists identify three cultures in the region: Cohonina, Kayenta, and Sinagua.

The San Francisco volcanic field was appropriately named "Sierra sin Agua"—mountains without water—by Spanish explorers in 1598 (Bancroft 1888:139). The Pueblo Revolt of 1680 drove the Spanish out of the northern Southwest for a short time. Their journals sparked interest in Spain about the riches of the area, and in 1692 they returned. By the 1830s Anglo explorers arrived in the Flagstaff area, finding the Yavapai and Hualapai hunting there, but reported no permanent villages. Soon thereafter important pueblos like Wupatki and remains of villages like Turkey Tanks were reported. Sheep ranching prevailed until 1882 when the Atlantic and Pacific Railroad brought cattle ranchers, loggers, and many others. Dr. Harold S. and Mary-Russell Ferrell Colton honeymooned in Flagstaff in 1912. By 1938 Dr. Colton established the name Sinagua for the Ancestral Puebloan people who lived in the region of the black sands (volcanic ash and lava) of the Sierra Sinagua (Colton 1946). Weaver (2014–2015:40) describes the Northern Sinagua development pattern in the Flagstaff-Anderson Mesa region as starting ca. A.D. 600 with small scattered pithouses followed by larger settlements and masonry pueblos before ending by A.D. 1400.

Many Southwestern archaeologists and ethnographers tried to understand who was where and when

Picture Canyon • Robert Mark

based on pottery types, lithics, settlement patterns, burial practices, and material culture, but rarely on the petroglyphs and pictographs at their sites. The Coltons were exceptions. They first photographed and sketched petroglyph designs of various Picture Canyon panels during their excavation project in 1919. They visited Willow Springs (Tutuveni), north of Flagstaff near Tuba City, with Edmund Nequatewa, a Hopi who identified many of the petroglyph designs as clan symbols (Colton and Colton 1931). In 1928 they established the Museum of Northern Arizona to continue their research on the pottery and lifestyle of the Sinagua and provide a local safe place for items they collected. Many artifacts of the region were previously sent to other institutions, and locals wanted their own museum (Stein 2014–2015:34–36).

Dr. Colton (1932:24) published a survey of sites near Flagstaff that included Picture Canyon, noting that it "was named for the large number of petroglyphs which cover the basalt rocks; indeed, a notable array. It is a typical site of the people who made the Flagstaff red pottery." Colton's 1960 book *Black Sand: Prehistory in Northern Arizona* synthesized 42 years of analyzing pottery, lithics, structures, tree ring dates, migrations, trading, and petroglyphs. Figure 31 in the chapter "Drawings on Rock" compares ten classes of drawings from the Kayenta, Sinagua, and Cohonina areas. He suggested several reasons for the imagery but concluded that "the drawings do not represent any system of hieroglyphic writing. However, the drawings deserve much more study than has been given them and may in the future make more sense to us" (Colton 1960:84).

In the intervening 60 years the number of recorded archaeological sites in the Sierra Sinagua, many of which have petroglyphs and/or pictographs, has increased dramatically. There have been comprehensive rock art documentation projects on National Park Service, National Forest, Reservation, state, city, and private lands. However, paraphrasing Einstein, the more we learn, the less we know. To my knowledge, no comprehensive study of the distribution of specific design elements over the entire Sierra Sinagua Region has been published.

As Hays-Gilpin and Weaver (2012:19) observed, "Many of the images seen at Picture Canyon are ubiquitous across the prehistoric Southwestern landscape, but a few appear to be diagnostic of Sinagua rock art. Among the quintessentially Sinagua petroglyphs are anthropomorphs with prominent, round bellies, as well as complex geometric designs resembling those found on pottery and textiles."

What is clear is that many different groups of people over the centuries left their marks and paintings on the rocks in the Sierra Sinagua, and some current tribes maintain connections with their ancestral imagery. Tribal representatives shared information with our Picture Canyon Working Group's archaeology team that could be made public. Interpretive signage (see page vi) at the area of petroglyphs that most Picture Canyon Natural and Cultural Preserve visitors see reflects some of their observations:

Hopi consultants recognized the waterbird as the crane clan symbol and spirals as migration symbols.

Havasupai people, whose ancestors lived in or traveled through the Picture Canyon area, believe that some of the quadruped petroglyphs with curved horns are bighorn sheep, the guardians of the Grand Canyon.

The Zuni people believe the stick figure anthropomorphs that appear to have a tail represent the emergence of their people into this world from a watery underworld. Octavius Seowtewa, Zuni Tribal consultant, noted "Petroglyphs are the library for Zuni; it's how we know we were here."

Gertrude Smith, Yavapai Culture Director, said, "It is accepted that we, the Yavapai People, were known around the region as the People of the Sun."

References Cited

Bancroft, Hubert Howe
1888 *Arizona and New Mexico 1530–1888.* History of the Pacific States of North America, Volume 12. The History Company, San Francisco. (Also published with identical text and pagination in 1889 as *History of Arizona and New Mexico 1530–1888,* The Works of Hubert Howe Bancroft, Volume 17, The History Company, San Francisco.)

Colton, Harold S.
1932 *A Survey of Prehistoric Sites in the Region of Flagstaff, Arizona.* Bureau of American Ethnology Bulletin 104. Smithsonian Institution, Washington, D.C.

1946 *The Sinagua: A Summary of the Archaeology of the Region of Flagstaff, Arizona.* Museum of Northern Arizona Bulletin 22. Northern Arizona Society of Science and Art, Flagstaff Arizona.

1960 *Black Sand: Prehistory in Northern Arizona.* University of New Mexico Press, Albuquerque, New Mexico.

Colton, Mary-Russell F., and Harold S. Colton
1931 Petroglyphs, the Record of a Great Adventure. *American Anthropologist* 33(1):32–37.

Downum, Christian E.
2012 Hisat'sinom and the Sierra Sin Agua: Ancient Peoples and Places of the San Francisco Peaks. In *Hisat'sinom: Ancient Peoples in a Land without Water,* edited by Christian E. Downum, pp. 1–4. School for Advanced Research Press, Santa Fe, New Mexico.

Hays-Gilpin, Kelley, and Donald E. Weaver, Jr.
2012 Marks on the Land: Rock Art of the Sierra Sin Agua. In *Hisat'sinom: Ancient Peoples in a Land without Water,* edited by Christian E. Downum, pp. 16–25. School for Advanced Research Press, Santa Fe, New Mexico.

Stein, Pat
2014–2015 Picture Canyon: A Pivotal Point for Harold. S. Colton. *Plateau* 8(1–2):34–37.

Weaver, Donald E., Jr.
2014–2015 Picture Canyon's Petroglyphs and Ancient People. *Plateau* 8(1–2):38–47.

Rock Art of Dinétah:
Stories of Heroes and Healing

Richard Jenkinson

The Navajo rock art of the Largo Canyon area was made recently enough that ethnography can aid in identification of much of the artwork. This essay will look at this Navajo rock art in relation to Navajo mythology and ceremonies. Even today, Navajos would immediately associate many of these rock art images with particular characters and stories in their mythology.

This project started when I went on a URARA field trip to Dinétah led by Dave Manley and Tom Hahl. I had spent fourteen years on the Navajo reservation at the beginning of my teaching career, but I had never been to the Largo Canyon area to look for rock art. As I looked at the images on the rock surfaces, I realized that, for a change, I actually knew the cultural connections related to the rock art. I had taught Navajo traditional stories to Navajo students for years, and during that time I read everything I could find on the subject, as well as talking to Navajo elders in my community. I have looked at fantastic panels of Archaic rock art and wished I knew the stories and ceremonies connected to them, but this time, with the Navajo images, I actually felt that I knew some of the cultural connections to the iconography.

Dinétah is the old Navajo homeland. The word literally means "among the people" (Young 1980:817). Dinétah is located in northwestern New Mexico, east of Farmington and south to about Chaco Canyon. It is focused around the Largo and Gobernador drainages. Included are two sites very sacred to the Navajo, Gobernador Knob, birthplace of Changing Woman, and Huerfano Mesa, the place where her children, the hero twins, were raised.

In the 1600s and 1700s Dinétah was occupied by Athabaskan speakers who were joined by Puebloans, many of whom were seeking refuge from the Spanish around the time of the Pueblo Revolt of 1680. These two cultures coalesced to form the culture that is today's Navajo culture. Many of the Navajo ceremonies are considered to have originated during the occupation of Dinétah. Images of Navajo deities and other important cultural material are depicted in rock art at locations throughout the canyons where the ceremonies took place. In the late 1700s the Navajo left Dinétah and moved west to an area centered around Canyon de Chelly. Images for ceremonies were then made only in sandpaintings, a practice that continues into the present (Schaafsma and Tsosie 2009:18–19).

Since the core of Navajo culture has remained relatively stable since it was first observed by anthropologists in the late 1800s (Matthews 1883, 1897, 1902; Stevenson 1886), it is possible to examine the cultural context of the rock art imagery by using ethnographic materials. My approach is therefore ethnological, not archaeological. I taught Navajo literature to Native students

Richard Jenkinson
Kanab, Utah

in Kayenta, Arizona. As most Navajos would do, when I look at the rock art imagery I immediately think of the stories that are associated with the characters depicted. Navajo literature is indeed voluminous. If all of these stories and the others that branch off from them were told in their fullest versions, they would fill a few thousand pages. They provide a solid foundation for Navajo culture, for its history, spirituality, morality, and much more. As we look at the rock art of Dinétah, we have to see it in this cultural context. This essay will relate the rock art of Dinétah to the traditional stories, which are still very much alive in Navajo culture.

The Navajo Origin Story

It's time to review the basics of the Navajo origin story in order to give the rock art images some cultural context. These stories are still very much alive in today's Navajo culture. The stories vary with each storyteller and with each clan, but the essential elements are consistent. The origin story has appeared in print in many versions (Benally 1982; Fishler 1953; Haile 1981; Klah 1942; Matthews 1897; O'Bryan 1956; Zolbrod 1984). My two primary sources for this summary are Zolbrod (1984) and O'Bryan (1956). In the 1980s and early 1990s, I taught Navajo literature, including traditional stories, in Kayenta, Arizona, using Zolbrod as my primary text. The Zolbrod text is a rewrite of the myth as it appears in Washington Matthews's 1897 *Navaho Legends*. Matthews was a physician and a well-respected pioneering ethnologist, but he was not a skilled writer. Zolbrod cleaned up his text and provided proper Navajo orthography. Matthews's collaborator was Hatathli Nez or Tall Chanter. O'Bryan provides a more concise and coherent account of the first four worlds. His collaborator was Sandoval.

Most of the Navajo clans believe that today we are in the fifth world. A few agree with the Pueblo belief that we are in the fourth world. Each world is associated with a color. The first world was black. First Man and First Woman were there, along with two Coyotes and many insects. These are all supernatural beings. Human beings will not be created until the fifth world. The first world is crude with a great deal of fighting, so everyone moves up to the second world.

The second world is blue. The new creatures here are birds. The Navajo word for blue is "dootłʼizh," which encompasses both blue and green. The birds found in the second world have blue and green colors, including blue jays and swallows. Again there is too much fighting and everyone moves up to the third world.

The third world is yellow. There are rivers and sacred mountains. After a while the men and women get angry with each other and decide to live on opposite sides of the river, feeling that they can get along without each other. Their separation results in unnatural births, creating monsters that will have to be dealt with by the hero twins in the fifth world. After the men and women are reunited, Coyote steals the babies of the water creature, Tééhoołtsódii. She becomes enraged and floods out the third world, causing everyone to escape up a reed into the fourth world.

The fourth world is white. Coyote returns the babies to the Water Creature and the flooding stops just below the surface of the fourth world. This world is soggy from the flooding below and looks to be sterile. Everyone moves on up to the fifth world.

The fifth world is our present-day world. It is the multicolored or glittering world. The place of emergence is thought to be a small island in the middle of a lake in southwestern Colorado. Early in the fifth world a lot of basic things are established. Coyote creates death. Day and night are agreed upon. The sacred mountains are set in their places. The sun and moon are created, along with other things that are fundamental to life on earth. The well-known Coyote stories take place, culminating in the tragic story of Changing Bear Woman. The people encounter the Great Gambler in Chaco Canyon, just south of Dinétah, and an epic gambling battle takes place. We will look at some of these stories in relation to rock art images below.

Eventually Changing Woman, the primary figure in Navajo myth, is born. Her parents are Mother Earth and Father Sky, but she is raised by First Man and First Woman. She is called Changing Woman because of her age. Her age is cyclical, just like the seasons in nature. So sometimes she is old and then becomes young again. When she is born she is proportioned like an adult, but the size of a baby. She matures very rapidly and is soon impregnated by the rays of Jóhonaa'éí, the Sun Carrier. He is a character much like Zeus in Greek mythology. We will see his image in the rock art. Changing Woman gives birth to the hero twins, Monster Slayer and Born for Water. Their job is to rid the world of monsters in preparation for the creation of human beings. The slaying of the monsters is a major epic, parts of which are depicted in Dinétah rock art.

Some humans are created by First Man, First Woman, and the yé'ii. The yé'ii are a class of very powerful supernatural beings. They put ears of corn under a blanket. They sing and dance over this blanket and Niłchʼi, the wind, comes and blows through the new people and brings them to life, as the wind continues to do to this day. We can see the evidence of the wind blowing through us in the swirls of our fingertips and toes and the swirl of hair on top of our heads. Changing Woman creates other people by rubbing skin from her body and molding humans from it.

The story continues with the creation of the clans and finally works its way into what we would consider to be history.

Two Yé'ii

There are a few easily recognizable characters who appear repeatedly in the rock art of Dinétah. Probably the easiest to identify is Gháá'ask'idii (Figure 1), known in English as Humpback. He is identified by his hump, mountain sheep horns, and a staff or digging stick (Hadlock 1980; Schaafsma 1980:317–318). The hump is a cloud held in place by a rainbow, which is often fringed with eagle feathers (Young and Copeland 2018:20). The hump contains mist and seeds. Humpback is one of the Mountain Sheep People and is associated with the harvest. As we see in Figure 2, he can appear without horns or a staff, but he always has the hump.

The Navajo yé'ii are immortal supernatural beings who reside in a world parallel to ours. The term "yé'ii" is usually translated "Holy People," which is actually the translation for "Diyin Dine'é" (Young 1980:918). I prefer the more literal translation of "Supernatural Powers People" for "yé'ii" (Young 1980:756). The word "holy" implies that they are always good and pure, which is often not the case for the yé'ii.

Song, dance, and visual imagery are used to attract the yé'ii to healing ceremonies so that they can return the patient to proper physical and spiritual balance. Humpback is most closely associated with the Nightway and the Mountainway (Faris 1990; Hadlock 1980:185; Reichard 1950:443), but he has a lesser role

Figure 1. Two images of Gháá'ask'idii, the Humpback Yé'ii. He has mountain sheep horns, a digging stick, and a hump on his back that is filled with seeds and mist.

Figure 2. Humpback can appear without the mountain sheep horns or the staff.

in many other ceremonies.

Zaha'doolzhaaí is another yé'ii commonly seen in Dinétah (Figures 3 and 4). The English translation is Fringe Mouth. The name comes from the fringe of fur around the mouth of the mask worn by his (or her) impersonators at ceremonies (Olin 1979:146). Fringe Mouth is most easily identified by the head and torso having different colors on the right and left sides. There is often a pointed cap (Schaafsma 1980:318). Fringe Mouth is not one person, but a class of beings. There are Fringe Mouths of the Land and Water (Reichard 1974:438–439; Young and Copeland 2018). Olin

Figure 3. (a) Fringe Mouth has different colors on the right and left sides of his or her face and torso. There is often a rattle in one hand and a bow in the other. (b) DStretch LAB enhancement.

Figure 4. (a) Fringe Mouth often has a conical hat. (b) DStretch YRD enhancement.

(179:148) says the Fringe Mouth of the Land is red on one side and black on the other, and the Fringe Mouth of the Water is yellow and blue. Ceremonies involv-ing Fringe Mouth include Nightway, Big Godway, Plumeway, Coyoteway, Beadway, and Waterway (Olin 1979:146) Both Fringe Mouth and Humpback are often depicted in the rock art in lines of dancers that are associated with ceremonies.

The Hero Twins

Images of the hero twins of Navajo mythology are very common in Dinétah. Most often they are represented by their symbols (Figure 5). Naayéé' Neizghání is Monster Slayer, the elder of the twins and the aggressive one. His symbol is the bow. Tóbájíshchíní, Born For Water, is the younger of the twins and is more passive than his brother. His symbol is the hourglass figure or scalp knot. The masks worn by ceremonial

Figure 5. Symbols of the hero twins from Crow Canyon. Monster Slayer is represented by the bow. Born for Water is represented by the hourglass or scalp knot.

impersonators of the twins (Figure 6) reveal some of their physical characteristics. Monster Slayer (Figure 6a), on the left, has lightning arrows as his most potent weapon. The lightning is occasionally seen on his face (Figure 7). His bow is next to his mask. Born for Water (Figure 6b) is usually depicted in red and his face is decorated with the hourglass figure.

Monster Slayer can be depicted in a wide variety of ways. He can have his bow in his hand like a warrior

Figure 6. Head and face masks of the hero twins Monster Slayer on the left and Born for Water on the right (Haile 1947:64).

Figure 8. Monster Slayer with bow in hand. Crow Canyon.

Figure 7. Monster Slayer with lightning depicted on his face.

(Figure 8) or he can have the bow symbol on his clothing or his shield (Figure 9). In Figure 10 he is behind the flint shield given to him by his father. The twins are an important part of most of the ceremonies. They appear in many of today's sandpaintings.

One interesting image from Largo Canyon is a petroglyph/pictograph combination (Figure 11). It is about four feet tall. On the face of the image is the symbol of both of the twins (Figure 12). So who is this? Perhaps it could be their mother, Changing Woman. She is rarely depicted in rock art or sandpaintings, but this might be one of those rare occasions. It might also be their father, the Sun Carrier.

Sun and Moon

The carriers of the sun and moon are depicted in a Dinétah canyon within about one hundred meters of one another. Jóhonaa'éí is the Sun Carrier (Figure 13).

Figure 9. Monster Slayer with bow symbol on his shield.

He is a young, vibrant man with long, shiny hair. Like Zeus, his weapon is the lightning bolt, and again like Zeus, he is a bit of a jerk. He has impregnated females all over the earth, including Changing Woman. His sons,

Figure 10. Shield figure of Monster Slayer with his flint armor.

the hero twins, seek him out far to the east. When they meet him he tries to kill them. When they are able to withstand his attempts, he acknowledges that they are in fact his children. He gives Monster Slayer lightning arrows and flint armor so he can kill the monsters. The first monster the twins go after, however, is Yé'iitsoh or Big Giant, who is also a son of Jóhonaaʼéí. After a gruesome battle, Jóhonaaʼéí himself kills his giant son with a lightning bolt.

The Moon Carrier, Tłʼehonaaʼéí, has a minor role in the myths. He is depicted as an old man with gray hair (Figure 14). These characters are just carriers of the sun and moon, not the actual sun and moon. Like Apollo, Jóhonaaʼéí carries the sun across the sky each day and returns to his home in the east. Tłʼehonaaʼéí carries the moon each night.

Animals

Animals play a prominent role in Navajo stories, and they appear in the rock art throughout Dinétah. In mythological times, animals had more human characteristics. They could talk and help make important decisions. Mąʼii the Coyote is the best-known animal character in the Navajo stories (Figure 15). The Navajo

Figure 11. Large petroglyph/pictograph with characteristics of both of the hero twins.

Figure 12. Detail of Figure 11 showing on the face both the bow symbol of Monster Slayer and the hourglass symbol of Born for Water.

coyote stories are used to teach children proper behavior by providing examples of where bad behavior leads, but there are also very serious stories involving Coyote, and he is a part of some important decision-making. After everyone emerges into the present fifth world, Coyote invents death (Zolbrod 1984:82–83). He says

Figure 13. (a) The Sun Carrier is a young man with long, shiny hair. (b) DStretch ʏʙᴋ enhancement.

Figure 14. (a) The Moon Carrier is an old man with gray hair. (b) DStretch ʏʀᴅ enhancement.

Figure 15. Mą'ii the Coyote is a prominent character in Navajo stories.

he takes a bit of his fur and decorates each one, creating our pubic hair.

The tracks of Shash the Bear are depicted in Figure 16. I suspect that you probably don't really think that those look like bear tracks. But, of course, there is a very well-known story to explain why those are indeed bear tracks. Bear is a very human-like creature, proportioned like us and able to stand on two legs, so it is not surprising that his footprints might resemble our handprints. But if we put our hands out in front of us our thumbs are on the inside, whereas in Figure 16 the thumbs or short toes are on the outside. Bears do, indeed, have their thumb-like toes on the outside, and this story explains why. It also explains the origin of day and night.

Early in the fifth world basic things were being established. The day-time animals wanted it to be day all the time, but, naturally, the night-time animals wanted it to be night all the time. They decided to gamble for it, winner take all. The game they played is called the Shoe Game or Moccasin Game. It is still commonly played today, usually on long winter nights with a large number of exuberant players on each team. The game goes on all night. Each team has four shoes, boots, or moccasins, a small ball that will be hidden in one of them, and 102 yucca stick counters. One team hides the ball in a boot and then fills all four boots with sand. The other team guesses which boot the ball is in. While they are deciding which boot to pick, their opponents sing the Shoe Game songs as loudly as they can to distract them. If they get it on the first guess, they get a number of the other team's yucca stick counters. If they get it on the

we need death because without it there would be too many of us.

We all carry a bit of Coyote with us. When the first human beings are created, First Man, First Woman, and the others are putting the finishing touches on the human body (Zolbrod 1984:177–179). They fashion the sex organs and put them on the male and the female. But Coyote thinks they don't quite look right, so

Figure 16. These handprints with thumbs on the outside are the tracks of Bear.

second or third guess, they get fewer sticks. The object of the game is to get all of the other team's yucca stick counters, so usually no one wins. But there is a lot of betting on the side to keep things interesting.

In the first shoe game with the day-time animals against the night-time animals, Bear provided his large feet to be used as his team's boots. The game went on all night with no one getting far ahead. Everyone was so absorbed in the game that they didn't notice that it was getting light out. The night animals were afraid to be caught out in daylight, so they all rushed out of the hogan when they saw the sun was about to come up. Bear quickly grabbed his shoes and was in such a hurry that he put them on the wrong feet. So his feet have been on backwards ever since. And a petroglyph with thumbs on the outsides of the hands is the human-like tracks of Bear.

Jaa'abaní is the bat (Figure 17). "Jaa" is "ear," and "aba" is "buckskin", so the name for bat is "buckskin ears." The story of how Bat Woman got her name brings us into the story of the hero twins and the slaying of the monsters (Zolbrod 1984:236–241). But first we need some background on the bat and the buckskin ears.

Figure 17. The image of a bat evokes the story of Bat Woman.

Early in the fifth world when things were being established, First Man, First Woman, and the other leaders decided it was time for the animals to decorate themselves. Different types of coverings were provided and all the creatures were called together to choose what they wanted to wear. The mammals liked the fur, the reptiles preferred the scales, and the birds went for the brightly colored feathers. Everyone had a great time and at the end of the day they all went home. But Bat Woman missed the whole thing! She slept all day in a cave and forgot to show up to get her feathers. When she came out at dusk everyone was gone and the only things left were a few pieces of ratty buckskin. She put the buckskin on herself and felt terrible about the way she looked. She decided that she would never let anyone see her. She would sleep in hiding all day and only come out when the day animals have gone home to sleep through the night. In our terms, she has a major problem with self-esteem based on how she feels about the way she looks.

Bat Woman also plays a role in the story of the twins and the monsters. After slaying the Big Giant and the Horned Monster, the twins decide to go after the Monster Birds. These birds live on top of Shiprock, known in Navajo as the Rock with Wings. The Monster Birds pick up a person, fly to Shiprock, and dash the person against a cliff at the top of the rock. The dead person falls to the base of the cliff, providing food for the baby monster birds below. Monster Slayer allows himself to be picked up by one of the adult birds, but because he has supernatural help he is not injured when he is thrown against the cliff. He talks to the baby birds and they tell him when their parents will return. When they come back he slays the adult birds and turns the baby birds into the raptors that we have in the world today.

Everything is going well for our hero until he realizes that he is on top of Shiprock with no way to get down! As it is getting dark he sees Bat Woman down below. He calls to her three times, asking for her to help him get off of Shiprock. She refuses each time. She doesn't want anyone to see her, and certainly not a macho hero like Monster Slayer. She would be totally humiliated in his presence. The fourth time, though, he makes an offer she can't refuse. He tells her if she helps him get down, he will give her the magnificent feathers of the monster birds, feathers of every possible color and shade. So she agrees, but on one condition. He cannot open his eyes the entire time she is carrying him down. He agrees, and she flies up with a large basket that he will ride in. On the way down, however,

Monster Slayer opens his eyes. Bat Woman is infuriated and totally embarrassed. The mighty Monster Slayer has seen how ugly she is! He keeps his end of the bargain and gives her the large bag of feathers. And he tells her not to walk through the field of sunflowers nearby. She says that he didn't comply with her request, so she won't comply with his, and she walks right into the sunflower field with the bag of feathers on her back. What she doesn't realize is that as she walks through the sunflowers, the little birds of the world are pouring out of the bag, all decorated in the spectacular colors of the monster birds. When she finally notices what is happening, she looks in the bag to see that all the feathers are gone. So Bat Woman remains her ugly self, and to this day she sleeps all day in caves and comes out only at night so that no one will see her.

What does this have to do with rock art images? Even today, seeing an image of a bat will bring this story to the mind of almost any Navajo. The cultural trappings of these images go far beyond the simple idea of representing a bat with a picture.

Constellations

Patterns of dots appear on rock art panels throughout Dinétah. They are easy to ignore, but many of them depict constellations, and, of course, every constellation has its story. A great deal has been written about Navajo starlore (Chamberlain and Rogers 2001; Haile 1947; Maryboy and Begay 2010; Salabye and Manolescu 2015; Young and Copeland 2018). But much of this information is difficult to apply to the night sky. Young and Copeland (2018:63), however, have provided a clear explanation of a starlore panel in Blanco Canyon (Figure 18). The images at the upper and middle right of the panel shaped like an inverted L are what we know as the belt and sword of Orion. To the Navajo it is called First Slim One, Átsé Ets'ózí. The two dots close together in the upper middle are known as the Pinching Stars. The seven dots in a V shape in the middle of the panel are Dilyéhé, known to us as the Pleiades. The word "dilyéhé" means "seed-like sparkles" (Maryboy and Begay 2010:40). It is the most prominent constellation in Navajo art, appearing often in sandpaintings. The pattern in the lower right is the Rabbit Tracks, Gah Hahat'ee. The circle on the left is Hastiin Sik'ai'ii, Man with his Legs Spread Apart, corresponding to the Western constellation Corvus.

So how did all these constellations get up there? First Man and Black God were making the stars and putting them in place in careful, meaningful arrange-

Figure 18. Constellation panel from Blanco Canyon.

ments. Many of the stars were already in place and the others were on a blanket, awaiting placement. But Coyote, the embodiment of impatience, just couldn't wait that long. He grabbed the blanket and flung the stars up into the air. They remained where they landed, and now the sky has a few carefully placed constellations and the rest of the stars are just a big mess (Zolbrod 1984:92–93). Coyote is symbolic of chaos, and the stars are symbolic of the relationship between order and chaos in the Navajo universe (Chamberlain and Rogers 2001:57). The Athabaskan hunter-gatherer roots of Navajo culture mix with the orderly, agricultural Pueblo roots in the patterns of stars above us.

The Kicker

Figure 19 is a large, complex panel. Much could be discussed here, but I will focus on one image that appears to illustrate a well-known Navajo myth. The detail (Figure 20) shows an upside down person with wild hair. He appears to me to be falling. Navajo rock art images generally don't show any details of loose, unruly hair, so this emphasis on hair is something out of the ordinary. I think this falling man is Tsé Dah Hódziiłtałii, known in English as the Kicker.

The story is part of the epic cycle of the slaying of the monsters by the hero twins. It has appeared in print in many versions (Klah 1942:92–93; Mat-

Figure 19. A large, complex panel that appears to contain a reference to the story of Monster Slayer and the Kicker.

Figure 20. Detail of Figure 19 showing the Kicker falling down the cliff.

thews 1897:122–123; O'Bryan 1956:94–95; Reichard 1950:445–446; Zolbrod 1984:242–244). We have already been introduced to one of these stories, the story of the Monster Birds and the rescue of Monster Slayer by Bat Woman. Later in the epic, Monster Slayer decides it is time to go after the Kicker, who spends his time sitting alongside a trail at the top of a mountain pass. He appears to be friendly as travelers approach him, but as they pass, he kicks them off the trail and over a cliff. They fall to their death, and the Kicker's children, who are waiting at the bottom of the cliff, eat them. Monster Slayer confronts the Kicker and has no trouble killing him. When he throws him off the cliff, he finds that the Kicker's long hair has grown into a crack in the rock, which is why no one has been able to defeat him by throwing him off the cliff. Monster Slayer cuts the hair and throws the Kicker down. Precisely this moment is captured in the rock art image. The Kicker is falling down with his long hair showing. When he lands at the bottom, his children eat him. Monster Slayer goes below and kills all of the children but the last one, which he turns into a buzzard.

The Great Gambler

Another unusual petroglyph illustrates a scene from a well-known Navajo myth. The image (Figure 21) shows a man with a large hoop. The person in the petroglyph has a look and posture that is very uncharacteristic of Navajo rock art imagery. Older photos show that he had an erect phallus that someone has since tried to rub out. While an erect phallus is common in Ancestral Puebloan rock art, I have never seen it in Navajo artwork. Roessel (1983:119) has associated this site with the story of the Great Gambler, and I agree. The main character in the story of the Great Gambler is a foreigner who causes a lot of trouble.

The story is one of the most commonly shared of the Navajo narratives, told, I'm sure, because of its moral of the evils of greed and self-centeredness. It appears in most of the collections of Navajo stories (Matthews 1897:82–87; O'Bryan 1956:48–62; Rock Point Community School 1982:62–69; Zolbrod 1984:99–112). The story takes place in Chaco Canyon, which is just southwest of Dinétah. The main character is Nááhwíiłbįįhí, which means "He Always Wins." He is described as being light-complected, blonde-haired, blue-eyed, and cocky (Beeshligai 2014:9). He speaks a different language, but is able to communicate.

The Gambler challenges everyone to play games against him and bet heavily. True to his name, he always wins. He is a really good cheater. He wins all of the Chaco people's possessions, their wives, their children, and ultimately all the men of Chaco as well. He orders the men to build more large buildings, including

Figure 21. Image depicting the Great Gambler of Chaco Canyon.

man in the petroglyph has a hoop in one hand and a decorated staff in the other hand, which may be the pole he throws through the hoop. The large hoop might also represent the large turquoise disc. In terms of the potential connections between Chaco and gambling, the cover story of a recent edition of *American Archaeology* highlights the unusually large number of gambling materials that archaeologists have found at Chaco (Witze 2018:12–17).

Navajo Ceremonies

Many rock art sites in Dinétah are thought to be associated with ceremonies. Schaafsma (1980:310) reports that a Navajo resident of the area indicated to her that ceremonies were still conducted at sites in Dinétah until the 1950s. Navajo ceremonies are conducted for healing. There are seasonal restrictions, but, unlike Pueblo ceremonies, Navajo ceremonies are not tied to the calendar. They are performed when a patient needs help or, in the case of the Blessingway, to prevent future harm.

What needs to be cured is not just the physical illness a patient might have. The issue at root is spiritual imbalance and the problems it brings. Images are made to attract the supernaturals to the ceremony so that they can help in the healing. "Supernaturals" includes the yé'ii, but also other supernatural beings that aren't yé'ii. We were introduced to the yé'ii above when we looked at Humpback and Fringe Mouth, the two easiest yé'ii to identify. There are images of other yé'ii or supernaturals, ones not as easy to identify, throughout Dinétah. Four of them appear in Figure 22.

Presumably these images were originally made on rock at places where ceremonies were to be held in order to attract the supernaturals to the site. In time, sandpaintings took the place of rock art images. Figure 23 shows four yé'ii with a plant in the middle. The yé'ii are standing on a long rectangular platform. In sandpaintings, this is called a foundation bar. This image looks like a sandpainting put on a rock face (Schaafsma and Tsosie 2009:21; Wyman 1983:40). After the center of Navajo settlement moved from Dinétah to the Canyon de Chelly area around 1750, rock art images of the Navajo deities were no longer made, replaced by sandpainting images.

his house, which we call Pueblo Alto. The Navajo name for it is Gambler's House. The greatest possession the people of Chaco have is a huge turquoise disc. After he wins the disc, the Sun Carrier asks the Gambler to give it to him, but the Gambler says, "I won't give it to you, but I will gamble with you for it!" This act of hubris sets the rest of the story in motion.

The sun calls together the yé'ii and other powerful supernatural beings and they hatch a plan to defeat the Gambler. A young man is chosen and trained in how to beat the Gambler in all of his favorite games. The young man will, of course, have plenty of supernatural help. All of the games are played, and the Gambler loses every one. On the last game he bets himself, which is all he has left. And he loses again. The young man, with the help of some of the supernatural beings who aided him in the games, ties the Gambler to a huge arrow and puts it on a bow equally large. The whole time this is going on the Gambler is cursing everyone and saying that he will return to get revenge.

The Gambler is launched into the sky and disappears from sight. He lands near the moon at the home of Begochídí, a mysterious and mischievous Navajo deity. Begochídí helps him out and sends him back to earth in Mexico, where he is said to become the leader of the Mexicans. If so, he does indeed return for revenge when the Spanish and Mexican troops come north to raid the Navajos for slaves.

Looking again at the petroglyph, I think the image depicts the Gambler at one of his favorite games, hoop and pole. In this game, a large hoop is rolled out and the player has to throw the stick or pole through it. The

Figure 22. Four unidentified yé'ii or other supernaturals.

in Dinétah, but as yet archaeologists have found no evidence of sandpainting in the area.

It is quite possible that the ceremonial use of rock art was similar to today's ceremonial use of sandpaintings. Leland Wyman (1970b:7) discussed the function of sandpaintings.

> In summary, the purpose of the drypainted pictures of Holy People and their activities is, first, to attract these beings (for they enjoy seeing their portraits made) so that they may help to cure the patient. Secondly, the sacred pictures are used to identify the patient with Holy People by seating him on the figures and applying their sands to his body. Finally, this procedure provides a two-way path (between the patient and the symbols in sand) for the exchange of good and evil, health and sickness, immunity and susceptibility; thus, man is able to partake of the nature of divinity.

Rock art at ceremonial sites in Dinétah may have been used in much this same way.

The goal of all ceremonies is to bring the patient back into spiritual balance. "Navajo oral traditions recount that during the creation, the Holy People were immediately present among the Navajo, and they taught the Navajo the ceremonies necessary for survival and readied the world for living. A central theme of their teaching was how to achieve and maintain hozho—beauty, balance, and harmony" (Schaafsma and Tsosie 2009:15). Ceremonial narratives involve a hero or heroine who undergoes trials, gets injured or ill, is cured by the supernaturals, and then returns to teach the healing ceremony to the Navajo. Five of these ceremonial stories are discussed below in relation to the associated ceremonies: Blessingway, Nightway, Beadway, Mountainway, and Beautyway. It is impor-

The transition to sandpaintings was made in part because sandpaintings are easy to control. The images are made, used for healing, and then ritually removed and discarded. Because they are permanently displayed on the rock surface, the power of rock art images could be improperly used for evil purposes, for witchcraft (McPherson 2014:144–145). With sandpaintings, these potent images could be controlled. It is possible that both rock art and sandpainting images were used

Figure 23. The Four Yé'ii panel is very similar to a sandpainting composition.

tant to remember that the story is the taproot of every ceremony. Any sandpaintings or rock art associated with a ceremony are in some way related to the story of the ceremony.

The two most important words in Navajo philosophy are "hózhǫ́" and "k'é." As mentioned above, "hózhǫ́" refers to beauty, balance, and harmony. Not physical beauty and balance, but spiritual beauty and balance. K'é is proper relationships, not just with people, but also with nature and the spiritual world. The goal of all ceremonies is to bring the patient back into hózhǫ́ and k'é.

Healing is achieved through the arts, primarily through song, visual art, and dance. The sandpainting and presumably the rock art panel are portals or membranes through which the patient can directly encounter the supernaturals and be cured (Wyman 1983:33). Today the patient sits in the middle of the sandpainting and sometimes the sand is rubbed all over his or her body. Obviously a person couldn't sit in a rock art panel on a cliff face, but the location of the rock art was a place where the supernaturals could be met.

Ceremonies can last as long as nine nights. There is singing by the medicine man, known in Navajo as a hataałii or singer, all night. The songs recount the narratives associated with the ceremony. Copeland (1998:58) writes that every ceremony has a Monster Slayer song. Some of the major ceremonies have a dance with impersonators of the supernaturals that can be attended by the public. Most of the remainder of the ceremonial activities are attended by family and people close to the patient.

There are several locations in Dinétah that appear to be associated with particular ceremonies. We will look at some of the associated rock art and the story connected to each ceremony.

Blessingway

Hózhǫ́ǫ́jí is a commonly performed ceremony, known in English as the Blessingway. It is an anomaly among Navajo ceremonies in that it is not done for healing. The ceremony is performed as a blessing in association with births, weddings, new homes, and other life transitions. The purpose is to provide health and spiritual balance for the future. Brugge (1977:15) notes that the Blessingway is one of the ceremonies most closely tied to the Athabaskan root of Navajo culture. This difference might explain why it has a different orientation from the other ceremonies.

The Blessingway is associated with plants and the earth, which are depicted in rock art. Anderson Hoskie (2017:6) identifies two of the main panels at Crow Canyon as being related to Blessingway. Figure 24 shows one of those panels. The small comma-like things are germinating seeds. Nearby is the other panel (Figure 25), part of one of the best-known sites in Dinétah. A corn plant is centered. On the viewer's right is Humpback, the harvest deity. The concentric circle next to him is identified as a cornfield. The original Navajo cornfields were round. There are two hourglass symbols of Born for Water. The three zigzag lines on the left could be symbolic of flowing water or of Monster Slayer's lightning arrows.

Changing Woman, the primary character associated with this ceremony, is rarely depicted in rock art or sandpaintings. The purpose of the images is to attract the supernaturals to the scene of the ceremony. Changing Woman, the personification of the earth, is considered to always be present in all places (Schaafsma and Tsosie 2009:21). The myth associated with Blessingway is the myth of Changing Woman. The fullest versions of her story are found in Wyman (1970a) and Zolbrod (1984), but an account of all the stories would fill a very large book. Here I recount a short segment from the end of the story of the twins slaying the monsters (Zolbrod 1984:256–264). After the hero twins have killed many monsters, Monster Slayer returns home and, in frustration, tells his mother (Changing Woman) that he doesn't think he can kill them all. There are just too many. She tells him not to worry; she will take care of it.

Changing Woman goes outside of their mountaintop hogan. She has five hoops and five knives that the

Figure 24. A panel related to Blessingway with germinating seeds.

Figure 25. Blessingway-related panel with Humpback, a symbol of Born for Water, and a round cornfield.

with rainbow, the second with sunbeams, and the last two with sheet lightning and chain lightning. The storm rages on for days. When it is finally over, Monster Slayer cuts loose the protective layers of cloud and fog. First the two types of lightning shoot into the air. Then come the sunbeams and, finally, the rainbows. Changing Woman and the twins step outside under the rainbow-filled sky. What had before been lush, green meadows and mountains was now a beautiful, carved rock landscape. The erosion of the storm has created the landscape of the Colorado Plateau as we know it today. Only four monsters survived the storm: Old Age Woman, Cold Woman, Poverty, and Hunger. Those four are with us to this day.

This story is an indication of the power of Changing Woman, the same power that presides over the Blessingway.

Nightway

Tł'ééjí, the Nightway, is performed to cure paralysis, blindness, deafness, and maladies of the head (Faris 1990:32), which were ailments related to the trials experienced by the protagonists in the ceremony's origin stories (Denetclaw 2015; Faris 1990; Matthews 1902; Spencer 1957). The Nightway is also known as the Yé'iibichai, because that is the name of the public dance held on the last night of the ceremony. "Yé'iibichai" means grandfather or leader of the yé'ii. That personage

Sun Carrier gave to the twins. She rolls the white hoop to the east, the blue hoop to the south, the yellow hoop to the west, and the black hoop to the north. She spits through each hoop as she pushes it away. The fifth multicolored hoop she throws straight up into the sky and throws the knives after it.

A violent storm that she has created is about to begin. Monster Slayer covers the hogan with layers of cloud and fog. The first layer is fastened to the ground

is Haashch'éélti'í or Talking God, the leader of the yé'ii and the leader of the dance. The Nightway was the first Navajo ceremony to receive attention from ethnographers (Matthews 1902; Stevenson 1891). Caches of materials related to the Nightway have been found in Dinétah (Hester 1962:60; Schaafsma 1992:36).

Schaafsma has identified multiple rock art sites with imagery related to Tł'ééjí, the Nightway (Schaafsma and Tsosie 2009:20). Figure 26 shows a group of

Figure 26. Nightway panel with Humpback and Fringe Mouth.

yé'ii from one of the sites. Humpback is on the left, and Fringe Mouth is second left. This could be a group of dancers. Hadlock (1980:183–185) reports that Humpback is the main yé'ii associated with the Nightway.

A petroglyph site in Crow Canyon contains multiple Nightway-related images. Figure 27 has Humpback on the left and a large image of the female goddess of the Nightway, Ha'ashchííh ba'áád. She is wearing a mask with indentations on the sides. It is through these indentations that the wind can give her advice (Young and Copeland 2018:21). Other yé'ii at the site are shown in Figure 28.

As I mentioned above, the health problems that each ceremony cures are related to the trials that are experienced by the protagonist in the narrative associated with the ceremony. The character's ailments are cured by the yé'ii and other supernaturals that the character encounters in the story, and then he or she learns the ceremony that effected the cure and comes back to teach it to the Navajo people.

The main branch of the Nightway narrative is the story of the Visionary (Denetclaw 2015; Faris 1990; Matthews 1902; Spencer 1957). He is the youngest of several brothers. He has informative visions, but his brothers disregard them and show him no respect. He follows behind them when they are hunting and gets lost. When he tries to kill a mountain sheep, he is temporarily paralyzed. He is adopted by the sheep, who are the Mountain Sheep People, the group to which Humpback belongs. The Visionary has many other adventures (and misadventures) with the supernaturals, and his injuries are cured by them with their ceremonies. One of the adventures involves floating down the San Juan River inside a hollow log. He learns the ceremonies that cured him and returns to his people to teach them how to make the cures.

Figure 27. The female yé'ii of the Nightway is in the lower center.

Figure 28. Other Nightway-related yé'ii at the site.

A branch of the narrative is the story of the Stricken Twins (Matthews 1902:212–265). They are born to a poor girl; their father is Talking God. They are disobedient and get injured; one becomes blind, the other lame. The blind one carries the lame one on his shoulders and they travel looking for a cure. The supernaturals agree to cure them, but they are disobedient again and it takes a second try to get a cure. They return home and teach the ceremony to the people.

Beadway

Yoo'ee, the Beadway ceremony, is closely related to the Eagleway, and both ceremonies treat maladies caused by exposure to eagles. The illnesses treated include head diseases, skin diseases, anorexia, nausea, and swollen legs. People were usually exposed to eagles through hunting and trapping. Since eagle hunting and catching aren't often done anymore, the Beadway is seldom performed today (Wyman 1983:27).

A panel in Crow Canyon (Figure 29) is considered to be Beadway-related (Olin 1984:67; Young and Copeland 2018:41). It appears to illustrate a scene from the Beadway story (Spenser 1957:194–201; Olin 1984:69). The hero is often called Scavenger or Beadboy. He is captured by Pueblos. They force him to be lowered into an eagle's nest to steal eaglets. After he throws down the eaglets they are going to leave him there to die. After being lowered into the nest, he refuses to steal the eaglets and the eagles protect him. The eagles send dust to the Pueblo people below, causing disease. The eagles, with the help of Fringe Mouth and snakes, take Beadboy up through the sky hole to the home of the eagles and other animals and birds. It is this scene that is illustrated in the rock art. Beadboy is holding an eaglet while being lifted by an eagle.

While in the home of the eagles he is told not to do certain things. Of course, he does them, suffers the consequences, and is cured by the eagles. A few examples: he is turned into a coyote, captured by a spider, and he spills a water jar and causes rain. He is not thought of too highly by the eagles. But then he helps the eagle warriors defeat the stinging insects and rolling weeds. He is rewarded by being allowed to stay with the eagles and marry one of their maidens. He returns to earth and teaches his brother the Eagleway and Beadway ceremonies that the eagles used to cure him. While back home he cures the diseased Pueblo people and gets their valuable jewelry in return. Then he returns to live in the land of the eagles.

Mountainway

The last two ceremonies that I examine in relation to rock art are the Mountainway and Beautyway. They are related in that they both are connected to the same story, the tale of two sisters who don't marry well.

The story of Dziłátahji, the Mountainway, is well-documented (Matthews 1887; Spencer 1957; Wyman 1975). Two sisters are courted by old men whom they reject. Then two young, handsome men come to court them and the sisters agree to run off with them and marry. Afterwards, the two young men change back to the original old men—Bear and Big Snake.

The Mountainway narrative is the story of the older sister married to Bear. She is exposed to bear illness and illnesses from other animals she encounters. Bear-related illnesses are arthritis and mental disturbances. Illnesses from the other animals encountered are gastrointestinal and genitourinary problems (porcupine), cough (squirrel), skin disease (turkey), and deafness and eye trouble (mountain sheep) (Wyman 1983:26). She escapes from Bear and meets many supernaturals

Figure 29. Beadboy lifted into the sky by an eagle.

along the way. She suffers misfortunes and is healed, and she learns the ceremonies. After returning to Bear and escaping again, she returns home and shares the ceremonies—the Mountainway—that cure the maladies she experienced in her trials.

The Mountainway is one of the better known Navajo ceremonies, probably because it features the public Fire Dance, as well as ten other dances (Matthews 1887:441). Mountainway dancers can be recognized by headdresses that extend all the way to the ground (Griffin-Pierce 1992:10; Wyman 1975:90–94). Figure 30 shows such a dancer. In sandpaintings, males have round heads and females have rectangular heads, so I assume this dancer is female. The entire line of dancers (Figure 31) shows four female dancers with Humpback and Fringe Mouth on the right. This is some of the finest artwork that I have seen in the rock art of Dinétah. A closer look at the female dancers (Figure 32) shows that first a petroglyph was made and then paint was applied over it. This reminds me of a technique used in present day sandpaintings. When a person is made in a sandpainting, first a tan body is made. This is a naked person, which is then "dressed" with the colorful clothing that the viewer sees. In this rock art, the "naked" petroglyph is dressed with painted clothing. Note that all of the dancers are different and distinctive.

Figure 30. (a) Dancer showing the long headdress associated with the Mountainway. (b) DStretch YBK enhancement.

Beautyway

The story of Hoozhónee, the Beautyway, is the story of the other sister who married Big Snake. Remember that "hózhǫ́" means spiritual balance, harmony, and beauty. So Beautyway could just as easily be called Balanceway or Harmonyway. The ceremony cures snake-related issues: snakebite, snake nightmares, rheumatism, sore throat, stomach trouble, kidney and bladder trouble, and skin diseases or sores (Wyman 1957:16–17; 1992:26).

There is a great deal of snake lore and snake phobia in Navajo culture. My students associated snakes with lightning, and I think close to 100% of them were afraid of snakes. An informant of Franc Newcomb claimed that at the time of their creation, snakes traded their arms and legs for power over death (Newcomb 1940:19).

Figure 33 shows a petroglyph of a coiled snake. This is Endless Snake, a major character in the Beautyway story (Schaafsma 1992:30). Reichard points out that in Navajo art there is always a way out of the design so that the artist will not get trapped. Endless Snake is an embodiment of the enclosing circle, one that will not let you out and trap you for good (Reichard 1950:454). Figure 34 is a sandpainting design from the Beautyway showing Endless Snake (Wyman 1957:Plate 6). It is almost identical to the petroglyph. The diamond on the snake's forehead is the location of his power (Wyman 1957:190).

Big Snake is the character that our unfortunate sister in the story runs off with. Endless Snake is either a variant of Big Snake or a close relative (Reichard 1950:454). A consultant of Robert McPherson's identifies Comb Ridge as the embodiment of Big Snake in the landscape. Its alcoves are the holes through which he breathes (McPherson 2009:64–65). Figure 35 is a petroglyph depicting Big Snake. Big Snake is always depicted as a short, thick snake. Like most characters in Navajo mythology, Big Snake can appear in multiples and as either sex. A sandpainting image from the Beautyway showing Endless Snake (Figure 36) shows four Big Snakes (Wyman 1957:Plate 1). The crooked snakes are male; the straight ones female.

There are several sources for the story (Pavlik 2014:256–260; Spencer 1957:150–155; Wyman 1957:41–142). The Beautyway story is the account of the younger sister who ran off with and married Big Snake. She tries to escape, but fails. She is told not to do certain things but always does them. For example,

Figure 31. Line of dancers with Humpback and Fringe Mouth on the right.

Figure 32. (a) Detail of Figure 31 showing the fine worksmanship of the rock art. (b) DStretch LAB enhancement.

she is told not to light a fire at night, but she does so and looks around to see that she is surrounded by huge, coiled snakes. On another occasion she wanders from home and is shot with a dart by Toad. She is cured of the problems caused by her transgressions by the Beautyway ceremony, which she takes home and teaches to the people.

Final Remarks on Navajo Ceremonies

The five ceremonies that I have commented on in this section are but a fragment of the total number of Navajo ceremonies. Wyman and Kluckhohn (1938:36) listed 58 ceremonies in 1938. The Morgan and Young (1980:421) dictionary has names for 65. There is no way to determine how many ceremonies were active during the Navajo occupation of Dinétah.

Each ceremony ends with positive thoughts. The singer, the patient, and those present are all focused on a positive outcome for the ceremony and for the patient. I will close this section with some famous lines from a Navajo prayer from the Male Shooting Chant. Remember that "beauty" is "hózhǫ́," meaning spiritual balance, harmony and beauty.

Figure 33. Endless Snake from the myth of the Beautyway.

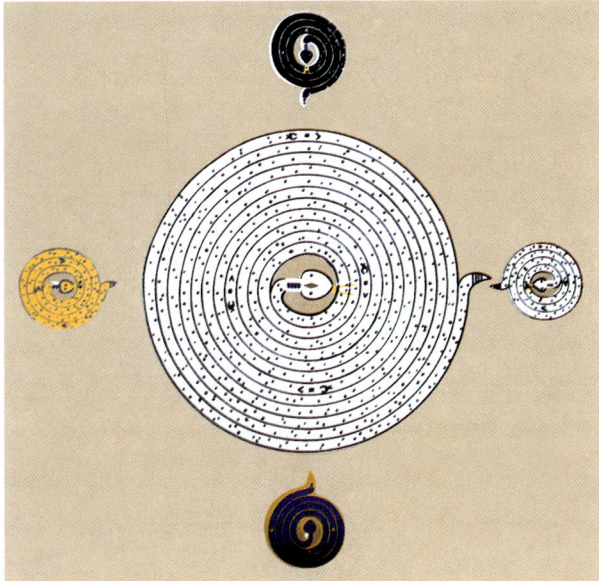

Figure 34. Endless Snake in a sandpainting from the Beautyway (Wyman 1957:Plate 6)

> *With beauty before me may I go about,*
> *With beauty behind me may I go about,*
> *With beauty beneath me may I go about,*
> *With beauty above me may I go about,*
> *With beauty all around me may I go about,*
> *With my speech under control may I go about,*
> *Restoration-to-youth According-to-beauty I have become,*
> *Restoration-to-youth According-to-beauty*
> *Perfection,*
> *These I have become again.*

Figure 35. Big Snake petroglyph in Largo Canyon drainage (Young and Copeland 2018:90). Photo by Bob Young.

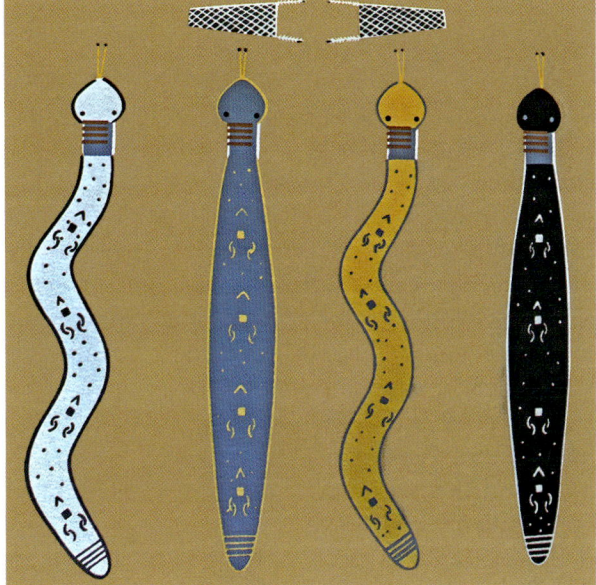

Figure 36. Sandpainting from the Beautyway ceremony with images of Big Snake (Wyman 1957:Plate 1).

> *These I have become again.*
> *These I have become again.*
> *These I have become again.*
> *It has become beautiful again.*
> *It has become beautiful again.*
> *It has become beautiful again.*
> *It has become beautiful again.*
> (Reichard 1944:93)

Conclusions

Like art in its traditional functions worldwide, paintings and carvings on stone are yet another form of visual legacy created to communicate and reaffirm symbols and metaphors of stories, cosmologies, and worldviews, projecting conceptual universes, cultural values, and social concerns. Within such complicated and dynamic frameworks, it was the role of the artist to create a network of metaphor and analogy connecting social and cosmological dimensions (Schaafsma 2013:4).

In this paper I have focused on traditional stories because that is what I know best in relation to Navajo culture. Joseph Campbell (1988:71) wrote, "I would say…the basic theme of all mythology [is] that there is an invisible plane supporting the visible one." In fact, Campbell's first book, written with Maud Oakes, was about Navajo mythology and sandpaintings (Oakes and Campbell 1943). The Navajo rock art of Dinétah often refers to that "invisible plane," and because the rock art was made in historic times and much is known about Navajo beliefs, we are able to use the rock art as a window into the intellectual and spiritual culture of the Navajo people.

Traditional stories bring with them a different way of thinking. We are accustomed to the hyperrational, scientific way of thinking established during the Enlightenment in Europe. But mythological thinking has a different logic. When I taught traditional Navajo stories some of my most traditional students thought primarily in the mythological mode. They did not speak English outside the classroom and there was no media at home pushing the white man's way at them. For them time was more cyclical than linear, logic was based on association, and that "invisible plane" was easily accessible. These students were usually confused by much of their schoolwork, but they were completely at home with Navajo stories.

Science is able to explain complex notions about the world through reduction and generalization. The natural world is too vast to grasp without simplification. But art, including rock art, takes a different approach. Through the use of metaphor, symbol, and analogy, the arts open us up into the mystery in all its complex, incomprehensible glory. Polly Schaafsma's quote at the beginning of this section identifies the role of the artist in pointing the way.

It is through the use of ethnography that we can get some of this insight into the "invisible plane." Taçon and Chippindale (1998:6–7) delineate two methods for rock art research. Informed methods gather direct information through ethnography. With ethnography we can "explore the pictures from the inside." Formal methods have no inside knowledge. The primary formal method is archaeology.

I was able to use ethnography and my own experience with Navajos to gain insight into the rock art of Dinétah. I am not in any way criticizing the use of archaeology. In most cases it is all we have to provide context for the artwork. But whenever it is possible to get information directly from the culture that made the artwork or from that culture's ethnographies, that information provides a more informed approach. David Whitley (2005:80) wrote, "All symbols have multiple levels of meaning, and identifying the social meaning of rock art is the goal of interpretation." It might not be the only goal, but it is certainly a primary one.

In this essay I have tried to identify the social and spiritual connections of the rock art of Dinétah to Navajo culture. Wouldn't it be wonderful if we could look at a site like the Great Gallery and be able to know the stories and ceremonies connected to it! But we can't. Those cultures are long gone. I feel privileged that I have been able to have experience with Navajo culture and pass on some of what I have learned to you.

Acknowledgments. I want to thank Dave Manley and Tom Hahl for leading URARA field trips into Dinétah. Dave led me on a second trip and shared his extensive knowledge of the area and the rock art.

References Cited

Beeshligai, Hastiin
   2014 The Gambler. *Leading the Way: Wisdom of the Navajo People* 12(9):8–9. September 2014.
Benally, Clyde.
   1982 *Dinéjí Nákéé' Nááhane': A Utah Navajo History*. San Juan School District, Monticello, Utah.
Brugge, David M.
   1977 The Ye'ii or Holy People in Navajo Rock Art. *Awanyu* 5(3):8–16.
Campbell, Joseph, with Bill Moyers
   1988 *The Power of Myth*. Doubleday, New York.
Chamberlain, Von Del, and Hugh Rogers
   2001 On the Trail of Dinétah Skywatchers: Patterned Dots and Scattered Pluses. In *American Indian Rock Art, Volume 27*, edited by Steven Freers and Alanah Woody, pp. 49–58. American Rock Art Research Association, Phoenix, Arizona.
Copeland, James Matthew
   2001 Dinétah Ceremonial Rock Art and Cultural Affiliation in Northwest New Mexico. In *American Indian Rock Art, Volume 27*, edited by Steven Freers and Alanah Woody, pp. 35–42. American Rock Art Research Association, Phoenix, Arizona.
Denetclaw, Dorothy
   2015 Bringing the Nightway to Diné Bikéyah. *Leading the Way: The Wisdom of the Navajo People* 13(12):2–5. December 2015.
Faris, James C.
   1990 *The Nightway: A History and a History of Documentation of a Navajo Ceremonial*. University of New Mexico Press, Albuquerque.
Fishler, Stanley A.
   1953 *In the Beginning: A Navaho Creation Myth*. University of Utah Anthropological Papers 13. Salt Lake City.
Griffin-Pierce, Trudy
   1992 *Earth Is My Mother, Sky Is My Father: Space, Time, and Astronomy in Navajo Sandpainting*. University of New Mexico Press, Albuquerque.

Hadlock, Harry L.
  1980 Gánaskĭdi: The Navajo Humpback Deity of the Largo. In *Collected Papers in Honor of Helen Greene Blumenschein*, edited by Albert H. Schroeder, pp. 179–210. Papers of the Archaeological Society of New Mexico 5. Archaeological Society Press, Albuquerque.

Haile, Berard
  1947 *Head and Face Masks in Navaho Ceremonialism*. St. Michael's Press, St. Michaels, Arizona. Facsimile reprint 1978, AMS Press, New York.
  1947 *Starlore Among the Navaho*. Museum of Navajo Ceremonial Art, Santa Fe. Facsimile reprint 1977, William Gannon, Santa Fe.
  1981 *Upward Moving and Emergence Way: The Gishin Biye Version*. Edited by Karl Luckert. University of Nebraska Press, Lincoln.

Hester, James J.
  1962 *Early Navajo Migrations and Acculturations in the Southwest*. Papers in Anthropology 6. Museum of New Mexico Press, Santa Fe.

Hoskie, Anderson
  2017 Why Dinétah is Important. *Leading the Way: The Wisdom of the Navajo People* 15(6):2–9. June 2017.

Klah, Hosteen
  1942 *Navajo Creation Myth: The Story of the Emergence*. Recorded by Mary C. Wheelwright. Museum of Navajo Ceremonial Art, Santa Fe.

Maryboy, Nancy C., and David Begay
  2010 *Sharing the Skies: Navajo Astronomy*. Fourth edition. Rio Nueva Publishers, Tucson.

Matthews, Washington
  1887 *The Mountain Chant: A Navajo Ceremony*. Fifth Annual Report of the Bureau of Ethnology 1883–'84, pp. 379–564. Facsimile reprint 1970, Rio Grande Press, Glorieta, New Mexico.
  1897 *Navajo Legends*. Houghton, Mifflin, Boston. Facsimile reprint 1994, University of Utah Press, Salt Lake City.
  1902 *The Night Chant: A Navaho Ceremony*. Memoirs of the American Museum of Natural History 6. Facsimile reprint 1978, AMS Press, New York.

McPherson, Robert S.
  2009 *Comb Ridge and Its People: The Ethnohistory of a Rock*. Utah State University Press, Logan, Utah.
  2014 *Viewing the Ancestors: Perceptions of the Anaasází, Mokwič, and Hisatsinom*. University of Oklahoma Press, Norman.

Newcomb, Franc Johnson
  1940 *Navajo Omens and Taboos*. The Rydal Press, Santa Fe.

Oakes, Maud, and Joseph Campbell
  1943 *Where the Two Came to Their Father: A Navaho War Ceremonial Given by Jeff King*. Third edition. Bollingen Series 1. Princeton University Press, Princeton.

O'Bryan, Aileen
  1956 *The Diné: Origin Myths of the Navaho Indians*. Bureau of American Ethnology Bulletin 163, pp. 1–194. Facsimile reprint 1993, Dover Publications, New York.

Olin, Caroline B.
  1979 Fringed Mouth, Navajo Yé'ii. In *Collected Papers in Honor of Bertha Pauline Dutton*, edited by Albert H. Schroeder, pp. 141–162. Papers of the Archaeological Society of New Mexico 4. Albuquerque Archaeological Society Press.
  1984 Early Navajo Sandpainting Symbols in Old Navajoland: Visual Aspects of Mythic Images. In *Collected Papers in Honor of Harry L. Hadlock*, edited by Nancy L. Fox, pp. 43–74. Papers of the Archaeological Society of New Mexico 9. Albuquerque Archaeological Society Press.

Pavlik, Steve
  2014 *The Navajo and the Animal People: Native American Traditional Ecological Knowledge and Ethnozoology*. Fulcrum Publishing, Golden, Colorado.

Reichard, Gladys A.
  1944 *Prayer: The Compulsive Word*. Monographs of the American Ethnological Society. University of Washington Press, Seattle
  1974 *Navajo Religion: A Study of Symbolism*. Second edition. Bollingen Series 18. Princeton University Press, Princeton.

Rock Point Community School (editors)
  1982 *Between Sacred Mountains: Stories and Lessons from the Land*. Rock Point Community School, Chinle, Arizona.

Roessel, Robert A.
  1983 *Dinétah*. Navajo Curriculum Center, Rough Rock, Arizona.

Salaybe, John C., and Kathleen Monalescu
  2015 Black God and the Constellations. *Leading the Way: The Wisdom of the Navajo People* 13(1):2. January 2015.

Schaafsma, Polly.
  1980 *Indian Rock Art of the Southwest*. School of American Research, Santa Fe, and University of New Mexico Press, Albuquerque.
  1992 *Rock Art in New Mexico*. Second Edition. Museum of New Mexico Press, Santa Fe.
  2013 *Images and Power: Rock Art and Ethics*. Springer, New York.

Schaafsma, Polly, and Will Tsosie
  2009 Xeroxed on Stone: Times of Origin and the Holy People in Canyon Landscapes. In *Landscapes of Origin in the Americas: Creation Narratives Linking Ancient Places and Present Communities*, edited by Jessica Joyce Christie, pp.15–31. University of Alabama Press, Tuscaloosa.

Spencer, Katherine
  1957 *An Analysis of Navaho Chantway Myths*. Memoirs of the American Folklore Society 48. American Folklore Society, Philadelphia.

Stevenson, James
  1891 *Ceremonial of Hasjelti Dailjis and Mythical Sand Painting of the Navajo Indians*. Eighth Annual Report of the Bureau of Ethnology 1886–'87, pp. 235–285. Government Printing Office, Washington, D.C.

Taçon, Paul S. C., and Christopher Chippindale
  1998 An Archaeology of Rock-Art Through Informed Methods and Formal Methods. In *The Archaeology of Rock-Art*, edited by Christopher Chippindale and Paul S. C. Taçon, pp. 1–10. Cambridge University Press, Cambridge, United Kingdom.

Whitley, David S.
  2005 *Introduction to Rock Art Research*. Left Coast Press, Walnut Creek, California.

Witze, Alexandra
  2018 When the Gambler Came to Chaco. *American Archaeology* 22(2):12–17.

Wyman, Leland C.
  1957 *Beautyway: A Navaho Ceremonial*. Bollingen Series 53. Pantheon Books, New York.
  1970a *Blessingway*. University of Arizona Press, Tucson.
  1970b *Sandpaintings of the Navaho Shootingway and The Walcott Collection*. Smithsonian Contributions to Anthropology No. 13. Smithsonian Institution Press, Washington, D.C.

1975 *The Mountainway of the Navajo.* University of Arizona Press, Tucson.

1983 *Southwest Indian Drypainting.* School of American Research, Santa Fe, and University of New Mexico Press, Albuquerque.

Wyman, Leland, and Clyde Kluckhohn
1938 *Navajo Classification of their Song Ceremonials.* Memoirs of the American Anthropological Association 50.

Young, Bob, and James M. Copeland
2018 *Images of Dinétah: Reflections of Past Life in the San Juan Basin of New Mexico.* Self-Published (Blurb).

Young, Robert W., and William Morgan
1980 *The Navajo Language: A Grammar and Colloquial Dictionary.* University of New Mexico Press, Albuquerque.

Zolbrod, Paul G.
1984 *Diné Bahane': The Navajo Creation Story.* University of New Mexico Press, Albuquerque.

Hoofprints and Footprints—The Grammar of Biographic Rock Art

David A. Kaiser and James D. Keyser

Biographic art occurs across the Plains of North America, stretching from Canada to Mexico. Using rock art, robe art, and ledger drawings, researchers over the last half century have rediscovered the lexicon of this narrative art tradition. Beyond the vocabulary of the objects and actions depicted, we examine the artistic conventions used and the structure of the narratives that aid in the understanding of this picture writing system.

> *Hoofprints and footprints,*
> *Deep ruts the wagons made,*
> *The victor and the loser came by here.*
> —Johnny Cash (1964)

Debate as to whether North American rock art is actually a language has continued since its first discovery by Europeans (e.g., Mallery 1893). But despite numerous spurious claims by various people that they have "cracked the code" (e.g., Martineau 1973; McGlone et al. 1993; Patterson 2004), the vast majority of North American rock art (well over 98 percent) clearly does not qualify as a written language, being largely spiritually and metaphorically oriented and ceremonial in nature.

However, some native writing systems do occur in rock art. Cree syllabics—a form of writing developed after that tribe had been in contact with Euro-Americans who helped them develop a syllabic written version of their own language—has been reported from a very few rock art sites in the Canadian Plains (Anonymous 1980:8, 31). Likewise, Sequoia's better-known Cherokee syllabary has also recently been identified in rock art in the southeast United States (Carroll 2017; Carroll et al. 2019). For pre-European contact rock art, however, the case is much less clear-cut.

Some Micmac incised rock art in Nova Scotia appears to have an explicitly narrative structure, with humans (some in canoes), animals, and mythic creatures routinely interacting with one another. In some compositions, projectiles fly between armed men in a canoe and their quarry (Mallery 1893:530–531). A few Micmac informants identified these scenes as mythological stories, further supporting their narrative function, and the possibility that they were a type of rudimentary picture writing. Unfortunately, for purposes of comparison with Plains narrative art, there are very few such images and even fewer ethnographic informants who professed knowledge of them.

Finally, the Archaic period great mural art of the Pecos River Tradition (Boyd 2003) has been shown to encode stories relating to the mythical quest

David A. Kaiser
Oregon Archaeological Society,
Portland

James D. Keyser
Oregon Archaeological Society,
Portland

to find and gather peyote. Current Huichol religious practitioners brought to some Pecos River paintings by Boyd have identified images of culture heroes and conventions linking them to various other objects in these expansive murals, whose stories can be understood once one is schooled in the meaning of many different symbols and their relationships. However, by itself, the art is not explicitly narrative (see Keyser et al. 2013) but rather relies heavily on metaphor and allegory to communicate the murals' tales of mythic journeys to those already initiated.

However, one native rock art tradition, whose roots undeniably predate Euro-American contact, and which then evolved significantly more complexity and detail over a span of slightly more than three centuries, meets the definition of picture writing. This is the Plains Biographic art tradition, which was used by numerous native groups over a long period and across a large geographic area that included the North American Plains and parts of the Columbia Plateau, Colorado Plateau, and American Southwest culture areas. Originally done as rock art, certainly as early as A.D. 1600, Plains Biographic art was later drawn on buffalo robes and as ledger drawings in the years between 1750 and 1920. Numerous early non-Indian observers commented on the communication potential of this Biographic art. Probably the most specific was Edwin Denig, chief factor (i.e., the agent in charge of commercial activities for an entire fur trade district) for the American Fur Company at Fort Union, who wrote:

> Most Indians can carve on a tree, or paint, who they are, where going, whence come, how many men, horses, and guns the party is composed of, whether they have killed enemies, or lost friends, and, if so, how many, etc., and *all Indians* passing by, either friends or foes, *will have no difficulty in reading the same, though such representations would be quite unintelligible to whites unless instructed* [Denig 1930:412–413 (italics ours)].

While the Biographic art tradition has long been recognized as a picture writing system (Ewers 1968; Smith 1949), in which information is stored by one person to be transferred to another in a different time or space, is it actually a written language? Like all writing systems, there needs to be a shared understanding between creator and reader in order to encode and decode the content. Written systems come in a variety of forms but are generally either pictorial, depicting objects and actions, or phonetic, which involves graphic representation of the spoken word (Kolers 1969:349).

Phonetic writing is generally divided into Alphabetic, with symbols representing each phoneme (or individual sound) in the spoken language (as in English); Syllabic, consisting of symbols representing syllables (as in Japanese katakana and the aforementioned Cree and Cherokee syllabaries); or Logographic in which a symbol represents an entire word or phrase (as in Chinese writing or Japanese Kanji characters). Finally, there are Ideographic or picture writings that directly represent images of objects and actions. Biographic tradition art would fall into this latter writing system.

Picture writing is composed of pictograms, graphic symbols that convey meaning through their resemblance to actual physical objects, though many seemingly straightforward images communicate much more than simply "picture equals object" because they are pregnant with symbolism and subtext. Also, pictorial writing does not necessarily conform directly to a specific spoken language, because the reader is reading pictures rather than words or syllables. Thus, even though many of the groups that drew Plains Biographic art were from the same few language families and necessarily shared many cultural practices and attributes, their visual system of communication (picture writing) did not correspond to any specific spoken utterances.

However, there are drawbacks to such a writing system, since pictorial writing cannot express the full range of human thoughts and ideas or convey all that is represented in spoken language. While detailed and intricate symbolism and conventions are often used, abstract concepts and tense can be difficult to convey. However, that is not to say that symbolism, and complex ideas cannot be represented.

Lacking the ability to communicate complicated or abstract ideas with the high degree of accuracy of a spoken language, pictorial writing is often considered only a "partial" writing system (Hill 1967). However, this form of communication also has advantages over what Hill terms "complete" writing systems in that it is not restricted to speakers of a specific language. Complete writing systems are self-contained constructions of components, including words, syntax, and grammar, whereas pictorial communication is comprehensible to a wider audience, the members of which share only generally similar cultural attributes and some understanding of how the communication system works.

Rather than being seen as a lesser or incomplete writing system, then, pictorial writing must be viewed as an entirely different form of written communication, which has been termed a discourse system (Hill

1967:92). Discourse communication is unique in that it does not require the reader to know the writer's spoken language, and instead relies largely on non-linguistic cultural knowledge. As such, discourse systems are a kind of pictorial pidgin language, a grammatically simplified means of communication that develops between two or more groups who do not have a language in common. Such pidgins are commonplace where different linguistic groups come into frequent contact, most often as trade languages such as Chinuk Wawa (or Chinook Jargon) in the Pacific Northwest and Plains Sign Language.

Biographic pictorial writing allowed communication amongst various tribal groups across the Plains who, while not necessarily sharing the same language, shared nearly identical lifeways and forms of warfare, which enabled them to understand its fundamental meaning. This is what allowed the spread of Biographic rock art from what is now Canada all the way to Mexico. According to Petersen (1971:269–308), who published what she termed a "pictographic dictionary," Biographic art became a graphic lingua franca (McLaughlin 2013:43), which explains in large part its widespread distribution across the North America Plains (and parts of adjacent regions). Subsequent authors (e.g., Greene 1985, 1996; Keyser 1987, 1996, 2000; Keyser and Klassen 2001; Keyser et al. 2013, 2015; Parsons 1987), while recognizing the flexibility of this picture writing system, have added significantly to the understanding of what its component parts are and how it functioned.

The construction of this picture writing without ties to specific linguistic utterances is what allows modern scholars, who do not speak the traditional indigenous languages, to still "read" Biographic compositions. In part, this occurs because some of the pictures are self-explanatory to anyone. Such things as bullets streaming from a gun's muzzle or horse hoofprints leading up to a horse being ridden into battle are readily understandable to anyone, even those without knowledge of Plains warfare. However, understanding Biographic art is not simply looking at pictures that are readily intelligible to everyone. Instead, reading these "texts" requires that we filter the images through the proper cultural and historical contexts in order to understand the connotations as well as the denoted meanings of the images (Keyser 1987:52). As such, these pictorial writings have been described as "'High Context' messages, which can be fully understood only by cultural insiders who already understand the messages' larger contextual references" (McLaughlin 2013:44). In this regard, we agree with McLaughlin that some specifics (e.g., locations, tribal identity of participants, individuals' names, and other elements that might be considered the composition's backstory) are beyond our understanding for many biographic compositions (cf. Keyser et al. 2013). However, as archaeologists whose work has involved the notoriously imperfect archaeological record, we prefer to emphasize what can be read in these compositions by understanding the lexicon that has been developed through the use of the direct historical approach and other archaeological and ethnographic techniques.

Discourse systems also have an advantage in that some ideas can be related in a more condensed manner that provides a quicker reading through pictorial representation than by the written word. The use of simplified or exaggerated imagery increases the speed of recognition (Ryan and Schwartz 1956). Modern examples include the use of gendered silhouettes on restrooms, an image of someone falling in order to warn us of slippery floors, or a sign indicating a slick road (Figure 1).

Figure 1. Road sign with ideogram conveying a warning of a possible slick road.

As in other pictorial writing systems, some of these images would be readily comprehensible across diverse language groups and levels of technology (a falling human), but understanding the meaning behind others (gendered silhouettes) would require understanding of the cultural context (indoor, gender-specific toilets, with sex indicated by gender-specific dress), and still others would require significant familiarity with appropriate technology (fast-moving automobiles and paved roads). Hence, just as we sometimes struggle to understand the implication of the figures in Biographic rock art, the creators of this art would often be equally confused by our modern use of the same sorts of images.

Discourse systems like Biographic art are a more participatory form of communication than simply reading a book. Therefore, deciphering the content is less a matter of following a strict set of rules than it is of active interpretation, where the "reader" must take in the entire image while at the same time breaking down individual details for their content, conventions, and cultural implications, and then piecing these back together to arrive at the intended narrative. But doing this today is neither simple nor easy, because observers lack familiarity with many aspects of the technology (old-style weaponry, horse gear, and elements of clothing and accessories) and they are not fully conversant with either the Plains war complex or the overall cultural milieu in which it was practiced. Therefore, many of the conventions and connotations that provide the context for the art have not yet been elucidated. Furthermore, understanding rock art sites often has an added difficulty resulting from the imperfection of the record caused by natural erosion of, and modern cultural damage to, the original images. Thus, we are left trying to decipher a narrative that might simply be lacking key elements that were originally present.

As previously stated, however, pictorial writing is particularly suited for documenting real world objects and narratives, which is exactly the content of Biographic rock art, with its focus on a complex system of war honors, including actual fighting, coup counting, horse theft, sexual capture, and to a lesser extent hunting prowess. This relatively narrow focus of Biographic art results in a limited corpus of images with repeated conventions and compositional structures. However, these compositions can be arranged in a variety of ways that the reader needs to unravel. Additionally, with repeated depictions of similar actions, a process of shortcuts and abstractions occurred in the historic development of Plains Biographic art, leading to reduced detail and greater conventionalization, as well as the development of abstract ideograms. This evolution began to move the pictorial language[1] away from direct representations, easily readable by people immersed in the cultural context, to a more specialized communication requiring culturally specific knowledge of the abstract symbolism. Understanding this level of abstraction today requires readers to carry more culturally specific knowledge with them, reducing the pictorial writing's advantage of easy interpretability. But condensation and abstraction also show the beginnings of a gradual development into a more complex writing system with the introduction of logograms (signs representing words, phrases, or ideas) and more formal structure.

Apart from the cultural knowledge needed to identify some of the objects and events in Biographic art, the way in which the art is composed can sometimes confuse or obfuscate the intended meaning for someone not versed in the rules informing Plains Indians' ideas about perspective and narrative. To this end, as modern readers, we need to understand the variety of non-Western perspectives as well as differing compositional narrative structures that are used in the creation of Biographic art.

Narrative art tells the story of a single event or sequence of events. However, narratives are told over time (diachronic) whereas static images, such as rock art, are seen all at once (synchronic). Therefore, reading a narrative embedded in a pictographic image requires the understanding of certain conventions and organizing principles. These principles define the direction and order of the narrative. While these organizational components are key to understanding a pictorial narrative, they are not regulated by hard and fast rules like most other writing systems.

First, the reader is required to identify the objects depicted. This can be as simple as recognizing a human figure, or involve more culturally specific recognition that the object on the human's head is a "wolf hat," or require intimate and detailed knowledge of the Biographic art lexicon to know that a Crow warrior's mark **X=** meant counting third coup. Moreover, one also needs to be aware of the social and cultural implications of the object depicted. For instance, the wolf hat is a sign that the person pictured served as a scout for a war party.

Understanding how multiple objects relate to one another adds even further complexity. However, there are some overall keys to reading the narrative that include types of perspective and the structure of narrative expression, and these clues can help unlock a composition's content and meanings.

Perspective in Plains Indian Warrior Art

Plains Indian warrior art is characterized by several different types of perspective and an overall artistic convention that differ markedly from our Western European ideal of linear, geometric perspective that characterizes modern realism.[2] These include X-ray perspective (with the corollary of unseen details), twisted perspective, stacked perspective, bird's-eye/aerial view perspective, hierarchical perspective, and expanded space/empty center perspective, and the convention of synecdoche (a rhetorical trope in which a part of something is used to symbolize the whole of an object or action).

Initially, *X-ray perspective* is commonly used to depict humans and animals in the Ceremonial tradition,[3] but it also occurs on some humans and animals in early examples of the Biographic tradition. In this type of perspective, internal organs are illustrated, somewhat as if the figure's body was shown as an X-ray. Such internal organs are not necessarily realistic, often neither accurately portrayed nor positioned, although sometimes the ribcage in particular can be quite lifelike. These organs include ribs and heartline (which is not an actual entity since it includes the esophagus, which often, but not always, has an abstract heart-like organ at its terminus), and a kidney "belt" or kidneys shown as dots. In Plains Indian spiritual beliefs, all these organs were thought to be locations in which supernatural power resided. Outside the body—so not truly in X-ray perspective—artists also drew primary sexual characteristics including penis and sometimes testes for a man and vulva and/or breasts for a woman. A few shield bearers and other warriors engaged in early Biographic combat scenes (Keyser and Poetschat 2014:61) are the most common examples of X-ray perspective in Biographic art, but there are a few late Biographic tradition humans drawn an X-ray style. One classic example is a rectangular-body style human with a heartline and kidneys at DgOw-29 in southern Alberta, shown grappling with an hourglass-body style figure and taking his gun (Figure 2). Another Biographic art scene with internal organs depicted is the larger armored horse at Arminto (48NA991), which has an obvious heartline (Figure 3).

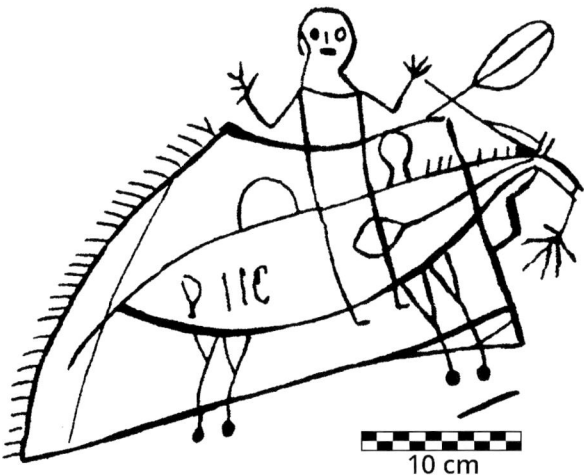

Figure 3. This armored horse with rider at Arminto, Wyoming (48NA991), shows X-ray perspective with the animal's heartline evident. The rider's far leg is visible through the horse and the leather armor cover was also depicted as if transparent.

Figure 4. This combat scene from DgOv-2 at Writing-on-Stone, Alberta, shows both legs of the rider, and a greatly outsized spear with which the rider counts coup on his pedestrian foe.

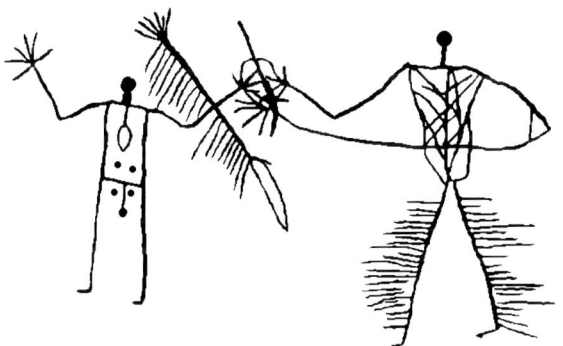

Figure 2. These fighting warriors at DgOw-29 at Verdigris Coulee, Alberta, illustrate a typical coup count—the capture of a weapon (a gun) in hand-to-hand combat. The warrior at left shows a heartline, dot kidneys, and penis and testes characteristic of X-ray perspective.

Corollary to this X-ray perspective is depiction of "unseen" details, even though these would not actually be visible to the observer. In this type of depiction, the artist "knows" what really exists and draws those details despite the fact they are hidden from view. Thus, a Plains Indian horseman with both legs depicted (Figure 4) is not riding side-saddle, but instead has his "off-side" leg drawn specifically because the artist understood that one leg does not really go away simply because it is hidden from the viewer behind the horse's body (Keyser and Minick 2018:13). Again, the Arminto armored horse (Figure 3) shows the armor itself as see-through as well as depicting the rider's far leg as seen through the horse's body. An equally common occurrence is the "see-through" shield that allows a shield-bearing warrior's body outline (sometimes even with his internal organs shown in X-ray perspective!) to show through his shield as if it were transparent (Keyser and Poetschat 2014:10, 61, Figure 4f). This certainly does not represent reality—such hide shields could not actually have been transparent—but rather is another instance of unseen detail, where the reality of what the Indian artist *knows* to exist overrules what his eye actually sees.

We are fortunate to have a diary entry by the Swiss artist Rudolph Friederich Kurz that clarifies the reason for such X-ray illustrations. While Kurz was at Ft. Union on February 26, 1852, he engaged in a debate with a Lakota warrior-artist about the merits of the European artistic tradition. In their discussion, the Lakota artist noted that Kurz's manner of representing a rider with his off-side leg not drawn because it was not visible since it was behind the horse "was not at all satisfactory" because everyone knows that "a man has two legs" (Kurz 1937:301).

Finally, some images are illustrated with what we term unseeable attributes. Sometimes this is a visible representation of sound, where a line or lines are drawn exiting the mouth of a bull elk to represent the bugling sound an animal does in the rut (Figure 5). Likewise, lines issuing from a human's mouth can be drawn to represent a spoken utterance. Human "voice" lines occur rarely in rock art (two are known at the Joliet site, 24CB402), but a line from the mouth or head is commonly used in ledger art and winter counts to connect a person to his/her name glyph—an image representing their spoken name. Still another example of "voice" is in a Cheyenne pictographic "letter" drawn about 1880, where lines from the mouth indicate a spoken invitation (Mallery 1893:363–364).

Figure 5. This Lakota drawing of an Elk Dreamer ceremony, ca. 1900, shows the elk's bugling "voice" as dark, fan-shaped lines issuing from its mouth. Drawing adapted from Wissler (1912:87).

Other unseeable attributes include supernatural indicators or disease (which was believed to have supernatural causation). These can include spirals or zigzag lines associated with humans or animals to denote a being's "spirit aura," or the possession of animal body parts for a part human/part animal therianthropic figure to indicate the transformation of a human into his animal spirit. In some winter count images, spirals or lines in a filigree pattern were used to represent the dyspepsia (including nausea, bloating, stomachache, and other symptoms) that accompanied many epidemic diseases. Such "disease lines" were drawn in the abdominal region for dyspepsia, exiting the belly to indicate borborygmus or flatulence, or exiting the mouth to indicate vomiting.

In rock art, such unseeable details are typically drawn for Ceremonial tradition imagery (Figure 6), presumably to indicate shamans or other supernaturally powerful individuals, but occasionally an image that clearly has biographic intent will utilize such conventions. A classic example is the Elk Dreamer/Dancer carved at the Elk Dreamer site in southeastern Montana. This human figure shows elk antlers and what appear to be cloven hooves, in an image that clearly has both Ceremonial and Biographic aspects. As such, this drawing appears to occupy a position that to some extent bridges both traditions (Keyser and Sundstrom 2015:132–133). A woman drawn at Picture Canyon in southeastern Colorado has her body covered with circles and a small filigree at her mouth. This has been identified as a depiction of epidemic disease (Renaud 1936:34, Plate 13) but it has yet to be verified.

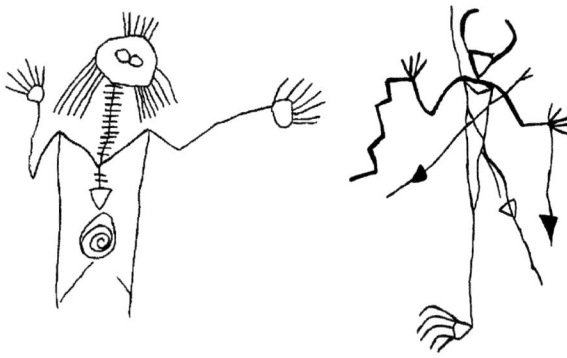

Figure 6. Plains Ceremonial tradition art often shows "unseen" details such as the spiral and neck vertebrae as well as bear-paw hands on figure at left and a bear-paw foot on the figure at right. (a) 24PR2317; (b) 24RB165.

Twisted perspective, where one or more parts of a figure or composition are drawn in one or more different planes than the rest of the drawing, also differs greatly from our ideal of Western realism, although we readily accept its use in some modern art and comic strips (Keyser 2011). The simplest sort of twisted perspective illustrates a figure in two separate planes, often at right angles to one another, so that an animal's body (including head and legs) is seen in side profile, while another part (usually horns, antlers, eyes, or ears) are shown frontally, as if being viewed head-on (Figure 7). The most common example of using two-plane twisted perspective in Biographic rock art is illustrating a horse completely in side profile except for its hooked or C-shaped hooves (which are a representation of the animal's one-toed, C-shaped track) turned 90 degrees so as to be shown in plan view. More complex examples of twisted perspective can include three or even more planes. A classic Biographic art example of three-plane twisted perspective is a horse at the Musselshell site (24ML1049) in Montana, shown in side profile with C-shaped hooves shown as plan view hoofprints, but with two eyes showing pendant tear-streak face paint drawn on the near side of the head, as if in front view (Figure 7c).

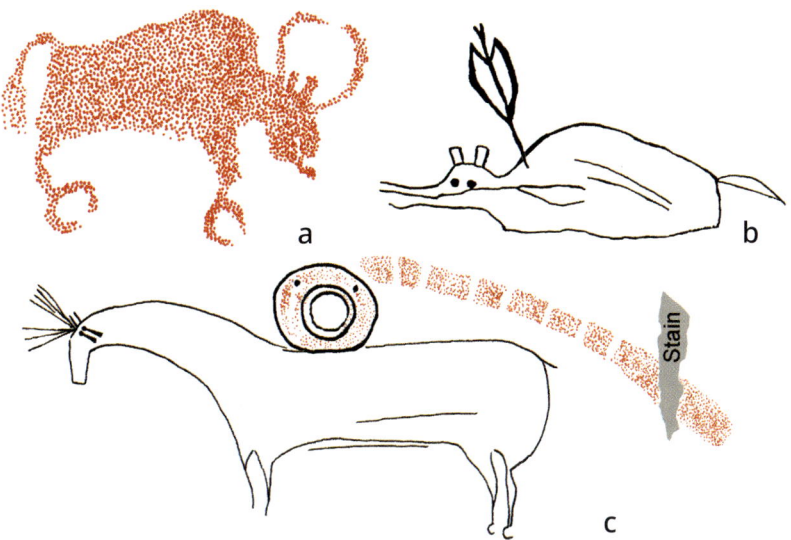

Figure 7. Twisted perspective is relatively common in Plains Ceremonial and Biographic rock art. (a) and (c) both show "three-plane" perspective with body and legs in side view (plane 1), horse's eyes and tear streaks and bison's horns and ears in front view (plane 2), and hooves in plan view (plane 3). Bear in (b) shows "two-plane" perspective with face and ears in front view while body is in side view. (a) 24FH1006; (b) 48SW83; (c) 24ML1049.

Horseback shield bearers also occasionally exhibit twisted perspective. Since the horse is always in side profile, we can assume that the rider astride the animal was most often meant to be viewed in the same way. But a few mounted men (especially shield-bearing warriors) have either facial features or a headdress that indicates their head is drawn as if looking directly at the viewer. Sometimes we cannot determine if this is merely a case of the rider being depicted as if turning his head to face the viewer, but there are figures whose arms and legs are clearly drawn to indicate that the human is in front view while the horse is just as clearly in side view (Keyser and Poetschat 2009:Figure 13a). Several of these are early mounted warriors who presumably were drawn in this manner because their creators were unfamiliar with horses and how to artistically integrate the horse and rider into a single image.

Plains Indian artists portrayed distance in a composition far differently than is typically done in the linear geometric perspective of western realism. To show relative distance from the observer, Plains artists usually used *stacked perspective*, in which images are placed successively higher in a composition to denote those that are further away. Likewise, the upper figures are often the same size as those below them, not smaller as if further from the viewer. The result is often quite confusing for a western observer, who fails to comprehend the relationship between components of a scene that sit one atop the other. For instance, in the scene shown in Figure 8, an observer unschooled in stacked perspective sees a riderless, saddled horse surmounted by a horse with rider who has a long line extending out from his shoulder area, and who in turn has a small cluster of seven short, side-by-side lines (five with small drilled dots at their upper end) placed far above his head. To this presumably untrained observer, the composition makes no sense, other than a possible assumption that the two horses are somehow interacting. But by understanding stacked perspective, the observer can see the unmounted horse and behind it (just slightly further away) a second horse with a rider who reaches out to touch the saddled horse with a long rod (likely a coup stick). The seven

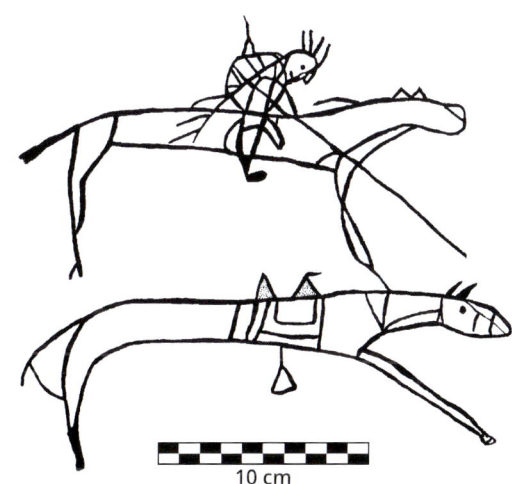

Figure 8. This horse capture scene at La Barge Bluffs, Wyoming (48LN1640), is a conventionalized view with stacked perspective, used to show the horseman behind the riderless horse and the bullets moving even further beyond the horseman.

lines are then seen as flying bullets (fired either by the dismounted rider of the saddled horse or his comrades who are not pictured) that have flown wide past their intended target—the horseman. Combined with two standard Biographic art conventions—(1) the fusillade of fire and (2) claiming ownership of a riderless horse in battle by being the first to touch it with a coup stick or similar implement—the stacked perspective here renders this readily understandable as a horse capture scene, almost identical to others in ledger drawings (Figure 9).

Bird's-eye/aerial view perspective is found exclusively in Biographic art, where it is used only occasionally, but particularly to illustrate large-scale battle scenes, a type of "sexual capture" that shows both the man and woman as complete people with the woman lying on her back as the man crawls up to touch (i.e., "capture") her vulva (Keyser et al. 2006:59), some villagescapes, and entrenched war parties. Merging to a slight degree with stacked perspective in some cases, bird's-eye/aerial view perspective can range from a steeply angled bird's eye view to a straight down plan view, and in some cases several angles can occur in a single composition. Thus, a battle scene at DgOv-43 at Writing-on-Stone (Figure 10) has a horse, a gun, and a human depicted almost as if seen in side profile or front view by an observer on the same level ground line but tipis in the camp circle under attack are shown both as if seen from a very shallow bird's-eye view angle and as an asterisk-like form as though seen from directly above. Another nearby battle scene at the same site is reduced to its basic elements, showing a gun, horse tracks, and opposing forces as if seen from directly above (Figure 11).

In another example, a dance scene at Joliet shows two women, each with her dress pulled up to expose her genitalia. One interpretation has one or both of the women squatting as if "giving birth" to the Crow Hot Dance (McCleary 2008:43–44), but it appears a second artist visiting the site understood the scene and added a man with an exaggeratedly erect phallus reaching up to touch the vulva of the larger of these women (Figure 12). When we compare the modified scene to other Biographic art scenes of "sexual capture" (Keyser

Figure 9. This scene from the Tie Creek ledger shows the same action as Figure 8. Note how the evolution of Biographic art has begun to change some ideas of perspective. While the red horse is still slightly higher than the blue one, its front legs now overlap the closer animal, but remain completely visible in X-ray perspective. Flying bullets litter the scene above and behind the horseman. Note the horseman's name glyph (highlighted in inset), a large and very faint bison extending back above his war bonnet, drawn in pencil and connected to his mouth with a curved line. Image courtesy of Mike Fosha.

Figure 10. Several perspectives are evident in this battle scene at DgOv-43 at Writing-on-Stone, Alberta. Humans defending villages are shown in side view, tipis are shown in steeply angled bird's eye view, with central structure in lower village shown from directly above. Weapons of both forces shown in side view, but man in front of horseman shown upside down. Tracks of horses and pedestrians shown in plan view.

Figure 11. A second battle scene at DgOv-43 at Writing-on-Stone, Alberta, is painted on the roof of a small overhang. In this scene the participants have been reduced to two ranks of short dashes and their tracks and horses' hoofprints. A single gun fires a shot at a horseman who circles in front of one of the groups of warriors.

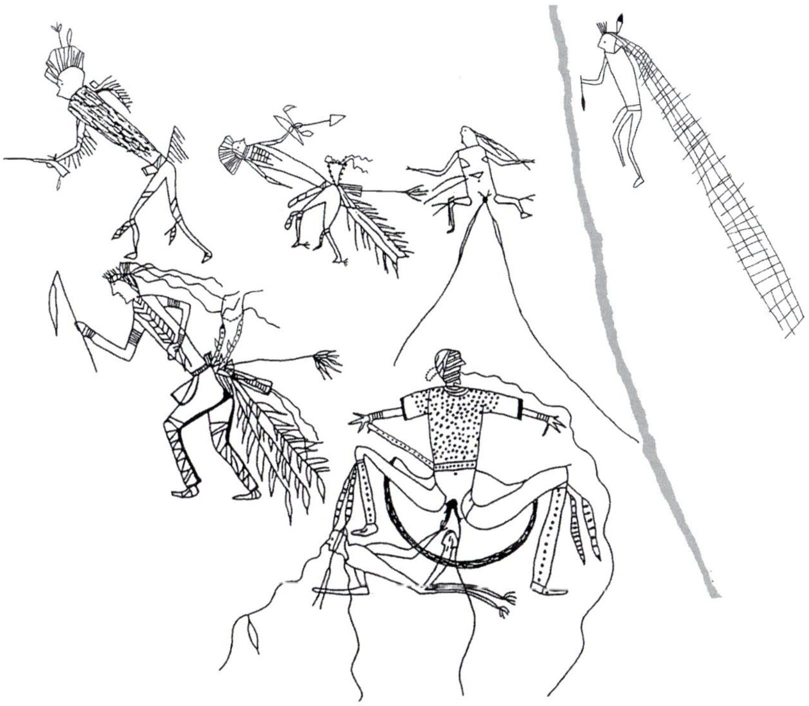

Figure 12. The Hot Dance scene at Joliet, Montana (24CB402), shows the larger woman being sexually captured by a reclining man below who reaches up to touch her vulva with one hand. Such sexual symbolism represents a thrown-away wife, who is dressed in all her finery, including an elk-tooth-decorated dress and leggings and brass bracelets, and with her face painted with lines to represent her husband's coups.

et al. 2006), it is clear that the later artist structured his sexual "coup" with the woman shown in plan view as if lying on her back with knees pulled up. This is the pose typical of other sexual capture scenes, which are shown from above with the man who is "capturing" the woman illustrated as if he were crawling up to reach under her dress and touch her genitalia (Figure 13).

Finally, groups of entrenched combatants encircled by a line are by definition seen as if from directly above. Some of the combatants themselves, either within or outside the fortification, might be lying down, but horses—when shown—are always in side profile (Figure 14). In later ledger art, sometimes a group of entrenched enemies was shown in a more realistic, relatively shallowly angled bird's-eye view (Afton et al. 1997:118–119).

Hierarchical perspective occurs when the size of a figure or an item, or its position in the composition, was used to indicate its relative importance. In the stylized hierarchical perspective of Medieval European art the evident hierarchy was often based on religious importance. But in battles, important generals are sometimes shown larger than life and in a central position in the fight, and in Egyptian art royal figures are shown larger than those serving them. The hierarchy in Biographic art can reflect several different things, including: (1) spiritual power (such as an outsized shield looming over a combat scene that attests to the spiritual potency of the owner's vision in which he obtained the heraldic design [Figure 13]); (2) superior killing ability (hence, an outsized spear or its metal point to indicate its greater efficacy as a killing implement); (3) the centrality or the exaggerated size of the artist's self-portrait (which designates him as the originator of key actions in the scene); or (4) the relative importance of a person or item to the storyline of the narrative (hence, an outsized gun that emphasizes it was taken by the protagonist in hand-to-hand combat and represents one of the four major coups).

One other aspect of hierarchical perspective deserves mention. Plains Biographic rock art routinely shows combat between two participants

Figure 13. This scene at 39HN217 in South Dakota's North Cave Hills shows a warrior's coups including his capture of a woman's reproductive potential as shown by his crawling up to touch the woman's vulva. Next to this a large decorated shield floats over a scene in which its owner is shown holding a smaller version of the same shield, appropriate to his size.

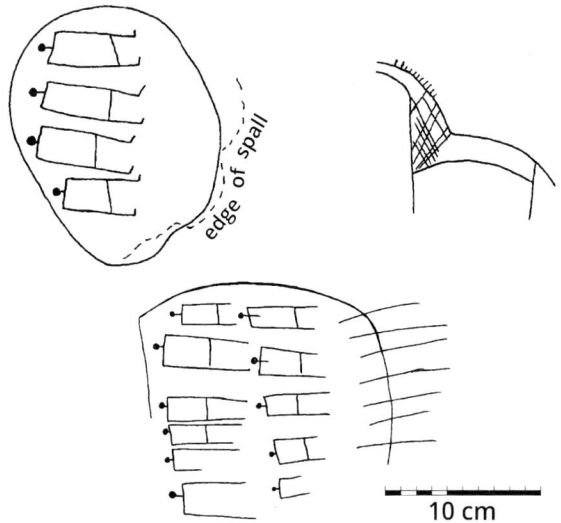

Figure 14. These fortification scenes at DgOw-32 at Verdigris Coulee, Alberta, show humans lying down, an attacker's horse in side profile, and attackers' weapons extending into the lower fortification.

one or both of whom wield a weapon of greatly exaggerated length (Figure 4). While such elongation might reflect superior killing power or spiritual potency, in some cases it simply appears that the weapon's length was exaggerated in order to explicitly "connect" the two participants who are being drawn some distance apart so they do not overlap or otherwise interfere with one another. Sometimes this occurs with both participants on a single ground line, but other times it occurs in stacked perspective. In this same concept of needing connection, some scenes of sexual intercourse show two people in front-view pose on an inferred ground line sexually connected by a man's greatly elongated penis looping down below the figures and turning back up to the woman's vulva (Figure 15).

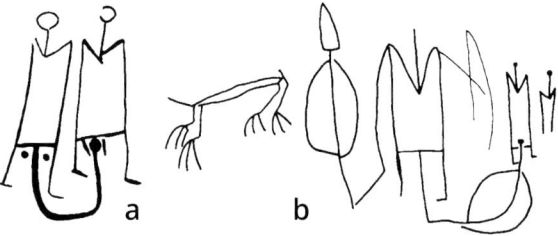

Figure 15. Hierarchical perspective often includes an explicit connection between two participants. In these scenes of sexual intercourse, the man's elongated penis extends down and curves upward to the woman on the right. Note the explicit hierarchy of the participants in (b) shown by the larger size of the man and his weapons. Also note the visual pun where his penis is "fletched" like the arrow he holds. (a) Castle Gardens, Wyoming (48FR108); (b) DgOv-133, Writing-on-Stone, Alberta.

The last type of perspective occurring in this art is what we term the *expanded space/empty center* organization (or for an easy mnemonic—the "donut-hole" perspective). This perspective derives largely from the fact that Biographic art has a non-linear depth perception and is essentially non-realistic in proportions for the actors. The donut-hole perspective combines an expansion of space required to illustrate all the actors in a complex scene (most or all of whom are essentially equal-sized, and some of whom are often mounted) while focusing the action that really occurred in a limited central space, which includes only key storytelling elements such as flying projectiles, human footprints and horse tracks, and floating weapons. The result is that a fight scene will often be drawn so that it appears to occupy a broad field of battle with participants riding or running toward one another, and shooting at one another from what seem to be great distances; when in fact, the artist well knew (and fully intended to depict) that this was hand-to-hand combat at close quarters. Thus, in order to illustrate just such a fight, while remaining true to the principles of illustrating complete details of weaponry, costume, horse tack, and sequent actions, the artist directs and focuses an observer's attention to this central area by marking it with clusters of flying bullets or arrows, the paths of humans and/or horses, and even a capture hand or floating weapon. Hence, what the observer first notes is the actors drawn in great detail but spread out at the margins of the scene. Only secondarily can the viewer truly understand the full extent and actual nature of the actions these combatants are undertaking by closely observing the seemingly almost empty space in the composition's center and comprehend the relationship of the much simpler marks and figures there to the greater whole.

When combined with an understanding of the various conventions that characterize Biographic art, this enables an observer to understand a composition in detail.

Several very detailed Biographic art compositions clearly show the "donut-hole" perspective. One of the simplest is the Castle Butte (24YL418) combat scene (Figure 16), in which two warriors engage one another

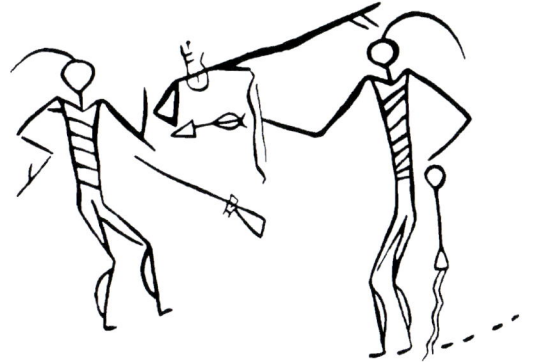

Figure 16. These fighting warriors at Castle Butte, Montana (24YL418), tell a complete and compelling story using a minimum of images drawn with exquisite detail.

without touching, although a very detailed flintlock rifle (shown twice) and a bow and flying arrow occupy a space (the donut-hole) between the two warriors that is large enough to contain the bodies of two additional men drawn to the same dimensions as the combatants. The floating flintlock at the top of the scene is clearly a gun taken by the victor (the warrior on the right) and then turned around to strike his foe—all in hand-to-hand combat after he shot an arrow at the man. Certainly, this weapon capture and coup-strike happened at close quarters, but had the artist tried to illustrate the hand-to-hand struggle, the ensuing take-away of the flintlock, and then its reuse to strike the foe, as it actually happened, the resultant tangle of bodies, arms, and weapons would have been an unintelligible mishmash of lines in this type of art. Instead, by leaving the protagonists at the margins of the scene and having the weapons move about in a simultaneous narrative in the "donut-hole," the action is fully understandable, and the artist was able to illustrate all the salient details of participants and their weaponry.

Another extreme example of illustrating the "donut-hole" spatial organization is the Rocky Coulee battle scene (DgOv-57) at Writing-on-Stone (Figure 17). This battle composition is one of the premier examples of Biographic rock art narratives on the Northern Plains (Kaiser and Keyser 2015:174–175; Keyser 1977, 1987; Keyser et al. 2013), showing detailed combat between five pedestrian warriors attacking four mounted warriors who ride out to defend their camp. In this scene, the concentration of "bullets" and human footprints in the upper center of the actual combat composition focuses the observer's attention on this otherwise unoccupied area of the drawing, and clearly indicates this is where the action involving five of the nine participants really took place. At the scale of this drawing, there simply was insufficient space to illustrate all five fighters in a narrative of close quarter combat with the detail required for this type of composition. Thus, the five men were drawn surrounding this central area and their bullets and footsteps show where the actual action occurred.

Synecdoche—the Implied Actor

One of the most common Biographic conventions is the use of synecdoche, in which a part of something symbolizes the whole object or action. Biographic art is replete with examples of synecdoche, where a floating weapon stands for the person wielding it, flying bullets indicate unseen guns firing, hoofprints stand for a horse's path into the fight, and busts of enemy warriors touched by floating weapons tally vanquished enemies. And although we can often see the development of these shorthand depictions in the evolution of this art (Figure 18), where recognizable things gradually get more abstract over time, these are still paired with fully explicit depictions in most scenes. This practice continued into the latest Biographic art (including historic ledger and robe drawings), produced as late as the first decades of the 1900s.

In this synecdoche convention the narrative's protagonist often does not appear as a complete

Figure 17. The Rocky Coulee battle scene (DgOv-57) at Writing-on-Stone is a classic example of the "donut-hole" perspective. The "empty" center, marked by the light grey circle, is actually the area where nearly all of the action took place as indicated by the clustering of more than 30 bullets there and the tracks of three participants running into that part of the scene. The only actors entirely within the empty center are the swordsman and his opponent on whom he has counted coup in addition to scalping and taking his gun. Tracks to the right of the gunmen show that group's route of travel to this engagement.

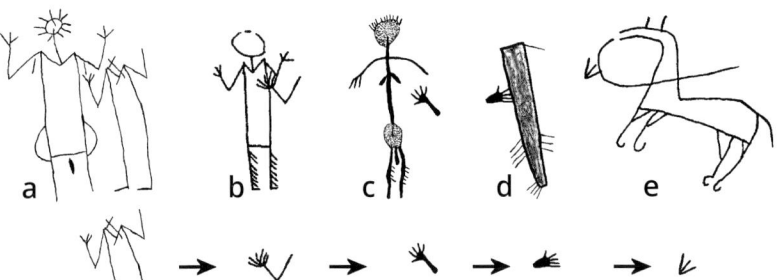

Figure 18. The development of the capture hand in Biographic art from a full human figure through various stages to a small trident. All examples but (c) can reasonably be attributed to Blackfoot artists. (a) and (b) Bear Gulch (24FR2); (c) Red Canyon (48FR2508); (d) Malcolm Robe, Blackfoot, ca. 1830s (Lycett and Keyser 2018); (e) DgOw-32 at Writing-on-Stone.

physical being. Instead, in such compositions, we see an abbreviated version of the character or object, such as a floating capture hand to stand in for the entire protagonist (Figure 19), or the holding of a quirt

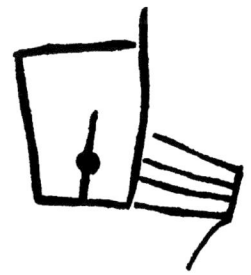

Figure 19. This stylized vulva with a Crow/Hidatsa style capture hand at 39HN893 is the ultimate in shorthand signs to indicate sexual capture.

symbolizing the riding of an unseen horse (Figure 16). Elsewhere, the protagonist is not depicted at all, only the results of his actions, which can be ascribed to him only because we recognize his weapon performing an action or his or his horse's tracks moving through a scene (Figure 20).

Figure 20. This vignette scene from a coup count tally at Ellison's Rock (24RB1019) is the epitome of synecdoche in Biographic rock art. Here the protagonist is shown by his horse's hoofprints and his quirt, used to strike the enemy as he rode by. The foe is shown only as a human bust with lines of a tattoo or body paint design on his upper torso.

Structurally, much narrative art can be viewed in terms of subject, verb, and direct object, such as "I stole a horse." In the grammar of null-subject languages, such as Spanish or Russian, an independent clause is permitted to lack an explicit subject if said subject is re-trievable from context. In Biographic art, the protagonist in a null-subject structure is only implied—as if he were "offstage." Thus, we see the horse that was stolen, or the enemy that was struck, but not the actor who performed these actions. Like the footprints of the iconic invisible man, in some scenes we see only the hero's tracks or his horse's hoofprints guiding us through the action. In others, a floating weapon is held by his unseen hand to strike coup upon a foe.

Narrative Detail

The use of synecdoche, and the removal of explicitly depicted subjects or actions is a key component in the structure of Biographic art. However, this is often a point of confusion for the reader, who must often "fill in the blanks" to complete the narrative. This need to read such narratives intertextually leads to their classification into three levels—*Explicit*, *Implied*, and *Inferred* narratives (Keyser et al. 2013; 2015)—based on the portrayal of movement and interaction between figures, the association of elements and their placement in a composition, and the use of standardized and repeated conventions.

Explicit Narrative

Sometimes the images and actions in a composition are sufficiently uncomplicated and clearly enough arranged so it is obvious to any observer that what is being depicted is a narrative story. In its most direct form, events and actors in an Explicit narrative are so unambiguously portrayed interacting with one another in postures showing obvious movement that any observer will recognize the basic storyline (Figure 21). Actions and participants are shown in adequate detail to be readily identified, and the story's content can be understood—at least in its basic outline—without the need for additional cultural knowledge. The artist might even use simple conventions, such as track sequences to show movement through the depicted scene, adding additional detail that can be readily understood by anyone if the larger action is portrayed in a sufficiently straightforward manner.

Touching an enemy with your weapon or your bare hand was the primary coup for Plains warriors, who depicted the act in multiple ways. Figure 22a shows an explicit depiction of the horseback protagonist being

Figure 21. This petroglyph of a man spearing another is an example of an explicit narrative any observer would recognize. Site DgOv-60 at Writing-on-Stone, Alberta.

The content of an explicit narrative can be significantly expanded if the observer has access to culturally relevant contextual information referenced earlier. But such information is "external" to the narrative composition, in that it is not present in the images themselves. Such contextual information might include ethnographic, ethnohistoric, historic, or oral history information or even archaeological evidence associated with a Biographic tradition rock art site. This sort of information would have been possessed by the artist of the composition and his contemporaries as part of the cultures in which they participated. Thus, information as divergent as which elements of clothing and costume accessories were considered ethnic identifiers, the rationale behind cutting a notch in a horse's ears or tying up his tail, and the reasons for and practices associated with slave raiding might serve to significantly increase the information about a particular composition, but today this can only be acquired through extensive study of Plains cultures.

Implied Narrative

However, not all narratives are drawn at the explicit level; sometimes details of the action are missing even though there is still a strong implication that the artist meant to portray a detailed narrative. Such cases can lack explicit markers of movement or unambiguous portrayals of action between component figures, but there are associations between figures or the use of conventions that strongly hint a storyline was intended by the original artist. Figure 22b takes away the image of the actor, using only synecdoche to reduce him to his horse's tracks, and then his footprints running up to the enemy, and finally his coup stick striking the enemy bowman. Figure 22c reduces the entire action to its two component parts, a standing enemy touched by a disembodied hand representing the scene's protagonist. For such implied narratives the only way to flesh out their narrative content—the storyline—is through an understanding of Biographic conventions and other evidence external to the composition itself. This necessitates a familiarity with the practices of Plains In-

wounded. Using synecdoche, we see him dismounting, his path represented by his footsteps. He runs up to touch the bowman and another enemy with his hand. Then, as he continues on, we see him run by three other enemy warriors, each of whom he has stabbed with a large spear.

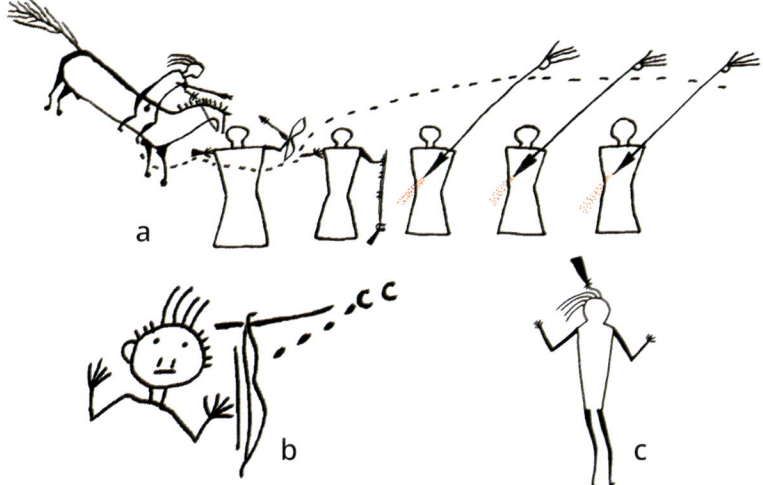

Figure 22. These Biographic art scenes illustrate the same act (touching an enemy to count coup) using explicit narratives: (a) shows the movement of the wounded horseback protagonist and his dismounting and running through the lineup of enemies to count coup by touching with his bare hand and stabbing with a lance; (b) shows this same action in a much more shorthand way, where the off-stage protagonist is represented only by his horse's tracks, his own footprints, and the coup stick he used to strike his enemy; (c) shows only the enemy with the protagonist's bare hand touching his head. (a) Mandan war shirt, ca. 1820; (b) Ellison's Rock petroglyph; (c) Schoch war shirt, ca. 1830 (Keyser and Brady 1993).

dian warfare, the objects (weapons, costume, and horse tack) illustrated by the artist, and also the reasons for drawing Biographic art.

For example, as mentioned above, in some scenes the protagonist himself is not shown. At other times, we may have to understand the action that took place by its end result. Both would be the case in a drawing showing a horse picketed at a tipi (Figure 23a). The subject of such a horse scene is the artist, and the implied action is his act of bravery in sneaking into an enemy's camp to take one of their best horses, which were tied up at their owners' tipis. Likewise, a horse shown with a cut lead rope also indicated such a war honor (Figure 23b). Taking a horse in this manner was a highly esteemed war honor among Plains tribes, but this scene could easily be misinterpreted if one saw the picture and assumed the subject was either the horses or the tipi, since the protagonist is not shown.

Inferred Narrative

Just as the protagonist in Biographic rock art must sometimes be inferred from the actions he performed, occasionally the existence of the narrative itself is obscure and can only be inferred. In such cases, without specific action there is no overt narrative; however, some images are so detailed and full of symbolic associations that the viewer feels there must be more of a story associated with the image. Such inferred narratives lack any markers for storyline or any indication suggesting to an uninitiated observer (one not schooled in the cultural milieu from which this art arose) that it represents a narrative event. Winter counts—calendars often recorded on a buffalo robe—depict a single memorable incident as a marker for the entire year, and often have only an iconic image that acts as a mnemonic device to remember a narrative. No clear action is shown. The narrative must be inferred. In such a case, the observer is entirely reliant on external evidence consisting of culturally specific knowledge not available to the modern viewer without extensive study. But, after study, such evidence, if carefully considered and conscientiously applied to a drawing, often can reveal incredible narrative storylines for even quite basic compositions.

As an example, two small, spatially isolated compositions carved adjacent to one another at Writing-on-Stone (Figure 24) were completely undecipherable

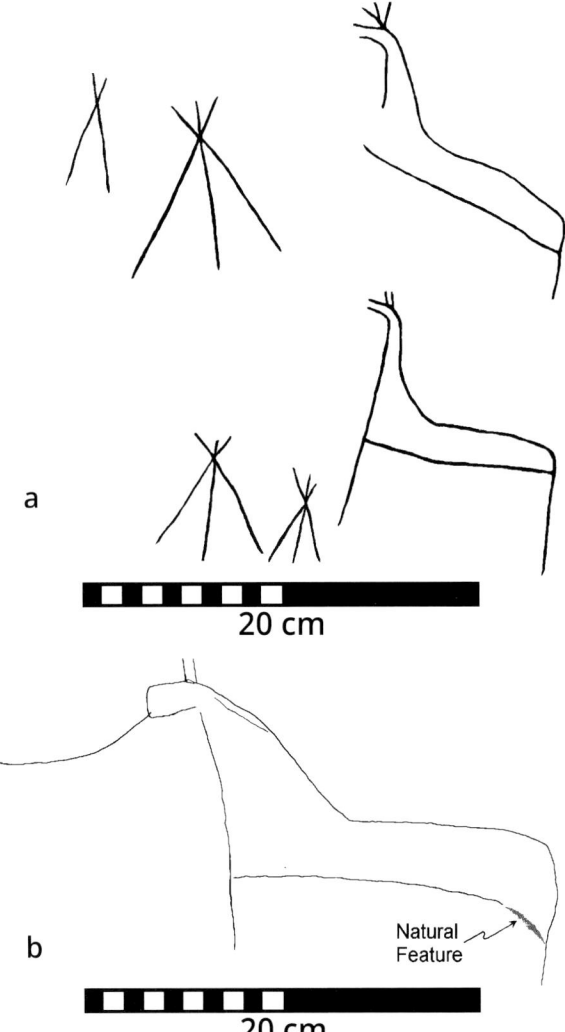

Figure 23. Stolen horses are recorded in a variety of ways in Biographic rock art: (a) horses shown picketed in front of a tipi, DgOv-2, Writing-on-Stone, Alberta; (b) horse with cut picket rope, Two Medicine Petroglyph (24GL1718), Montana.

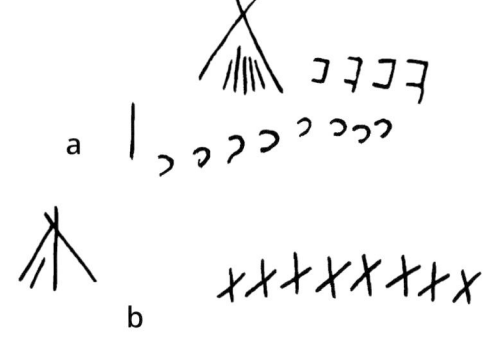

Figure 24. These ideographic compositions, consisting of a tipi with various symbols carved next to it, are tallies of Blackfoot men's war honors. They are carved at DgOw-27 at Writing-on-Stone, Alberta. The vertical line in (a) is a picket pin juxtaposed with eight horse tracks indicating horses taken from within an enemy village. The four backward squared C-shapes denote leadership of four war parties. The Xs in (b) signify eight picket pins each representing a horse stolen from in front of an enemy's tipi.

when first recorded. Neither was suspected of being a narrative. Each shows a tipi associated with small geometric forms; Xs in one case and small open-sided rectangles, reverse Cs, and a vertical slash in the other. Only after research two decades later that exposed the junior author to Blackfoot Biographic art ideograms for picketed horses, picket pins, and horse raids (Wissler 1911) was the narrative content of these two compositions revealed (Keyser and Klassen 2003).

Another example is a portrait of a Ute warrior fully outfitted with fancy clothing and weapons (Figure 25). No action is shown, but we can infer that this warrior would have been readily identified by his contemporaries based on his detailed regalia and hairstyle, and it seems likely that his deeds were well known. Unfortunately, in the absence of culturally specific knowledge, we have been unable to determine this man's identity, so the storyline associated with his portrait is now unknown to us. Possibly, additional ethnographic work will provide information enabling us to know this man's story.

Narrative Structure

In addition to the continuum of Narrative detail, from explicit to implied and inferred, the structure of how the composition itself was organized varies considerably. There is no single organizing principle in the overall depiction of narratives in Biographic rock art. This same lack of universal structure is found in a variety of narrative art around the world and throughout history. This is why narrative art is often said to be interpreted rather than read, in its strictest sense.

The study of visual narratives has been the subject of multiple disciplines including archaeology, art history, narratology, and semiotics. These different disciplines have often created their own taxonomies and have not generally looked outside their own fields to develop more universal classifications; however, they have recognized a variety of methods used to communicate a narrative through pictures (Horváth 2016). Most pertinent to our current analysis is study of the structure of ancient Greek and Roman narrative art (Stansbury-O'Donnell 1999; Von Dippe 2007) as well as early Buddhist art (Dehejia 1990).

The classification of narrative types is based on how many times the subject occurs, as well as the number of timeframes or locations depicted (Table 1). These different structural methods, though recognized up to this point primarily in Classical Greek, Roman, and Asian-Indian art, occur in narrative art around the world, including Plains Biographic art. However, previous classification schemes have not taken into account the use of synecdoche and implied and inferred

Figure 25. This fully outfitted Ute warrior is carved at McKee Springs along the Green River in Dinosaur National Monument, Utah. While this portrait would undoubtedly have been recognized by the artist's peers, the biographic story it was intended to tell is now lost.

Table 1. Types of Pictorial Narration.

Narrative Type	No. of Pictures	Characters	Time	Space
Monoscenic	1	No Repeats	One Moment	One
Simultaneous	1	No Repeats	Multiple	One
Progressive	1	No Repeats	Multiple	Multiple
Cyclical	2+	Repeats	Multiple	Multiple
Continuous	2+	Repeats	Multiple	One Landscape
Serial	2+	No Repeats	Multiple	Multiple

(Adapted from Stansbury-O'Donnell (1999), Table 1)

narratives. The model therefore is not an exact fit for Biographic rock art, but can be used as a guide, with a deeper abstract/implied component. Our model of narrative structure is based on a subset of the taxonomy of narrative discussed in some detail and summarized by Stansbury-O'Donnell (1999:1–6, Table 1-1).

While these categories are academic classifications that would not have consciously occurred to the creator of the art, the varieties of narrative construction show that similar methods were used to visually communicate complex ideas in widely different cultures. Thus, it is not necessarily important that the reader be able to classify the structure of the pictures they are interpreting, but awareness of the differing kinds of narrative structure gives clues to the organizing principles of the images and how to read them.

Monoscenic Narrative

Like an explicit narrative, the simplest and most direct depiction of a narrative is Monoscenic. This is a simple picture that depicts an action that takes place in a single time and place, in which the characters are shown only once (Figure 21).

As mentioned above, this simple, direct narrative can have additional complexity when elements are abbreviated, abstracted, or implied. However, the key feature is that a Monoscenic narrative depicts a single event in time and space, without duplication of subjects, objects, or action. So you can have a Monoscenic implied narrative, such as a warrior at Bear Gulch (24FR2) depicted holding a spear as well as a bow with a quiver of arrows, but he is shown in a falling defeated posture with a double-spike mace hitting him on the head (Figure 26). The warrior who wielded the weapon is not shown. He is only implied by his weapon and the results of his actions.

However, even Monoscenic narratives can be more complex than initially recognized. A single scene can be used to represent a much larger narrative in which the overall story needs to already be known by the viewer, thus acting as a mnemonic device. In rock art this is commonly found in non-narrative Ceremonial imagery in which mythological figures, who have their associated stories, are shown. But it also occurs in Biographic art, where it has long been known that many of the specific details of any scene were left to the narrator (Wissler 1911:38–39). On the Plains, such Monoscenic narratives are one of the prime features of Winter Counts (Figure 27). These incidents are sometime iconic individual images, but can also be Biographic

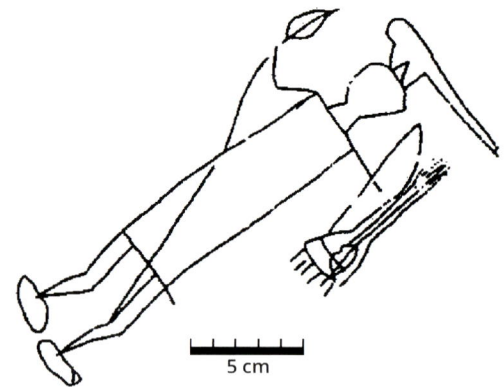

Figure 26. This vanquished warrior at Bear Gulch, Montana (24FR2), is armed with both a bow and arrows and a spear. He topples over in the loser's posture after being hit on the head with a floating double-spiked mace.

Figure 27. This monoscenic vignette from American Horse's winter count is a biographic scene documenting a memorable incident for his tribe for the year 1854–1855. The scene records the killing of Conquering Bear (indicated by name glyph attached to head) in a fight where the Lakota killed 30 U.S. army soldiers. The soldiers are indicated by the black dashes arranged in three ranks behind the hat-wearing soldier's bust, while Conquering Bear's death is indicated by a bullet streaming from one of the four muzzle blasts, which causes a chest wound to bleed profusely. Adapted from Mallery (1893:562).

narratives. The full details surrounding these narratives are rarely shown, but are remembered by the calendar keeper or community as a whole.

Simultaneous Narrative

Some narrative rock art, upon initial viewing, seems to have little discernable structure, being a jumble of different images in which the story is obscured. This is often the case with Simultaneous narrative, one of the most common narrative compositional structures found in Biographic art. Like a Monoscenic narrative, this is also a single picture where the characters are not repeated. However, in a Simultaneous narrative, multiple events of a single story are combined into a single picture. Often a central scene is shown, to which images or events from the past and/or future are appended. The result is a sequence of narrative moments in a single event that are conflated into a single image. Different moments in time are shown simultaneously. Sometimes the order of events is clear, such as a line of footprints leading to a subject, but other times no direct order of causality is shown. The use of images from different times can show different tenses, or a narrative progression in a single image.

At the Manual Lisa site (24YL82) in Montana an equestrian warrior holds a decorated shield and a spear (Figure 28). The spear stabs or hits a pedestrian. Immediately next to this figure is another pedestrian in a

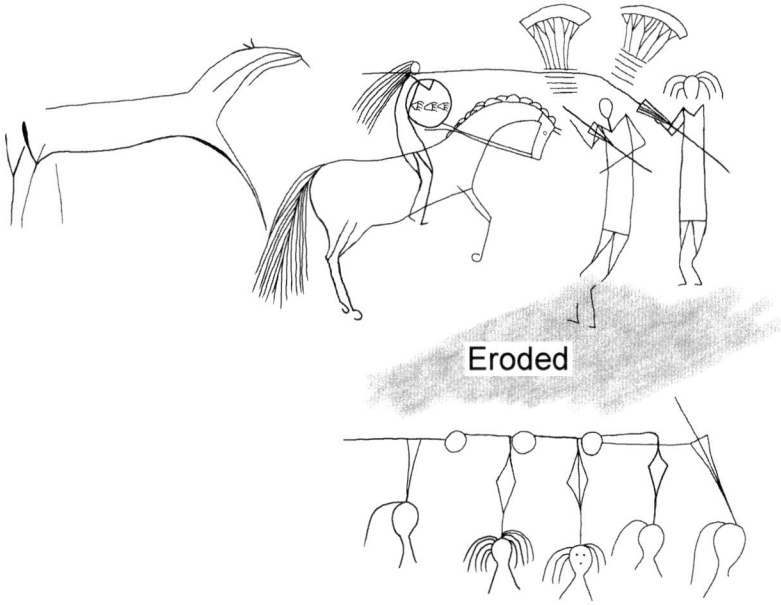

Figure 28. A Crow man's tally of his coups as recorded in a petroglyph at the Manuel Lisa site (24YL82). In the scene above he counts coup on two enemies with a long spear. The lineup of human busts (below) shows a spontoon tomahawk counting coup on four figures and a spear touching the head of the fifth. A horse and two war bonnets juxtaposed with the horseman indicate captured war trophies.

leaning defeated posture also hit by another depiction of the same lance and spear tip. However, this second depiction of the spear is abbreviated, showing only the matching spear point and part of the shaft. The narrative shows the explicit battle between two enemies, to which a confrontation with a second warrior is appended. Two actions at different moments in time are shown in this single image.

A more complex panel at Castle Butte (Figure 16) shows two fighting warriors. While each of them is shown only once, the narrative depicts actions from various times in their encounter. The warrior on the right—a bowman—has a series of footprints showing him entering the scene. However, he also holds a quirt. While this could be seen as a simple snapshot of the action, it misses the significance of the past implied action—the quirt signifying that its carrier rode to the location, but dismounted from his horse before entering the fight. In Plains warfare, giving up the advantage provided by one's horse in such a fight was considered to add to the bravery inherent in such a deed, and hence to increase the prestige of one who engaged an enemy in this manner. As he approaches the enemy he shoots an arrow, but apparently misses.

The warrior on the left is armed with a flintlock long gun and a coup stick, but he leans back in a defeated posture. His gun is the only element shown twice in the scene, indicating different points in the timeline. In one depiction it floats just out of the loser's hand, pointed toward his attacker, while the second time it is floating between the opponents but facing the opposite direction. The first position shows the gun was captured by the bowman, while the second position shows that the victor turned the enemy's gun back on him to strike coup by using it to touch the vanquished man. Various narrative elements are conflated into this one scene. Events both before and after the central conflict portrayed are signified by synecdoche and other conventions. The main action involving the two warriors directly clashing in hand-to-hand combat functions as a synchronic fulcrum for the past (dismount, run up, shoot arrow) and future actions (take gun, turn it around, and strike enemy with it) of this diachronic narrative.

This use of conflated time requires us to begin inferring parts of the narrative, as we must deduce elements of the action based on clues depicted, without the full action being shown. Moreover, interpretation can be further complicated when significant elements, like the subject himself, are only implied either by synecdoche or the result of an action (Figure 29).

Progressive Narrative

Like a Simultaneous narrative, a Progressive narrative is quite similar in that it depicts multiple narrative events within a single image, without repetition of the

Figure 29. Vignette scene from a coup count tally at Ellison's Rock (24RB1019) showing a protagonist's footprints running up to count coup on an enemy with a bow. The victor then took his foe's spontoon tomahawk, which floats away out of the man's hand.

character(s). The difference between the two is that in a Progressive narrative the events depicted can occur not only at different times but in multiple locations as well. This type of composition commonly shows a warrior's accomplishments over a significant time span (occasionally his entire lifetime).

A composition at Ten Sleep Canyon in Wyoming shows such a progressive narrative (Figure 30). The protagonist, identified in the scene only by his horse's tracks, his own footprints and weapons, and the capture hand convention, first rides by a pedestrian warrior who carries a shield and spear to strike him with the horseman's own spear. Then, in another battle action (note the tracks crossing themselves), our hero rides up on his horse, dismounts and runs up to count coup on a second enemy with a special type of metal-bladed tomahawk known as a Missouri war axe. In still another action the hero's capture hand is shown taking three arrows. Finally, a scalp pole with suspended enemy scalp drawn above the entire scene indicates the attainment of another war honor. In this composition, the protagonist is shown only through synecdoche, but his multiple deeds from different times and places—as indicated by different weapons, different enemies, and the layout of the composition—illustrate his prowess as a warrior.

Sometimes the nature of a progressive narrative in Plains Biographic art is only made clear by the depiction of an unreasonable number of coups to have been counted in a single engagement; the presence of too many weapons to have been used in a single fight; or by a representative image accompanied by tallies showing similar events to have occurred multiple times.

Cyclical Narrative

Larger compositions can show a single story with multiple pictures showing different events within the larger action. Some of the events within a Cyclical narrative can even be from the viewpoint of different

Figure 30. This coup count tally at Ten Sleep Canyon, Wyoming, is a progressive narrative. Beginning at upper right the artist shows himself (represented by his horse's tracks and his spear) counting coup on a pedestrian warrior carrying a shield and spear. Just below the horse tracks is another pair of horse tracks with footprints (indicating the hero's dismounting and running up to an enemy) extending to the left to a Missouri war axe tomahawk that counts coup on the second human. Between the two humans are three arrows taken by a capture hand. At the top left is a scalp pole with a suspended scalp at the upper end.

actors. Thus, in a Cyclical narrative one or more characters are shown more than once, taking part in multiple scenes that happened in multiple locations. Such narratives are a collection of individual pictures each telling a part of a larger story.

A ledger drawing from the 1880s by Elk Head, a Gros Ventre prisoner incarcerated in the territorial prison at Deer Lodge, Montana, depicts a collage of significant moments in the story of his life (Bottomley-O'looney 2012:45). Within the same illustration he shows himself both as a baby being carried by his mother, who is being shot at, as well as his accomplishments as an adult warrior.

At La Barge Bluffs (48LN1640) in Wyoming a large Biographic composition shows numerous warriors on horseback and assorted combat scenes, as well as objects such as a railroad train (Figure 31). Within this large petroglyph the distinct representation of a woman wearing a dress with a long elk-tooth-decorated sash

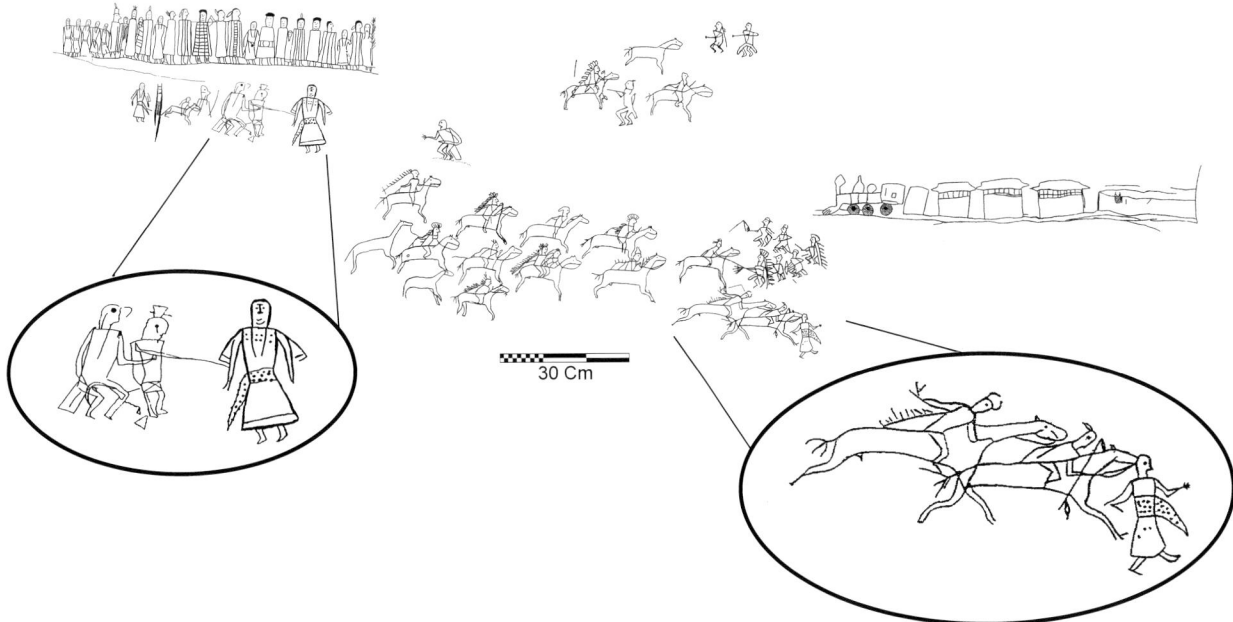

Figure 31. This scene at La Barge Bluffs, Wyoming (48LN1640), is a cyclical narrative showing a running battle near a train and a later adoption ceremony in which a captured woman is taken into the victorious group. Enlargements of the two scenes showing this same woman are shown in the oval areas.

occurs twice. In one scene, as part of a larger battle, she is running from two pursuers on horseback, who capture her. Elsewhere on the panel she stands in front of a line of dancers where two men, almost certainly the same who were riding her down, touch her with a coup stick or lance to recount her capture as part of her adoption into the group (Keyser and Poetschat 2005:35–37).

Continuous Narrative

A Continuous narrative has the same elements as a Cyclical narrative, showing multiple representations of the subject at various times, but it all occurs on a single depicted landscape. However, plants, natural features, or other landforms are rarely illustrated in Biographic rock art, so the "landscape" is often indicated by a tipi camp, buildings, or structures of some sort. Vegetation, such as trees, is sometimes depicted in horse stealing scenes, to show the copse of trees near the enemy village where the warrior hid awaiting his chance to sneak out in the night and steal the best horse. In other cases, location or landscape is often only implied—by the physical setting of the art, or even by the topography of the rock surface itself.

This Continuous narrative subset was created by those studying Roman and Hellenistic art in which the landscape and architecture often featured prominently. We know of no example of Continuous narrative in Plains Biographic rock art but it occurs in some of the latest ledger drawings made by Southern Plains Indian artists incarcerated as prisoners of war. For example, Howling Wolf illustrates a horse race in which two horses compete along a winding course (Petersen 1968:54–55). The riders' movement through the landscape of hills, trees, and open plains is shown by their horses' hoofprints. In addition to showing the main horses in full gallop, they are also shown at the starting line. The winning horse is identifiable by its color and two horizontal lines branded or painted on its hindquarters. Here we have multiple representations at different points in time, all contained within a landscape composition. Though rare in biographic art due to the frequent lack of landscape details, it shows the further variety that was employed to communicate a visual story.

Serial Narratives

Like a newspaper comic strip, Serial narratives are individual pictures that are separate, divided episodes of a single, larger story. Each of these discreet images shows a single event from a continuous story, and characters occur only once per frame. The separation of panels in this fashion does not occur in Plains rock art, but became common in later robe art where scenes were separated by lines demarcating individual panels in a larger narrative (Brownstone 1993, 2007; Dempsey

2007; Ewers 2011:106). These divisions were added either by the artist/authors or sometimes by Euro-Americans who annotated the art as it was described to them. Just such a painted elk skin robe was created by Big Nose, a Blackfeet warrior, ca. 1893 to show his various militaristic accomplishments throughout life (Brownstone 2007). The individual scenes are divided with lines separating each engagement (Figure 32).

Likewise, individual images in ledger art also were sometimes demarcated with dividing lines. However, more often individual pages in a ledger book each contained an individual scene as part of the larger narrative of an individual's or group's accomplishments or experiences, the separate pages acting as structural divisions. Winter counts, in which a group's communal history was recorded by a single image representing a memorable event for each year, were organized in such a serial sequence (Burke 2007). These images could be fully narrative or simply mnemonic devices to jog the memory, but structurally each of these images acts as separate panels in a larger community history, similar to Serial narratives. While winter counts were created for use within their community, lines dividing scenes in robe and ledger art were often employed to aid interpretation for the Euro-American consumers of this commercially produced art (Ewers 2011:106). These demarcations were deemed necessary for those who were not used to deducing order out of a seeming jumble of images; in other words, someone not adept at reading Biographic art.

Summary

Unlike written languages that conform to specific utterances and have clearly defined syntax, Biographic art is a writing system that requires more inference on the part of the reader and much more interaction with the "text." The reader must bring to the task of understanding these stories a detailed cultural knowledge that enables identification of objects and their associ-

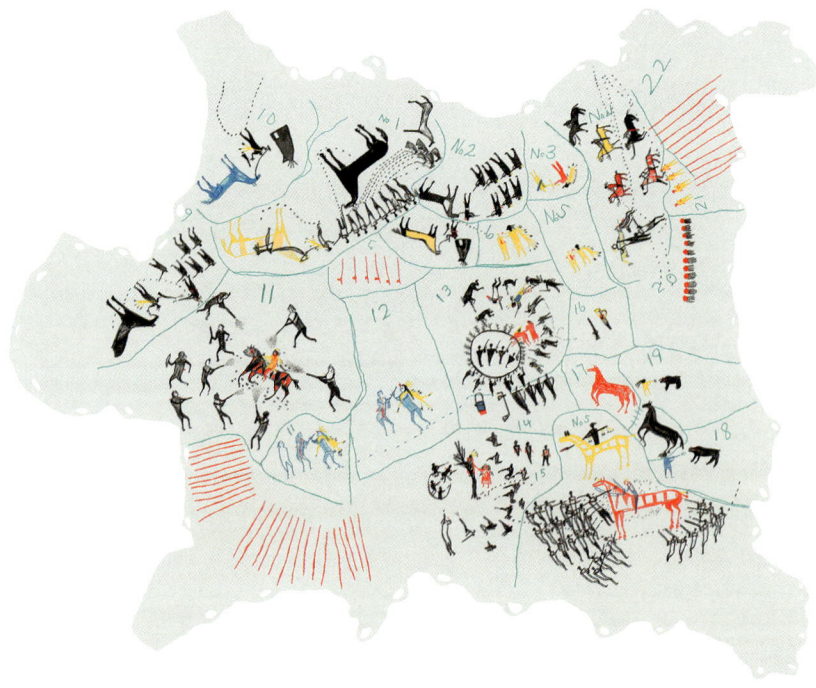

Figure 32. Painted elk skin robe by Blackfeet artist Big Nose, ca 1893. Note the lines demarking individual scenes of this serial narrative. Image courtesy Arni Brownstone.

Figure 33. Coup count tally from Ellison's Rock in Montana, showing multiple Plains Biographic art conventions and narrative structures.

ated meanings and subtext. In short, the less information explicitly depicted, the more knowledge the reader must bring to it.

Ellison's Rock in Montana (Keyser 2014; Keyser et al. 2015) demonstrates how these various Biographic art perspectives, conventions, and narrative structures are used to communicate a warrior's accomplishments across time (Figure 33). Synecdoche is used in the partial depiction of what is likely the warrior artist in the lower left of the image, as well as his enemies and his actions. His tracks run up to an enemy warrior to strike him with a bow (thereby counting a coup). During or shortly after the coup-strike, the protagonist also took the enemy's spontoon tomahawk, which is shown floating away from the vanquished man's hand. By itself, this is a classic Simultaneous narrative. But the tally of the warrior's deeds continues, creating a Progressive narrative with additional events from multiple times and places indicated. Hoofprints show his path, riding a horse and whipping the enemy with his quirt. Elsewhere the tracks reveal him riding into battle, then dismounting to bravely confront the enemy on foot with a variety of weapons. Each vignette is a brief narrative using not only synecdoche but also various conventions including floating (captured) weapons, falling/inverted defeated posture, and track conventions (which themselves are aerial views), which, when combined with the front-facing warriors, created a twisted, multiplane perspective.

These varying conventions and narrative structures, as well as their subtextual meanings, may complicate interpretation of this and other Plains Biographic art, but through careful study using the methods we have offered here (as well as others, e.g., Afton et al. 1997:322–323; Keyser 1987; Parsons 1987; Petersen 1971:267–308, 1988:xvii), we believe that these images can still communicate specific messages across cultures and through the depths of time.

Notes

1. While Plains Biographic art may not technically be a language, as it does not relate specifically to spoken utterances (as described above), we use the term Biographic or picture language as a convenient shorthand for discussing the pictographic writing system.

2. Within our own culture, however, we are comfortable and conversant with several different perspectives, from the Medieval use of stylized hierarchical perspective (where the size of a figure or its position in the composition was used to indicate its importance relative to other figures), to the cubism of Picasso and other artists, to the "twisted perspective" in some modern day comic strips (Keyser 2011). Our comfort with these is probably because many of us do not consider such art to be realism.

3. Plains Ceremonial tradition art, first defined by Keyser (1977) and then refined by Klassen (1995, 1998) and Keyser and Klassen (2001), began in the Late Prehistoric Period and continued into the last years of the Historic period. It shows shield-bearing warriors and a variety of other human figures usually juxtaposed with one another and with simple animal figures into simple static compositions drawn primarily to communicate with the spirit world. Such imagery was drawn to represent sacred themes including supernatural beings and medicine visions.

References Cited

Afton, Jean, David Fridtjof Halaas, and Andrew E. Masich
  1997 *Cheyenne Dog Soldiers: A Ledgerbook History of Coups and Combat*. University Press of Colorado, Boulder.

Anonymous
  1980 *Story on Stone*. Archaeological Society of Alberta, Lethbridge Centre.

Bottomley-O'looney, Jennifer
  2012 The Art of Storytelling: Plains Indian Perspectives. *Montana: The Magazine of Western History* 62(3):42–55, 94–95.

Boyd, Carolyn E.
  2003 *Rock Art of the Lower Pecos*. Texas A & M University Press, College Station.

Brownstone, Arni
  1993 *War Paint: Blackfoot and Sarcee Painted Buffalo Robes in the Royal Ontario Museum*. Royal Ontario Museum, Toronto.

  2007 Big Nose and His Painted Elk Skin. *Plains Anthropologist* 52(202):195–207.

Burke, Christina E.
  2007 Winter Counts in the Smithsonian. In *The Year the Stars Fell*, edited by Candace S. Green and Russell Thornton, pp. 12–58. Smithsonian Institution, Washington, D.C.

Cash, Johnny
  1964 Apache Tears. Song from the album *Bitter Tears: Ballads of the American Indian*. Columbia Records, New York.

Carroll, Beau Duke
  2017 *Talking Stone: Cherokee Syllabary Inscriptions in Dark Zone Caves*. Master's Thesis, University of Tennessee, Knoxville.

Carroll, Beau Duke, Alan Cressler, Tom Belt, Julie Reed, and Jan F. Simek
  2019 Talking stones: Cherokee Syllabary in Manitou Cave, Alabama. *Antiquity* 93(368):519–536.

Dehejia, Vidya
  1990 On Modes of Visual Narration in Early Buddhist Art. *The Art Bulletin* 72(3):374–392.

Dempsey, L. James
  2007 *Blackfoot War Art: Pictographs of the Reservation Period, 1880–2000*. University of Oklahoma Press, Norman.

Denig, Edwin Thompson
  1930 *Indian Tribes of the Upper Missouri*. Forty-Sixth Annual Report of the Bureau of American Ethnology 1928–1929, pp. 375–654. Smithsonian Institution, Washington, D.C. Facsimile reprint 2000 under the title *The Assiniboine* with a new Introduction by David R. Miller, University of Oklahoma Press, Norman.

Ewers, John C.
  1968 Plains Indian Painting: The History and Development of an American Art Form. Introduction to *Howling Wolf: A Cheyenne Warrior's Graphic Interpretation of His People*, edited by Karen D. Petersen, pp. 5–19. American West Publishing Company, Palo Alto, California.

  2011 A Century and a Half of Blackfeet Picture Writing. In *Plains Indian Art: The Pioneering Work of John C. Ewers*, edited by Candace S. Green, pp. 95–110. University of Oklahoma Press, Norman. Slightly revised reprint from *American Indian Art Magazine* 8(3):52–61, 1983.

Greene, Candace S.
  1985 *Women, Bison, and Coup: A Structural Analysis of Cheyenne Pictographic Art*. Ph.D. Dissertation, University of Oklahoma, Norman.

1996 Structure and Meaning in Cheyenne Ledger Art. In *Plains Indian Drawings, 1865–1935*, edited by Janet Catherine Berlo, pp. 26–33. Harry N. Abrams, New York.

Hill, Archibald A.
1967 The typology of Writing Systems. In *Papers in Linguistics in Honor of Leon Dostert*, edited by William M. Austin, pp. 92–99. Mouton, The Hague.

Horváth, Gyöngyvér
2016 A Passion for Order: Classifications for Narrative Imagery in Art History and Beyond. Visual Narratives—Cultural Identities (special issue), edited by Jacobus Bracker and Clara Doose-Grünefeld. *Visual Past* 3(1):247–278. University of Hamburg.

Kaiser, David A., and James D. Keyser
2015 Delving Into the Details: Further Discoveries at Writing-On-Stone. In *American Indian Rock Art, Volume 41*, edited by David A. Kaiser and James D. Keyser, pp. 167–182. American Rock Art Research Association, San Jose, California.

Keyser, James D.
1977 Writing-On-Stone: Rock Art on the Northwestern Plains. *Canadian Journal of Archaeology* 1:15–80.

1987 A Lexicon for Historic Plains Indian Rock Art: Increasing Interpretive Potential. *Plains Anthropologist* 32(115):43–71.

1996 Painted Bison Robes: The Missing Link in the Biographic Art Style Lexicon. *Plains Anthropologist* 41(155):29–52.

2000 *The Five Crows Ledger: Biographic Warrior Art of the Flathead Indians*. University of Utah Press, Salt Lake City.

2011 The Bedolina Horsemen: A New Twist in Perspective. In *American Indian Rock Art, Volume 37*, edited by Mavis Greer, John Greer, and Peggy Whitehead, pp. 173–181. American Rock Art Research Association, Glendale, Arizona.

2014 A Crow Warrior's Coup Count Tally at the Ellison's Rock Petroglyphs. *Archaeology In Montana* 55(2):1–15.

Keyser, James D., and Timothy J. Brady
1993 A War Shirt from the Schoch Collection: Documenting Individual Artistic Expression. *Plains Anthropologist* 38(142):5–20.

Keyser, James D., and Michael A. Klassen
2001 *Plains Indian Rock Art*. University of Washington Press, Seattle.

2003 Every Detail Counts: More Additions to the Plains Biographic Rock Art Lexicon. *Plains Anthropologist* 48(184):7–20.

Keyser, James D., and David L. Minick
2018 *Horse Raiders in the Missouri Breaks: Eagle Creek Canyon Petroglyphs, Montana*. Oregon Archaeological Society Press, Publication 25. Portland.

Keyser, James D., and George Poetschat
2005 *Warrior Art of Wyoming's Green River Basin: Biographic Petroglyphs Along the Seedskadee*. Oregon Archaeological Society Press, Publication No. 15. Portland.

2009 *Crow Rock Art in the Bighorn Basin: Petroglyphs at No Water Wyoming*. Oregon Archaeological Society Press, Publication 20. Portland.

2014 *Northern Plains Shield Bearing Warriors: A Five Century Rock Art Record of Indian Warfare*. Oregon Archaeological Society Press, Publication 22. Portland.

Keyser, James D., and Linea Sundstrom
2015 The Elk Dreamer Site: Themes of Change and Continuity in Northern Plains Rock Art. In *American Indian Rock Art, Volume 41*, edited by David A. Kaiser and James D. Keyser, pp. 127–145. American Rock Art Research Association, San Jose, California.

Keyser, James D., Livio A. C. Dobrez, Don Hann, and David A. Kaiser
2013 How is a Picture a Narrative? Interpreting Different Types of Rock Art. In *American Indian Rock, Volume Art 39*, edited by William D. Hyder, pp. 82–99. American Rock Art Research Association, Glendale, Arizona.

Keyser, James D., David A. Kaiser, and Livio A. C. Dobrez,
2015 Biographic Rock Art Tallies: Explicit, Implicit, or Inferred Narrative? In *American Indian Rock Art, Volume 41*, edited by David A. Kaiser and James D. Keyser, pp. 69–85. American Rock Art Research Association, San Jose, California.

Keyser, James D., Linea Sundstrom, and George Poetschat
2006 Women in War: Gender in Plains Biographic Rock Art. *Plains Anthropologist* 51(197):51–70.

Klassen, Michael
1995 *Icons of Power, Narratives of Glory: Ethnic Continuity and Cultural Change in the Contact Period Rock Art of Writing-on-Stone*. Master's Thesis, Trent University, Peterborough, Ontario.

1998 Icon and Narrative in Transition: Contact-period Rock Art at Writing-On-Stone, Southern Alberta, Canada. In *The Archaeology of Rock Art*, edited by Christopher Chippindale and Paul S. C. Taçon, pp 42–72. Cambridge University Press, Cambridge, United Kingdom.

Kolers, Paul A.
1969 Some Formal Characteristics of Pictograms. *American Scientist* 57(3):348–363.

Kurz, Rudolph Friederich
1937 *Journal of Rudolph Friederich Kurz*. Translated by Myrtis Jarrell, edited by J. N. B. Hewitt. Bureau of American Ethnology Bulletin 115. Smithsonian Institution, Washington, D.C.

Lycett, Stephen J., and James D. Keyser
2018 Beyond Oral History: A Nineteenth Century Blackfoot Warriors' Biographic Robe in Comparative and Chronological Context. *International Journal of Historical Archaeology* 22(4):771–799.

Mallery, Garrick
1893 *Picture-writing of the American Indians*. Tenth Annual Report of the Bureau of Ethnology 1888–'89, pp. 1–822. Smithsonian Institution, Washington, D.C. Facsimile reprint 1972 (in two volumes), Dover Publications, New York.

Martineau, LaVan
1973 *The Rocks Begin to Speak*. KC Publications, Las Vegas, Nevada.

McCleary, Timothy P.
2008 Writing on the Wall: Crow Interpretation of the Joliet Rock Art Panels. *Archaeology In Montana* 49(1):35–62.

McGlone, William R., Phillip M. Leonard, James L. Guthrie, Rollin W. Gillespie, and James P. Whitall, Jr.
1993 *Ancient American Inscriptions: Plow Marks or History?* Early Sites Research Society, Sutton, Massachusetts.

McLaughlin, Castle
2013 *A Lakota War Book from the Little Bighorn: The Biographic "Autobiography of Half Moon."* Peabody Museum Press, Cambridge.

Parsons, Mark L.
1987 Plains Indian Portable Art as a Key to Two Texas Historic Rock Art Sites. *Plains Anthropologist* 32(117):257–274.

Patterson, Carol
2004 Gesture and Sign Language: Reading the Rock Art. In *Utah Rock Art, Volume 23*, edited by Steven J. Manning, pp.15–43. Utah Rock Art Research Association, Salt Lake City.

Petersen, Karen Daniels
   1968 *Howling Wolf: A Cheyenne Warrior's Graphic Interpretation of His People*. American West Publishing Company, Palo Alto, California.
   1971 *Plains Indian Art from Fort Marion*. University of Oklahoma Press, Norman.
   1988 *American Pictographic Images: Historical Works on Paper by the Plains Indians*. Morning Star Gallery, Santa Fe, New Mexico.

Renaud, Etienne B.
   1936 *Pictographs and Petroglyphs of the High Western Plains*. Archaeological Survey of the High Western Plains, Eighth Report. Department of Anthropology, University of Denver.

Ryan, T. A., and Carl B. Schwartz
   1956 Speed of Perception as a Function of Mode of Representation. *The American Journal of Psychology* 69(1):60–69.

Smith, DeCost
   1949 *Red Indian Experiences*. George Allen & Unwin, London.

Stansbury-O'Donnell, Mark D.
   1999 *Pictorial Narrative in Ancient Greek Art*. Cambridge University Press, Cambridge.

Von Dippe, Roger David
   2007 *The Origin and Development of Continuous Narrative in Roman Art, 300 B.C.–A.D. 200*. Ph.D. Dissertation, University of Southern California.

Wissler, Clark
   1911 *The Social Life of the Blackfoot Indians*. Anthropological Papers of the American Museum of Natural History, Volume 7, Part 1.
   1912 *Societies and Ceremonial Associations in the Oglala Division of the Teton-Dakota*. Anthropological Papers of the American Museum of Natural History, Volume 11, Part 1.

Where are the Hohokam Leaders? An Examination of Complexity of Rock Art Anthropomorphs at Cocoraque Butte, Arizona

Janine Hernbrode

Archaeological work in Southern Arizona reveals many ways the ancient native people changed over time. They changed in transition from Early Agriculture to Hohokam and from Classic Hohokam to Historic O'odham. During just the Hohokam millennium (450–1450 C.E.) they changed their residential architecture, their mortuary treatments, their agricultural cooperation, and their social connections. The more than 11,000 petroglyphs at the Cocoraque Butte Complex span all of these transitions including the rapid change periods that have been characterized as having upheaval and conflict. With anthropomorphic forms at the Cocoraque Butte Complex being consistent through time (Hernbrode 2019), are there detectable changes evident in the complexity or embellishment of anthropomorphs? Some archaeologists argue that there were charismatic leaders leading great projects and trading networks that spanned the Southwest. Are there discernable changes in the imagery as a result of the growing complexity, cooperation, trade, and conflict during this period of societal growth and aggregation? In an analysis of the 1067 anthropomorphs at the Cocoraque Ranch portion of the site the author scored the number of embellishments to the basic form of anthropomorph in three levels of repatination representing three cultural phases of the Ancestral O'odham: Archaic/Early Agriculture, Hohokam, and Historic O'odham. This paper discusses embellishment of anthropomorphs within the cultural phases, the implications of the data analysis, and criteria and evidence for identifying leadership-focused panels of rock art.

Cocoraque Butte (Figure 1) is set in the tremendously diverse Sonoran Desert where the giant saguaro cacti make up forests of prickly sentries, where ironwood trees have wood so dense it sinks in water rather than

Janine Hernbrode
Arizona Archaeological and Historical Society

Figure 1. An inselberg that is one of the loci for Cocoraque Butte is a visible part of this landscape of the Sonoran Desert.

floats, where the animal population has exotic names like "Gila monster," "tarantula," and "sidewinder" in addition to the more familiar desert tortoise, mule deer, mountain lion, and antelope jackrabbit (Dimmitt 2000:9). In this setting, Arizona's ancient people came together through the millennia to mark their place in this world at the Cocoraque Butte Complex. The water source surrounded by the dry desert may have been the primary attractant, but it was not the only one. The archaeological site's landscape provided appropriate places to celebrate emergence into the present world (Hernbrode and Boyle 2018), the combination of flowers, brilliant color, and the sound of bells anthropologists have called the "Flower World" (Hernbrode and Boyle 2013, 2016, 2017), and to recognize the spirits of the ancestors. This rugged and dry landscape is primarily a ceremonial place rather than a habitation site. Stone-outlined enclosures are scattered throughout the site with the largest numbers of them on the north and south slopes of the main Butte, away from the rock art concentrations (Gillespie 2019:2). Habitation occurred here, but the ceremonial landscapes and petroglyphs appear to have much greater longevity and importance.

Archaeological Contexts

Cocoraque has been the focus of a 4.5-year project (January 2014 to November 2018) sponsored by the Arizona Archaeological and Historical Society to record its more than 11,000 petroglyphs, the largest rock art site known in Southern Arizona. Encompassing a combination of public land administered by the Bureau of Land Management as the Ironwood Forest National Monument and the privately owned Cocoraque Ranch, the site can be generally described as monumental piles of dark rounded granodiorite boulders located on smaller hills at the base of the large Cocoraque Butte. This sacred site is located just outside the official boundary of the Tohono O'odham Nation. Even though the area of the current Nation is the second largest Native American property in the United States, it is abundantly clear that their historic lands are much greater than the set-aside and that Cocoraque was an important gathering place for the ancients. Historical accounts make clear that this sacred site was likely used by the Historic O'odham at least until the water source was claimed by Hispanic ranchers in the 1890s (Gillespie 2018). Some modern imagery that is consistent with other reports of O'odham imagery (Martynec and Martynec 1995, 2003) has been attributed to the O'odham through analysis of pecking styles and patination (Hernbrode 2019). Although the site bears no evidence of current use, there is traditional knowledge that it was used into more modern times as a stopover on pilgrimages to the Mission San Xavier del Bac for an annual December feast day. One of the O'odham tribal members visiting the site with T. J. Ferguson (2008:7) remembered doing so in his youth.

Surface artifacts (Figure 2) found by volunteer rock art recorders in the course of either moving among the petroglyph-covered hills, or at the base of the petroglyph boulders themselves, indicate the site has been in use since 4,000 to 5,000 years B.P. The oldest artifacts, from the Middle Archaic (3000 to 2000 B.C.E.), are Gypsum stemmed points (Mabry and Stevens 2014:124) found in the vicinity of the petroglyphs but not among the boulders. The presence of Early Agricultural Period (2000 B.C.E. to 50 C.E.) (Sliva 2015:36) points and a

Figure 2. Surface artifacts from the Cocoraque Ranch site indicating periods of use. Middle Archaic through Early Agricultural Period artifacts 3000 B.C.E to 50 C.E.: (a) Cortaro point; (b) Early Agricultural Period pipe bowl, 800 B.C.E. to 50 C.E.; (c) San Pedro point, 1200 to 800 B.C.E.; Hohokam artifacts: (d) Hohokam Pioneer Point, 450 to 750 C.E.; (e) Conus shell pendant and beads from unidentified shells; (f) Classic Period sherd, 1150 to 1450 C.E.; (g) ceramic spindle whorl found near Tanque Verde Phase ceramics, 1150–1300 C.E.

pipe bowl (Adams 2005:112) among the boulders gives an indication some of the oldest petroglyphs may date from that period (Figure 3). A Conus shell pendant and

Figure 3. Some of the Archaic style imagery is completely repatinated and only visible by using the angle of the sun to aid viewing.

unidentified shell beads (Vokes 2008:343–345) likely date from the Hohokam occupation when trading networks and the Salt Journey could account for shell this far inland. Painted sherds from the site were identified by Henry Wallace (personal communication 2018) as Hohokam Rincon Period (950 to 1150 C.E.) as well as Classic Period (1150 to 1300 C.E.). Plainware and Classic Period sherds were more abundant. Although archaeologists have identified the Archaic cultures, the Hohokam, and the Historic O'odham as having separate characteristics, the O'odham themselves along with many archaeologists believe these are the same people through time (Loendorf and Lewis 2017; Lopez 2007) and, following Loendorf and Lewis, I will refer to them as Ancestral O'odham.

During the 4,000 to 5,000 years this site was in use, the native people made vast changes in their lifeways. The Middle Archaic is described by Mabry and Stevens (2014:132) as a time of increased rainfall, more reliable water sources, and regular floods leading to increases of edible plants in riparian areas and better hunting. The highly mobile hunter-gatherers making seasonal rotations of living areas to search for plant foods (cactus buds, fruit, and pads; tree legumes; edible grasses; and seeds) and supplementing their diets though hunting (Reid and Whittlesey 1997:44) found conditions that allowed for some reduced mobility (Mabry and Stevens 2014:132). Mortuary customs became burials within habitation areas (Mabry 2008:14). Petroglyphs from this time period have been classified as Western Archaic Tradition (Wallace 2008), a collection of circles, grids, and abstracts accompanied by anthropomorphs with outstretched arms and occasionally patterned bodies, many of those with vertical stripes. Henry Wallace (2008:206) states that the mobile lifestyle of these people limited their capabilities to transport material goods, elaborate clothing, and ritual paraphernalia. Examples of the imagery are generally broad-lined and imprecise. Cocoraque has imagery from this time period (see Figure 3) but as of this publication the study of it is incomplete.

During the Late Archaic/Early Agricultural Period, Cocoraque was within the estimated boundaries of the San Pedro Complex, which is identified by the presence of San Pedro artifacts (1200–800 B.C.E.) to the west of the Santa Cruz River corridor. During this time, irrigation is evident in the Tucson area as early as 2100 B.C.E. with almost continuous use from about 1250 to 750 B.C.E. (Mabry 2008:22). The size of the irrigation system for distribution of water to adjacent plots in the Tucson area implies that a larger population could be supported by the increased crop yields in this location and that cooperation among the residents was necessary to maintain such a system (Mabry et al. 2008:235).

Cocoraque is on the periphery of these developments, about 12 miles from the nearest large settlements along the Santa Cruz River. At Cocoraque, structures on the steep hillside of the largest Cocoraque Butte above the public petroglyph sites include a rubble-filled wall in the middle of a drainage (Figure 4) that, along with a constructed channel evident some distance below it, suggests an attempt to control the movement of water from higher on the Butte to its base, presumably for agricultural purposes even in this non-riverine environment. However, Cocoraque's water source, presumably, would not have been adequate for extensive irrigation. The site shows evidence of limited agriculture (Suzanne Fish, personal communication 2015). An area just east of the site was still in use by an O'odham farmer growing beans without irrigation in 1909 (Gillespie 2018).

The artifacts found among the petroglyph boulders at Cocoraque Ranch are from the San Pedro Phase of the Late Archaic/Early Agricultural Period. The San Pedro Phase in the Tucson area is identified with more than irrigation; the people also constructed more permanent pit-style living structures, storage pits, pottery, and ceramic figurines. During this period tropical cultigens like maize and squash arrived from Mexico, indicating contact with people far to the south, and canal networks requiring coordinated labor were beginning to be built (Mabry and Stevens 2014:132).

Figure 4. Peter Boyle and Paul Fish examine a Hohokam rubble-filled wall built in the middle of a drainage. The wall is approximately halfway to the top of the main Cocoraque Butte.

Figure 5. Center of photo shows a vegetation-covered Hohokam ballcourt as it appears today. The courts represented many hours of hand labor and are thought to be places for gatherings, games, gambling, and trade.

The "Hohokam Millennium" from 450 to 1450 C.E. (Fish and Fish 2007:8) is marked by increases in societal complexity. During this time these remarkable people were creating public works and spaces by moving tons of dirt to build canal networks up to 22 miles in length, irrigating up to 70,000 acres of land (Fish and Fish 2007:5). They also constructed public architecture like "ball courts" (Figure 5) and multistory buildings (Figure 6). The courts usually consisted of two parenthesis-like mounds enclosing an elongate sub-surface oval in their villages, thought to be places to play games, gamble, and trade. Later during this same period, they constructed rectangular mounds with residences on top (Fish and Fish 2007:5). Their trading networks connected to Mexico and across the Southwest (Vokes and Gregory 2007:320). They had both agricultural and settlement stability with some settlements persisting in one place for up to several hundred years (Fish and Fish 2007:6).

The Hohokam millennium ends, according to O'odham oral history, in conflict between rival factions. The archaeological record supports the end of the Hohokam lifeway as coming between 1450 and 1500 C.E. when the traditional networks that traded ceramics and obsidian across the Southwest disappeared (Mills et al. 2013).

Figure 6. Stabilized great house at Casa Grande National Monument shows the building skill and the size of some Hohokam construction projects.

To distinguish between the Hohokam and the people whose lifestyle and social organization was different after 1450 C.E., I will refer to the later people as "Historic O'odham." There is a disagreement as to what led to people giving up the Hohokam lifestyle. Some speculate about nutritional stress (Fink 1991) or other factors leading to reduced fertility (Hill et al. 2004) as causes of a dwindling population leading to a smaller labor pool for maintaining elaborate systems and producing crop yields to feed many mouths. Others, looking at climatic changes and environmental factors, theorize that sustained drought and floods causing erosion of river channels changed the reliable delivery of water to irrigation systems (Doyel 1991:234; Gregory 1991:186; Masse 1991:215). Warfare along with the threat of conflict and migration (Hill et al. 2004:690, 694; Reid and Whittlesey 1997:106–107) have also been suggested as causes. Though we do not fully understand what happened during that period, ultimately, when the Spanish priests arrived in the Tucson area around 1690 C.E., they found people living in more modest farming villages along the Santa Cruz River (Fish and Fish 1991; Fontana 2010:5).

Along with these historic period river valley O'odham farmers there were also O'odham people who successfully made a living in much drier areas away from the Santa Cruz River valley. These people were very efficient in harvesting and using limited water. Ak chin methods directed alluvial water to fields and sometimes to small reservoirs. Natural rainwater catchments were also utilized both for drinking and for watering crops. When the water was used up they harvested and moved on (Fontana 1981:37). These people are among the most recent group to make petroglyphs at Cocoraque. Glyphs with light patination have been attributed to the Historic O'odham. Even now, the O'odham are resident immediately south of the Cocoraque area (Hernbrode 2019).

Leadership and Status in Hohokam Culture

There is considerable discussion in the literature regarding the degree of social stratification in Hohokam society. Wright (2014:216) has reviewed evidence that "focal villages" along irrigation canals may have been centers for multiple forms of leadership including political, economic, hydraulic, defensive, and religious leadership (Abbott 2000; Bostwick et al. 2010; Elson and Abbott 2000). Craig (2010) argues that power was concentrated in the hands of a few "aristocratic houses" whose members were tied together by the large irrigable tracts, property, and place. However, there is considerable evidence that centralized organization may not always have been necessary, for example, in the case of irrigation systems (Elson and Abbott 2000; Woodson 2010; Wright 2014).

There are clearly situations where leaders do not accumulate material possessions (Elson and Abbott 2000). But in other cases, there are reasons to suspect that Hohokam society included individuals with special leadership status who did accumulate possessions.

Doyel (2007:84) has proposed that leadership emerged to manage the distribution and control of surplus crops. During the Classic Period, in some areas, walled platform mounds were constructed where ceremonies were performed by religious leaders, likely in seclusion from the community at large, in contrast to earlier time periods where religious practices were more open and participatory (Wright 2014:211–212).

Evidence indicating that there were individuals with special status are burials with exceptional goods and items of fine craftmanship. These burials signify great differentiation even in death (Doyel 2007:86–87). One elaborate burial has been called a "Hohokam Sarcophagus" at Casa Grande National Monument in Arizona. The burial was investigated by Jesse W. Fewkes (1912:108–109), who found the body accompanied by the trappings of both a warrior and a medicine man lying supine in a specially constructed tomb (Rice 2016). Rice mentions that the burial included an unusual circular ax, which he suggests may be a symbol of office. He speculates that this may have been the burial of a ruler similar to the kind described in O'odham oral histories about Casa Grande ruins and other platform mound sites of the 13th and 14th centuries (Barr et al. 1994; Fewkes 1912; Teague 1993).

Overview of the Cocoraque Butte Petroglyphs

It appears that virtually all of the glyphs at Cocoraque, with the exception of a few very modern additions, are Ancestral O'odham. As the artifacts found among the petroglyph boulders at Cocoraque Ranch were from the San Pedro Phase of the Late Archaic/Early Agricultural Period (2000 B.C.E. to 50 C.E.), I classify the most darkly patinated petroglyph forms of anthropomorphs as dating from this and, taking into account the older stemmed points, possibly the previous Middle Archaic Period (3000 to 2000 B.C.E.).

Operationally defined by a mid-range repatination level, Hohokam petroglyphs make up a substantial portion of the 11,200 glyphs at the Cocoraque Butte Complex. Overall petroglyph production rates calculated using the patination data for 9,021 petroglyphs at Cocoraque Ranch, show that 28 percent of the glyphs were made during the Archaic/Early Agricultural Period and 62 percent during the briefer Hohokam times (450 to 1450 C.E.). This suggests the effects of agriculture and sedentism led to greater numbers of people in larger groups using Cocoraque as a sacred site.

Focusing on the anthropomorphs only, the Archaic and Early Agricultural Period anthropomorphs identified by dark patination are again comparatively few (n=79) of the total 1,067 anthropomorphs. However, the two later periods, Hohokam and Historic O'odham, differentiated also by patination, have almost equal numbers of anthropomorphs. The Hohokam collection of anthropomorphs consists of 495 petroglyphs with medium patination. The Historic O'odham have 493 anthropomorphs with light patination.

Cocoraque's petroglyphs and sacred site not only have imagery showing a continuance of the same traditions into modern times but additionally have modern motifs showing drawings of missions with crosses on top, decorated crosses, initials, horses, and possible brands that bring the site into the nineteenth and twentieth centuries (Hernbrode 2019). One petroglyph is claimed by two cultures. There is a "European style" labyrinth (Astroth 2019:104) that also is claimed by the O'odham as a "maze" that fits their tradition as "one of the old ones" (O'odham tribal member, personal communication 2018). This glyph was visited by O'odham elders in 2008 and reported by T. J. Ferguson (2008:2–3).

The rock art of the Ancestral O'odham is not greatly detailed, or as carefully executed, or located on boulders that are easy to mark with details, as those found on the easier-to-use sandstone cliffs of some other cultures. Nevertheless, with practice, detail that is individualistic and rich in variety can be noticed and scored among the abundant petroglyphs. In examining the anthropomorphs for continuity through time, the anthropomorphs were classified into nine categories in 2019 with one category providing for miscellaneous forms to include those with unusual or spirit-like properties. The finding that the forms were consistent through the entire period that the site was used made it clear that tradition is important and consistent for the Ancestral O'odham (Hernbrode 2019).

Focus and Purpose

The evidence discussed above suggesting that there were people with special status and perhaps leadership duties in Hohokam society who had access to special goods led to my hypothesis that this status would be reflected in the extensive petroglyphic record of anthropomorphs at Cocoraque Ranch. Body shape styles persisted for as much as 4,000 years (Hernbrode 2019). During that time, vast changes in Ancestral O'odham lifeways and organization took place, possibly showing evidence of the increase in the complexity of the people's rituals and, with full sedentism, also their ritual paraphernalia. I assume that some higher status individuals should be identifiable in rock art as they have been identified in burials. Cocoraque's extremely long use and its remarkable number of petroglyphs is a rarity for petroglyph sites and consequently an unusual opportunity to investigate this matter.

This paper examines stability and variance in the way the petroglyphs portray people during three segments of time based upon patination data. Do the anthropomorphs produced and embellished when they were essentially hunting and gathering and supplementing their diets with an opportunistic farming plot differ from the way they are portrayed when they were cooperatively building great structures, supporting large villages by irrigating a thousand acres of land, and trading widely across the Southwest? Do these two segments also differ from the Historic O'odham? If there were Hohokam special status individuals who have been identified in burials, are they also immortalized on the boulders? I hypothesize that there will be a rise in embellishment of anthropomorphs in the Hohokam culture when the higher status burials took place.

Methods

This study attempts to measure two dimensions to determine a possible relationship between time period (Pre-Hohokam, Hohokam, Post-Hohokam) and the relative frequency of high-status anthropomorphs. In operational terms, time period is determined by repatination levels and status is measured by the amount of embellishments on anthropomorphic figures.

Using the gray scale portion of the IFRAO (International Federation of Rock Art Organizations) November 2001 centimeter measure and color scale, I judged three levels of patination as (1) equal to or lighter than the very slightly gray color, (2) between the lighter gray scale up to the mid-gray scale, and (3) equal to or darker than the mid-gray scale. Of course, repatination is a crude measure of time given the influence of differential weathering resulting from position, orientation, and other variables. At the same time, the present study has the advantage of a large sample size (n=1067) and only one observer making all patination judgments.

To differentiate between the status of anthropomorphs, I hypothesize that there are discernable differences in elaboration of the anthropomorphs and the attachments to the anthropomorphs' basic forms. Higher status Hohokam burials contain jewelry that may be evident in rock art. Rice (2016) reports jewelry in the forms of shell and turquoise beads; pendants of shell and stone; shell rings, bracelets, and tinklers; ear spools or nose plugs; and bone hairpins as artifact categories. Beads, by far the most ubiquitous single personal item found in burials, made up 70 percent of the artifact totals and yet were in just 17.4 percent of the burials. Rice notes that jewelry is neither practical nor necessary for duties and thus is a measure of material wealth of a household. Rice does mention that the special circular ax in the Casa Grande burial may have been a symbol of office.

Bostwick et al. (2010) report four Hohokam villages with what appear to be shaman-priest burials containing materials that may be apparent in rock art. In addition to items listed above, Bostwick et al. mention a stone pipe, a turtle carapace, hawk bone tubes, bone awls, a stone ax, marine shells, ceramic vessels, a woven bag, an incised bone wand, and bird wings.

Ruth Underhill (1939:188–189) studied O'odham traditions in the early 20th century. Burial customs called for the dead to be buried in his/her best regalia and paint, including warriors with headdresses and paint, and enemy-slayers with faces painted black and white. However, the ruler-priest of the village was not buried with his/her regalia, nor with special rain fetishes, because those items were considered hereditary. Rain fetishes may not be identifiable in rock art but special headdresses resembling Wikita ceremonial dress are evident at Cocoraque. A leadership staff similar to the Tohono O'odham flag that has been on display at Himdag Ki Cultural Center in Topowa, Arizona, may also be identifiable in rock art.

It should be mentioned that some anthropomorphic figures may not in fact represent humans. Bostwick (2002) has discussed attributes of anthropomorphs that may depict spirit beings rather than humans. In his analysis attributes suggesting spirit beings include large size, unusual or exaggerated form, and distorted bodies. In the present study I observed only four anthropomorphs that appear spirit-like. One legless figure appears ghost-like without an outline and represented by gossamer dots placed over other imagery. Another legless figure has exaggerated arms and a skull-like head. A third rises from a crack with a wave-like body. The fourth has very long arms and unusual leg positions. Whether these are spirit beings or humans is a matter of interpretation; in either event there are only four such glyphs, and it does not materially affect the analysis reported here.

To identify the level of anthropomorphic embellishment, each of the 1,067 anthropomorphs was scored by giving one point for the basic human form: two legs and two arms, a line for the body, and a solidly pecked head (see Figures 7 and 8). Additional points were earned by having provided details in specific sections of the body.

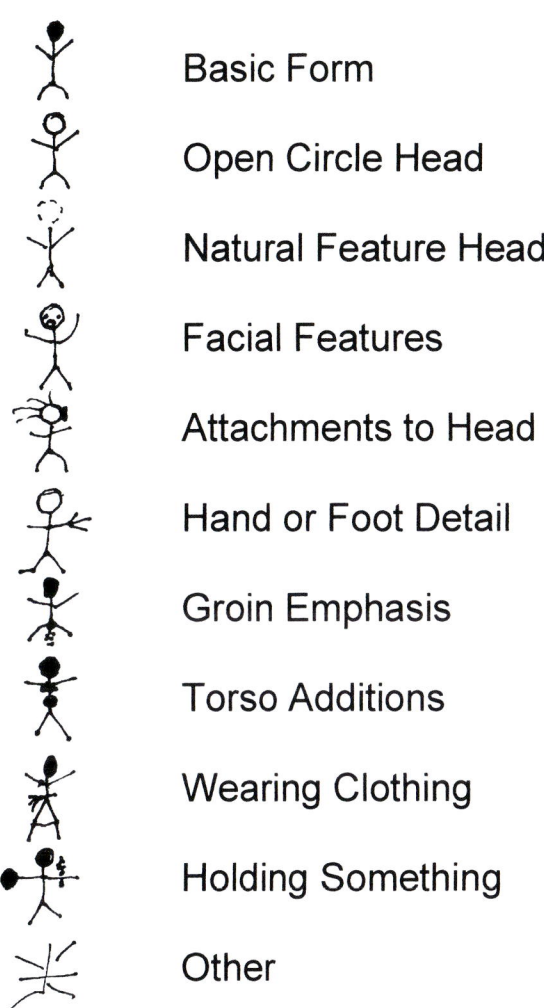

Figure 7. Eleven details used to score the complexity of Ancestral O'odham anthropomorphs. Each detail is worth one point.

Figure 8. Anthropomorphs in the simplest form: a solid head, a single line for the body, four lines for limbs.

Partial anthropomorphs, like portrait heads without bodies, did not receive the point for the basic human form. Additional points were given for the head being an open circle rather than a solid dot, for added facial features, for locating the head over natural bumps and other aberrations that look like facial features in the rock, and for attachments to the outside of the head where special goods may be in evidence (Figure 9). Attachments could be ears, earbobs, hats, hair both free

Figure 9. The heads of Ancestral O'odham anthropomorphs can be rich in detail as is this one with facial features. This figure also has one hand attached to a crack while the other is formed by a circular spall. One foot is also attached to a spall. More detail is provided by a groin emphasis and a torso bulge.

Figure 10. Exceptionally long-fingers provide an additional point for this anthropomorph.

and appearing tied in some fashion, feather-like projections, and multiple similar projections that could be special headdresses. A head with a dot in the middle or divided into a pie shape was given a point for this small complexity in the "Other" category. None of the figures were so complicated that there were multiple things attached to the head, though the figure may have received a point for facial features, another for lines from the top of the head, and yet another for using an open circle to represent the head.

Another point could be scored by providing hand and/or foot detail (Figure 10). The most common form was lines for fingers and/or toes on at least one limb. Four limbs of fingers and toes did not earn multiple points. A few instances of circles at the end of arms or legs and/or a straight line almost perpendicular to the leg or arm was considered enough of an indication of hands and feet to earn a point. A variation in the trunk of the body could earn another point. Sometimes trunks are made of stacked circles or a double line that would earn another point (Figure 11). A bulging body, breasts, and a line across the body were all trunk varia-

Figure 11. A trunk formed by two, rather than one line, adds to this anthropomorph's complexity.

tions earning points. Indications of clothing earned a point. The most common were a triangle shape over the lower body, perhaps indicating a kilt, and a robe-like rectangle with either lines or fringes or a line across the body with fringes resembling a sash. A necklace or other jewelry earned a point.

The last way to earn a point is to be holding some cultural material. Some figures hold what appear to be birds (Figure 12), others circular items and things that look like weaponry, particularly war clubs. Since buri-

Figure 12. This anthropomorph extends his right arm from the shoulder to make accommodation for a large bird.

als of the elite were identified by the number, detail, and craftsmanship of the funerary objects, it is reasonable to expect the same differentiation in detail of anthropomorphic figures.

This analysis assumes that status is reflected in the degree of embellishment of the anthropomorphs because high-status individuals, at least in some situations, are associated with attributes such as body decoration in the form of jewelry and special possessions such as birds and other objects placed in burials.

Results and Discussion

Embellishments Over Time

The basic figure of an anthropomorph, a stick figure with a solid head and without added detail, occurred only 53 times out of a total of 1,067 anthropomorphs. At the other end of the spectrum, there is one example of an anthropomorph given the basic form point in addition to nine embellishments. In between these two extremes is the most common human-like petroglyph at Cocoraque, the basic form with three details in 269 examples (the distribution is shown in Figure 13). Figure 14 shows the frequencies of each embellishment in each of the three time periods covered by this study, each of which I discuss below.

The most popular detail added to basic figures was a groin emphasis (see Figure 15 for an example). That included 54 percent of the darkest anthropomorphs, 59 percent of the medium anthropomorphs, and 51 percent of the lightly colored anthropomorphs. The glyphs appear to show representations of genitals and something being emitted from a groin-located hole or spall or darkened area. I believe these are likely natural processes like birth, urination, menses, ejaculation, and defecation; or possibly as Kelley Hays-Gilpin (2004:33) suggests, alterations to the penis like circumcision or subincision. Of course, the significance of this emphasis and its metaphorical meanings are buried in the past.

The use of an open circle for an anthropomorph's head, rather than a solid dot, is used in 25 percent of the darkly patinated Archaic anthropomorphs. This increases through time to 45 percent of the Hohokam anthropomorphs and then 55 percent of the Historic O'odham anthropomorphs. Of all of the traits, this one shows the greatest difference through time (Figure 14). In a search for leaders, this does not appear to be a distinguishing characteristic.

The addition of facial features also increases through time. The Archaic glyphs of anthropomorphs have distinguishable facial features 35 percent of the time. Hohokam glyphs have facial features 53 percent of the time and the trait increases to 59 percent for the Historic O'odham. On the newest glyphs some of the eyes and mouths are finely scratched, suggesting that some of the gap between the Archaic and Historic anthropomorphs might reflect the difficulty in observing completely repatinated scratches on the varied surfaces of the granodiorite boulders. In addition to the solid head and the open circle head, there are also heads formed by a natural feature. This is often an old spall or slight circular indentation that has a darker patination than the glyph itself. It is apparent that sometimes the glyph maker has searched the boulders for aberrations in the surface that appear to be facial features and then utilized that place to make an anthropomorph. Additional anthropomorphs on the same panel do not ben-

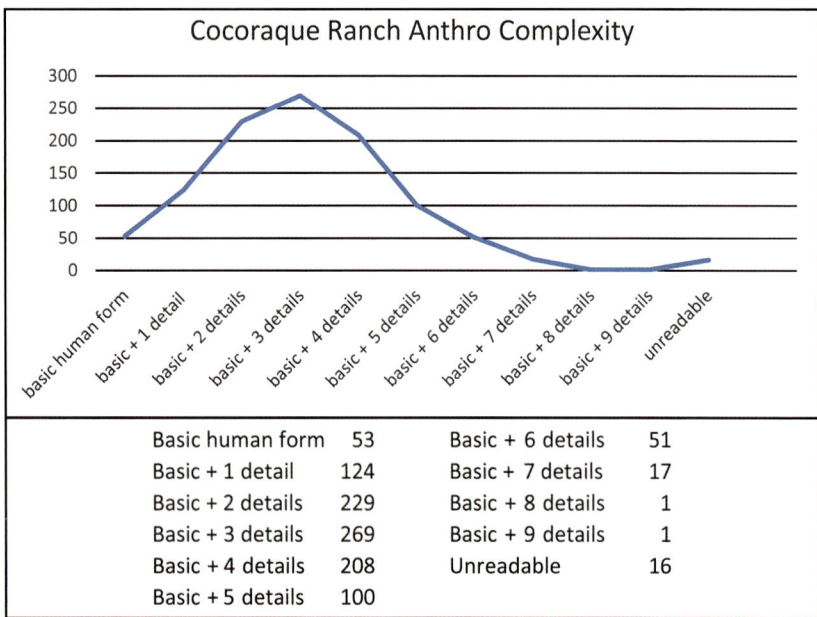

Figure 13. Graph showing the number of details added to anthropomorphic figures (n=1067) at Cocoraque Ranch peaks at the basic form plus three embellishments.

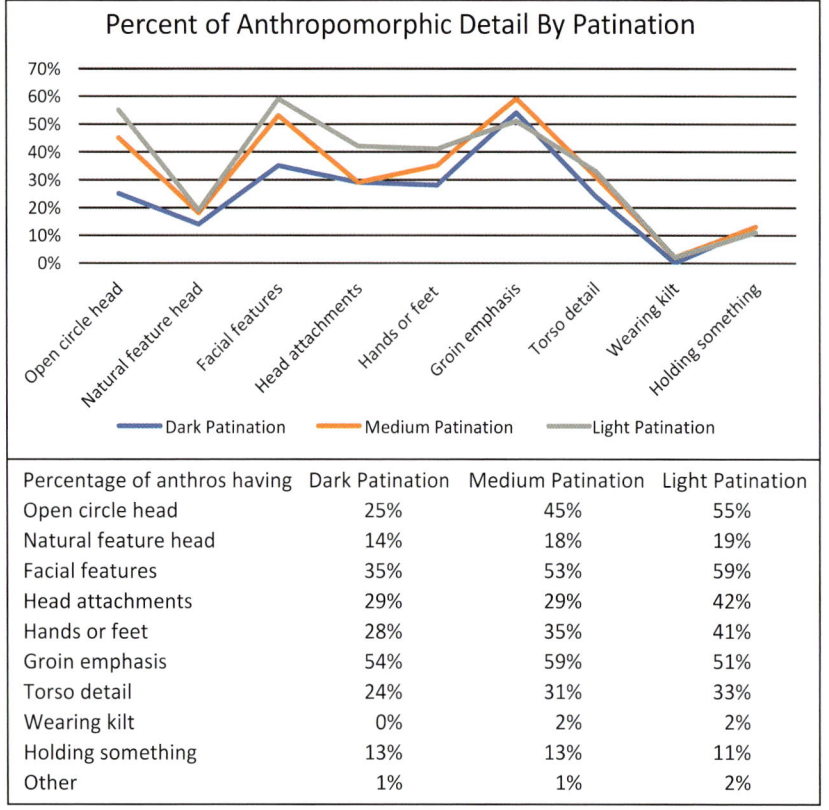

Figure 14. Graph comparing anthropomorphic embellishments across the three levels of patination of petroglyphs.

efit from this anomaly. The most common facial features are eyes, often placed at the circle margins rather than a short distance from the center that is more common in the Euro-American culture. Mouths are almost always open circles, sometimes very open, and located low on the face as though there was no chin. Some observers of modern culture will be relieved to know that the "smiley face" apparently did not exist during the marking of Cocoraque.

There are five anthropomorphs with open circle heads with lines or dots in the center that do not appear to be facial features. Two of them have central circles or dots in the center of the face (Figure 16), two are divided into pie shapes like a divided-circle motif, and one is flower-like. Our proposal that the circle-dot and divided circle can represent abstract flowers (Hernbrode and Boyle 2013) is strengthened by the flower-like human head petroglyph. Although there are many flower shapes among the glyphs at Cocoraque, only one has a human body attached. On the Sand Altar of the kiva murals of Awatovi (Smith 1952:Plates F and I) these two symbols (circle-dot and divided circle) are present and were later identified as symbolic flowers or corn (Sekaquaptewa and Washburn 2010:147, 154). Perhaps the flower and corn songs of the O'odham, the private songs of power, the songs of curing, the songs of narrative (Hill 1992:124), represent a more widespread idea that traveled north to Hopi and is evident in Awatovi. The Uto-Aztecan origin of concentric circle or circle-dot faces has been noted in Coso (California) rock art by Mukhopadhyay and Garfinkel (2016:58). They report the motif may represent either transcendent corridors or a "divine eye" to connect to layers of the cosmos as an axis mundus. This particular interpretation is also given strength by Hernbrode and Boyle's (2018) paper detailing the significance of landscape features representing an emergence site, and thus an axis mundus at this location. These are not elements

Figure 15. The most popular detail added to basic figures was a groin emphasis. Fifty-five percent of all anthropomorphs at the site had this detail.

signs and dots. But they did pay attention to hair. Both male and female dancers were selected for their long glossy hair, which they wore loose for the dancing (Underhill (1946:28). Carl Lumholtz (1912:345) mentions that a "luxuriant growth" of hair was a sign of beauty in men. It is possible the anthropomorph heads with long radiant lines are signs of beauty.

Radiant lines might also represent the feathers of a very special costume for the Wikita (or Vikita) Ceremony (Lumholtz 1912:92). In 1910 the head covering for this costume was made of burlap with a painted or woven rectangular motif on the face and small openings for the eyes. The top of the head covering held a mass of feathers, stylistically similar to figures on a stunningly beautiful and very large Hohokam ceramic bowl located at the Akimel O'odham's Huhugam Heritage Center near Phoenix. Cocoraque has no rock art of such stunning beauty or clarity as the bowl, but there is one image that also may represent this costume (Figure 17).

Figure 16. Anthropomorph with a concentric circle head. The interior circle has an eye-like shape with radiant lines, perhaps either (or both) a flower or a divine eye connecting levels of the cosmos.

that are unique to Cocoraque. They have been found in other Ancestral O'odham sites.

In Ancestral O'odham rock art, much of the detail of the anthropomorph is about the figure's head. The most common attachment to the outside of the circular head was long or short vertical lines. The lines may represent hair, though it could be feather headdress displays too. Ruth Underhill, an ethnologist who lived with the O'odham periodically from 1931 to 1935, reported that the tribe made little attempt to costume themselves, preferring to paint exposed skin with de-

Figure 17. Anthropomorph with special headdress resembling the O'odham Wikita Ceremony costume.

Long-fingered hands and feet with long toes also showed an increase over time from 28 percent in the Archaic to 41 percent for the Historic O'odham. In order to qualify for an added point, the figure need only have this detail on one limb. It is clear there was no attempt to provide five fingers or five toes because these numbers are a rarity. Some hands, and occasionally feet too, were circles or 45- to 90-degree lines at the ends of arms or legs.

Torso details are expressed in variations from a single-line torso. It is tempting to assign pregnancy to abdominal bumps but this feature could also represent abundance of food supplies or some distressing ailments. There was one panel with both a pregnant-looking anthropomorph and a birth scene where their juxtaposition made the idea more convincing. Forty-one of the anthropomorphic images had breasts, expressed as either two circles or dots on either side of the midline or two triangles pointing outward from the midline.

Some of the 338 (or 32% of 1,067) torso attachments could be sashes but, if so, they did not hang beside the anthropomorph in the way I would expect a woven sash to drape. Instead, these illustrations have a line across the body extending out at a 90-degree angle. When these lines had fringes at the end they were judged to be sashes and put into the clothing category.

A kilt was the only clothing identified other than the sashes. Twenty-one anthropomorphs wore kilts or sashes, none of them during the Archaic Period, and a mere 2 percent of the totals in the Hohokam and Historic O'odham times. One anthropomorph has a necklace. From looking at the data, this embellishment was not important for the general populace.

Anthropomorphs held a variety of cultural objects in their hands. The percentages of imagery devoted to this was consistent through time with 13 percent of the anthropomorphs attached to cultural material for both the Archaic and Hohokam time frames and 11 percent for the Historic O'odham. Unless the role of leaders was consistent across the time periods represented at Cocoraque Butte, the even percentages through time seems to eliminate this category as status markers. If the social complexity and hierarchy associated with ballcourts and mound-building was present at this site, it does not appear to be manifested in anthropomorphic embellishment. Although it reaped much information, analysis of the complexity of the anthropomorphs is either not an adequate method to identify higher status members of the community, or such high-status individuals were not marked through rock art, or they did not exist at this site.

Size and Possessions of Anthropomorphs

Given that embellishments in general did not significantly vary over time, I shifted my focus to possessions. If the leaders and the elites can be identified by their possessions in death, then perhaps the leaders and elites can be identified on rock art panels at ritual sites by their possessions. I would not expect offerings of food or water as in the mortuary treatments, but other grave goods that are mentioned in the literature might be recognizable, like jewelry, special tools, and images representing accomplishments in hunting or warfare. In the data from Cocoraque there were 128 anthropomorphs found to be holding 133 objects. Twenty-eight of those objects could only be classed as "something." Another 28 were holding a circular object, possibly a shield or a basket or another circular object.

Recorders reported 19 anthropomorphs as possibly holding birds. Nine were eliminated as too obscure. The remaining ten anthropomorphs are associated with objects that appear to be birds, possibly a metaphor for an altered state of consciousness "flight" or a transition to the Lower World in death. However, unlike a metaphorical flight image that would act as a conveyor for flight and transformation to the Lower World, the impression of this imagery is not that the human is being transported but that the birds are pets perched on shoulders instead (see Figure 12). This idea is given strength by the positions of the arms of the anthropomorphs. The anthropomorph extends the arm horizontally from the shoulder to the elbow to provide adequate space to enable a larger bird to perch on its shoulder. Gilman et al. (2014:105) found macaws and parrots were elite signs of ritual power and social standing in a similar time period for the Mimbres of New Mexico. If the Hohokam and early Historic O'odham had a version of this same tradition, the bird species were not limited to parrots and macaws. Macaw bones have been found in Hohokam contexts but they are very few in number. Other birds are well represented in the archaeological record. William B. Gillespie (1995:704–707) found roadrunner, macaw, raven, quail, owl, and hawk remains at Los Morteros, a site along the Santa Cruz River within 12 miles of Cocoraque. People with birds in the Cocoraque imagery appear to have a similar array of owls, parrots, quail, and other less identifiable birds. In the petroglyph panels, anthropomorphic bird-holders stand in confident positions, defined as a stance showing characteristics like hips slightly thrown to the side, eyes slightly diverted, thick bold lines, broad shoulders, and feet firmly planted. These are in contrast to the vulnerable spread-eagle position of many of the anthropomorphs. Of the ten anthropomorphs associated with identifiable bird-like objects, none are of the darkest patination, seven have patination levels within the Hohokam occupation, and three have the brighter patination of the Historic O'odham. For perspective, there were virtually the same number of anthropomorphs recorded in the Hohokam versus Historic O'odham occupations (495 and 493, respectively) so the difference in the number of birds associated with anthropomorphs is noteworthy. If this was a Hohokam cultural tradition representing a sign of social standing, it diminishes markedly after Hohokam times.

In addition, I tabulated the number of anthropomorphs associated with other possible indicators of power, specifically staffs and clubs. As discussed above, staffs and clubs have been interpreted as indicating higher social status in burials. There were four such images, all dating to the Hohokam based on patination. None of these were holding birds and are therefore incremental to the figures discussed above. It is worth mentioning that only one anthropomorphic image included jewelry but it also included a bird; this image is already discussed in the preceding paragraph.

Taken together, the data suggest that images of possessions may be of value in identifying high status individuals. Combining the data on birds and staffs or clubs, there were zero of these in Pre-Hohokam times, eleven in Hohokam times, and three in Post-Hohokam times. This is interesting because differentiation by social status was highest in the Hohokam culture.

Another criterion of interest is size of the glyph, based on the assumption that prominent individuals would be depicted in a larger format. Image height data is available for 13 of the 14 anthropomorphs holding birds, staffs, or clubs that may depict high-status individuals. The mean height of these 13 glyphs is 31 cm versus a mean height of 20 cm for the 1,040 remaining anthropomorphs, supporting the interpretation that these are high-status individuals.

Illustrations of High-Status Individuals

Figures 18–22 show five of the fourteen glyphs that may depict high-status individuals defined by their possessions, either in hand or nearby, and the size of the anthropomorphic image. All of these particular petroglyphs and many of the others occupy places on the landscape where the image is visible from below, as in Figure 23.

The individuals in Figures 18, 19, 20, and 22 appear to be either holding or associated with a nearby depiction of a bird. Figure 18's bird, formed from pecked and natural aberrations in the boulder, appears so large the anthropomorph's arm is positioned to extend the shoulder to accommodate the large animal. Figures

Figure 18. One of the fourteen candidates for leadership or high status indicated by evidence of possessions and size. In this case the anthropomorph has a bird over its right shoulder, a circular object in its right hand, and at 36 cm is taller than the 20 cm mean height for anthropomorphs at Cocoraque Ranch.

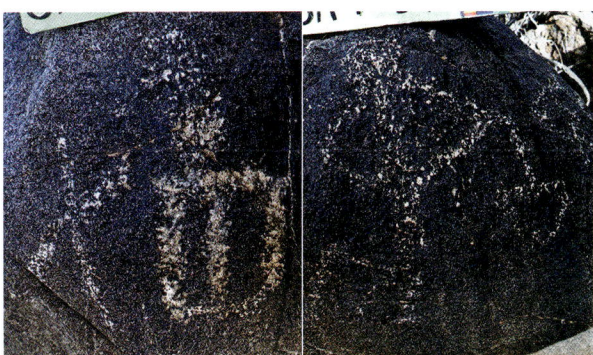

Figure 19. Illustration of a higher status individual with shield and arrow, an association with a bird, and measurement of 31 cm. Left and right sections of panel photographed separately and placed here in approximate natural relationship.

19 and 20 show individuals with adjacent birds, one perched on a squarish object, the other flying between the anthropomorph and a triangular shape.

Figure 20 shows imagery that may indicate leadership in hunting because the anthropomorph is associated with a jackrabbit. Cocoraque is home to some of the largest hares in North America: antelope jackrabbits and black-tailed jackrabbits. These 8- to 10-pound

Figure 20. The rabbit image to the left of the anthropomorph may indicate hunt leadership. The unembellished figure is also associated with a flying bird. Conventional image combined with DStretch LDS enhancement (Photoshop hue blending mode).

Figure 21. The large circular object attached to the anthropomorph's left hand could be a shield signifying "enemy-killer" status, one of the Tohono O'odham ways of gaining power. It is among the tallest of the anthropomorphs at 42 cm. The figure conveys confidence, is located at a very visible place on the landscape (see Figure 23), and is inscribed over older glyphs.

Figure 22. The sparsely pecked necklace on this anthropomorph is the only element interpreted as jewelry we found at Cocoraque Ranch. High status of this individual is also supported by possessions, including a skull under the right elbow, a very lightly pecked bird, and many less identifiable things. The confident stance and prominent location on the landscape strengthen the case for this being a high-status figure. Details identify elements identified by the author as (a) flying bird, (b) skull, and (c) necklace.

animals evade predators with speed and jumping ability (Merlin and Siminski 2000:494). Jackrabbits were not only significant meat animals to the O'odham but their importance is supported by ethnographic accounts detailing men participating in communal ceremonial rabbit drives. There was also a communal deer drive but the hunt chief's title "topetam" literally translates to "rabbiter" (Underhill 1946:96).

The anthropomorphs in Figures 19 and 22 appear to have possessions related to warfare, one of the three ways Underhill (1946:19) reported that Tohono O'odham men could gain power. The anthropomorph on the right in Figure 19 looks to have a shield in front of its upper body with arms showing through as though the shield is transparent, a practice also common in other cultures. The figure also has an arrow or spear. Figure 22's anthropomorph appears to have a skull under its right elbow that might qualify the person depict-

ed as an "enemy slayer." There is another possible explanation for the skull image, however; reports of ancestor veneration or ancestor worship could account for this item. Archaeologists have cited ancestor worship as a belief for the Hohokam, supported by ubiquitous small clay human-like figurines found starting in the 7th century C.E. (Wallace 2007:18–19). This skull image does not have a violent aspect or drips coming from the bottom as do decapitated heads in the Fremont Culture (Simms and Gohier 2010:94) and as is illustrated on a bowl from the Mimbres Culture (Creel and Anyon 2010:32). Other skulls are illustrated at Cocoraque, indicating this subject deserves a thoughtful study.

In addition to the skull, the interesting anthropomorph in Figure 22 appears to have a necklace, a bird,

where one of the categories of elaboration was introduced during a later period.

However, subsequent analysis suggests that a few characteristics may distinguish high-status individuals. The presence of possessions, specifically birds, staffs, and clubs, as well as the size of the anthropomorph, may be significant. These anthropomorphs are 50 percent larger than other anthropomorphs at the site and are often situated in highly visible locations. Anthropomorphs that included these characteristics were much more common in the Hohokam time frame than they were in the preceding and subsequent time periods. This time frame coincides well with the period of greatest cultural complexity covered by this study—Hohokam times.

Acknowledgments. The author gratefully acknowledges the following photographers and illustrators for their contributions: Lance K. Trask – Figures 3, 4a, 6, 8, 9, 11, 12, 14, 23, composite illustration Figure 2; Gordon P. Hanson – Figures 1, 16; Logan T. White – Figures 10, 17; Henry D. Wallace – Figure 5, courtesy Archaeology Southwest; William B. Gillespie – Figure 2, shells photos. The remaining figures and illustrations are by the author.

References Cited

Abbott, David R.
 2000 *Ceramics and Community Organization Among the Hohokam.* University of Arizona Press, Tucson.

Adams, Jenny L.
 2005 Early Agricultural Period Grinding Technology. In *Material Cultures and Lifeways of Early Agricultural Communities in Southern Arizona*, edited by R. Jane Sliva, pp. 99–119. Anthropological Papers 35. Center for Desert Archaeology, Tucson, Arizona.

Astroth, Kirk
 2019 Elusive, Enigmatic Labyrinth Glyphs of the American Southwest. In *American Indian Rock Art, Volume 45*, edited by Ken Hedges and Anne McConnell, pp. 103–113. American Rock Art Research Association, San Jose, California.

Barr, Donald M., Juan Smith, William Smith Allison, and Julian Hayden
 1994 *The Short Swift Time of Gods on Earth.* University of California Press, Berkeley.

Bostwick, Todd W.
 2002 *Landscape of the Spirits: Hohokam Rock Art at South Mountain Park.* University of Arizona Press, Tucson.

Bostwick, Todd W., Stephanie M. Whittlesey, and Douglas R. Mitchell
 2010 Reconstructing the Sacred in Hohokam Archaeology: Cosmology, Mythology, and Ritual. *Journal of Arizona Archaeology* 1(1):89–101.

Craig, Douglas B.
 2010 Modeling Leadership Strategies in Hohokam Society. *Journal of Arizona Archaeology* 2010 1(1):71–88.

Figure 23. A portion of the prominent hillside at Cocoraque Ranch where some petroglyph panels are positioned to be seen at a distance from below. Note the location of the boulder for the panel illustrated in Figure 21.

and additional less identifiable things. Even if none of the possessions were identifiable, the image exudes capability, confidence, and importance. It is the largest image on the boulder and is surrounded by possessions.

Conclusions

The initial hypothesis that there would be changes in the complexity of anthropomorphs reflecting social changes over time was not confirmed. Despite the vast changes in living conditions from 5000 B.P. to the mid-twentieth century, this study finds that the Ancestral and post-contact O'odham embellishment of anthropomorphs at the Cocoraque Ranch remained relatively constant. The types of embellishment are the same over time, no new ways appear with the changes in living circumstances from hunting and gathering to agriculture, to aggregation into larger communities and building of great structures requiring cooperative projects, and then to smaller villages with less elaborate agricultural systems. This research found no instances

Creel, Darrell, and Roger Anyon
   2010 Burning Down the House: Ritual Architecture of the Mimbres Late Pithouse Period. In *Mimbres Lives and Landscapes,* edited by Margaret C. Nelson and Michelle Hegmon, pp. 29–37. School for Advanced Research Press, Santa Fe, New Mexico.

Dimmitt, Mark A.
   2000 Biomes and Communities of the Sonoran Desert Region. In *A Natural History of the Sonoran Desert,* edited by Steven J. Phillips and Patricia Wentworth Comus, pp. 3–18. Arizona-Sonora Desert Museum Press, Tucson, and University of California Press, Berkeley.

Doyel, David E.
   1991 Hohokam Cultural Evolution in the Phoenix Basin. In *Exploring the Hohokam: Prehistoric Desert Peoples of the American Southwest,* edited by George J. Gumerman, pp. 231–278. Amerind Foundation Publication, University of New Mexico Press, Albuquerque.

   2007 Irrigation, Production, and Power in Phoenix Basin Hohokam Society. In *The Hohokam Millennium,* edited by Suzanne K. Fish and Paul R. Fish, pp. 82–89. School for Advanced Research Press, Santa Fe, New Mexico.

Elson, Mark D., and David R. Abbott
   2000 Organizational Variability in Platform Mound-building Groups in the American Southwest. In *Alternative Leadership Strategies in the Prehispanic Southwest,* edited by Barbara J. Mills, pp. 117–135. University of Arizona Press, Tucson.

Ferguson, T. J.
   2008 Cocoraque Butte: Signs of History in the Storied Landscape of the Tohono O'odham. Unpublished report prepared for the Arizona Open Lands Trust, Tucson, Arizona.

Fewkes, Jesse W.
   1912 *Casa Grande, Arizona.* Twenty-Eighth Annual Report of the Bureau of Ethnology. Smithsonian Institution, Washington, D.C.

Fink, T. Michael
   1991 Prehistoric Irrigation Canals and Their Possible Impact on Hohokam Health. In *Prehistoric Irrigation in Arizona: Symposium 1988,* edited by Cory D. Breternitz, pp. 61–86. Soil Systems Publications in Archaeology No. 17, Phoenix.

Fish, Suzanne K., and Paul R. Fish
   1991 Hohokam Political Organization and Social Organization. In *Exploring the Hohokam: Prehistoric Desert Peoples of the American Southwest,* edited by George J. Gumerman, pp.151–175. Amerind Foundation Publication, University of New Mexico Press, Albuquerque.

   2007 *The Hohokam Millennium.* School for Advanced Research Press, Santa Fe, New Mexico.

Fontana, Bernard L.
   1981 *Of Earth and Little Rain: The Papago Indians.* Northland Press, Flagstaff, Arizona.

   2010 *A Gift of Angels.* The University of Arizona Press, Tucson.

Gillespie, William B.
   1995 Vertebrate Remains from Los Morteros. In *Archaeological Investigations at Los Morteros, a Prehistoric Settlement in the Northern Tucson Basin,* edited by Henry D. Wallace, pp. 673–719. Anthropological Papers No. 17, Part 2. Center for Desert Archaeology, Tucson, Arizona.

   2018 O'odham and Cocoraque—Documentary Accounts. Unpublished report prepared for the Cocoraque Petroglyph Complex Site Report submission to the Bureau of Land Management. Tucson.

   2019 Cocoraque Features—Preliminary Report. Report prepared for the Cocoraque Petroglyph Complex Site. Unsubmitted.

Gilman, Patricia A., Marc Thompson, and Kristina C. Wyckoff
   2014 Ritual Change and the Distant: Mesoamerican Iconography, Scarlet Macaws, and Great Kivas in the Mimbres Region of Southwestern New Mexico. *American Antiquity* 79(1):90–107.

Gregory, David A.
   1991 Form and Variation in Hohokam Settlement Patterns. In *Chaco and Hohokam: Prehistoric Regional Systems in the American Southwest,* edited by Patricia L. Crown and W. James Judge, pp. 159–193. School of American Research Press, Santa Fe, New Mexico.

Hays-Gilpin, Kelley A.
   2004 *Ambiguous Images: Gender and Rock Art.* Alta Mira Press, Walnut Creek, California.

Hernbrode, Janine
   2019 Rock Art After the Hohokam: Elements, Style, and Continuity of the Tohono O'odham at Cocoraque Butte. In *American Indian Rock Art, Volume 45,* edited by Ken Hedges and Anne McConnell, pp. 89–101. American Rock Art Research Association, San Jose, California.

Hernbrode, Janine, and Peter Boyle
   2013 Flower World Imagery in Petroglyphs: Hints of Hohokam Cosmology on the Landscape. In *IFRAO 2013 Proceedings, American Indian Rock Art, Volume 40,* edited by Mavis Greer and Peggy Whitehead, pp. 1077–1092. American Rock Art Research Association, Glendale, Arizona.

   2016 Petroglyphs and Bell Rocks at Cocoraque Butte: Further Evidence of the Flower World Belief Among the Hohokam. In *American Indian Rock Art, Volume 42,* edited by Ken Hedges, pp. 91–105. American Rock Art Research Association, San Jose, California.

   2017 Broad Distribution of Flower World Imagery in Hohokam Petroglyphs. In *American Indian Rock Art, Volume 43,* edited by Ken Hedges and Mark A. Calamia, pp. 75–83. American Rock Art Research Association, San Jose, California.

   2018 Becoming Human: Rock Art Depictions of Transformation in Landscapes of Emergence. In *American Indian Rock Art, Volume 44,* edited by David A. Kaiser and James D. Keyser, pp. 97–110. American Rock Art Research Association, San Jose, California.

Hill, Jane H.
   1992 The Flower World of Old Uto-Aztecan. In *Journal of Anthropological Research* 48(2):117–144.

Hill, J. Brett, Jeffery J. Clark, William H. Doelle, and Patrick D. Lyons
   2004 Prehistoric Demography in the Southwest: Migration, Coalescence, and Hohokam Population Decline. *American Antiquity* 69(4):689–716.

Loendorf, Chris, and Barnaby V. Lewis
   2017 Ancestral O'odham: Akimel O'odham Cultural Traditions and the Archaeological Record. *American Antiquity* 82(1):123–139.

Lopez, Daniel
   2007 Huhugam. In *The Hohokam Millennium,* edited by Suzanne K. Fish and Paul R. Fish, pp. 117–121. School for Advanced Research Press, Santa Fe, New Mexico.

Lumholtz, Carl
   1912 *New Trails in Mexico: An Account of One Year's Exploration in North-Western Sonora, Mexico, and South-Western Arizona 1909–1910.* Charles Scribner's Sons, New York.

Mabry, Jonathan B.
2008 Introduction. In *Las Capas: Early Irrigation and Sedentism in a Southwestern Floodplain,* edited by Jonathan B. Mabry, pp. 1–34. Anthropological Papers 28. Center for Desert Archaeology, Tucson, Arizona.

Mabry, Jonathan B., James P. Holmlund, Fred L. Nials, and Manuel R. Palacios-Fest
2008 Modeling Canal Characteristics and Trends. In *Las Capas: Early Irrigation and Sedentism in a Southwestern Floodplain,* edited by Jonathan B. Mabry, pp. 235–247. Anthropological Papers 28. Center for Desert Archaeology, Tucson, Arizona.

Mabry, Jonathan B., and Michelle N. Stevens
2014 Beyond the Cochise Culture: New Views of Archaic Foragers and Early Farmers in Southeastern Arizona. In *Between Mimbres and Hohokam: Exploring the Archaeology and History of Southeastern Arizona and Southwestern New Mexico,* edited by Henry D. Wallace, pp. 115–164. Archaeology Southwest, Tucson.

Martynec, Richard, and Sandy Martynec
1995 Did the Tohono O'odham Make Petroglyphs? In *Rock Art Papers, Volume 22,* edited by Ken Hedges, pp. 81–87. San Diego Museum Papers 33. San Diego Museum of Man, San Diego.

2003 Petroglyphs at a Temporal Site in the Growler Mountains, Southwest Arizona. In *Rock Art Papers, Volume 16,* edited by Ken Hedges, pp. 39–46. San Diego Museum Papers 41. San Diego Museum of Man, San Diego.

Masse, W. Bruce
1991 The Quest for Subsistence Sufficiency and Civilization in the Sonoran Desert. In *Chaco and Hohokam: Prehistoric Regional Systems in the American Southwest,* edited by Patricia L. Crown and W. James Judge, pp. 195–223. School of American Research Press, Santa Fe, New Mexico.

Merlin, Pinau, and Peter Siminski
2000 Mammal Accounts. In *A Natural History of the Sonoran Desert,* edited by Steven J. Phillips and Patricia Wentworth Comus, pp. 459–508. Arizona-Sonora Desert Museum Press, Tucson, and University of California Press, Berkeley.

Mills, Barbara J., Jeffrey J. Clark, Matthew A. Peebles, W. R. Haas, Jr., John M. Roberts, Jr., J. Brett Hill, Deborah L. Huntley, Lewis Borck, Ronald L. Breiger, Aaron Clauset, and M. Stephen Shackley
2013 Transformation of Social Networks in the Late Pre-hispanic US Southwest. *Proceedings of the National Academy of Sciences* 110(15):5785–5790.

Mukhopadhyay, Tirtha Prasad, and Alan P. Garfinkel
2016 Patterned Body Anthropomorphs of the Cosos: How Might Concentric Circle Psychograms Function in Ethnographic Schemes? *Expression* 13(3):54–70.

Reid, Jefferson, and Stephanie Whittlesey
1997 *The Archaeology of Ancient Arizona.* University of Arizona Press, Tucson.

Rice, Glen E.
2016 *Sending the Spirits Home: The Archaeology of Hohokam Mortuary Practices.* University of Utah Press, Salt Lake City.

Sekaquaptewa, Emory, and Dorothy Washburn
2010 Living in Metaphor: Hopi Traditions in Song and Image. In *Painting the Cosmos,* edited by Kelley Hays-Gilpin and Polly Schaafsma, pp. 139–177. Museum of Northern Arizona Bulletin 67, Flagstaff.

Simms, Steven R., and François Gohier
2010 *Traces of Fremont: Society and Rock Art in Ancient Utah.* University of Utah Press, Salt Lake City.

Sliva, R. Jane
2015 *Projectile Points of the Early Agricultural Southwest: Typology, Migration, and Social Dynamics from the Sonoran Desert to the Colorado Plateau.* Archaeology Southwest and Desert Archaeology, West Press, Tucson, Arizona.

Smith, Watson
1952 *Kiva Mural Decorations at Awatovi and Kawaika-a with a Survey of Other Wall Paintings in the Pueblo Southwest.* Reports of the Awatovi Expedition, Report No. 5. Papers of the Peabody Museum of American Archaeology and Ethnology 37. Harvard University, Cambridge, Massachusetts.

Teague, Lynn S.
1993 Prehistory and the Traditions of the O'odham and Hopi. *Kiva* 58(4):435–454.

Underhill, Ruth M.
1939 *Social Organization of the Papago Indians.* Columbia University Contributions to Anthropology 30. Columbia University Press, New York. Facsimile reprint 1969, AMS Press, New York.

1946 *Papago Indian Religion.* Columbia University Contributions to Anthropology 33. Columbia University Press, New York. Facsimile reprint 1969, AMS Press, New York.

Vokes, Arthur W.
2008 The Shell Assemblage. In *Life in the Foothills: Archaeological Investigations in the Tortolita Mountains of Southern Arizona,* edited by Deborah L. Swartz, pp. 343–353. Anthropological Papers 46. Center for Desert Archaeology, Tucson, Arizona.

Vokes, Arthur W., and David A. Gregory
2007 Exchange Networks for Exotic Goods in the Southwest and Zuni's Place in Them. In *Zuni Origins: Toward a New Synthesis of Southwestern Archaeology,* edited by David A. Gregory and David R. Wilcox, pp. 318–357. University of Arizona Press, Tucson.

Wallace, Henry D.
2007 Hohokam Beginnings. In *The Hohokam Millennium,* edited by Suzanne K. Fish and Paul R. Fish, pp. 13–21. School for Advanced Research Press, Santa Fe, New Mexico.

2008 The Petroglyphs of Atlatl Ridge, Tortolita Mountains, Pima County, Arizona. In *Life in the Foothills: Archaeological Investigations in the Tortolita Mountains of Southern Arizona,* edited by D. L. Swartz, pp. 159–231. Anthropological Papers No. 46. Center for Desert Archaeology, Tucson, Arizona.

Woodson, Michael Kyle
2010 *The Social Organization of Hohokam Irrigation in the Middle Gila River Valley, Arizona.* Ph.D. Dissertation, School of Human Evolution and Social Change, Arizona State University, Tempe. University Microfilms, Ann Arbor, Michigan.

Wright, Aaron M.
2014 *Religion on the Rocks: Hohokam Rock Art, Ritual Practice, and Social Transformation.* University of Utah Press, Salt Lake City.

Portable X-ray Fluorescence Analyses at the Meyers Spring Pictograph Site

Karen L. Steelman, Charles W. Koenig, Amanda M. Castañeda,
Jerod L. Roberts, and Victoria L. Roberts

As part of the documentation of the Meyers Spring pictograph site (41TE9), Shumla Archaeological Research & Education Center utilized portable X-ray fluorescence spectroscopy to non-destructively analyze the art panel in situ. Meyers Spring contains many historic era pictographs such as horses, churches, crosses, and shield-bearing warriors in addition to hundreds of examples of historic graffiti. As such, we were interested in the composition of the paint used by native and non-native peoples during the contact period. As we have seen for other paintings in the Lower Pecos Canyonlands region, red paintings were primarily painted with ochers of iron mineral pigments and the few black paintings at the site were painted with manganese mineral pigments. The most interesting discovery was elevated zinc levels for three yellow-orange paintings of an avian figure and two handprints, likely painted by indigenous peoples, suggesting commercial paints may have been used for these paintings. In addition, numerous locations on the panel have been damaged from target shooting and we were able to confirm that the fractures and black residue on the panel were the result of lead bullets and shot damaging the panel. This X-ray fluorescence study at Meyers Spring highlights the advantages of this non-destructive spectroscopy used in conjunction with rock art documentation.

Shumla Archaeological Research & Education Center (Shumla) performed portable X-ray fluorescence (pXRF) analyses during rock art documentation at Meyers Spring (41TE9) (see Koenig et al. 2019 for a description of the Alexandria Project). Located in the Lower Pecos Canyonlands of southwest Texas (Figure 1), the Meyers Spring rockshelter (Figure 2) contains a variety of rock art imagery including Pecos River style pictographs, historic (post-contact) indigenous pictographs, historic non-native graffiti, and modern graffiti. In conjunction with the intensive photographic documentation of the rock art at Meyers Spring, Shumla used pXRF to assay 110 individual locations on the shelter wall for painted pictographs (red, yellow, black, and white), painted graffiti (red and black), suspected bullet impacts, and unmodified rock backgrounds. Meyers Spring is one of the most important Historic-era rock art sites in the region, and afforded a unique opportunity to employ non-destructive, in situ pXRF spectroscopy to identify the inorganic pigments in the paintings, as well as characterize the chemical signatures for suspected bullet impacts.

Previous pigment studies relating to Lower Pecos Canyonlands rock art have primarily focused on Pecos River style pictographs using non-destructive pXRF (Koenig et al. 2014) and destructive laboratory-based methods such as X-ray diffraction (XRD) (Hyman et al. 1996; Zolensky 1982) and inductively coupled plasma mass spectrometry (ICP-MS) (Bu et al. 2013; Russ et al. 2012). XRF and ICP-MS are elemental analysis techniques, whereas XRD is a crystallographic technique that provides molecular identification. For example, an elemental analysis technique would indicate the presence of

Karen L. Steelman,
Charles W. Koenig,
Amanda M. Castañeda,
Jerod L. Roberts, and
Victoria L. Roberts
Shumla Archaeological Research & Education Center, Comstock, Texas

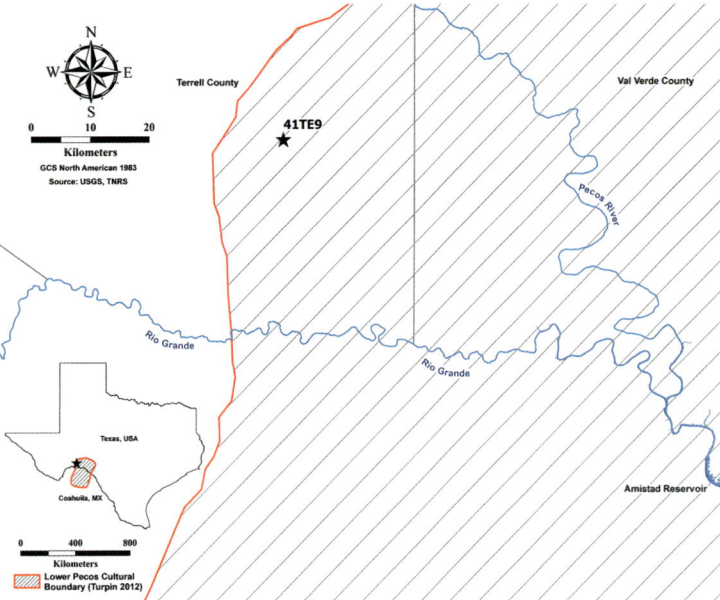

Figure 1. Map showing the approximate location of the Meyers Spring pictograph site (41TE9).

iron (Fe), but a molecular analysis technique is able to identify a specific mineral such as hematite ($\alpha\text{-Fe}_2\text{O}_3$) or goethite ($\alpha\text{-FeOOH}$). Solveig Turpin initiated pigment studies in the region by analyzing Pecos River style paint samples with XRD, concluding that red and yellow pictographs were made with iron mineral pigments (hematite, goethite, maghemite, lepidocrocite, etc.) and black pictographs were made with manganese mineral pigments (pyrolusite or manganite) (Hyman et al. 1996; Zolensky 1982). Subsequently, these results have been expanded upon as Shumla began conducting chemical analyses to identify pigments in Lower Pecos parietal and mobiliary art using pXRF (e.g. Castañeda et al. 2019a; Castañeda et al. 2019b; Koenig et al. 2014). For example, Koenig et al. (2014) analyzed parietal art at 10 rock art sites and determined that pXRF is a useful tool for determining the elemental composition of pigments, specifically differentiating whether black paintings were made with manganese-mineral or charcoal pigments. While pXRF is purely an elemental analysis technique, it has the advantage that it is non-destructive, and can be carried to sites to analyze the pictographs in situ.

Worldwide, researchers have applied pXRF to the study of rock art to address different research questions (e.g., Beck et al. 2014; Bedford et al. 2018; Dostal and Smith 2015; Huntley 2012; Huntley et al. 2015; Lins and Price 2011; Miller et al. 2011; Newman and Loendorf 2005; Olivares et al. 2013; O'Regan et al. 2019; Robinson et al. 2015; Roldán et al. 2010; Rowe et al. 2011; Sepúlveda et al. 2015; Wesley et al. 2014). With pXRF, numerous locations on a single pictograph panel can be analyzed over the course of hours, whereas only a few samples might be removed from a rockshelter wall and collected for laboratory-based methods. Further, a large pXRF dataset can be easily collected for an entire archaeological region including multiple styles of rock art, allowing archaeologists to develop hypotheses about rock art styles and pigment usage that might not be explored otherwise (Koenig et al. 2014).

Meyers Spring is an important location for pigment analyses because not only is the site the westernmost known example of Pecos River style pictographs, but it also contains hundreds of post-contact indigenous paintings as well as historic and modern graffiti. Prior to this study, Shumla had not analyzed any historic pictographs or graffiti in the region with pXRF and we viewed the fieldwork at 41TE9 as a new opportunity to learn more about the rock art of the region using chemical analysis. At 41TE9, we explored three different research questions with pXRF:

1) Are any of the historic-era indigenous images executed with paints containing commercial in-

Figure 2. Looking upstream at the Meyers Spring rockshelter. The pictographs span the entire shelter wall, including the surface above the holding tank.

gredients (e.g., lead, zinc, titanium)?

2) What are the chemical signatures of the paints used to produce the historic graffiti?

3) Can we confirm the presence of bullet impacts using chemical signatures?

During our analyses, Shumla identified three yellow-orange paintings with elevated zinc and iron levels suggesting the use of commercial paints (Di Bernardo 1945). For the remainder of the indigenous pictographs, the use of iron (red/yellow) and manganese (black) mineral pigments for pictographs at Meyers Spring is consistent with previous analyses for pictographs in the region (Koenig et al. 2014). Regarding the historic graffiti, red and black painted graffiti had elevated iron levels, but no measurable levels of titanium, zinc, or lead, suggesting either a lime-based commercial paint or mineral-based paints similar to those used for the pictographs. Finally, pXRF detected elevated levels of lead in the areas on the limestone wall containing fractures and black residue suspected to be from gunshot damage.

Meyers Spring (41TE9)

Meyers Spring (41TE9) is on the northwestern limit of the Lower Pecos Canyonlands archaeological region, located on a private ranch approximately 10 miles northeast of Dryden in Terrell County, Texas (Figure 1). Listed on the National Register of Historic Places, 41TE9 is comprised of a variety of prehistoric features including pictographs, burned rock middens, stone alignments, cairns, and bedrock mortars (Houk 2009; Stone 2009). In addition, the site contains several historic features such as a holding tank (constructed with mortar and limestone blocks in 1901, located just below the spring openings and still collecting water), several dams, a corral, and a paddock (Johnson 2010; Walter and Johnson 2010). Based on rock art imagery and point types, the site has been utilized from the Middle Archaic to modern times (Stone 2009). Nearby is the historic Camp Meyers, a military outpost for Fort Clark in Brackettville, Texas. The site is closely tied to the history of the Indian Wars and U.S. military in west Texas, and is perhaps best known for its association with the Black Seminole Indian Scouts (Walter and Johnson 2010).

The main rock art panel at Meyers Spring spans 95 meters on a limestone shelter wall immediately downstream of a spring (Figure 2) and consists of poorly preserved Pecos River style pictographs (Figure 3) superimposed by Historic period pictographs, historic

Figure 3. The best-preserved Pecos River style figure at Meyers Spring as seen in (a) real-color and (b) DStretch YDS enhancement. This figure is a polychrome anthropomorph with a probable rabbit-ear headdress, wrist adornment, loaded atlatl, and additional darts.

graffiti, and gunshot damage (Figure 4). The lower portions of the panel are in very poor condition due to water scouring and occasional standing water. Historic imagery at the site includes shield-bearing warriors, guns, horses, crosses, and mission-style churches. The Historic pictographs show a resemblance to Plains Biographic Tradition art (Peel 2009). This tradition was brought to the Southern Plains during the southern migration of the Comanche, Kiowa, Kiowa Apache, and others (Keyser and Klassen 2001; Peel 2009). Turpin (1986) suggests that the anthropomorphs at 41TE9 (and those at another Lower Pecos rock art site, 41VV666)—with circular heads, rectangular bodies, bent legs, shield symbols, and single feather headdresses (Figure 5)—are characteristic of Early Biographic Art dated between 1775 and 1830, proposing that these figures were introduced by the movement of Plains Indians into the region. In addition to the Comanche, Kiowa, and Kiowa Apache, other native groups in the area who could have produced the rock art at Meyers Spring include the Jumano, Patarabueye, Apache, Ute, Arapahoe, Pawnee, Cheyenne, and Caddo, all of whom

Figure 4. Historic pictographs on the central portion of the panel at Meyers Spring. There is historic graffiti incised into the red paintings as well as numerous bullet impacts.

Figure 5. Probable Plains Biographic rock art depicting a line of "dancers" high above on the shelter wall.

traveled through the area (Kenmotsu and Wade 2002). In addition, there are red and orange anthropomorphic figures, handprints, zoomorphs, and other elements that lack historic iconography; Kirkland referred to these figures as "middle-period paintings" (Kirkland and Newcomb 1967:113). We suspect that much of this rock art is also post-contact, even though not all of these paintings depict imagery clearly associated with unquestionably diagnostic historic imagery.

Meyers Spring has been the subject of archaeological investigations since the 1930s when A. T. Jackson (1938:146–157) and Forrest and Lula Kirkland (Kirkland and Newcomb 1967:112–123) first documented the rock art. In 1972, the National Park Service visited Meyers Spring to evaluate the site, which resulted in the National Register nomination (Bell 1972). In June 2003, the Texas Archeological Society's Rock Art Task Force documented the pictographs at Meyers Spring (on file at the Texas Archeological Research Laboratory, The University of Texas at Austin). From 2007 to 2009, Texas Tech University conducted the most extensive documentation of both the historic and prehistoric components of the site with support from the Rock Art Foundation (Houk 2009; Johnson 2010; Stone 2009; Walter and Johnson 2010).

Methods

For portable X-ray fluorescence spectroscopy, an X-ray tube source in the instrument emits primary (incident) X-rays that interact with atoms in a sample with sufficient energy to eject low-energy inner shell electrons, creating an unstable ion. When this occurs, an electron from a higher-energy, outer orbital fills the vacancy, releasing energy in the form of secondary (fluorescent) X-rays measured by a solid-state diode detector. The energy of these secondary X-rays is characteristic of a specific element, allowing qualitative identification of elements present in a sample. In addition, the detector also counts the number of secondary X-rays from the sample, allowing quantitative elemental concentrations to be determined under advantageous conditions. We direct readers to Huntley (2012:79–80) and Koenig et al. (2014:171–174) for discussions on the considerations and limitations of pXRF analysis for the study of rock art. The variability of pXRF measurements on thin paint layers is due to a number of reasons, which combine to make pXRF results qualitative or semi-quantitative at best. It must be emphasized that the concentration units (ppm) displayed by the instrument are for rough, relative comparisons only (Rowe et al. 2011).

We used a hand-held Innov-X Systems Alpha Series pXRF device with a silver (Ag) anode X-ray tube source and a SiPIN diode detector, powered by a Li-ion rechargeable battery. The instrument was operated in Soil mode, which uses a 40 kV excitation energy, to analyze for elements from Ti to Bi. We used Alloy 316 provided by the manufacturer for standardizing the pXRF upon each instrument start-up and selected 60 second analysis times for each pXRF reading. Compton Normalization calibration calculations converted measured characteristic line intensities for each element into weight percent concentrations. A Hewlett Packard iPAQ personal digital assistant was used in the field to control the instrument and store data, which were exported into a spreadsheet for data analysis. During data collection, elemental concentrations are displayed on the palmtop computer screen attached to the instrument. This type of feedback in the field is satisfying, as results can be discussed immediately with collaborators.

A single person can collect pXRF data, but it is more efficient with up to four people. One team member operates the pXRF instrument (the pXRF is held flush against the rock wall), another fills in the pXRF database form, the third takes context photographs, and the remaining person holds a laser pointer to mark the pXRF location in the context photographs (Figure 6). Though results are exported into a spreadsheet for data analysis once back at the office, we have developed a pXRF database form that we fill in on electronic tablets in the field. Fields include pXRF reading ID number, paint color, sample type (infilled, line, fine line), parts per million (ppm) Fe, ppm Mn, ppm Other (any other notable element), context photograph numbers, and notes. This form can then be queried by color or any of the other fields to aid in data analysis.

At 41TE9 we analyzed 110 locations using pXRF: 36 pictographs, 8 historic graffiti, 11 suspected bullet impacts, and 55 unpainted background control locations. When possible, painting locations >1 cm^2 were tested to ensure that the instrument window is placed completely over a painted surface. Each paint location selected dealt directly with one of the three research questions we wanted to investigate. In addition, a nearby location of unpainted wall was analyzed for comparison.

Results and Discussion

For the 110 measurements across the panel at Meyers Spring, the pXRF instrument analyzed for elements from Ti to Bi (atomic number 22 to 83). Results for manganese (Mn), iron (Fe), strontium (Sr), and barium (Ba) are shown in Table 1 (page 76) for all analysis locations. Results for chromium (Cr), copper (Cu), selenium (Se), cadmium (Cd), tin (Sn), mercury (Hg), and lead (Pb) are shown in Table 2 (page 78) and were only found at suspected gunshot locations. Zinc (Zn) was only detected for three yellow-orange paintings (Figure 7). All other elements for analysis locations were reported as <LOD (limit of detection), which is defined as the lowest amount of substance present in a sample that can be reliably detected and distinguished from the absence of that substance in a sample (i.e., the zero level). LOD is estimated from replicate analyses (typically n=20) of a blank sample (not containing the analyte of interest) and is defined as three times the standard deviation of a blank. During factory calibration, pXRF manufacturers analyze interference-free standards to determine LODs that are programmed into the analyzer software. Of interest to our study, instrumental LODs for all elements discussed are ~100 ppm.

Unpainted Rock Backgrounds

In order to determine background thresholds, we collected 55 control measurements on unpainted

Figure 6. The pXRF team collecting data at Meyers Spring: Karen Steelman runs the pXRF instrument while Charles Koenig inputs data into the database and Victoria Roberts takes context photographs.

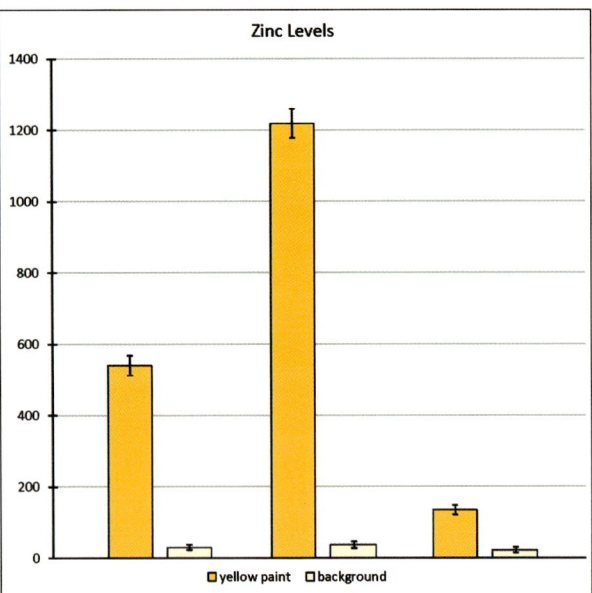

Figure 7. Zinc levels (ppm) for three yellow-orange pictographs and associated background control measurements. Error bars represent the ±1s instrumental error of the pXRF. From left to right, yellow avian shield figure, well-preserved positive handprint, and poorly preserved positive handprint (see Figure 9).

limestone directly adjacent to each pXRF analysis location for painted (or bullet-impacted) stone. For the unpainted rock, the only elements detected above the instrumental limit of detection were manganese, iron, strontium, and barium (Table 1). Manganese levels averaged 200 ppm Mn and iron levels averaged 1000 ppm Fe. The only other element consistently detected for all measurements was strontium, with an average of 300 ppm Sr, which is a component of the rock substrate. The element strontium is below calcium in the periodic table as it has a similar reactivity and substitutes for calcium in the crystal lattice of limestone (Kulp et al. 1962). For a handful of locations, barium (also aligned below Ca in the periodic table) was detected and is also commonly found in limestone as barite, a barium sulfate salt (Stanienda 2016).

Historic Pictographs

Thirty-six pXRF assays were recorded for indigenous pictographs at Meyers Spring: 33 images of red, orange, or yellow shades, one white image, and two images painted in black. The only two elements consistently detected above background levels were manganese and iron (Table 1). Previous studies have demonstrated that these two elements are the most common in Lower Pecos prehistoric paints (Koenig et al. 2014). For the 33 Historic pictographs of various shades of red, orange, and yellow, iron levels are significantly elevated as the measurements for the painted areas and the unpainted control backgrounds do not overlap at two standard deviations. One white painting (Table 1: P016-20190319) had a similar spectrum as the unpainted rock, suggesting either a calcium carbonate (same mineral as the rock substrate) or clay pigment (the pXRF does not detect Al or Si). In addition, two black paintings of an avian (Figure 8) and paint remnant did not have elevated iron levels, but instead had significantly elevated levels of manganese (Table 1: P034-20190319 and P038-20190319). The use of red iron and black manganese mineral pigments for pictographs at Meyers Spring is consistent with analyses for red and black pictographs in the region (Castañeda et al. 2019b; Koenig et al. 2014), though some charcoal-pigmented paintings of an unidentified style have been studied in the Lower Pecos Canyonlands (Koenig et al. 2014).

The most interesting discovery was elevated zinc levels (see Figure 7) for three yellow-orange paint-

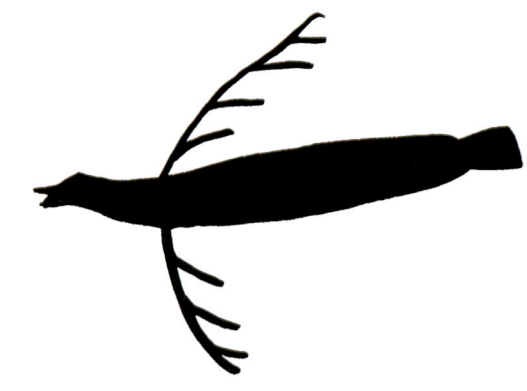

Figure 8. Black historic pictograph of avian painted with manganese mineral paint. (a) DStretch LXX 0.04_1.14_0.36 enhancement and (b) idealized interpretive illustration.

ings of an avian figure and two handprints (Figure 9); suggesting commercial paints may have been used for these paintings. Zinc was not detected in measureable levels at any other location on the rockshelter wall. For commercial paints, colored pigment is mixed with a base white paint to create the desired color and opacity. Common commercial white paints include lead white, zinc white, titanium dioxide white (not available until 1921), and lime white (Ashok 1993). For these three yellow-orange paintings, the presence of zinc and iron suggests a commercial paint consisting of an iron pigment mixed with zinc white. While the elevated zinc levels do not conclusively confirm the use of commercial paints, it is an interesting observation that warrants further consideration and study.

Historic Graffiti

There is a variety of historic graffiti from the 19th and 20th centuries scattered across the rockshelter wall. The graffiti was painted, carved, or scratched into the rock, and in many cases the writing is superimposing pictographs. For the eight pXRF measurements on historic graffiti, both the red (Figures 10a–d) and black paintings (Figures 11a–b) have elevated iron levels (Table 1). Manganese, strontium, and barium were detected at levels comparable to associated background control measurements, and are, thus, part of the rock substrate. No other elements were detected in the historic graffiti above instrumental LODs. Interestingly, the historic graffiti with the highest iron content was a painted black "J" in "J.D. STINEBA OCT 1896" (Figure 11a), whereas another black graffiti had only slightly elevated iron, most likely due to the fragmentary nature of the remaining thin paint layer (Figure 11b). Surprisingly, neither of the two black graffiti paintings contained elevated manganese above background levels, which is a common mineral-pigment for prehistoric black pictographs in the area (Koenig et al. 2014). Further, none of the analyzed red or black graffiti had elevated levels of titanium, zinc, or lead that would be expected in commercial paints (Ashok 1993; Di Bernardo 1945). If a commercial paint was used to create the historic graffiti, lime white paint as a base with an added iron-mineral pigment to

Figure 9. (a) A probable Plains Biographic avian figure painted in yellow and orange/red with a "shield" in the center of the body and (b) two handprints painted in a yellow-orange. The avian figure and the handprints had elevated Zn levels.

Figure 10. (a) Red historic graffiti underneath a black accretion. (b) Historic graffiti painted in 1877 by Company B of the 10th Infantry and Company C of the 10th Cavalry with elevated iron levels. (c) Red historic graffiti "D.C." (d) Red historic graffiti.

Figure 11. (a) Name and date of 1896 painted in black with the highest level of iron detected for historic graffiti. (b) Faded black historic graffiti.

create the red and black colors was likely used because titanium, zinc, and lead were not detected. Calcium is not detected by this particular pXRF instrument and is also the main constituent of the limestone ($CaCO_3$) rockshelter wall, so we cannot confirm this possibility with the pXRF technique. As elevated iron was the only element detected by the pXRF, the other alternative is that the historic graffiti was made similar to indigenous paint recipes using locally-sourced mineral pigments.

Of the more than 100 people who recorded their names at Meyers Spring, only nine have been positively identified (Walter and Johnson 2010). This historic graffiti consists primarily of names and dates. A pXRF measurement was obtained for the "D" in "Davis Co B 10th Inf" (Figure 10b). Directly below and in the same red color "Willis Cook Co C 10th Cav 1877" is painted. From 1873 to 1879, Company B of the 10th Infantry was stationed at Fort McKavett. And, in 1877 and 1878, they were in encounters with the Apache on both sides of the Rio Grande. Likely, it was during these military actions that Company B was at Meyers Spring. In addition, the 10th Cavalry regiment of Buffalo Soldiers was stationed at Fort Concho from 1875 to 1885, with different companies posted at various locations in the area (Walter and Johnson 2010). An interesting anecdote about the graffiti appears in the diary of Burr Duvall, a prospector of the region who traveled with Bullis and his scouts in 1879 (Woolford 1962:509): "Confound the stupid idiots, and their stupid officers who permitted such vandalism. I noticed my own name, 'Duvall' in large, black letters on the most prominent part of the cliff and mentally consigned the owner of it, (who seems was a 'private in Company B') to a hotter place than I care to mention." Because some of the graffiti is from U.S. military personnel, future research of historical records might shed light on the paints that were readily available to soldiers around Camp Meyers.

Bullet Impacts

Eleven areas of suspected bullet impacts had elevated lead levels (Table 2), confirming that the wall fractures and black staining are due to shooting damage (Figure 12). Manganese, iron, strontium, and barium were detected at levels comparable to associated background control measurements, and are part of the rock substrate and not from bullet residue (Table 1).

Figure 12. Fracturing and black residue left behind from gunshot damage on top of and surrounding a historic red pictograph.

Interestingly, elements that were detected in bullet impact locations but *not* in the control locations include chromium, copper, selenium, cadmium, tin, and mercury (Table 2). These are all elements associated with lead smelting and lead alloys, and are expected to be present in gunshot residue (Wallace 2018). Each bullet impact location had different amounts of these six elements, with no apparent patterns. Further, several locations with elevated lead did not have measureable levels for any of the six trace elements. We suspect that the variation observed is due to the low levels in the thin residues left on the rockshelter wall. In fact, it is the black residue within and around fractures that has the higher levels of lead and associated trace elements. Only the major elements present in the bullets, such as lead, would be consistently detected with pXRF when analyzing thin residues. Interestingly, a black area (P023-20190320) located on the head of a red iron-pigmented avian (P025-20190320 and P027-

20190320) contained the highest lead content measured on the panel, but there is no obvious fracturing of the rock substrate (Figure 13). We cannot rule out that this black color, where an eye would be painted, may be from a lead-based paint. However, the same trace elements observed for other black residues associated with fractured bullet impacts on the panel suggest that this black color may be due to gunshot vandalism.

Figure 13. Avian pictograph with the highest lead levels for the black area on the head.

It is important to note that every time a sizable lead peak is observed, an elevated arsenic signal is also invariably reported by the instrument even when there is no arsenic present in a sample because of a software artifact (Rowe 2013). Due to overlap of the Pb $L_{\alpha 1}$ and As $K_{\alpha 1}$ peaks at 10.6 keV, the InnovX software incorrectly reports the levels of arsenic. The $K_{\beta 1}$ peak of arsenic at 11.7 keV, which is not coincident with a lead peak, was investigated for the presence of arsenic (Figure 14). There was no visible peak at 11.7 keV for any of the spectra; therefore, arsenic is not present in measureable levels for any analysis locations.

Unfortunately, there is not sufficient data to identify the type or date of ammunition used. From 1929 photographs (Houk 2009) and photographs from *Picture-Writing of Texas Indians* (Jackson 1938:Plates 98–112), the majority of the shooting vandalism at the Meyers Spring pictograph site predates the 1930s. The gunshot damage that we see across the panel is most likely due to early vandalism of the site by U.S military units stationed at Camp Meyers in the late 1800s and early 1900s as well as local ranchers and visitors who used the site as a favorite camp and picnic spot (Houk 2009).

Conclusions

As part of Shumla's documentation at Meyers Spring (41TE9), we expanded our ongoing Lower Pecos pXRF pigment analyses to include historic pictographs. Prior to this analysis, we had no expectations regarding the paint ingredients in historic pictographs. We determined that iron-mineral pigments were used to create red paintings and manganese-mineral pigments were used to create black paintings for historic pictographs at Meyers Spring. This is consistent with the analyses for red and black pictographs in the region (Koenig et al. 2014). The most interesting discovery was elevated zinc levels for three yellow-orange paintings of an avian figure and two handprints, suggesting commercial paints may have been used for these paintings.

The Meyers Spring pictograph site and spring were visited and utilized from prehistoric times to the present by both indigenous peoples and western settlers. Historic graffiti at the site had elevated iron levels, but no measureable levels of titanium, zinc, or lead that would be expected in commercial paints. Thus, if a commercial paint was used to create the historic graffiti, lime white paint with an iron-mineral pigment added for color is the most likely possibility for these names and dates. For suspected bullet impacts, we determined that lead as well as chromium, copper, selenium, cadmium, tin, and mercury were present, even within fractures that did not have the tell-tale black

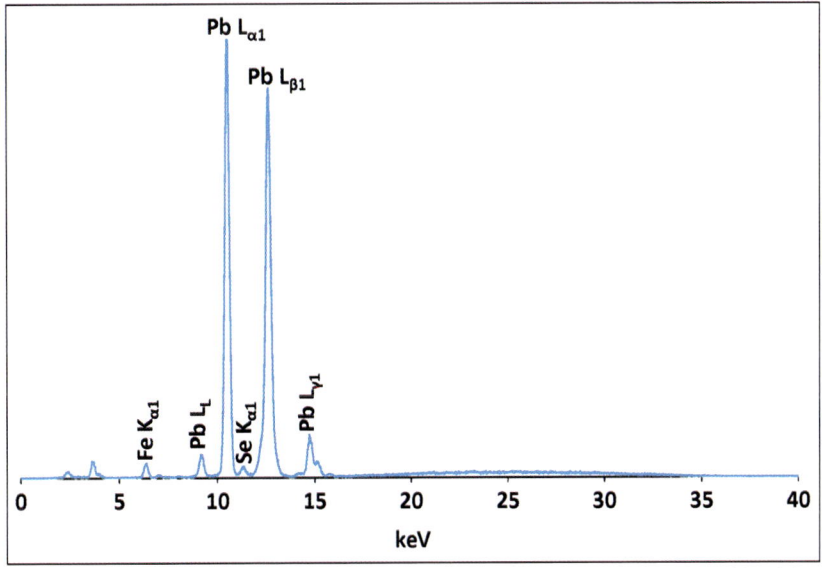

Figure 14. X-ray fluorescence spectrum for a bullet impact location with elevated lead, but no arsenic present.

residue often left behind from gunshot damage.

Elemental analysis using pXRF has provided some information about the pictographs, graffiti, and gunshot vandalism at Meyers Spring, but has not answered all our questions. Future work at Meyers Spring and other Historic period rock art sites using additional portable technologies such as Fourier Transform infrared and Raman spectroscopies (Olivares et al. 2013) or destructive laboratory-based methods such as scanning electron microscopy with energy dispersive spectroscopy (SEM-EDS) and plasma oxidation AMS radiocarbon dating (Bonneau et al. 2012; Steelman et al. 2019) may provide more comprehensive data. What is remarkable about this study's pXRF research is that we were able to collect 110 spectra across the entire panel in less than two days of fieldwork to obtain preliminary data on the elemental analysis of the rock art at Meyers Spring. We found some interesting clues, such as the elevated zinc for the three yellow-orange paintings and elevated lead for the black gunshot residues. And, unlike laboratory benchtop methods, which require removing a small sample of pigment from the rockshelter wall, non-destructive and in situ techniques such as pXRF allow us to analyze numerous paintings across the landscape. As researchers, we encourage pXRF analysis and other portable, non-destructive chemical techniques to become a routine part of rock art recording and documentation efforts at sites around the globe, just as digital cameras and DStretch on our phones has now become a standard procedure. You never know what you will learn until you look.

Acknowledgments. We appreciate the support of Dr. Marvin Rowe, Professor Emeritus of Chemistry, Texas A&M University and the Office of Archaeological Studies, Center for New Mexico Archaeology, Santa Fe, for supplying us with the pXRF analyzer. Thank you to the landowner, Thad Steele and family, for access to the site for research. As a non-profit research center, we are grateful for the organizations and foundations who have provided funding for the Alexandria Project including Abell-Hanger Foundation, Brown Foundation, Mitchell Foundation, Still Water Foundation, Summerlee Foundation, Texas Historical Commission, Val Verde Community Foundation, and many more individual donors.

References Cited

Ashok, Roy (editor)
    1993 *Artists Pigments: A Handbook of their History and Characteristics.* Volume 2. National Gallery of Art, Washington, D.C.

Beck, Lucile, H. Rousselière, J. Castaing, A. Duran, M. Lebon, B. Moignard, and F. Plassard
    2014 First Use of Portable System Coupling X-ray Diffraction and X-ray Fluorescence for In-situ Analysis of Prehistoric Rock Art. *Talanta* 129:459–464.

Bedford, Clare, David W. Robinson, and Devlin Gandy
    2018 Emigdiano Blues: The California Indigenous Pigment Palette and an In Situ Analysis of an Exotic Color. *Open Archaeology* 4(1):152–172.

Bell, Wayne
    1972 National Register of Historic Places Inventory Nomination Form. Submitted to U.S. Department of the Interior, Reference No. 72001373. Manuscript on file at the Texas Historical Commission, Austin.

Bonneau, A., D. G. Pearce, and A. M. Pollard
    2012 A Multi-technique Characterization and Provenance Study of the Pigments Used in San Rock Art, South Africa. *Journal of Archaeological Science* 39(2):287–294.

Bu, Kaixuan, James V. Cizdziel, and Jon Russ
    2013 The Source of Iron-Oxide Pigments Used in Pecos River Style Rock Paints. *Archaeometry* 55(6):1088–1100.

Castañeda, Amanda M., Charles W. Koenig, Marvin W. Rowe, and Karen L. Steelman
    2019a Portable X-ray Fluorescence of Lower Pecos Painted Pebbles: New Insights Regarding Pigment Choice and Chronology. *Journal of Archaeological Science: Reports* 25:56–71.

Castañeda, Amanda M., Charles W. Koenig, Jerod L. Roberts, Victoria L. Roberts, Jay D. Franklin, Carolyn E. Boyd, and Karen L. Steelman
    2019b Portable X-ray Fluorescence Spectroscopy of Black Red Linear Style Paintings at 41VV1000. In *Bulletin of the Texas Archeological Society, Volume 90*, edited by Britt Bousman and Sarah Morris, in press. Texas Archeological Society, Austin.

Di Bernardo, Joseph D.
    1945 *Painting and Decorating: A Handbook of Tools, Materials, Methods, and Directions.* Van Nostrand Company, New York.

Dostal, Chris, and Morgan Smith
    2015 *A Report on Analysis of Rock Art Panels at Big Bend Ranch State Park by Means of Portable X-Ray Fluorescence.* Report prepared by Texas A&M University, College Station, for Texas Parks and Wildlife Department, Austin.

Houk, Brett A. (editor)
    2009 *Inventory and Assessment of the Prehistoric Cultural Resources at Meyers Spring, Terrell County, Texas.* Occasional Papers in Archaeology, Number 1. Department of Sociology, Anthropology, and Social Work, Texas Tech University, Lubbock, Texas.

Huntley (née Ford), Jillian A.
    2012 Taphonomy or Paint Recipe: In Situ Portable X-ray Fluorescence Analysis of Two Anthropomorphic Motifs from the Woronora Plateau, New South Wales. *Australian Archaeology* 75(2):78–94.

Huntley, Jillian A., Maxime Aubert, June Ross, Helen Brand, and Michael J. Morwood
    2015 One Colour, (At Least) Two Minerals: A Study of Mulberry Rock Art Pigment and A Mulberry Pigment "Quarry" from the Kimberley, Northern Australia. *Archaeometry* 57(1):77–99.

Hyman, Marian, Solveig A. Turpin, and Michael E. Zolensky
    1996 Pigment Analyses at Panther Cave, Texas. *Rock Art Research* 13:93–103.

Jackson, A. T.
    1938 *Picture-Writing of Texas Indians.* University of Texas, Austin.

Johnson, Faith
   2010 *Camp Meyers Spring (41TE9): An Investigation of a 19th Century Military Outpost*. Masters Thesis, Department of Anthropology, Texas Tech University, Lubbock.

Kenmotsu, Nancy A., and Mariah F. Wade
   2002 *Amistad National Recreation Area, Del Rio, Texas, American Indian Tribal Affiliation Study, Phase I: Ethnohistoric Literature Review*. Archeological Studies Program, Report No. 34. Texas Department of Transportation, Austin; National Park Service, Del Rio, Texas.

Keyser, James D., and Michael A. Klassen
   2001 *Plains Indian Rock Art*. University of Washington Press, Seattle.

Kirkland, Forrest, and W. W. Newcomb
   1967 *The Rock Art of Texas Indians*. University of Texas Press, Austin.

Koenig, Charles W., Amanda M. Castañeda, Carolyn E. Boyd, Marvin W. Rowe, and Karen L. Steelman
   2014 Portable X-ray Fluorescence Spectroscopy of Pictographs: A Case Study from the Lower Pecos Canyonlands, Texas. *Archaeometry* 56 (Suppl. 1):168–186.

Koenig, Charles W., Amanda M. Castañeda, Victoria L. Roberts, Karen L. Steelman, and Carolyn E. Boyd
   2019 Around the Lower Pecos in 1,095 Days: The Alexandria Project. In *American Indian Rock Art, Volume 45*, edited by Ken Hedges and Anne McConnell, pp. 147–160. American Rock Art Research Association, San Jose, California.

Kulp, J. Laurence, Karl Turekian, and Donald W. Boyd
   1952 Strontium Content of Limestones and Fossils. *Bulletin of the Geological Society of America* 63(7):701–716.

Lins, A., and B. Price
   2011 *Final Report on the Non-Invasive Analysis of Pictographs and on Analysis of Graffiti at the Hueco Tanks State Park and Historic Site, Texas Parks and Wildlife Department, El Paso County, Texas*. Report prepared by the Philadelphia Museum of Art for the Texas Parks and Wildlife Department, Austin.

Miller, Myles R., Lawrence L. Loendorf, and Leonard Kemp
   2011 *Picture Cave and Other Rock Art Sites on Fort Bliss*. Cultural Resources Report No. 10–36. Report prepared by Geo-Marine, Inc., El Paso, Texas, for Directorate of Public Works, Environmental Division, Fort Bliss Garrison Command.

Newman, Bonita, and Lawrence L. Loendorf
   2005 Portable X-Ray Fluorescence Analysis of Rock Art Pigments. *Plains Anthropologist* 50(195):277–283.

Olivares, Maitane, Kepa Castro, Ma Soledad Corchón, Diego Gárate, Xabier Murelag, and Alfredo Sarmiento
   2013 Non-invasive Portable Instrumentation to Study Palaeolithic Rock Paintings: the Case of La Peña Cave in San Roman de Candamo (Asturias, Spain). *Journal of Archaeological Science* 40(2):1354–1360.

O'Regan, Gerard, Fiona Petchey, Rachel Wood, Andrew McAlister, Fiona Bradshaw, and Simon Holdaway
   2019 Dating South Island Māori Rock Art: Pigment and Pitfalls. *Journal of Archaeological Science: Reports* 24:132–141.

Peel, Reeda
   2009 Assessment of the Condition of the Rock Art at Meyers Spring. In *Inventory and Assessment of the Prehistoric Cultural Resources at Meyers Spring, Terrell County, Texas*, edited by Brett A. Houk, pp. 17–34. Occasional Papers in Archaeology, Number 1. Department of Sociology, Anthropology, and Social Work, Texas Tech University, Lubbock.

Robinson, David, Matthew J. Baker, Clare Bedford, Jennifer Perry, Michelle Wienhold, Julienne Bernard, Dan Reeves, Eleni Kotoula, Devlin Gandy, and James Miles
   2015 Methodological Considerations of Integrating Portable Digital Technologies in the Analysis and Management of Complex Superimposed Californian Pictographs: From Spectroscopy and Spectral Imaging to 3-D Scanning. *Digital Applications in Archaeology and Cultural Heritage* 2(2–3):166–180.

Roldán, Clodoaldo, Sonia Murcia-Mascarós, José Ferrero, Valentín Villaverde, Esther López-Montalvo, Inés Domingo Sanz, Rafael Martínez Valle, and Pere Miquel Guillem Calatayud
   2010 Application of Field Portable EDXRF Spectrometry to Analysis of Pigments of Levantine Rock Art. *X-Ray Spectrometry* 39(3):243–250.

Rowe, Marvin W., Robert Mark, Evelyn Billo, Margaret Berrier, Karen L. Steelman, and Eric Dillingham
   2011 Chemistry as a Criterion for Selecting Pictographs for Radiocarbon Dating: Lost Again Shelter in the Guadalupe Mountains of Southeastern New Mexico. In *American Indian Rock Art, Volume 37*, edited by Mavis Greer, John Greer, and Peggy Whitehead, pp. 37–47. American Rock Art Research Association, San Jose, California.

Rowe, Marvin W.
   2013 pXRF Analysis of Arsenic When Lead Is Present: A Cautionary Tale. In *Archaeological Chemistry VIII, ACS Symposium Series 1147*, edited by Ruth Ann Armitage and James H. Burton, pp. 269–276. American Chemical Society, Division of History of Chemistry, Washington, D.C.

Russ, Jon, Kaixuan Bu, Jeff Hamrick, and James Cizdziel
   2012 Laser Ablation-inductively Coupled Plasma-mass Spectrometry Analysis of Lower Pecos Rock Paints and Possible Pigment Sources. In *Collaborative Endeavors in the Chemical Analysis of Art and Cultural Heritage Materials*, edited by Patricia L. Lang and Ruth Ann Armitage, pp. 92–121. American Chemical Society Press, Washington, D.C.

Sepúlveda, Marcela, Sebastian Gutierrez, José Carcamo, Adrian Oyaneder, Daniela Valenzuela, Indira Montt, and Calogero M. Santoro
   2015 In Situ Fluorescence Analysis of Rock Art Paintings along the Coast and Valleys of the Atacama Desert, Northern Chile. *Journal of the Chilean Chemical Society* 60(1):2822–2826.

Stanienda, Katarzyna
   2016 Strontium and Barium in the Triassic Limestone of the Opole Silesia Deposits. *Archives of Mining Sciences* 61(1):29–49.

Steelman, Karen L., Eric Dillingham, Margaret Berrier, Lennon N. Bates, Robert Mark, and Evelyn Billo
   2019 Radiocarbon Dating the Guadalupe Red Linear Style in the Guadalupe Mountains, New Mexico. In *American Indian Rock Art, Volume 45*, edited by Ken Hedges and Anne McConnell, pp. 115–129. American Rock Art Research Association, San Jose, California.

Stone, Kevin
   2009 *Meyers Springs: Archaeological Investigations at an Inter-Regional Site*. Master's Thesis, Department of Anthropology, Texas Tech University, Lubbock.

Turpin, Solveig A.
   1986 The Meyers Springs and Bailando Shelters: Iconographic Parallels. *La Tierra* 13(1):5–8.

Wallace, James Smyth
   2018 *Chemical Analysis of Firearms, Ammunition, and Gunshot Residue*. CRC Press, Boca Raton, Florida.

Walter, Tamra L., and Faith Johnson
  2010 *Inventory and Assessment of the Historic Cultural Resources at Meyers Spring, Terrell County, Texas.* Occasional Papers in Archaeology, Number 2. Department of Sociology, Anthropology, and Social Work, Texas Tech University, Lubbock, Texas.

Wesley, Daryl, Tristen Jones, and Christian Reepmeyer
  2014 Pigment Geochemistry as Chronological Marker: The Case of Lead Pigment in Rock Art in the Urrmarning 'Red Lily Lagoon' Rock Art Precinct, Western Arnhem Land. *Australian Archaeology* 78(1):1–9.

Woolford, Sam
  1962 The Burr G. Duvall Diary. *Southwestern Historical Quarterly* 65(4):487–511.

Zolensky, Michael E.
  1982 Analysis of Pigments from Prehistoric Pictographs, Seminole Canyon State Historical Park. In *Seminole Canyon: the Art and the Archaeology,* edited by Solveig A. Turpin, pp. 277–284. Texas Archeological Survey Research Report No. 83. The University of Texas Press, Austin.

Table 1. Portable X-ray fluorescence readings for manganese, iron, strontium, and barium in parts per million (ppm) for analyzed locations at Meyers Spring. For the pictographs (grey), the numbers in parentheses after the description refer to plate numbers in Kirkland and Newcomb (1967). For the historic graffiti (orange), descriptions include figure numbers referring to photographs of the graffiti in this paper. Readings of <LOD are displayed as -- in the table.

pXRF Reading	Description	Mn	±	Fe	±	Sr	±	Ba	±
P010-20190319	orange church (71)	161	48	10337	276	309	10	--	--
P011-20190319	background	--	--	1398	85	391	12	--	--
P012-20190319	red anthropomorph with bow (71)	333	65	22840	522	212	28	--	--
P013-20190319	background	--	--	609	59	550	36	--	--
P014-20190319	orange priest (72)	324	56	9224	253	400	12	--	--
P015-20190319	background	--	--	2575	113	346	11	--	--
P016-20190319	white face of priest (72)	--	--	947	68	268	9	--	--
P017-20190319	background	--	--	2327	111	265	9	--	--
P022-20190319	red anthropomorph (72)	--	--	3451	135	757	21	--	--
P023-20190319	background	--	--	1960	93	745	18	--	--
P024-20190319	red shield (73)	--	--	23566	522	351	16	--	--
P025-20190319	background	--	--	2268	101	324	10	--	--
P026-20190319	red dancer (73)	--	--	4170	167	504	15	--	--
P027-20190319	background	--	--	1686	88	670	17	--	--
P028-20190319	red cross on church (73)	521	74	19347	479	281	10	--	--
P029-20190319	background	--	--	1945	97	223	8	--	--
P030-20190319	red cross on church (73)	286	56	8369	245	370	11	--	--
P031-20190319	background	--	--	3198	138	371	12	--	--
P032-20190319	impaled anthropomorph (73)	217	55	9383	273	321	13	1295	348
P033-20190319	background	--	--	1685	87	329	10	--	--
P034-20190319	black avian (73)	20992	533	1313	135	256	9	--	--
P035-20190319	background	217	45	1342	77	309	10	--	--
P038-20190319	black remnant paint (73)	36829	818	1559	163	384	11	1288	351
P039-20190319	background	445	57	1468	81	253	8	1145	302
P044-20190319	red anthropomorph on horse (74)	275	67	30958	699	278	10	--	--
P045-20190319	background	167	43	2245	102	226	8	--	--
P046-20190319	red buffalo (74)	325	60	16859	401	267	11	--	--
P047-20190319	background	176	44	2076	98	283	9	--	--
P048-20190319	red anthropomorph on horse (74)	--	--	26431	565	221	8	--	--
P049-20190319	background	<LOD	114	2719	111	222	8	--	--
P050-20190319	red avian - thunderbird (74)	--	--	39569	790	256	10	--	--
P051-20190319	background	--	--	884	67	272	9	--	--
P005-20190320	red horned anthropomorph (74)	--	--	4732	160	202	10	--	--
P006-20190320	background	261	47	4050	137	282	9	--	--
P007-20190320	red zia sun symbol (74)	187	59	27450	607	348	11	--	--
P008-20190320	background	254	51	4248	151	379	11	2034	378
P009-20190320	red zia sun symbol (74)	304	61	22105	498	284	11	--	--
P010-20190320	background	884	79	4323	154	341	10	--	--
P013-20190320	yellow/orange winged shield figure (75)	217	52	5640	193	233	9	--	--
P014-20190320	background	137	42	4522	150	374	11	--	--
P015-20190320	red armored horse (75)	--	--	4490	166	242	9	--	--
P016-20190320	background	479	60	2551	111	277	9	--	--
P017-20190320	anthropomorph with shield (75)	183	52	21297	464	239	8	--	--
P018-20190320	background	131	40	1945	95	267	9	--	--
P021-20190320	red handprint (75)	--	--	6294	194	255	11	--	--
P022-20190320	background	--	--	1620	82	290	9	--	--
P025-20190320	red horizontal avian (76)	--	--	10722	291	239	9	--	--
P026-20190320	background	215	46	4213	140	279	9	1010	294
P027-20190320	red horizontal avian (76)	293	74	54945	1108	258	11	--	--
P028-20190320	background	--	--	1834	91	271	9	--	--
P029-20190320	red enigmatic with crosses -possible church (76)	--	--	8053	234	249	13	--	--
P030-20190320	background	--	--	2305	102	312	10	--	--
P033-20190320	red/orange blown paint around stencil (77)	--	--	6444	192	391	24	--	--
P034-20190320	background	158	44	2637	114	456	13	--	--
P037-20190320	red horizontal zigzag (77)	208	53	20938	444	341	10	--	--

pXRF Reading	Description	Mn	±	Fe	±	Sr	±	Ba	±
P038-20190320	background	--	--	1325	81	383	12	--	--
P041-20190320	red rider on horse (77)	184	46	6136	183	412	13	--	--
P042-20190320	background	166	43	2803	116	554	14	--	--
P043-20190320	red rider on horse - duplicate of P041 (77)	193	51	7959	232	479	13	--	--
P044-20190320	background	229	45	3448	123	600	14	--	--
P045-20190320	red antlered deer (78)	320	62	16376	402	304	10	1223	348
P046-20190320	background	--	--	1061	72	276	9	--	--
P049-20190320	yellow/orange handprint (not depicted in 78)	--	--	7796	220	614	17	--	--
P050-20190320	background	--	--	1044	79	765	21	--	--
P051-20190320	yellow/orange handprint (not depicted in 78)	--	--	1213	76	316	10	--	--
P052-20190320	background	--	--	562	52	306	19	--	--
P053-20190320	red rider on horse with shield (78)	--	--	9500	268	604	16	--	--
P054-20190320	background	--	--	1229	76	617	16	--	--
P055-20190320	yellow/orange anthropomorph (79)	168	44	5202	162	519	13	--	--
P056-20190320	background	--	--	970	70	503	26	--	--
P061-20190320	yellow/orange horse (79)	409	59	8320	234	206	10	--	--
P062-20190320	background	217	49	2214	109	275	10	--	--
P002-20190319	red lettering (Figure 10a)	--	--	2931	120	290	9	--	--
P003-20190319	background - black accretion	143	43	1106	74	294	10	--	--
P004-20190319	red lettering - replicate of P002 (Figure 10a)	--	--	2671	116	409	12	--	--
P005-20190319	background	--	--	2699	114	432	12	--	--
P006-20190319	red lettering - replicate of P002 (Figure 10a)	--	--	3137	123	280	9	--	--
P007-20190319	background - black accretion	--	--	1380	78	267	9	--	--
P040-20190319	red "Davis Co B 10th Inf" (Figure 10b)	178	50	5575	193	221	11	--	--
P041-20190319	background	--	--	2423	108	281	9	--	--
P039-20190320	red "D.C." (Figure 10c)	--	--	3494	134	448	13	932	304
P040-20190320	background	153	44	1130	74	462	13	--	--
P059-20190320	red lettering (Figure 10d)	287	54	6972	211	409	12	--	--
P060-20190320	background	165	43	3539	128	454	12	--	--
P035-20190320	black "J.D. Stineba 1896" (Figure 11a)	--	--	19627	457	317	10	--	--
P036-20190320	background	--	--	4007	149	342	11	--	--
P057-20190320	black lettering (Figure 11b)	213	48	2108	105	278	10	--	--
P058-20190320	background	136	40	1877	91	508	13	--	--
P008-20190319	black residue below church (71)	391	94	1818	121	237	12	--	--
P009-20190319	background	404	60	1853	100	266	9	--	--
P018-20190319	black residue/fracturing right of priest's shoulder (72)	--	--	1810	112	344	13	--	--
P019-20190319	background	--	--	1922	91	516	13	--	--
P020-20190319	black residue/fracturing 30 cm right of priest (72)	--	--	1313	99	259	12	--	--
P021-20190319	background	196	42	1212	72	291	9	--	--
P036-20190319	black residue/fracturing on leg of 4th anthropomorph from left in a series of 11 impaled anthropomorphs (73)	306	57	3025	127	321	11	--	--
P037-20190319	background	218	44	1750	86	402	11	--	--
P042-20190319	black residue/fracturing from possible bird shot near left horse with rider (74)	--	--	2258	106	295	10	--	--
P043-20190319	background	--	--	2375	113	220	8	--	--
P003-20190320	black residue/fracturing left of square-bodied anthropomorph left of sun symbol (74)	--	--	322	57	413	15	1435	436
P004-20190320	background	327	52	2649	109	316	10	1096	306
P011-20190320	black residue/fracturing lower-left center of sun symbol (74)	221	54	833	70	434	13	--	--
P012-20190320	background	--	--	1137	77	334	11	1112	328
P019-20190320	black residue 30 cm below red anthropomorph with shield (75)	247	63	1402	93	227	10	1529	380
P020-20190320	background	736	69	4232	145	240	8	--	--
P023-20190320	black residue on head of horizontal red avian (76)	534	161	19345	717	144	13	3294	804
P024-20190320	background	310	55	1971	103	282	10	--	--
P031-20190320	black residue/fracturing to right of red enigmatic with crosses - possible church (between 76 & 77)	543	96	3262	165	229	12	1674	471
P032-20190320	background	--	--	2571	122	223	9	--	--
P047-20190320	black residue/fracturing above body of large antlered deer (78)	365	76	2520	125	307	12	1609	416
P048-20190320	background	--	--	2405	103	324	10	1157	307

Table 2. Lead and associated trace elements detected for suspected gunshot locations. See Table 1 for more detailed locational descriptions. All readings are in parts per million (ppm). Readings of <LOD are displayed as -- in the table.

pXRF Reading	Description	Cr	±	Cu	±	Se	±	Cd	±	Sn	±	Hg	±	Pb	±
P008-20190319	black residue	416	137	--	--	265	26	--	--	--	--	253	50	50157	1192
P009-20190319	background	--	--	--	--	--	--	--	--	--	--	--	--	--	--
P018-20190319	black residue/fracturing	--	--	--	--	--	--	--	--	--	--	--	--	4694	127
P019-20190319	background	--	--	--	--	--	--	--	--	--	--	--	--	--	--
P020-20190319	black residue/fracturing	--	--	129	29	116	17	--	--	--	--	--	--	22512	541
P021-20190319	background	--	--	--	--	--	--	--	--	--	--	--	--	--	--
P036-20190319	black residue/fracturing	--	--	--	--	--	--	--	--	--	--	--	--	6387	140
P037-20190319	background	--	--	--	--	--	--	--	--	--	--	--	--	--	--
P042-20190319	black residue/fracturing	--	--	--	--	--	--	--	--	--	--	--	--	4858	109
P043-20190319	background	--	--	--	--	--	--	--	--	--	--	--	--	--	--
P003-20190320	black residue/fracturing	--	--	--	--	--	--	--	--	870	65	--	--	27762	652
P004-20190320	background	--	--	--	--	--	--	--	--	--	--	--	--	--	--
P011-20190320	black residue/fracturing	--	--	--	--	--	--	--	--	--	--	--	--	3842	96
P012-20190320	background	--	--	--	--	--	--	--	--	--	--	--	--	--	--
P019-20190320	black residue	--	--	--	--	--	--	--	--	--	--	95	25	14983	332
P020-20190320	background	--	--	--	--	--	--	--	--	--	--	--	--	--	--
P023-20190320	black residue	802	233	--	--	464	50	161	46	--	--	296	89	114918	3460
P024-20190320	background	--	--	--	--	--	--	--	--	--	--	--	--	--	--
P031-20190320	black residue/fracturing	--	--	--	--	168	23	--	--	--	--	148	43	39605	953
P032-20190320	background	--	--	--	--	--	--	--	--	--	--	--	--	--	--
P047-20190320	black residue/fracturing	--	--	110	28	191	20	--	--	653	57	171	36	33381	699
P048-20190320	background	--	--	--	--	--	--	--	--	--	--	--	--	--	--

Re-Imagining Fremont:
A Color Palette for the Ages

James D. Keyser and David L. Minick

Given the prevalence of "shorthand" Fremont anthropomorphs, which seem likely to have been augmented with fugitive pigments, it seems obvious that Fremont artists must have used a far broader color palette than the red and white colors typically known today. A few sites protected from weathering and cultural damage have recently revealed Fremont images painted in a spectrum of striking pastel colors. In 2018 we visited Nine-Mile Canyon, Utah, and photographed Fremont images painted in six different colors. Using this color palette, we make some educated guesses as to how it may have enriched the Fremont world.

While photographing the Daddy Canyon site we also recognized two episodes of spatter painting done by throwing some sort of grey-white, muddy pigment onto the panel at different times. While not being "fugitive" pigment, such spatter painting (using a variety of pigments) appears to be more common than is typically reported, and researchers are urged to pay greater attention to this behavior.

It has long been recognized that Fremont rock art in the Uinta style zone (Figure 1) must have had a far broader color palette than the various shades of red and occasional white pigments that characterize the great majority of painted Fremont figures known today. This color discrepancy is best demonstrated by the dozens of "shorthand" Fremont anthropomorphs[1] whose "missing" body forms are presumed to have been originally colored in with fugitive pigments of various hues (Keyser 2015; Keyser et al. 2018; Manning 2004; Reagan 1931:169, 174, 179, 195). Such shorthand anthropomorphs are characteristic of the Uinta style zone (Keyser et al. 2018:145), where they are present at dozens of sites (Table 1). Such fugitive pigments embellishing a few Fremont figures that would otherwise be classified as shorthand anthropomorphs have recently been demonstrated with the use of DStretch and various other photographic enhancement techniques (Keyser et al. 2018; Manning 2004). Likewise, a few sites that have been protected from both natural and cultural degradation by their location in the recently opened Range Creek area have revealed Fremont images painted in red, white, and pastel green pigments (Simms and Gohier 2010:50–51). These complement the pastel pink, white, and blue pigments used on various types of mobiliary artifacts (e.g., Simms and Gohier 2010:66, 98–99).

During a recent visit to Nine-Mile Canyon, on our way to the 2018 ARARA meeting in Grand Junction, Colorado, we visited several sites in the areas of Daddy Canyon and Cottonwood Canyon. By using DStretch at three of these sites (42Cb829, 42Cb239, and 42Cb974) we were able to view a number of Fremont images at fairly well-protected panels that show pigment colors including red, brown, white, green, blue, and black. Coupled with other recent discoveries (e.g., Keyser et al. 2018), this evidence enables us to

James D. Keyser
*Oregon Archaeological Society,
Portland, Oregon*

David L. Minick
*Oregon Archaeological Society,
Portland, Oregon*

Re-Imagining Fremont: A Color Palette for the Ages

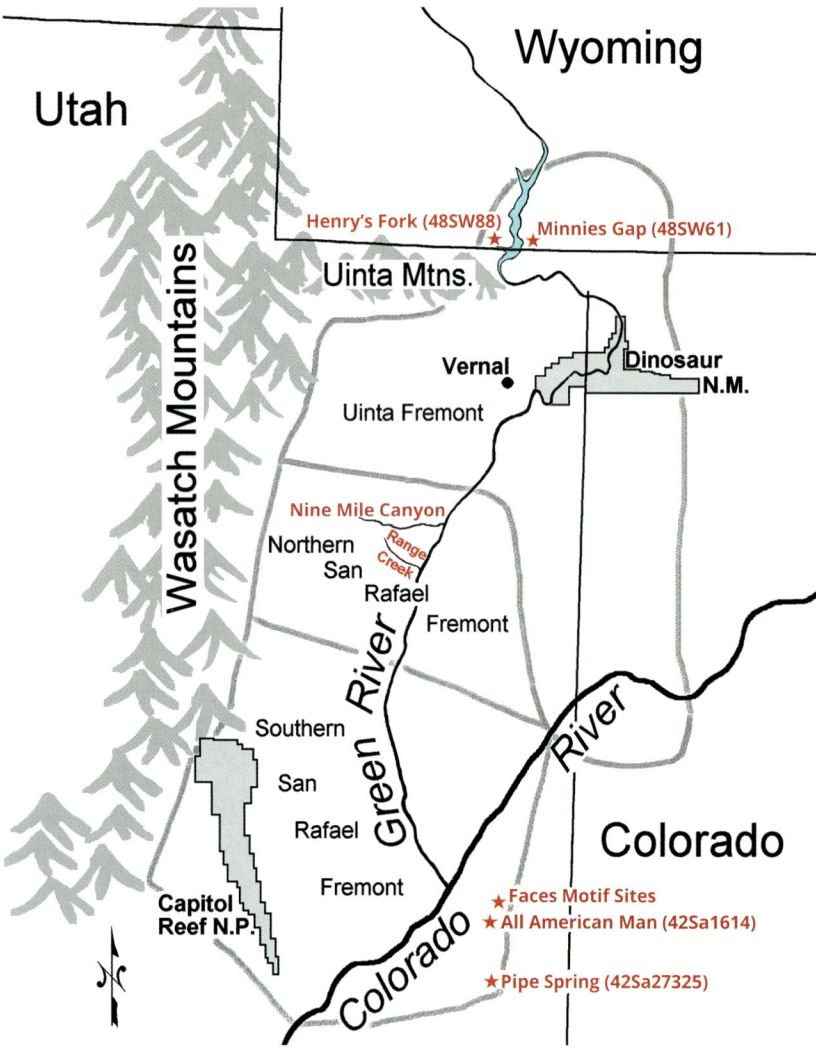

Figure 1. The eastern Fremont area, extending from southwestern Wyoming to southeast of Capitol Reef National Park in Utah, is separated into the Uinta style zone at the north, Northern San Rafael style zone centered on Nine Mile Canyon, and the Southern San Rafael style zone at the south (border expanded southeast of Colorado River based on Conti et al. 2018). Sites and site concentrations referred to in article are shown in red.

imagine what some of the most spectacular collections of Fremont imagery in Wyoming might have looked like when freshly made.

Color Evident at Some Nine Mile Canyon Sites

We visited half a dozen different sites in our trip down Nine Mile Canyon. Several of these are among the best-known sites in this area of Utah. Among these are two sites, The Daddy Canyon site (42Cb829) and The Great Hunt Panel site (42Cb239), which have well-protected rock art panels showing Fremont pictographs painted in a broad range of colors. A third site (42Cb974) contains two important pictographs painted with white or red and white pigments.

Daddy Canyon Elk Panel: 42Cb829

The first site we photographed in our research is 42Cb829 at the confluence of Daddy Canyon and Nine Mile Canyon, approximately three kilometers (two miles) west of Cottonwood Canyon, which contains our other two sites of interest. The site is located on a panel directly above the dry streambed only a short distance northeast of the Daddy Canyon parking lot. The painted panel itself is out of reach from the current ground surface, so our examination was by photography only. Good photographs could be obtained by standing on a large boulder in the dry streambed a short distance away from the panel. This enabled the photographer to get significantly closer to the images with a better angle for eliminating parallax.

There are seven rock art elements of interest at the site (Figure 2). Most prominent are four large animals. The largest is a large red-painted ovoid without legs that appears to represent a style C zoomorph as defined by Hurst and Louthan (1979), which appears to relate to Schaafsma's (1971) Northern San Rafael Style. In her discussion of that style, Schaafsma (1971:33) notes that these animals tend to have a rounded body and long outstretched neck, and some are headless (possibly the head was originally painted with a fugitive pigment). The bulky body is approximately one meter long, with a thin extension at the left but no tail at the rounded right end. No obvious legs are present, but at the left end, pointing downward on the lower side, are what might be curved horns. Although inverted animals are not particularly common in Fremont art, for a person more familiar with Plains rock art, this resembles an upside-down, legless bison, with its tongue extended (Figure 3)—one of the more common conventions for bison.

The unique figure at the site is an elk, approximately 75 cm long from nose to tail, painted with a pastel

Table 1. Shorthand Fremont Anthropomorphs

	Sites	N Anthropomorphs
Uinta Style Zone		
Southwestern Wyoming	3	8
Browns Park	3	12
Yampa River	1	2
Echo Park (Dinosaur NMon)	4	30+
Vernal	1	6
Cub Creek	1	20
Ashley/Dry Fork	6	60+
Brush Creek	1	2
Total	20	140+
Northern San Rafael Style Zone		
Nine Mile Canyon	8	15+
Desolation Canyon	1	4
Range Creek	2	4
Total	11	23+
Southern San Rafael Style Zone		
Fremont River	3	16+
Fish Creek	1	7
Capitol Wash	1	3
Pipe Spring	1	4
Total	6	30+

Data taken from Castleton (1984), Hartley et al. (1993), Keyser and Poetschat (2017), Manning (2004), and Schaafsma (1971)

Figure 2. Daddy Canyon Elk Panel at 42Cb829 showing four animals and a stamped handprint. Pigments include red, white, and green. Three spattering episodes are evident on the panel. (a) DStretch LABI enhancement; (b) color-replacement phototracing made from several different DStretch enhancements. The spoked circular elements indicate bullet scars.

green pigment. The animal has an outlined, rounded, "bean-shaped" body formed of approximately finger-

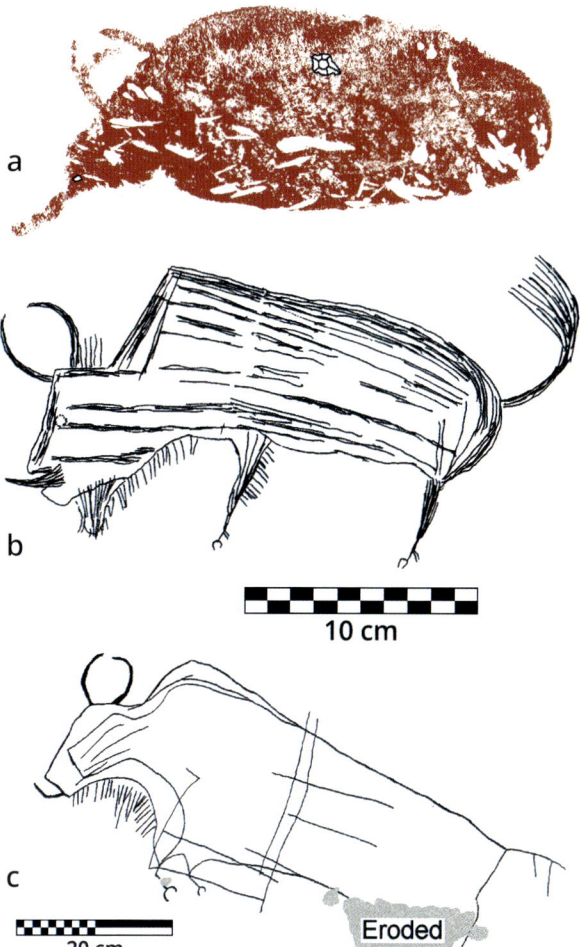

Figure 3. (a) Red animal at 42Cb829 inverted to show similarity to Plains-style bison forms; (b) Bear Gulch, Montana (24FR2), image mirrored to correspond to orientation of Daddy Canyon animal; (c) Lucerne Valley, Wyoming (48SW82).

width lines, stick legs without hooves, a short tail, a long neck, and an elongate, bulky head crowned with outsized antlers. The rear legs, along with the rump area and tail, are nearly eroded away, though DStretch enables us to pick out enough faded pigment in those areas to determine their shape. The neck and head are slightly out of proportion to the rest of the animal and the rear of the body appears to have been much less lightly pigmented than the front.

DStretch enhancement reveals the figure was first outlined and then had pigment smeared heavily in the neck and front quarters area and much more lightly along the back and underneath the original neck and belly lines. Whether the darker front quarters, neck and head, and lighter rear half of the body were intended to portray the actual coat coloration of an elk cannot be determined, but it is suggestive. Paired front and remnant rear legs are straight and semi-realistically portrayed in a "walking" position as two inverted V-shapes. Antlers show long, straight main beams rising perpendicular to the neck line, each with five side tines. Both show a slight disjointedness where they connect to the crown of the head. What appear to be two short, slightly downcurved ears project forward just above the animal's forehead. A short, sketchy, oblique line sticks into the animal's upper back just at the slight shoulder hump.

About equidistant, both above and slightly to the right and below and to the left of the green elk, are a pair of barely visible white elk scratched and painted with white pigment. Each of these animals has an elongate, ovoid body with exaggeratedly long neck, though only their front quarters are readily visible. For the upper elk, the hindquarters disappear in an area that has been abraded away by extreme erosion; much of the lower animal is nearly obscured by smeared, grey-white, muddy pigment that resulted from smearing of pigment that was spattered over the panel after all the Fremont figures were painted. For both animals their outline and antlers (and the rudimentary single-line legs of the upper elk) appear to be lightly and incompletely scratched, but their bodies are filled in with a thin wash of white pigment. What appears to have happened is the figures were drawn with a raw lump of white pigment whose hard edge (or a harder inclusion within the natural "chalk") left a scratch where the artist focused on drawing specific lines (e.g., body outline, antlers, legs). Then the white pigment was lightly "chalked" (and then smeared?) into the body outline to create a filled-in body. If the pigment was smeared it was probably done using fingertips or a soft tool of some sort (hide pad?). For the lower animal, the filled-in body essentially disappears into the smeared grey-white pigment that superimposes it.

These elk have a much more gracile, streamlined form than the green-painted one, with bodies that are less rounded and relatively longer necks that taper markedly to where the head is attached. Heads are relatively much smaller (that of the upper animal is mostly obscured by two grey-white pigment splatters), and the antlers are relatively much longer and more sinuous than those of the green elk. They also show more tines on each main beam. The antlers show main beams perpendicular to the line of the neck for the upper animal and laid back at a much flatter angle for the lower one. Each main beam has multiple side tines—between ten and a dozen for the three most visible antlers. For the upper animal the tines are on the front side of each main branch, though the top tine in each case has a corresponding tine extending to the rear. For the lower animal the tines come off opposite sides of main branches, like the configuration on the green elk. No ears are drawn on either animal, and the rudimentary front legs of the upper one are nothing more than two short, straight lines. These elk are not readily noticeable when one initially views the panel, since the observer's attention is first captured by the large red and green animals. Careful observation revealed the upper animal to us (and a red handprint over which it is superimposed) but we did not see the lower one until we enhanced the panel with DStretch to look at all the images. Given the later bombardment of the upper white elk with the grey-white, clay-like, episode 2 spatter pigment (below), we infer that these white animals were more visible when freshly drawn.

Underneath (that is, *superimposed by*) the head and antlers of the upper white elk is a stamped red handprint of an adult left hand. This handprint is angled up to the right. Once observed with DStretch, the handprint can be readily seen with the naked eye, but because the red pigment is much more faded than that of the large animal, the handprint does not stand out during one's initial look at the panel.

Superimposed on all images at the site and across much of the rest of the apparently otherwise unpainted vertical cliff surface here is a dense spattering of grey-white, clay-like pigment that was clearly applied to the panel in multiple episodes. The earliest of these episodes occurred as multiple events of pigment spattering done from at least two directions. Spatter marks are angled up from opposite sides of the panel (Figure 4, arrows 1 and 2), based on their elongated shapes and patterned placement across the cliff surface. These spatters seem focused on the large red animal, although some few extend far above it both to the left and right (above the green elk). Then while that application was either still damp, or dry and powdery but spreadable, the material appears to have been smeared on the panel's lower reaches, resulting in a large, chalky, grey-white cloud below the red animal and on the lower part of its body (Figure 4, number 3). Because the panel is out of reach from the current ground surface, we could not determine whether this smudge was caused naturally (e.g., by an animal rubbing against the panel) or by intentional cultural smearing, though closer examination of the panel might clarify this.

Then, at some time after this first, multiple-event episode of spattering, a slightly thicker clay-like pigment of essentially the same grey-white color was spattered

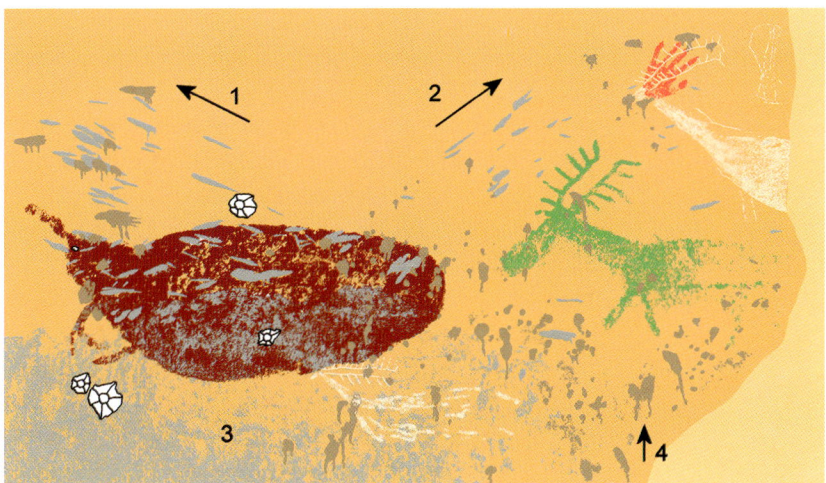

Figure 4. Spattering episodes on Daddy Canyon Elk Panel. Arrows show orientation of three different episodes: 1 and 2 are earliest but we cannot determine which was first; 3 indicates smearing of first two spatter mark episodes across lower part of red animal and below on panel; and 4 indicates last spattering episode with larger blobs, many of which have long "tails" below, indicating the liquid clay ran after contacting the panel surface.

onto the panel from a position directly in front of and below it (Figure 4, arrow 4). These spatter marks are rounder, and the larger ones typically have emphatic dribbles extending down below. These spatters cover almost all the rock surface on which the animals are painted and a few even mark the overhanging roof of the small sheltered area in which the panel is situated. Dozens of these "mud balls" were thrown against the panel in a fairly focused effort to blemish the red animal's body, the green elk, and the head of the upper white elk, but more than 50 such mud balls were impacted onto a restricted area about the size of the red animal but just to the left of it. We can see no figure in that area, and DStretch reveals nothing there, so the reason for disfiguring that specific part of the panel remains a mystery. Finally, four bullet scars mar the panel, two through the white smudge, one through the white smear over the lower part of the red animal, and one just above the red animal.

Spattering pigment onto Fremont panels occurs at other sites in Nine Mile Canyon. One of the most impressive examples is at nearby Rasmussen Cave (42Cb16), just to the west of 42Cb829 in the Daddy Canyon site complex, where both red and white pigments are spattered over several panels in much the same manner as the clay-like pigment occurs at 42Cb829. The original Claflin-Emerson expedition excavations at Rasmussen Cave actually recovered flattened clay "blobs" and although they claimed not to have found evidence that these were thrown against the cave's wall or ceiling, modern archaeological inspection shows abundant evidence that this practice had occurred (Spangler and Aton 2018:181). In short, the flattened clay blobs in Rasmussen cave are "spent ammunition" from people throwing them against the cliff wall and ceiling.

The occurrence of "mud-ball" spattering in Rasmussen Cave, complete with finding the spent mud balls in archaeological context, lends credence to the activity having occurred at 42Cb829, and this is especially relevant in light of an historic photograph of the green elk figure. In 1929 Noel Morss visited the site and photographed the green elk (Spangler and Aton 2018:179). In the Morss black-and-white photograph the elk seems unnaturally boldly colored, since we know it is actually significantly faded. Further examination of the Morss photograph shows that only a few of the largest, thickest spatter marks are visible and several of these have different shapes than they do in modern photographs (one of which is printed directly below the Morss photograph).

We contacted Jerry Spangler to ascertain if he might be aware of some explanation for the mysterious "disappearance" of the spatter marks on this panel. We had posited that these might have been natural splatter resulting from flash flooding or transport of mud by nesting cliff swallows but rejected both of those possibilities based on a variety of factors. Initially, we felt these marks were far too high on the cliff face to have been splattered there by flash flooding, and Spangler concurred with that, based on his knowledge of the canyon's hydrology. Likewise, the amount of mud in many individual blobs seemed far too great for swallow transport, and getting some of the large blobs on the ceiling of the shallow rockshelter would seem to defy even a cliff swallow's most impressive aerial acrobatics. Additionally, there were no nests or remnant nests above the panel and not nearly enough bird droppings on the panel to indicate nests had been above.

Then we considered whether the spattering was essentially a modern activity, started by someone unknown, at some time before Morss photographed the panel (since some spatter mark blobs are visible) but continuing afterward and stopping sometime in the recent past. But this failed to account for the fact the spatter blobs visible in the Morss photograph were in the second spatter episode, while those in the first episode were not visible. And in addition, there are spatters from an identical activity in nearby Rasmussen Cave (42Cb16), which we know to be prehistoric based on archaeological recovery of the spent clay "ammunition" in the cave deposits.

Finally, however, Jerry Spangler (personal communication 2018) reminded us that early photographers frequently applied water (and even sometimes kerosene) to faded pictographs to make them appear more distinct in black and white photography. While we have no documentation that Morss did this at 42Cb829, the fact the faded elk seems far too boldly colored, coupled with the "washed out" appearance of the thickest spatter blobs, fits very well with this hypothesis. Furthermore, there is some support for the hypothesis that Morss was close enough to the panel to apply water to it, in the form of a partial chalk outline on the red animal's rump. In sum, we believe the spatter marks to be the result of prehistoric site users interacting with the panel in the same way they interacted with those at nearby 42Cb829. This interaction apparently involved multiple episodes done with clay "pigments" of different consistencies.

42Cb239: Panel 2

The second of three sites we photographed in detail is 42Cb239, located at the confluence of Cottonwood and Nine Mile canyons about 500 meters (one-quarter mile) south of Nine Mile Creek on the west side of Cottonwood Creek (Merritt 2017; Spangler 2007). Best known for its famous Panel 3 composition, called the Great Hunt Panel, 42Cb239 is actually a group of five rock art panels. Of these, Panel 2 contains a series of Fremont shield pictographs painted with a broad palette of pastel colors in a shallow rockshelter. These are superimposed by a few other zigzag images and a row of pecked animals. The most striking images are a group of five large circular shields and two much smaller ones, each with a complex geometric heraldic design.[2]

Unfortunately, all five larger shields have been partially filled in or outlined with modern chalk, but careful close observation combined with the use of DStretch enhancement enables us to determine that four different prehistoric pigments were used on these designs. Figure 5 shows these colors, all of which can be discerned with the naked eye. Other painted or pecked zigzags and pecked figures on this panel have also been quite heavily chalked, but the details of these do not concern us here, except as they impact the shields.

The large shields range from 60 to 68 cm in diameter, the two smaller are between 17 and 20 cm across. From left to right they are (Figure 5):

Shield 1. Outlined with a thin, spotty line of dark brown pigment, this shield has the top one-third painted red, and the remaining two-thirds painted white. A "yellow-colored" area starting on the red pigment in the upper right quadrant and extending outside the shield to the right is light pecking and likely does not relate to the shield's original design. There is a white chalked zigzag superimposed on a small dark red smear just below the shield. The site form indicates that this zigzag was originally pecked and then chalked, but we cannot confirm this from photographs. Shield diameter is 66–69 cm.

Shield 2. This is a small, very lightly incised and abraded, crudely circular shield with the bottom half filled in with light abrasion. Diameter is approximately 17 cm. If pigment was associated with this image, none has survived. This shield was illustrated by Spangler (2007; see also Merritt 2017:Figure 5 of 23), so we know it is not a recent addition to the panel, but it is unlike the other shields drawn here. It is neither mentioned nor illustrated in Reagan (1933:59–62), but his recording is woefully incomplete, lacking two of the other large shields, the smaller painted one, and most if not all of the pecked animals. Since there are so many scratched graffiti at this location, and no paint is associated with this shield, we are not completely convinced of its authenticity.

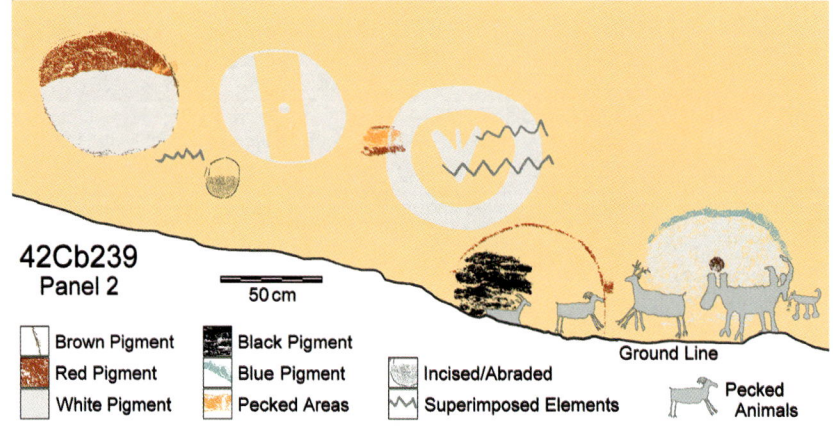

Figure 5. Color-replacement photo-tracing of shields on Panel 2 at 42Cb239.

Shield 3. An all-white painted shield is vertically divided into three approximately equal sized sections. The center section is blank, with a small white circle about 5 cm in diameter painted in its approximate center. The two side sections are painted white. This shield verifies the identification of white pigment, since neither the white-painted left section nor the central circle was filled in with modern chalk, yet they are still visible as a ghost-like very light grey color. Once the observer's eye becomes attuned to this light grey, it can then be seen between the chalk lines filling other colored sections of Shields 1, 3, and 5, and it even enables us to correctly identify the bottom margin of this shield where a vandal has "colored outside the lines." Shield diameter is 63–65 cm.

Shield 4. Just to the right of the third shield and partially superimposed on the fifth shield, there is the much smaller shield image. Only the upper two-thirds of what was apparently intended to be a small circular figure are still visible. This shows a narrow red-painted band on its upper central rim, a broad pecked area (which presents to the eye as a yellow color) occupying most of the top half of the circular image, and a narrow red band running across what would be the approximate midpoint band. There are small, scattered remnants of pigment in the yellow top half of the shield, suggesting that the pecking was done through a red-painted area. The bottom half was either unpainted or the pigment used therein was fugitive and has since disappeared. Such fugitive pigment is typical of many Fremont images at other sites. The superimposition here, between shields 4 and 5, is difficult to determine with certainty in the absence of microscopic examination that we were unable to perform. Chalking of Shield 5 has obscured much of the evidence available to the naked eye but in photographs it appears that this small shield (4) is superimposed on the larger Shield 5. Shield diameter is about 20 cm.

Shield 5. Painted in white pigment only, the color for Shield 5 is applied in a broad 10-cm wide band circumscribing the outer edge of the circle, creating a wreath-like effect. In fact, the band consists of two approximately 1- to 1.5-cm-wide, white-painted bands, between which white paint had been unevenly smeared so that the narrower bands themselves are clearly visible as distinct entities in some places. Inside, but not quite centered in the wreath form, is a white-painted "winged" figure that might represent some sort of bird or butterfly, but it also might simply be a geometric design.[3] Shield diameter is 58–60 cm.

Two long zigzag lines occur on this central figure and extend outside the edge of the shield to the right. From photographs alone we cannot determine if these zigzags are superimposed on or superimposed by the shield and central design element or were intended to be a part of the design. This is largely due to the overpainting by vandals who have chalked the zigzags. This chalking also makes it difficult to determine the order of superimposition between Shields 4 and 5.

Shield 6. Only a little more than the top half of Shield 6 is visible above the current ground line formed by the top of deposits that have "filled this once habitable [rockshelter] to a depth of several feet" (Reagan 1933:62). The top of the shield is shown as a semicircular, single-line, red-painted arc. The arc does not reach all the way to current ground level but stops approximately 10–15 cm above the deposit on the left side, and just a few centimeters above on the right. There is a roughly 4 x 4 cm red painted rectangle appended to the right side of the arc at what would be the approximate midpoint of the circular shield's right side. The left half of the shield interior is smeared with black pigment that continues down to the ground line. Across the lower part of this left half there are indications the area has been abraded, but we cannot determine whether this is of prehistoric or recent origin. The bottom half of the shield has been heavily impacted by the pecking of two large relatively deeply and solidly pecked bighorn sheep. While we cannot be certain, the fact that similar animals are clearly superimposed on neighboring Shield 7 suggests that they also superimpose Shield 6. Perhaps excavation of the buried portion of the design would clarify this. Shield diameter is 58–60 cm.

Shield 7. Just to the right of Shield 6 and at the same level is Shield 7, which is painted in a thick, solid, pasty-white pigment across its interior but has a wide arc of "blue" pigment outlining its upper edge. This blue pigment is most likely a mixture of some white base pigment mixed with charcoal, which is the common "recipe" used to achieve a bluish color for other Fremont and Anasazi paintings (Chaffee et al. 1994:777; Smith 1952:23).

A brown, solidly painted circle a bit larger than 5 cm in diameter is positioned in the upper center of the shield. Our photographs reveal no evidence of the "yellowish-gold border above" the blue arc, as is reported in the National Register nomination narrative, which is taken directly from Spangler's 2007 site form (Merritt 2017:7.7; Spangler 2007).

The bottom half of Shield 7 is almost completely removed by the row of deeply and solidly pecked animals, two pairs of which are superimposed as direct conjoined overlays. The left conjoined pair shows a left-facing elk or deer, whose only evidence of the underlying figure is an extra set of "front" legs (though oddly curved main antler tines hint at bighorn sheep horns for the underlying animal). The other conjoined pair is a probable left-facing canid, which is clearly superimposed on a right-facing bighorn sheep. However, below both conjoined pairs of animals, and just above ground level, one can see a remnant of the shield's thick white pigment. Shield diameter is 60–62 cm.

We can see no clear evidence either in ambient light or with DStretch enhancement of the area above and to the right of Shield 7 of the "yellow-gold pigment design and a circle of gray" as reported by Merritt (2017:7.7). There is a very ephemeral "ghost" image in this area in some DStretch enhancements, but despite intensive effort, we were unable to discern what this might represent, or even if it was actually pigment.

Animal figures pecked in the row at the bottom of the panel, from left to right are, two bighorn sheep, an elk conjoined over an unknown quadruped (probable bighorn sheep?), a canid conjoined over a bighorn sheep, a second canid, a bighorn sheep (positioned slightly above the row), and a bison (these last two animals are not shown on our figure). Other animals are shown to the right of the bison in the NRHP nomination form (Merritt 2017:Figure 7 of 23).

In summary, Panel 2 of 42Cb239 contains a relatively broad spectrum of Fremont colors, used to paint a group of shields in a shallow rockshelter. Parts of two of these shields appear to extend below the current ground surface. Other images superimposed on the shields are a row of deeply pecked animals, two of which have been further superimposed by later directly conjoined overlaid animals.

42Cb974: Miscellaneous Panels

Across Cottonwood Canyon from 42Cb239 is an extensive site containing both pictographs and petroglyphs scattered along the base of the high sandstone cliffs for several hundred meters. Of interest to our study are a red- and white-painted shield design and a yellow-painted Fremont-style human on one panel (Figure 6, which shows only the legs of the human figure at upper right), and a large white-painted shield-like design located on a different panel high above the current ground surface (Figure 7). Clearly, three of the

Figure 6. Red-and-white painted shield at 42Cb974. (a) Bright white pigment is probably historic addition; (b) original white pigment is visible as yellow-green within the shield in DStretch CRGB enhancement while historic white renders as pink. The legs of the yellow human and elongate drip are visible at upper right.

white "pie-wedge" triangles of the red and white shield have been overpainted in recent times, but close observation (confirmed by DStretch enhancement) shows that the shield originally had an interior white border and a pie-wedge design with red, white, and apparently uncolored segments (Figure 8). Being able to identify the very faded white pigment that has not been overpainted is another example of identifying coloration in Fremont rock art that is almost completely fugitive.

The bright yellow pigment on the nearby trapezoidal body Fremont figure appears to us to be too fresh to be prehistoric and there is an elongate yellow drip splashed just below the center of this figure indicating that the pigment was applied as a very thin liquid. There are also yellow spattered droplets to the right of the figure, further implying a somewhat hurried brush application. Given the obvious recent overpainting of the nearby white pictographs and the infilling of adjacent petroglyphs with bright white pigment, we suspect that the bright white and yellow colors are recent additions to the panel, done to "improve" the prehistoric colors,

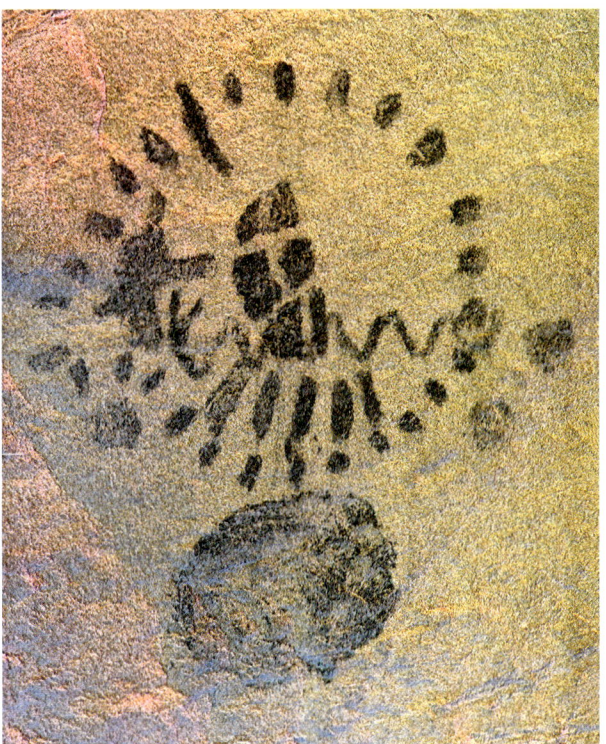

Figure 7. Complex, white-painted design high up on cliff at 42Cb974. Note zigzag snake with open mouth at left. DStretch LABI_AC further modified as negative/greyscale/negative/contrast-enhanced.

Figure 8. Color-replacement photo-tracing of shield at 42Cb974, showing red and white pigments, and apparently unpainted wedge shape (at 9–11 o'clock position) in shield.

but we have no proof of that. If this is modern yellow pigment, it implies the presence of prehistoric yellow pigment that someone thought needed "refreshing."

The white-painted design on the higher panel comprises two circular images, the upper one of which is more complex and interests us here. It shows two pairs of small white circles flanking a large circular design formed of short "rays" surrounding a central ovoid made of six segments. Below the ovoid is a fan of five lines and crossing the entire field of the circle from right to left is a zigzag snake with open, upward-pointing jaws at the left. Within the circle and above the snake's open mouth is a carefully painted shape that appears to have had some—now lost—meaning to the overall design. Taking the elements together it is easy to see how the central design could represent some sort of bird (with the fan shape being a tail) sitting on a snake, but the image is too high for our close examination. Regardless of what the design represents, it seems likely that there was fugitive pigment here that we can no longer see. Just below this complex circular image is a large, nearly solid, white-painted second circle.

Illuminating the Fremont Color Palette

Due to the use of several colors of pigments that apparently degraded more quickly than the common red ochre pigment we see today, modern observers tend to have a very "bland" view of the Fremont color palette—especially in the Uinta style zone. This is because the great majority of painted sites currently known in that area are limited to various shades of red with the occasional white pigment. And frequently these two colors are used only for parts of a figure. A deeper examination, however, focusing on a number of as yet incompletely documented sites in the Northern San Rafael style zone (and limited areas of the Southern San Rafael zone), demonstrates that this restricted color palette was not actually the one commonly used by Fremont artists. Instead, these artists lived in, and painted, a very colorful world. Fortunately, just enough of the colors typically used by Fremont painters in other areas have survived at protected sites in out-of-the-way places for us to determine how much broader their color scheme must have been. For example, from only three sites we photographed in Nine Mile Canyon we know they commonly used at least five other colors—brown, white, green, blue, and black—in addition to red. And almost certainly, more colors and color combinations await discovery and description. Accordingly, when we spoke with Jerry Spangler about this project (in the course of acquiring Nine Mile canyon site numbers and discussing the Daddy Canyon elk panel) he noted that there is a much greater variety of colors at Fremont sites in Range Creek Canyon than at the sites we photographed (Spangler, personal commu-

Figure 9. This panel of Fremont images in Range Creek Canyon shows the typically colorful palette used in that area. Photograph courtesy of Jerry Spangler.

nication 2018). As examples, he provided one image from Range Creek canyon (Figure 9) and directed us to the previously mentioned image published by Simms and Gohier (2010:50–51).

But our ultimate purpose here is not to publish an exhaustive list of colors in the Fremont palette. Rather, we simply wish to show that these people painted a far more colorful world than has survived—especially in the Uinta style zone. With that in mind, we select two classic Vernal style Fremont sites in the Green River basin of southwestern Wyoming (Keyser 2015; Keyser and Poetschat 2015) whose shorthand anthropomorphs imply that they must have originally been much more colorful and could even have been spectacular. Using current photographic enhancement techniques, we attempt to discover what, if any, evidence exists as to the previous presence of fugitive pigments. Then, using the color palette we already know Fremont artists were familiar with, we try to imagine how these anthropomorphs may originally have appeared.

Re-Analysis of Two Sites

Two sites situated almost directly on the border between Utah and Wyoming each show striking groups of Fremont anthropomorphs that range from the simplest phalanx of "shorthand" figures at one site to more complex groupings of carved and partially painted figures and other shorthand figures at the second site. All figures are carved on open south-facing cliffs exposed to all the vagaries of weather in this severe landscape.

Minnies Gap: 48SW61

Near Minnies Gap, Wyoming, site 48SW61 (Figure 1) shows a row of four almost human-sized, shorthand anthropomorphs (Figure 10) drawn in the Classic Vernal style on a large, bus-sized boulder detached and fallen from the dramatic escarpment above. Pecked side-by-side across the massive face of the detached boulder, all are quite similarly drawn, Classic Vernal style shorthand anthropomorphs (Keyser and Poetschat 2017:158, 161–162). Each has one or two pecked arc necklaces with earrings situated just above the upward-pointing ends and a horizontal belt-line or a trap-

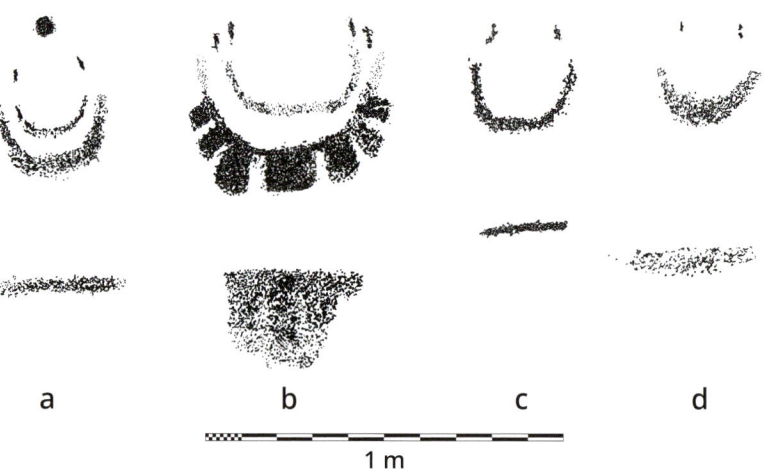

Figure 10. Direct tracings of figures in the phalanx of shorthand Fremont anthropomorphs at Minnies Gap, 48SW61. Superimposed images removed for clarity.

ezoidal breechclout pecked below. The simplest are the right-hand pair, each with a single necklace, paired earrings, and a belt. The most complex figure has a double necklace with the lower arc showing seven graduated sub-rectangular pendants. In addition, this anthropomorph has two earrings on each side of the head and a large trapezoidal breechclout incorporating a trilobed design. The only indication of a head on any of the four figures is a small pecked circle, apparently representing a headdress or hairstyle "bun" element above the earrings on the leftmost figure. Close field examination while tracing these figures showed no indication of pigment.

Henrys Fork Petroglyphs: 48SW88

Just north of the Utah-Wyoming state line on the west side of Flaming Gorge reservoir (Figure 1) is a large site complex containing the Henrys Fork petroglyphs, 48SW88 (Keyser 2015; Keyser and Poetschat 2015). Yet only partially recorded and reported in the professional literature, the Henrys Fork site contains eight classic Vernal style Fremont anthropomorphs (three of which are partial or classic shorthand variants), a spiral shield-bearing warrior, and three trophy heads associated with one shorthand anthropomorph (Figure 11). As a group, these anthropomorphs show archetypal Vernal style attributes including trapezoidal torso, necklace elements, headdress, hairbobs, facial features, and tear streaks. In fact, one figure apparently represents the same Fremont personage as is illustrated at the Steinaker Reservoir site, more than 50 km to the south, near Vernal, Utah (Keyser and Poetschat 2017:170–171). Field examination of these anthropomorphs showed limited areas of red pigment on two of them used for various headdress elements and different techniques (pecking, incising, and two different densities of abrading) used for body outlines and accoutrements (Keyser 2015; Keyser and Poetschat 2017). In addition, a very faint abrasion on the body area of the shorthand anthropomorph associated with the trophy heads suggested its body had been "chalked" in with a fugitive color by a prehistoric artist (Keyser 2015:208–210).

Photographic Examination

To ascertain if there was remnant fugitive pigment on the Fremont anthropomorphs from either of these sites, we used DStretch on photographs of all 12 anthropomorphs. The group from Minnies Gap was done both collectively and individually, while those from Henrys Fork were done as individuals. We found no indication of remnant fugitive color on any of them, though the two different shades of red pigment visible to the naked eye on two Henrys Fork anthropomorphs showed clearly in several DStretch color spaces (e.g., Figures 12, 13). DStretch did enable us to discover three things, however. Initially, on the rabbit-ear figure at 48SW88, using DStretch color space LABI we could see evidence of abraded ear bobs that had not been recognized in the original recording, and there was also evidence of two broader bands of very light abrasion across the body and head of this figure, which we later hypothesized were caused by the application of dry-applied pigment (Figure 12). Additionally, at 48SW61 we were able to demonstrate evidence of extreme water flow across the entire panel (Figure 14). Such water flow almost certainly is the reason the

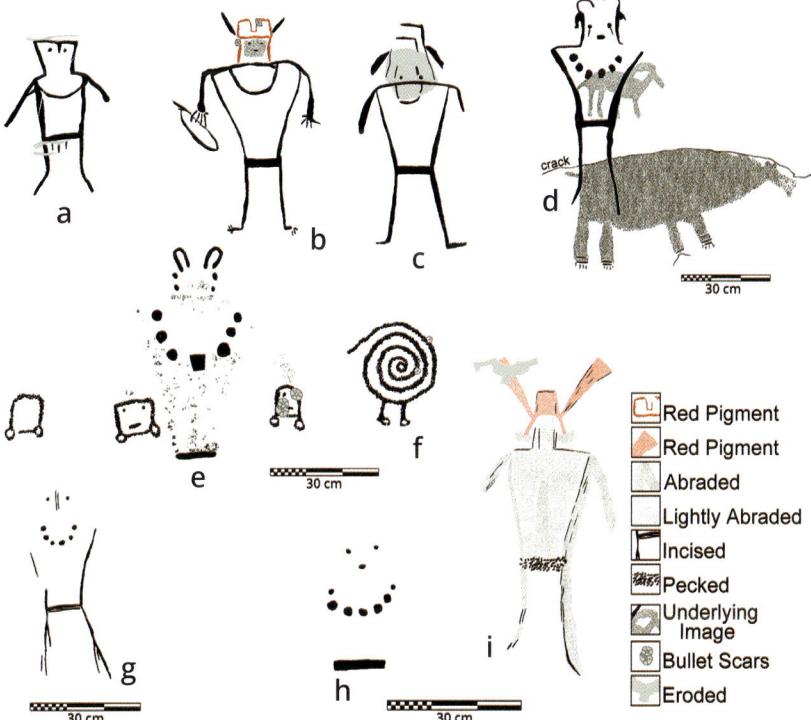

Figure 11. Fremont tradition images at Henrys Fork Petroglyphs, 48SW88. All are direct tracings, but images (e) and (i) are augmented by photo-tracings. Note that anthropomorph (d) superimposes archaic period bighorn sheep and bear images. Original red pigment still visible on anthropomorphs (b) and (i).

Figure 12. Rabbit-ear anthropomorph at 48SW88. Red pigment shows up as white and abraded areas as dark green in this DStretch enhancement LABI.

Figure 13. Red pigment for headdress on Fremont anthropomorph (cf. Figure 11b) at 48SW88 is emphasized in this DStretch enhancement LAB. Bluish pigment on some lines of body is modern sheep paint.

pigments that presumably filled in these shorthand figures no longer are visible—even with DStretch.

Re-Imagining the Sites

Certainly, without DStretch evidence for specific pigment color(s) on these anthropomorphs, any colors we propose for them are simply educated guesswork. However, in trying to "re-imagine" what these Fremont images may have looked like, we can use as a guide not only the Nine Mile Canyon sites we photographed, but also imagery from Range Creek Canyon (cf. Simms and Gohier 2010:50–51) and color schemes from other Fremont pictographs further south, such as those at Pipe Spring (Keyser et al. 2018), the All American Man shield-bearing warrior (Chaffee et al. 1994), and several Faces Motif style sites in the Canyonlands National

Figure 14. Overview of large panel of shorthand Fremont anthropomorphs at 48SW61. Note evidence of extensive water flow across all four anthropomorphs. DStretch YBR. Inset shows bar and three lobes incorporated into the breechclout of the seocnd figure from the left (Photoshop contrst enhancement).

Park area (Conti et al. 2018:137; Noxon and Marcus 1985:219–349; Schaafsma 1971:54).

Henrys Fork Petroglyphs: 48SW88

Initially, we believe the extremely light abrasion evident on the torsos of two figures at 48SW88—referred to here as the trophy-head and rabbit-ear figures respectively (Figure 11e, i)—is the result of pigment originally being dry-applied to their bodies in the form of colored "chalk." On both anthropomorphs the torso abrasion itself is so light as to be almost indistinguishable today (Figure 15), and it could not originally have

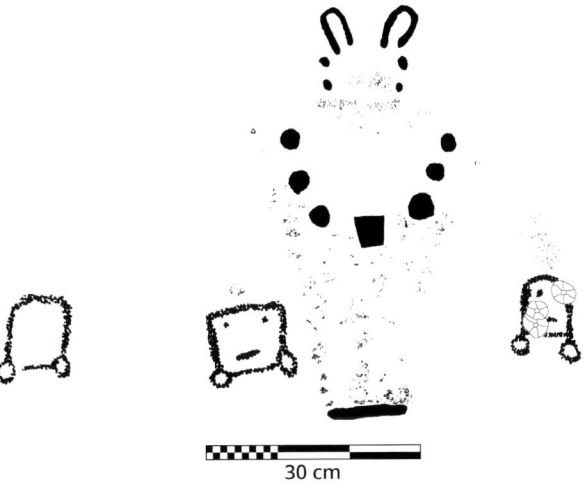

Figure 15. Trophy-head shorthand anthropomorph at 48SW88. Heavy stipple and solid line is direct tracing. Light stipple is abrasion identified in photograph and added from photo-tracing. Spoked circular elements on trophy head at right are bullet scars.

been much more significant. But pigment application by "chalking" a dry-applied color on these figures would have lightly burnished the surface of the relatively soft sandstone in the torso area as the color was left behind. Without a binder, however, whatever color was applied would soon wash off these figures, since the open-air cliff surfaces are completely unprotected and exposed to the elements, which feature numerous and repeated violent summer thunderstorms. Since the remaining red color on the rabbit-ear anthropomorph (Figure 11i) is very faded, the fact it does remain indicates either it was applied with some sort of weak binding agent or its chemical composition naturally binds better to the iron-rich sandstone than would other colors lacking a binder. Given the evident fading on this figure's red pigment, we favor the latter explanation.[4]

The torso areas of both figures show the most obvious abrasion (Figures 11i, 15), which we ascribe to pigment "chalking." For both figures it seems probable the head and arms were also colored, and for the rabbit-ear figure the hairbobs are also likely to have been infilled with pigment. The abrasion creating part of the body outline, legs, arms, and long rectangular breastplate for the rabbit-ear figure is notably heavier than that found in the rest of the torso area (Figure 11i). It is certainly possible that this heavier abrasion was sufficient to produce a white "streak" adequate to color that part of the image without pigment, but the body interior would not have been "colored" by only the abrasion now evident, and we believe this exceedingly ephemeral "buffing" was caused by chalking as has been proposed for the trophy head anthropomorph (Keyser 2015:208–210).

Although we have no idea what color(s) may have been applied to these two anthropomorphs, the simplest would have been white (Figure 16a). However,

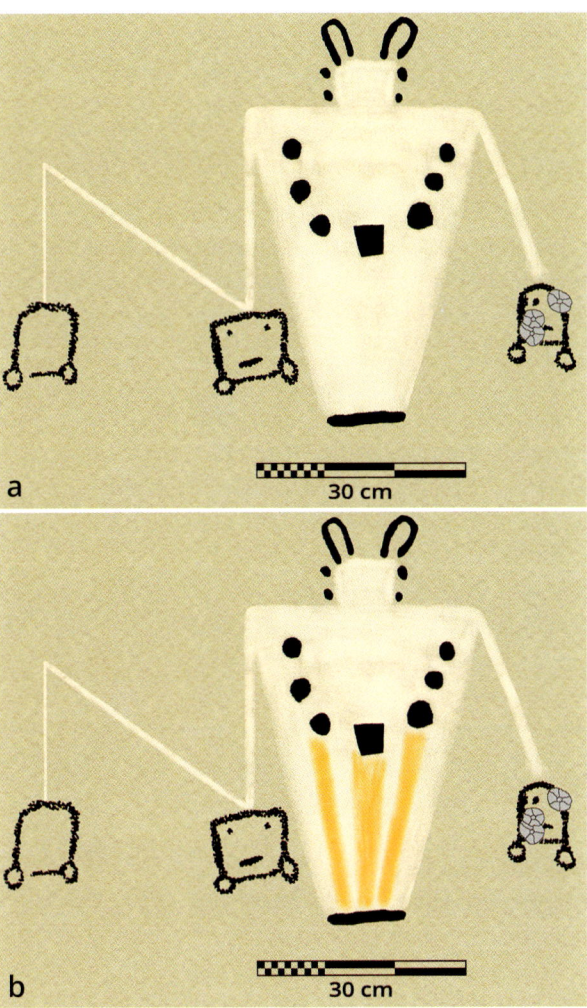

Figure 16. Two possible reconstructions of painted body and arms for trophy-head anthropomorph at 48SW88; (b) shows second color responsible for vertical stripes of slightly heavier abrasion in lower torso (cf. Figure 15). Arm position at left is consistent with other Vernal style anthropomorphs.

another color such as pastel yellow or green may equally well have been used, and if we view Faces Motif style figures or shield designs as models it is possible that more than one color was used to paint an anthropomorph's body with a more complex pattern (Figures 16b, 17). In fact, the hint of bands and other areas with different "densities" of abrasion in both figures suggests different colored areas whose "chalk" applicators had different compositions and thus created more or less abrasion during use.

Minnies Gap: 48SW61

The phalanx of four anthropomorphs at 48SW61 is a typical Vernal style composition, like those occurring at nearby 48SW88 (Figure 11a–d) and at numerous sites in the Dry Fork drainage (McConkie Ranch), Brush Creek, and Dinosaur National Monument (Castleton 1984:17–27, 35–39, 45–52; Schaafsma 1971:9–12) areas near Vernal, Utah. Given the sketchy nature of these figures at Minnies Gap, with only belt (or breechclout for one), necklace, and earrings/hairbobs common to each figure, it seems almost certain that they were originally painted. Otherwise, why go to the trouble of making such monumental art if the figures were intentionally so incomplete? But rain, and the lack of a binding agent, apparently combined to remove most of the original painted forms of these anthropomorphs, so if we wish to have some idea what they may have looked like to the artist who drew them we need to re-imagine them.

Using colors in a combination similar (though not identical) to a phalanx of anthropomorphs in Range Creek Canyon (Simms and Gohier 2010:50–51), we filled in the torsos and heads for these figures

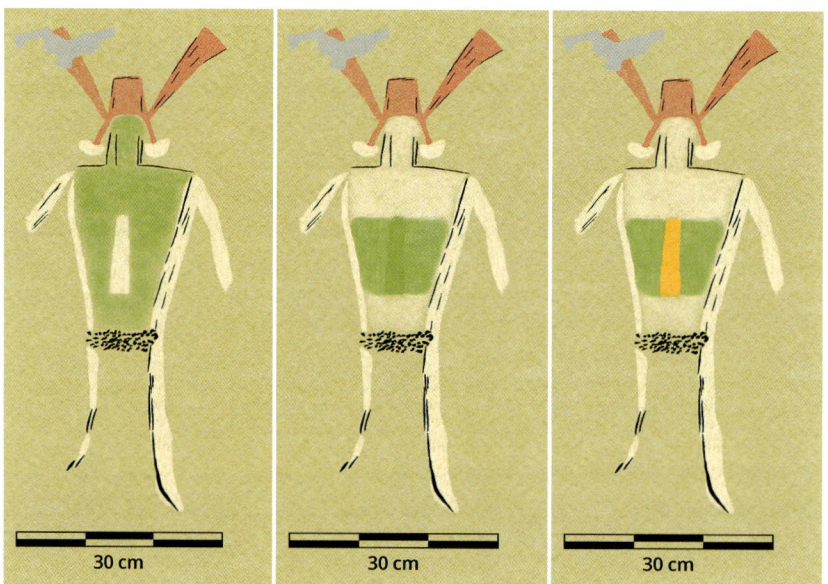

Figure 17. Three possible reconstructed body painting schemes for the rabbit-ear anthropomorph at 48SW88. These possibilities are based on the amount of abrasion observed at the site, in photographs, and in DStretch enhancements. Grey on upper left headdress element is broken area.

with pastel blue, white, and yellow pigments (Figure 18). Body shape was relatively easy to determine, given the trapezoidal form typical of the Vernal style as well as the belt-and-necklace configurations, which provided reasonably specific guidelines in light of the basic Vernal style homogeneity. We included straight arms, since most Vernal style anthropomorphs have arms, but did not include legs, hands, or different arm positions even though all are common in the Vernal style, because they all vary to such a degree and there was no pecked indication (armbands, feet, carried items, etc.) to provide any guideline as to their positioning.

We drew heads for these figures based on the position of the earrings/hairbobs and the topknot on the anthropomorph in Figure 18a. Head shapes

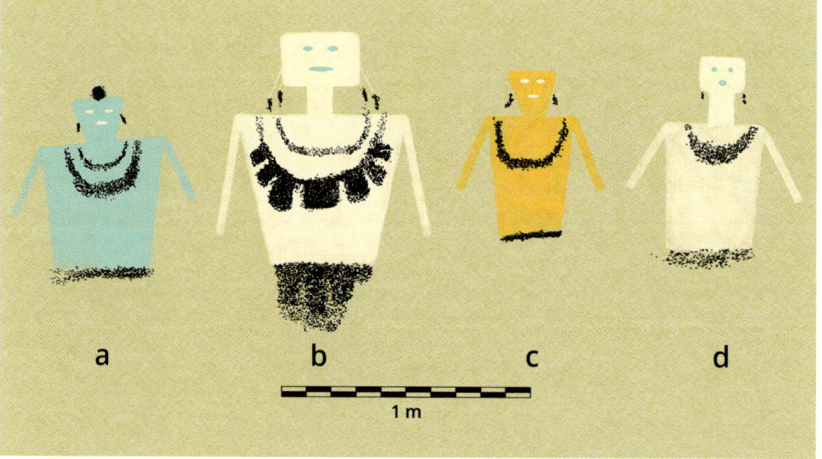

Figure 18. Possible reconstruction of painted bodies for phalanx of anthropomorphs at 48SW61 (cf. Figure 10). Although colors are speculative, similar combinations occur at other Fremont sites. Head and body shapes are based on positions of pecked belt, necklace, and earring/hairbob elements.

fitting these configurations were chosen from those most common to anthropomorphs at sites in the Vernal, Utah, area. Certainly, there are other head shape configurations that would fit, but slight differences in head shape—like changing the colors used—would not markedly change our end result. As with legs, we did not create any headdress elements, since other than the topknot on the anthropomorph (Figure 18a) there are no indications of headdress elements to provide any guidance, and anything we might draw could only be completely conjectural.

Conclusion

Observing Fremont rock art sites in the Uinta style zone, one is struck by the prevalence of petroglyphs classified as shorthand anthropomorphs or other only partially complete anthropomorphs—those lacking primary body parts common to others at the same sites (cf. Figure 11e, g, h). This has led many different scholars (Cole 2009:245; Keyser and Poetschat 2017:161, 169; Schaafsma 1971:8; Simms and Gohier 2010:115; Wellmann 1979:105) to surmise that these shorthand and incomplete figures were originally filled out with pigments that are termed "fugitive" because they are impermanent and lighten over time (even to the point of disappearing) when exposed to ambient environmental conditions. Recent research has, in fact, demonstrated the presence of such fugitive pigments on some well-protected figures that would otherwise be classified as shorthand anthropomorphs (Keyser et al. 2018; Manning 2004).

Probably the best example of a figure incorporating both paint and pecking in a way that clearly illustrates what shorthand anthropomorphs would have looked like before the pigment faded or disappeared is at Steinaker Reservoir, just north of Vernal, Utah. At this site, a large rabbit-eared figure is painted in a dark red pigment, but with the addition of a pecked belt, a pecked necklace, and two pecked eyes in the trophy head carried by the anthropomorph (Figure 19). Aside from the fact the image is so similar to the one we discuss at 48SW88 that it has been identified as likely representing the same Fremont personage (Keyser and Poetschat 2017:170-171), what makes the Steinaker Reservoir figure even more relevant to our study is that, were one to remove the red pigment, all that would be left are the pecked elements—in exactly the configuration of shorthand anthropomorphs found throughout the eastern Fremont area (Manning 2004).[5]

Finally, our recent photography of Nine-Mile Canyon sites combined with imagery from Range Creek

Figure 19. This anthropomorph at Steinaker Reservoir, just north of Vernal, Utah, shows both painted and pecked body elements. If the red pigment were to disappear all that would remain would be the pecked belt, necklace, and eyes of the trophy head. The result would be a classic shorthand anthropomorph. Modern bullet impact scars have heavily damaged the head and upper part of one leg of this figure. Photograph courtesy of David Sucec.

Canyon shows that the Fremont color palette was, in fact, quite colorful. Since we now know—from multiple sources—that Fremont artists possessed a very color-rich palette, we can make some educated guesses as to how it may have intensified their world. We have re-examined shorthand Fremont anthropomorphs at two sites in extreme southwestern Wyoming to discern if fugitive pigment was present. Though none was found, clues revealed by DStretch analysis at both sites lead us to believe that the shorthand anthropomorphs there were originally colored. We have used a graphic design program to re-imagine what these Fremont anthropomorphs might have looked like painted with pastel colors like those used at other sites. While we make no claims as to these being the actual true-color appearance of the figures in question, we suggest that they probably looked something like this. Certainly, they originally looked more like what we have created here than the stark black-and-white drawings showing only their pecked parts, which is the way they are illustrated in a typical archaeological report.

Acknowledgments. We thank Jerry Spangler for sharing his knowledge of both Nine Mile Canyon and Range Creek sites and providing a photograph used in this report. We also thank David Sucec for the photograph of the Steinaker Reservoir image. Field work at 48SW61 and 48SW88 was funded in part by the Oregon Archaeological Society and by David Easley through the Indigenous Cultures Preservation Society. David Kaiser, Angelo Fossati, Mike Taylor, Melissa Gentry, and George Poetschat assisted the senior author in recording the Wyoming images.

End Notes

1. The term "shorthand," when used to refer to a rock art image, often indicates a type of synecdoche where a part (or parts) of a whole stand for the entire image. Some well-known shorthand depictions are the single-line profiles of horses or rhinoceros in Paleolithic cave art (Chippindale 2001:259260) or the parallel-line "necks" used to represent horses in Plains Biographic art (Keyser 1977:35). These cases are a conventionalized reduction of a complete drawing to a shorthand representation reflecting the ultimate simplicity in the principle of canonical form (cf. Dobrez and Dobrez 2013).

In contrast, shorthand anthropomorphs, which are common as Fremont Vernal style petroglyphs, are not so easily categorized. These images were intended to show large, usually trapezoidal-body anthropomorphs, but what the observer sees today are only parts of the figure. The most complex show a pecked or incised head with facial features and headdress and/or hairbob elements, a necklace, a belt or kilt, and even bracelets or a trophy head held out where the end of the arm would be. Conversely, the simplest are reduced to a necklace, or even just headdress elements and a belt. When seeing one of these, the present-day observer usually mentally fills in the body and limbs—and for the simplest, even the head (cf. Keyser 2015:217)—to make a "complete" figure.

These Fremont images are regularly termed "shorthand anthropomorphs" although they cannot be automatically classified as synecdochic. Some may well have been made using only these petroglyph parts as a type of true shorthand—like the necks of Plains horses. For others, however, their present-day shorthand form may not have been a choice in production, but a consequence of fading over time of pigment that was originally used to draw the parts of the body that were not pecked or incised. Such degraded pigments are termed fugitive. Fugitive rock art pigment has not flaked off, instead it appears to have been a paint without a strong binding agent, so it did not bond well with the rock surface.

Several examples have been documented showing Fremont anthropomorphs with fugitive-pigmented body parts expressing various conditions of fading (Keyser et al. 2018:145-146). Thus, rather than being shorthand synecdochic representations, some of these Fremont anthropomorphs are better classified as "incomplete" in their present form. Unfortunately, it is often difficult to determine whether a particular example is incomplete, was painted with fugitive pigment precisely because the artist wanted the pigment to disappear, or was created as a conventionalized shorthand representation using only the pecked portions. Given the fact that the Fremont rock art color palette was far more extensive than previously documented in most of its range, and often far more susceptible to degradation, we have proposed some possible scenarios for original coloration of a few Fremont anthropomorphs in Wyoming if they were—in fact—originally painted.

2. As noted by Spangler (2007) this panel was first described by Reagan (1933:59–62). Interestingly, Reagan's illustration shows the panel upside down.

3. Although Reagan (1933:59–62) identifies this central image as a man (and later the shield as the sun), his upside-down illustration shows a "head" that is not visible by either ambient light or DStretch. We suspect that the "man" was a product of Reagan's imagination.

4. Unfortunately, Manning (2004:69) is mistaken when he states that the headdress of this anthropomorph is painted with red sheep paint. Close examination shows that the pigment predates the breakage of the eroded section of the left "ear" and there is even pigment in the small part of the ear remaining above the broken area. Furthermore, the painted headdress form is the same shape as nearly identical headdresses found on other similar figures at Steinaker Reservoir (Castleton 1984:34), with no "coloring outside the lines" as occurs with blue sheep paint applied to nearby Fremont figures at Henrys Fork. Finally, the pigment goes outside the obviously abraded area of the headdress to connect it to the hairbobs, something that only an artist intimately familiar with this style would have known to do. Our conclusion, therefore, is that no vandal or sheepherder painted this image in this way.

5. Manning (2004:76) also recognized the fact that this would have been an example of a shorthand anthropomorph had the pigment been fugitive.

References Cited

Castleton, Kenneth B.
  1984 *Petroglyphs and Pictographs of Utah. Volume One: The East and Northeast*. Utah Museum of Natural History, Salt Lake City.

Chaffee, Scott D., Marian Hyman, Marvin W. Rowe, Nancy J. Coulam, Alan Schroedl, and Kathleen Hogue
  1994 Radiocarbon Dates on the All American Man Pictograph. *American Antiquity* 59(4):769–781.

Chippindale, Christopher
  2001 Studying Ancient Pictures as Pictures. In *Handbook of Rock Art Research*, edited by David S. Whitley, pp. 247–272. AltaMira Press, Walnut Creek, California.

Cole, Sally J.
  2009 *Legacy on Stone: Rock Art of the Colorado Plateau and Four Corners Region*. Johnson Books, Boulder, Colorado.

Conti, Kevin, James D. Keyser, David A. Kaiser, and David L. Minick
  2018 Pipe Spring: Fremont-Anasazi Interaction in Southeastern Utah. In *American Indian Rock Art, Volume 44*, edited by David A. Kaiser and James D. Keyser, pp. 123–143. American Rock Art Research Association, San Jose, California.

Dobrez, Livio, and Patricia Dobrez
  2013 Canonical Form and the Identification of Rock Art Figures. In *American Indian Rock Art, Volume 39*, edited by William D. Hyder, pp. 115–129. American Rock Art Research Association, Glendale, Arizona.

Hartley, Ralph J., Anne Wolley Vawser, Alan R. Smith, and Mary A. Johnson
  1993 *Documenting Rock Art in Dinosaur National Monument*. United States Department of the Interior, National Park Service, Midwest Archaeological Center, Occasional Studies in Anthropology No. 29. Lincoln, Nebraska.

Hurst, Winston, and Bruce D. Louthan
  1979 *Survey of Rock Art in the Central Portion of Nine Mile Canyon, Eastern Utah*. Brigham Young University, Publications in Archaeology, New Series, Number 4.

Keyser, James D.
  1977 Writing-On-Stone: Rock Art on the Northwestern Plains. *Canadian Journal of Archaeology* 1:15–80.

  2015 Preliminary Recording of Images at the Henry's Fork Petroglyphs (48SW88). In *Seeking Bear: The Petroglyphs of Lucerne, Wyoming*, edited by James D. Keyser and George Poetschat, Appendix II, pp. 205–220. Oregon Archaeological Society Press, Publication 23. Portland.

Keyser, James D., and George Poetschat
  2015 *Seeking Bear: The Petroglyphs of Lucerne Valley, Wyoming*. Oregon Archaeological Society Press Publication 23. Portland.

  2017 Uinta Fremont Rock Art in Southwestern Wyoming: Marking the Fremont Northern Periphery. *Plains Anthropologist* 62:157–178.

Keyser, James D., Kevin Conti, and David A. Kaiser
  2018 Finding Faded Fremont: Shorthand Anthropomorphs and Fugitive Pigment at Pipe Spring, Utah. In *American Indian Rock Art, Volume 44*, edited by David A. Kaiser and James D. Keyser, pp. 145–158. American Rock Art Research Association, San Jose, California.

Manning, Steven J.
  2004 The Fugitive-Pigment Anthropomorphs of Eastern Utah: A Shared Cultural Trait Indicating a Temporal Relationship. In *Utah Rock Art, Volume 23*, edited by Steven J. Manning, pp. 61–177. Utah Rock Art Research Association, Salt Lake City.

Merritt, Christopher W.
  2017 *National Register of Historic Places Registration Form: The Great Hunt Panel*. On File at Utah State Historic Preservation Office, Salt Lake City.

Noxon, John, and Deborah Marcus
  1985 *Significant Rock Art Sites in the Canyonlands National Park, Southeastern Utah*. Document on File with Canyonlands National Park, Moab, Utah.

Reagan, Albert B.
  1931 The Pictographs of Ashley and Dry Fork Valleys in Northeastern Utah. *Transactions of the Kansas Academy of Science* 34:168–216.

  1933 Anciently Inhabited Caves of the Vernal (Utah) District, with Some Additional Notes on Nine Mile Canyon, Northeast Utah. *Transactions of the Kansas Academy of Science* 36:41–70.

Schaafsma Polly
  1971 *The Rock Art of Utah*. University of Utah Press, Salt Lake City.

Simms, Steven R., and François Gohier
  2010 *Traces of Fremont: Society and Rock Art in Ancient Utah*. University of Utah Press, Salt Lake City.

Smith, Watson
  1952 *Kiva Mural Decorations at Awatovi and Kawaika-a with a Survey of Other Wall Paintings in the Pueblo Southwest*. Papers of the Peabody Museum of American Archaeology and Ethnology 37. Harvard University, Cambridge, Massachusetts.

Spangler, Jerry D.
  2007 *IMACS Site Form (42Cb239)*. On File at Antiquities Section of the Utah Division of State History, Salt Lake City.

Spangler, Jerry D., and James M. Aton
  2018 *The Crimson Cowboys: The Remarkable Odyssey of the 1931 Claflin-Emerson Expedition*. University of Utah Press, Salt Lake City.

Wellmann, Klaus
  1979 *A Survey of North American Indian Rock Art*. Akademische Druck- und Verlagsanstalt, Graz, Austria.

A Leviathan in the Desert

Jon Harman

Deep in a nearly impenetrable canyon of the Sierra de Guadalupe in Baja California Sur there is a rockshelter painted with images of humans, animals, and sea creatures. Floating above all these images is a huge whale—an orca! The painting is life size—about 8 m long. It may be the largest pictograph of an animal in the world. The paintings are within the Great Mural Tradition but faded with age so that some are nearly invisible. I use DStretch (www.DStretch.com) to make the fantastic images found here visible. The life-sized image (in red) of the orca is superimposed on older yellow paintings. Also red painted human figures cover ones in yellow that are in a style similar to images found at the well-known site of San Borjitas, in the same mountain range. The superimpositions in San Borjitas indicate that the yellow figures are among the oldest Great Mural human figures. This site confirms the sequence seen in San Borjitas. Many typical Great Mural forms are present: human figures, deer, bighorn sheep, birds, mountain lions, turtles, and fish. An excellent reference on Great Mural art is Crosby, 1997.

In this paper I describe a Great Mural site in Baja California Sur. At this site is an amazing full-size pictograph of an orca (killer whale). Although fish are common subjects in Great Mural art (Crosby 1997; Gutierrez 2013), an orca is very unusual. The identification of the pictograph as an orca is secure, as will be seen after some background on orcas. Even for Great Murals, known for life-size and larger paintings of humans and animals, this is a bold statement by the artist. Compared to other famous Great Mural sites that contain dozens or even hundreds of paintings such as Cueva Pintada and Cueva Palmarito (Crosby 1997:67, 101) this site is relatively simple. The number of paintings is small (less than 40), and the sequence of painting is at least grossly apparent. Yellow figures appear underneath red paintings including the red orca. On each side of the site are paintings of human figures (called *monos* in the language of the Great Murals) in red over older yellow monos.

DStretch

Paintings at this site are faded with age. I use the program DStretch (Harman 2008) to make the paintings visible. DStretch has several different enhancements which can be used to best enhance different pigment colors. These enhancements typically have names with three or four letters such as LDS, LRE, etc. Enhancements used are indicated in the figure captions. The letters CF indicate that the DStretch "Color Fix" button (introduced in DStretch version 8.3) was applied after enhancement.

Orcas

Background

The orca (*Orcinus orca*, Figure 1), also known as the killer whale, is the largest member of the dolphin family (thus technically not a whale). It is the largest and most fearsome ocean predator and the most widely distributed cetacean in

Jon Harman
DStretch.com

A Leviathan in the Desert

Figure 1. Killer Whales Jumping. Photo by Robert Pittman (NOAA). Public domain.

the world (Reeves et al. 2002:436). Along the west coast of North America there are orca pods from the Bering Sea down to Baja California (Black and Ternullo 2009). Native groups along the coast noticed this fearsome animal and orcas played (and continue today to play) an important part in their mythology and art (Davidson and Steltzer 1994; Jonaitis 1986; MacDonald 1996).

Orcas in Native Art

The native tribes of the west coast of North America have included the orca in their mythology, ceremony, and art for centuries. Figure 2 provides some examples of orca depictions from native artists from the Haida, Tlingit, and Salish tribes. Note that the prominent dorsal fin is emphasized in all the depictions.

Orcas in Rock Art

Along the northwest coast of North America can be found several depictions of orcas in rock art located in the historic ranges of various Native cultures, but we should not assume the rock art was made by the historic inhabitants of these areas. At a San Francisco kayak club presentation in 2008 photographer Dan Kiely included the photo in Figure 3a from a kayak trip he made to the southeast Alaska coast. Faint red pictographs can be seen. I asked Dan for a copy of the photo which I then enhanced using DStretch to reveal the intricate

orca pictographs in 3b. Figure 4 illustrates orca depictions on Kosciusko Island and at Wrangell in southeast Alaska. Figure 5 shows orca depictions from the Olympic Peninsula at Wedding Rocks.

The Wedding Rocks depictions demonstrate orca characteristics that identify the petroglyphs as orcas: dorsal fin, whale tail, flippers, blunt head with mouth. The dorsal fin does not separate the animal from sharks or dolphins. The whale tail and flippers eliminate the possibility of sharks. The blunt head eliminates dolphins.

Orca Effigies

While researching orca images I found several beautiful orca effigies attributed to the Chumash (Hoover 1974). Unfortunately, I found that these effigies (Figure 6), with their naturalistic style, smiling faces, and shell bead inlay,

Figure 2. Orcas in Northwest Coast native art. (a) Salish wood carving, "Transformation—Human to Whale" by John Murphy (George and Anne Stoll collection). (b) Haida deerskin paint bag, ca. 1890 (Canadian Museum of History). (c) Tlingit caved bone amulet (Portland Museum of Art). (d) Tlingit ceremonial hat (Smithsonian Institution).

Figure 3 (a) Dan Kiely photograph taken along the southeast Alaska coast. (b) DStretch LRE CF enhancement.

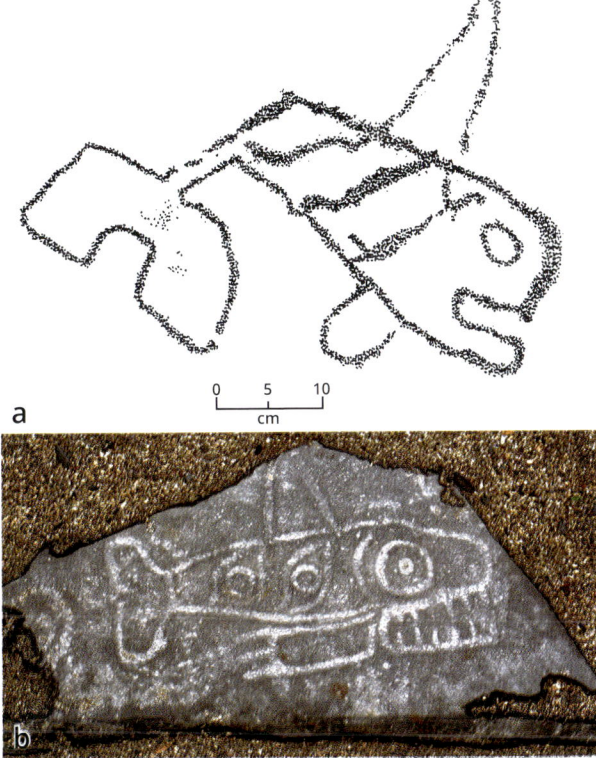

Figure 4. Orcas in southeast Alaska rock art. (a) Kosciusko Island (courtesy James D. Keyser); (b) Wrangell (photo courtesy Ken Hedges).

Figure 5. Orca petroglyphs from Cape Alava (Olympic Peninsula) "Wedding Rocks." Photo by Jon Harman.

were fakes (Gamble 2002; Koerper and Desautels-Wiley 2010:73–78; Lee 1993). Archaeological collections for the Canaliño area include a large number of genuine stylized and schematic effigies including orcas and whales, other forms of sea life, pelicans, and tabular forms interpreted as orca dorsal fins (Koerper and Desautels-Wiley 2010). Among early examples are orca effigies (Figure 7) collected on San Nicolas Island by León de Cessac in the 1870s (de Cessac 1882), an effigy (Figure 8a) collected on Catalina Island by Paul Schumacher in the 1870s (Put-

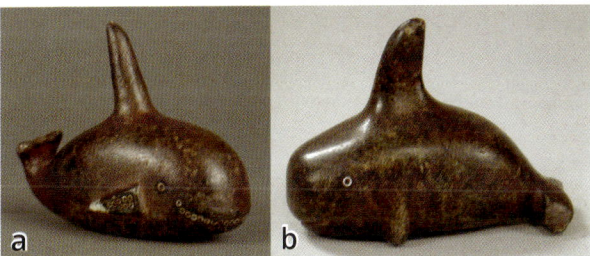

Figure 6. Fake Chumash orca effigies characterized by whimsical smiles and shell bead inlay in styles not found on genuine effigies. (a) Portland Museum of Art (no copyright restrictions); (b) Metropolitan Museum of Art (public domain).

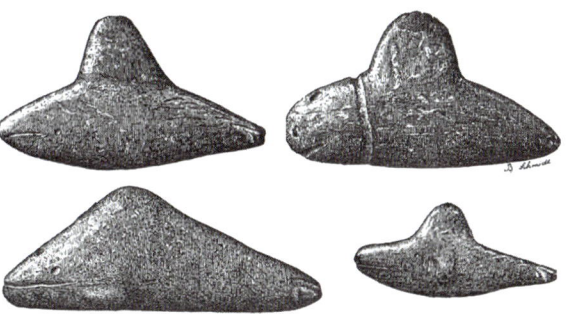

Figure 7. Orca effigies from San Nicolas Island, collected by León de Cessac (1882:31–32).

Figure 8. (a) Orca effigy collected on Catalina Island by Paul Schumacher in the 1870s (Putnam 1879:220). (b) One of two orca effigies excavated near Santa Barbara by David Banks Rogers in 1925 (Rogers 1929:Plate 74), Santa Barbara Museum of Natural History, Robert Hoover photo.

nam 1879:220), and examples found in archaeological excavations near Santa Barbara by David Banks Rogers (Figure 8b) in 1925 (Rogers 1929:Plate 74).

Toños Pictograph Site

Location

The pictograph site described in this paper is located inland in the rugged mountains of the Sierra de Guadalupe in Baja California Sur (Figure 9). Accompanied by my wife Sheila, I photographed it in 2009 as part of the INAH (Instituto Nacional de Antropología e Historia) project "Identidad Social, Comunicación Ritual y Arte Rupestre: El Gran Mural de la Sierra de Guadalupe B.C.S." The project was under the leadership of INAH archaeologist Maria de la Luz Gutiérrez Martinez. Our local guides were INAH guide Miguel Angel Aguilar and Manuel Vicente Rousseau. The site, named Toños after its discoverer (a local rancher), is located in a canyon filled with dense vegetation (Figures 10 and 11). As the crow flies it is only 5 km from the important and much-visited Great Mural site San Borjitas (Crosby 1997:113; Dahlgren and Romero 1951; Grant 1974:99; Gutiérrez 2013:250; Harman 2010,

Figure 9. Map of Baja California Sur showing locations of Toños and San Borjitas.

Figure 10. Canyon containing the Toños site.

Figure 11. Overview of the Toños site.

2011), but between the two places are extremely rugged mountain peaks and canyons. There are clear links between this site and San Borjitas in the style of the monos. The images at San Borjitas are mostly monos (by my count nearly 80 of them) and there is considerable overlap. This allows for the creation of a sequence of mono types. The monos at Toños can be fit into that sequence, as will be seen below. There are many sites in the Sierra de Guadalupe within a few kilometers of the site, but except for San Borjitas they are not open to the public. In my experience there is nothing unusual in the location (side of a canyon) of this site. At the time of my visit I did not see any water in the canyon.

Site Description

The paintings cover about 20 m along the side of the canyon. A rock fall has created a shelter under the paintings and there is some archaeological debris inside. There is a flat rock with a grinding slick and some (possibly recent) evidence of fire. To my knowledge it has never been excavated. There is a main panel containing the orca and other red paintings of fish over older yellow paintings (Figures 12a and b). In Figure 12b a DStretch enhancement is used that emphasizes reds. The large red orca can be seen as well as a red fish and two turtles beneath the orca. An idea of the huge scale of the orca pictograph can be judged from Figures 13a and b, where enhancement makes the tail more visible. The size of the orca is about 8 m, which makes it a candidate for the largest pictograph in the world! The next section describes the orca and associated paintings in more detail.

Left Part of Site

There are also several paintings to the left of Figure 12. Some of those can be seen in Figure 14a and in the enhancements, Figures 14b and c. This part of the site contains many typical Great Mural images including a mono at far left, a mountain lion with long tail (just above Sheila in Figure 14b), and two quadruped images done in yellow (Figure 14c). The rightmost quadruped in Figure 14c has the massive horns of a male bighorn sheep. I describe the mono in a subsequent section.

Orca Panorama

It was difficult to get the photo in Figure 12 because of vegetation and rock obstructions. It gives a somewhat distorted image of the orca. For a better view

Figure 12. (a) Toños main panel. (b) DStretch LRE CF enhancement showing orca and associated paintings in red.

Figure 13. (a) Tail of the orca with Sheila Harman and Manuel Vicente Rousseau. (b) DStretch LRE CF enhancement showing the size of the orca tail.

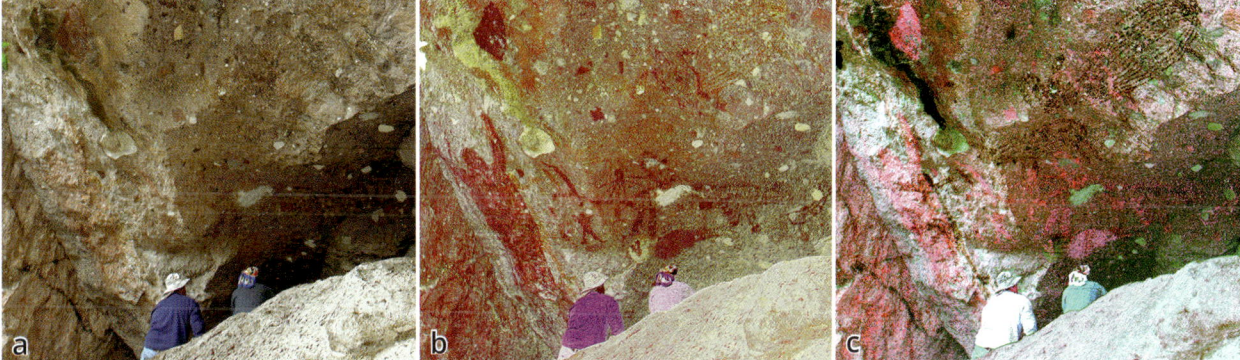

Figure 14. (a) Painted area to the left of main panel with Miguel Angel Aguilar and Sheila Harman. (b) Levels-adjusted DStretch LRE CF enhancement shows several typical Great Mural images. (c) DStretch YYE enhancement showing two quadrupeds painted in yellow.

Figure 15a is a panorama of the main panel made of several separate images. In Figure 15b the red painting is enhanced. Here the large dorsal fin of the orca is apparent, as is the whale tail and blunt head. Harder to see are the two flippers (pectoral fins) just to the right of the vertical fish. These characteristics (large dorsal fin, whale tail, flippers, blunt head) ensure the identification of the painting as an orca (Figure 15b). The orca has been painted over older figures done in yellow including a bird, fish, and probable bighorn sheep. These figures are discussed in the detailed description of the left side of the main panel below.

Figure 15. (a) Panorama of main panel. (b) DStretch LRE CF enhancement emphasizing red pigments. Arrows indicate defining characteristics of the orca image.

Detailed Description of the Paintings

Right Side of Main Panel

The DStretch enhancements in Figures 15 and 16 give a closer look at elements associated with the large orca. The red objects below the orca are, from left to right, a large turtle, after a space a smaller turtle with an unfinished fish tail below it, a large vertical fish, the two flippers of the orca, and finally two red monos. Above the flippers can be seen a small faint orca inside the large one. In Figure 16 the DStretch enhancement has been digitally altered to highlight

Figure 16. Detail of the left side of the main panel. DStretch LRE CF enhancement showing the red figures below the large orca, digitally altered to show the small orca in black.

the small orca. The small orca is facing to the left with only the bottom of the tail extending outside the larger orca. It can be seen between the heads of the two red monos. The identification of the small orca as an orca depends on the existence of a large dorsal fin. This fin is very hard to see even in the enhancement. The leading (left) edge of the fin can be seen above the vertical fish. It extends almost to the top of the large orca. The small orca does not have flippers.

Monos on Right

On the right side and below the orca are two monos in red superimposed on an irregular form in white pigment bordered in red (Figure 17a). Figure 17b emphasizes the red pigments. One fluke of the tail of the small orca falls between the heads of the monos. The mono on the left is a scarecrow (Dahlgren and Romero 1951:173) with a checkerboard pattern. The one on the right has a vertically divided pattern with one side empty, the other side filled with red. This type was named a bicolor (Dahlgren and Romero 1951:174). Examples of these two types of monos can be found at San Borjitas (Dahlgren and Romero 1951; Harman 2010) and other Great Mural sites in the Sierra de Guadalupe. The two red monos seem painted at the same time, but the checkerboard type is an older type in the San Borjitas sequence versus the bicolor type. An explanation of this anomaly could be that the red scarecrow mimicked the style of the older yellow scarecrow beneath it.

In Figure 17c an enhancement (LDS) is used that emphasizes yellows and demonstrates that there is yellow under the red pigments. The irregular white figure

Figure 17. (a) Monos on right side of main panel. (b) DStretch LRE CF enhancement showing checkerboard mono (1) and vertically divided mono (2) in red. (c) DStretch LDS enhancement showing yellow under the red figures and highlighting black squares alternating with red striped squares (3) in the checkerboard mono. (d) DStretch YYE enhancement rendering yellow as black to highlight the figures under the red monos; red mono on the left follows the checkerboard pattern and outline of the yellow one except for the head extended upward (4).

is also rendered as bright yellow in this enhancement. The red checkerboard mono has vertically striped squares, black squares, and alternating red and black lines in the head; the black is best seen in Figure 17c. Figure 17d uses the YYE enhancement that turns yellows into brown and reds into pink. This makes the yellow painting below the red monos visible. Two yellow monos are present, a crude one on the right and the checkerboard scarecrow on the left. The red monos were intentionally placed on top of the yellow ones. In fact, on the left the red mono follows the checkerboard pattern and the outline of the yellow one, with the exception that the head is extended upward. This gives evidence that the red painters were aware of the yellow painting and the overpainting was intentional. I return to a discussion of the mono types later when we describe the panel with monos to the left of the orca.

Left Side of Main Panel

I include two enhancements of the left side of the orca. Figure 18a emphasizes reds and Figure 18b emphasizes yellows. As was seen in the panorama, the red paint was placed on top of three yellow figures, rendered here in dark brown. They consist of a beautifully drawn bird (possibly an eagle or a vulture) on the left, a fish in the center, and a quadruped on the right. The painting of the quadruped is very similar to the yellow paintings in Figure 14c, hence it is probably a depiction of a bighorn sheep.

Mono Panel on Left Side of Site

Besides the main orca panel there are paintings to the left. Animals in yellow on this panel are discussed above (Figure 14c). Here we will focus only on the mono panel on the far left.

Figure 19a shows the panel. The red pigments are enhanced in Figure 19b. A large red mono has been placed over two older yellow monos. The red mono is a type called bicolor in Dahlgren and Romero (1951:174) and gingerbread men in Grant (1974:100). Details of the yellow monos can be seen in Figure 20.

These two yellow monos are "scarecrows" as defined by Dahgren and Romero (1951:172), and also mentioned by Grant (1974:98). Dahlgren defines the scarecrow type as having an elliptical head, straight arms, yellow or red paint, painted using stripes (i.e., not filled), legs with feet turned out. Dahlgren and Grant considered the scarecrows to be the oldest mono type at San Borjitas. Gutiérrez (2013:363) considers the scarecrow figures to be in the second out of three phases at San Bor-

Figure 18. (a) DStretch LRE CF enhancement of left side of main panel, emphasizing red pigments. (b) DStretch YYE enhancement emphasizing yellow pigments.

jitas. This site confirms that the scarecrows are an older type. It also reinforces the existence of paired monos as a repeated pattern in Great Mural art (Harman 2012).

Concluding Remarks

This example of an orca pictograph is unique (so far) in Great Mural art. There is no indication that the orca played a role in the mythology of the Great Mural painters at all similar to the important role played by orcas in the tribes of the northwest coast of North America. There is very little ethnographic data existing for the Great Mural artists; in fact, the relation between the painters and the inhabitants of the peninsula at the time of European contact is not known (Crosby 1997:210). Great Mural art could have preceded European contact, which may account for the lack of ethnographic descriptions of the rock art production.

Figure 19. (a) Left mono panel. (b) DStretch LRE CF enhancement emphasizing red pigments.

Figure 20. DStretch YYE enhancement of close-up of left mono panel, enhancing yellow pigments.

It is an interesting question to ask where the painters at this site could see an orca. Difficult and variable conditions on the Baja California Peninsula resulted in a highly nomadic lifestyle of its inhabitants (Harman 2016:126,127). The painters could have seen orcas on either coast of the peninsula. The site is closer to the Sea of Cortez (Gulf of California) than to the Pacific. Formal studies have produced records of orcas in the gulf from La Paz northward, with significant numbers in the Canal de Ballenas opposite Bahia de Los Angeles and occasional sightings as far north as Puerto Peñasco (Black et al. 1997:10, 30–34, Figure 1; Silber et al. 1994). Thus ample opportunities existed for sightings of orcas in the Sea of Cortez, but there is another possibility. Each year California gray whales make a long migration from their feeding grounds in the Bering Sea to their breeding areas in Baja California (Reeves et al. 2002:204). One of the lagoons that form a major part of the southern terminus of this migration is San Ignacio Lagoon, shown in Figure 9. Hundreds of gray whales gather in the Pacific coastal lagoons of the Baja California peninsula in the winter to breed and give birth. Orcas do not enter the shallow lagoons but follow the gray whale mothers and calves on their return trip in spring (Pederson 2016). Orca predation of the gray whales on the return trip is significant. Whether on the Pacific coast or in the Gulf of California, orcas easily could have been observed from land or from small boats known to be used by indigenous peoples.

Acknowledgments. The author acknowledges significant additions and revisions by Ken Hedges, ARARA Publications Chair, and the anonymous reviewers.

References Cited

Black, Nancy A., Alisa Schulman-Janiger, Richard L. Ternullo, and Mercedes Guerrero-Ruiz
  1997 *Killer Whales of California and Western Mexico: A Catalog of Photo-Identified Individuals.* NOAA-TM-NMFS-SWFSC-247. U.S. Department of Commerce, National Oceanic and Atmospheric Administration, National Marine Fisheries Service, Southwest Fisheries Science Center, La Jolla, California.

Black, Nancy A., and Richard L. Ternullo
  2009 *Ecology of Mammal-Hunting ("Transient") Killer Whales in Monterey Bay, California: A 22-Year Study.* Biology of Marine Mammals 18th Biennial Conference, Quebec, Canada, 12–16 October 2009 (poster).

Crosby, Harry W.
  1997 *The Cave Paintings of Baja California: Discovering the Great Murals of an Unknown People.* Revised and Expanded Edition. Sunbelt Publications, San Diego, California.

Dahlgren, Barbro, and Javier Romero
  1951 La Prehistoria Bajacaliforniana. *Cuadernos Americanos* 58:153–178.

Davidson, Robert, and Ulli Steltzer
  1994 *Eagle Transforming: The Art of Robert Davidson.* University of Washington Press, Seattle, and Douglas & McIntyre, Madeira Park, British Columbia.

de Cessac, León
  1882 Observations sur des fétiches de pierre sculptés en forme d'animaux découverts à l'île de San Nicolas (Californie). *Revue d'Ethnographie* 1:30–40. Paris.

Gamble, Lynn H.
  2002 Fact or Forgery: Dilemmas in Museum Collections. *Museum Anthropology* 25(2):3–20.

Grant, Campbell
    1974 *Rock Art of Baja California*. Dawson's Book Shop, Los Angeles.

Gutiérrez Martínez, María De La Luz
    2013 *Paisajes Ancestrales: Identidad, Memoria y Arte Rupestre en las Cordilleras Centrales de la Península de Baja California*. Ph.D. Thesis, Escuela Nacional de Antropología e Historia, México, D.F.

Harman, Jon
    2008 Using Decorrelation Stretch to Enhance Rock Art Images. DStretch.com. Electronic document, http://dstretch.com/AlgorithmDescription.html, accessed January 8, 2020.

    2010 Cueva San Borjitas: Birthplace of the Great Mural Tradition. Presented at Rock Art 2010 in San Diego, California, and the Balances y Perspectivas XI conference in Ensenada, Baja California, November 2010. Slides from the presentation are available on the web at http://www.dstretch.com/RA2010Web/index.html, accessed November 25, 2019.

    2011 The Monos of Cueva San Borjitas. Presented at SAA 2011 in Sacramento, California; and the ARARA 2011 conference in Idaho Falls, Idaho. Slides from the presentation are available on the web at http://www.dstretch.com/ARARA2011Web/index.html, accessed November 25, 2019.

    2012 Patterns of Figure Placement in Great Mural Art near Mission Santa Gertrudis. Presented at the INAH Balances Conference in Mexico City, September 24, 2012; Rock Art 2012 in San Diego, November 3, 2012; and IFRAO in Albuquerque, May 28, 2013. Slides from the presentation are available on the web at http://www.dstretch.com/IFRAO2013/index.html, accessed November 25, 2019.

    2016 Migrations of the Great Mural Artists. In *Rock Art Papers, Volume 18*, edited by Ken Hedges, pp. 101–114. San Diego Rock Art Association, San Diego.

Hoover, Robert
    1974 Some Observations on Chumash Prehistoric Stone Effigies. *Journal of California Anthropology* 1(1):33–40.

Jonaitis, Aldona
    1986 *Art of the Northern Tlingit*. University of Washington Press, Seattle.

Koerper, Henry C., and Nancy A. Desautels-Wiley
    2010 A Proposed New Genre for the Portable Cosmos of South Central Coastal California: The Dorsal Fin Effigy. *Pacific Coast Archaeological Society Quarterly* 46(1–2):39–112.

Lee, Georgia
    1993 Fake Effigies from the Southern California Coast? Robert Heizer and the Effigy Controversy. *Journal of California and Great Basin Anthropology* 15(2):195–215.

MacDonald, George F.
    1996 *Haida Art*. University of Washington Press, Seattle.

Pederson, Pete
    2016 Whale Birthing Lagoons of Baja California. Lindblad Expeditions-National Geographic Video. Electronic document, https://www.youtube.com/watch?v=reLHWUtEgao, accessed August 15, 2019.

Putnam, Frederick W.
    1879 *Reports upon Archaeological and Ethnological Collections from Vicinity of Santa Barbara, California, and from Ruined Pueblos of Arizona and New Mexico, and Certain Interior Tribes*. Report upon United States Geological Surveys West of the One Hundredth Meridian, in Charge of First Lieut. Geo. M. Wheeler, Volume 7—Archaeology. Government Printing Office, Washington, D.C.

Reeves, Randall R., Phillip J. Clapham, Brent S. Stewart, and James A. Powell
    2002 *Guide to Marine Mammals of the World*. Alfred A. Knopf, New York.

Rogers, David Banks
    1929 *Prehistoric Man of the Santa Barbara Coast*. Santa Barbara Museum of Natural History Special Publications 1. Santa Barbara, California.

Silber, Gregory K., Michael W. Newcomer, Patricia C. Silber, Héctor Pérez-Cortés, and Graeme M. Elle
    1994 Cetaceans of the Northern Gulf of California: Distribution, Occurrence, and Relative Abundance. *Marine Mammal Science* 10(3):283–298.

The Paintings of the Red Rock Shelter: An Example of Rock Graphics in the Central Coast of Sonora

César A. Quijada

In the territory of the Central Coast of Sonora, Mexico, which extends from the bay of Puerto Libertad in the north to the bay of Guaymas in the south, in the municipalities of Pitiquito, Hermosillo, and Guaymas, more sites with engravings and cave paintings have become known and registered in the last two decades than in the previous one hundred years. Although sites with rock art were already known to exist to the east of the Comcáac populations of Punta Chueca and El Desemboque, in 2016 a site with cave paintings was reported to the north of the fishing and tourist town of Kino Bay. The first results of the study of the site are presented here.

The archaeological tradition of the Central Coast of Sonora is defined for the west-central part of the state, in the northwest of Mexico. Thomas Bowen (1965:14) initially defined the concept, comprising territory from the Bay of Guaymas to the town of Puerto Libertad northwest of the mouth of the San Ignacio River near the community of Desemboque de los Seris, and a hundred kilometers inland at its widest part (Figure 1). The extent of this tradition has been defined by the distribution of archaeological vestiges such as hearths for the preparation of food and Tiburon Lisa (Tiburon Plain) ceramics, one of the most diagnostic types (Villalpando 1989:13). The Comcáac, also known as Seris, still live on the Central Coast, but nowadays in a very small territory. They were previously dedicated to hunting-gathering and fishing as a way of subsistence, taking advantage of the resources offered by nature, supported by an economy of appropriation.

One of the first references to the presence of archaeological sites with rock art in the Archaeological Tradition of the Central Coast is that of Thomas Bowen (1976:51–52), who mentions that there are caves with paintings known to the Seris. Richard White recorded one of them, described as two chambers connected by a passage, in the east hills of Desemboque. On the surface, a small number of Tiburon Lisa and Seri Historic sherds were found, along with some flakes and shells. He observed a large number of sherds, probably belonging to a single vessel, scattered on the slope below the site. There are seven painted panels, all but two of them located in the smaller chamber. Most of the figures are made in red, with yellow-orange, blue-black, and white used to a lesser extent (Bowen 1976:51–52, citing personal communication from White, date not specified).

For a long time we have known of the existence of sites with cave paintings to the north of Kino Bay, when it was mentioned that in the municipality of

César A. Quijada
*Centro INAH Sonora
Instituto Nacional de
Antropología e Historia,
México*

Figure 1. Territory of the Archaeological Tradition of the Central Coast of Sonora.
Figura 1. Territorio de la Tradición Arqueológica de la Costa Central de Sonora.

Hermosillo there are some sites near the Tastiota estuary, as well as on the Chichi Chora hill, north of Kino Bay, and in the hills near the Comcáac settlement of Punta Chueca (Quijada 2005:207). During 2016, the Red Rock Shelter site was located and recorded. It is about 10 km in a straight line northwest of Kino Bay, within the traditional Comcáac territory, in the municipality of Hermosillo (Figure 2).

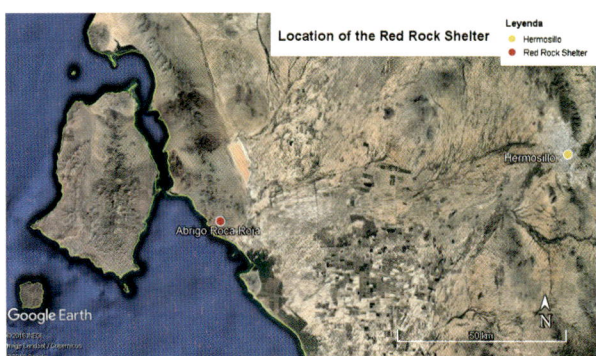

Figure 2. Location of the Red Rock Shelter site, northwest of Kino Bay, in the municipality of Hermosillo.
Figura 2. Localización del sitio Abrigo Roca Roja, al noroeste de Bahía Kino, en el municipio de Hermosillo.

The vegetation around the site with cave paintings consists of mesquite (Prosopis juliflora), ocotillo (Fouquieria splendens), saguaro (Carnegiea gigantea), palo verde (Parkinsonia aculeata), nopales (Opuntia spp.), and palo fierro (Olneya tésota), plus a variety of spiny shrubs (Figure 3). The orientation of the hill is from south to north, characteristic of the hills of the region. In the region there are archaeological sites known as concheros—the camps of hunters, gatherers, and fishermen—more than 4 km to the southwest and 9 km

Figure 3. Vegetation of the Red Rock arroyo.
Figura 3. Vegetación del arroyo de la Roca Roja.

and 20 km to the southeast, the last one on the eastern margin of the Santa Cruz estuary. The distance to the sea from the site with paintings, in a straight line, is just over 4 km. To reach the site, you start the ascent via the channel of a stream; in the middle of the slope you can see a rockshelter (Figure 4).

Figure 4. General view of the rockshelter from the stream.
Figura 4. Vista general del abrigo rocoso desde el arroyo.

This site consists of two shelters containing several panels with anthropomorphic and geometric figures (Figure 5). The largest shelter has a group of paintings on its northern wall (Figure 6), which we call the north panel. A few meters farther north is a second rockshelter whose floor is at a lower level, in relation to the base of the hill. In this hollow (Figure 7), there are three areas where there are cave paintings, also in red.

The main panel of the first shelter is 3 m long from east to west and less than 2 m high with a set of more than 20 paintings including anthropomorphic, partial anthropomorphic, and geometric figures of various

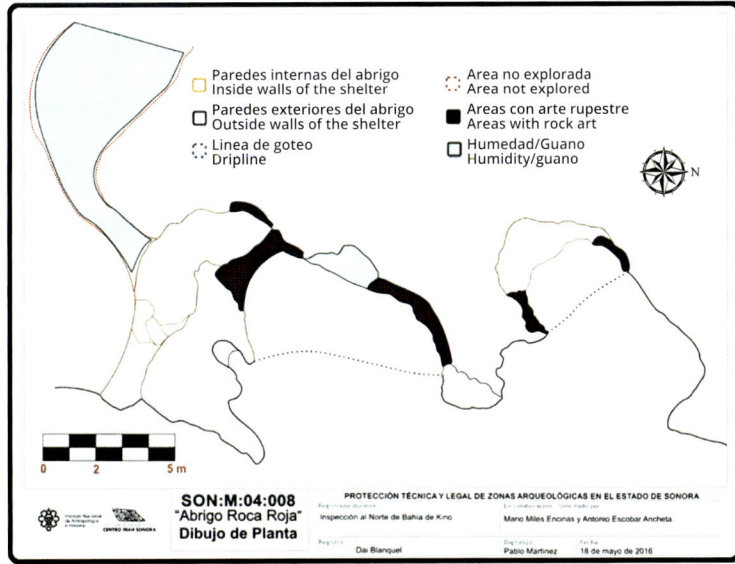

Figure 5. Plan drawing of the Red Rock Shelter archaeological site.
Figura 5. Dibujo del sitio arqueológico Abrigo Roca Roja.

Figure 6. Panoramic of the north panel of the first shelter.
Figura 6. Panorámica del panel norte del primer abrigo.

Figure 7. General view of the entrance of the second shelter.
Figura 7. Vista general de la entrada del segundo abrigo.

sizes, varying between 10 and 30 cm in height (Figure 8a). The representations appear to be made in the same period with uniform tonality seen in the painting. At first glance there are no apparent superimpositions, an opinion confirmed (Figure 8b) with the use of DStretch (Harman 2008).

The anthropomorphic paintings on the main panel are of different sizes, but they are all schematic and in red color. For example, in the center of the panel there is an anthropomorphic figure whose arms are disproportionate, in a ratio of 2 to 1, with respect to the legs (Figures 8 and 9a). There are two anthropomorphic figures, one above the other, with the one on the top having a very long thorax and oversized legs (Figure 9b). In the figure

Figure 8. (a) View of the bottom of the first panel. (b) DStretch LDS enhancement shows that there is no superimposition in the paintings of this panel.
Figura 8. (a) Vista de la parte inferior del primer panel. (b) Utilizando DStretch LDS se ve que no hay sobreposición en las pinturas de este panel.

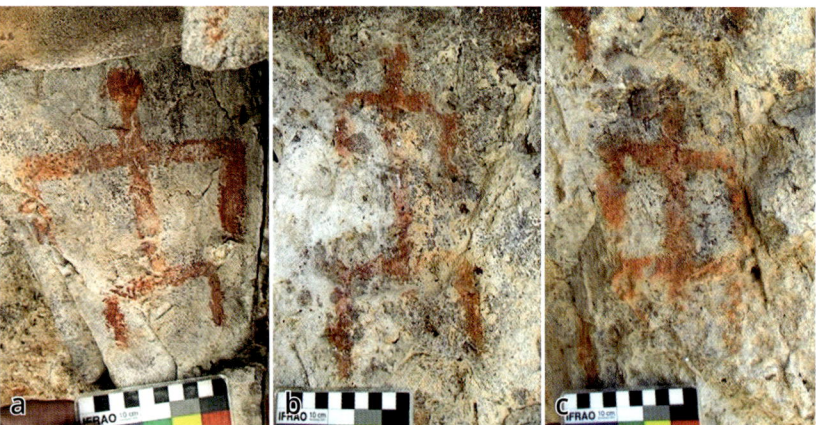

Figure 9. (a) Anthropomorphic painting with arms larger than legs. (b) Painting with a long thorax, equal to the legs. (c) Painting with proportional arms, thorax, and legs.
Figura 9. (a) Pintura antropomorfa con los brazos más grandes que las piernas. (b) Hay pinturas con un tórax largo, igual que las piernas. (c) También hay pinturas con brazos, tórax y piernas, de forma proporcional.

below, the sizes of the arms, the thorax, and the legs are proportional (Figure 9c).

In this panel, there are also anthropomorphic figures that have the head, arms, and thorax, but they do not have legs (Figure 10a). DStretch was used to examine the rest of the paintings to see if they were formerly complete (Figure 10b), but they were not, so we named these paintings partial anthropomorphic representations. The panel also has a group of eight geometric figures based on parallel lines (Quijada 2016:5) of different lengths but with a more or less homogeneous width of about two centimeters. It is proposed that they were made using several fingers at a time (Figure 11).

There is a tunnel in the southwest corner of the first

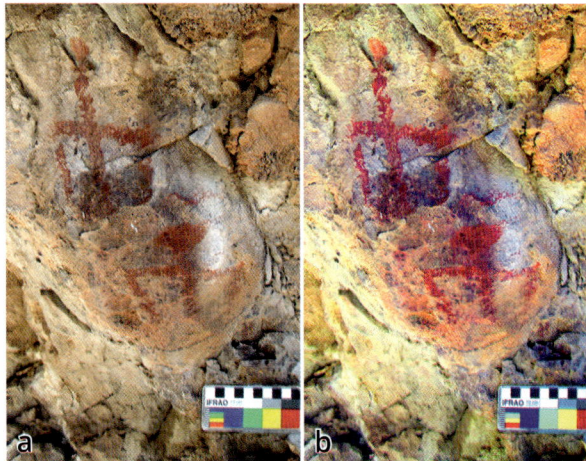

Figure 10. (a) Anthropomorphic paintings that give the impression that they do not have legs. (b). DStretch LDS enhancement confirms that the legs were not painted.
Figura 10. (a) Pinturas antropomorfas que dan la impresión no tiene las piernas. (b) Utilizando DStrech LDS se ve que no fueron pintadas las piernas.

shelter (Figure 12) with the upper part decorated with geometric paintings based on inclined and parallel vertical lines (Figure 13). This tunnel leads to a kind of funnel (see Figure 5), which could not be explored in its entirety because it is a shelter for bats with guano in all the hollows. The guano supports growth of a fungus which, if it reaches the lungs and they become infected, can cause the dangerous disease known as histoplasmosis, making a prolonged stay in the tunnel dangerous. Therefore, we limited ourselves to pointing out the existence of the cavity, without defining where it ends.

Near the entrance to the tunnel is another group of paintings consisting mostly of straight lines, but with one figure that stands out over the others: a stylized anthropomorphic figure with a height of 80 cm. The head, arms, and legs are small in proportion to

Figure 11. Geometric figure based on parallel lines.
Figura 11. Figura geométrica a base de líneas paralelas.

Figure 12. Entrance to the natural tunnel that exists on the site.
Figura 12. Entrada al túnel natural que existe en el sitio.

Figure 13. Lines at the top of the entrance to the tunnel.
Figura 13. Líneas en la parte superior de la entrada.

the length of the thorax (Figure 14a). Using DStretch, other paintings can seen in the upper right part of the large figure, such as two curved lines and one zigzag line (Figure 14b).

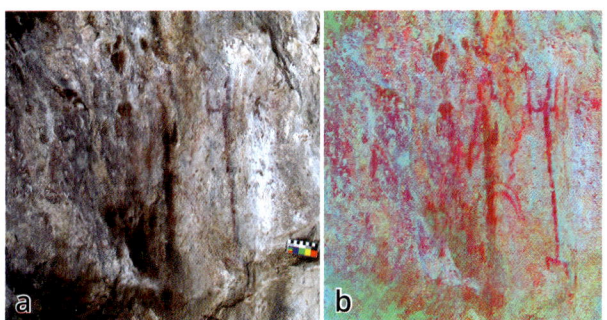

Figure 14. (a) Anthropomorphic representation 80 cm in length. (b) DStretch LRE enhancement reveals additional other paintings on the left and graffiti in black.
Figura 14. (a) Representación antropomorfa de 80 centímetros de largo. (b) Con DStretch LRE se aprecian otras pinturas en la parte izquierda y grafiti en color negro.

The second rockshelter is a few meters to the north, with a drop of one meter in relation to the hillside. The shelter measures 3 m from southwest to northeast and in its central part the depth is about 4 m. Upon examining the walls of the second shelter, we found fewer cave paintings, still mostly schematic anthropomorphs, made with the fingers as indicated by the width of the lines. On the north side wall, two schematic anthropomorphic figures stand out, one almost covering the other (Figure 15a), which have two dots below the arms, giving the composition the appearance of a face (Quijada 2016:5). But use of DStretch (Figure 15b) confirms that these are two superimposed anthropomorphic figures; we do not know why they are super-

Figure 15. (a) Two anthropomorphic paintings, one almost on top of the other. (b) DStretch LDS shows that there is superimposition in the paintings.
Figura 15. (a) Dos pinturas antropomorfas, una casi sobre la otra. (b) Con DStretch LDS se comprobó que si hay sobre posición en las pinturas.

imposed since they seem to be contemporary and there is ample space on the rock for two paintings.

On this same wall of the shelter, a little further down, there are composite lines, each representing half of a human figure (Figure 16a), but the representation of the head is no longer seen. DStretch (lsd) was used to determine whether the head was painted, but without success (Figure 16b).

Figure 16. (a) Possible representation of an anthropomorphic figure. (a) DStretch LDS enhancement reveals no evidence that the head was painted.
Figura 16. (a) Posible representación de figura antropomorfa. (b) Utilizando DStretch LDS no se encontró evidencia de que estuvo pintada la cabeza.

On the south wall of this second shelter is another group of paintings, mostly lines in various positions: vertical, horizontal, and inclined. In addition, at the bottom of the shelter on the south side, there are more paintings but they are difficult to distinguish (Quijada 2016:5).

Final Comments

In further research about the subject, we found that Thomas Bowen (1976:52) tells us that Campbell Grant (1967:128–129) recorded several pictographic sites in the Central Coast, including some on Tiburón Island. Apparently he recognizes two styles, one consisting of "game animals and stylized humans in red," and another of "animals and triangular human figures without legs" in black and white (Grant 1967:129), all characterized by being very simple. Bowen also mentions that the Comcáac consider a cave in the hills to the east of Desemboque, as well as other sites where there are paintings, to be places where you can seek visions. The Comcáac believe that the paintings are representations of spirits or forms shown to the vision seeker by the spirits (E. and M. Moser, undated personal communication, cited in Bowen 1976:52).

The Red Rock Shelter site consists of several panels where geometric figures are present, but stylized anthropomorphic representations in red predominate, as mentioned by both Grant and Bowen. I consider these paintings to be an example of rock art in the style of the Central Coast, but for now we do not have elements that tell us how old they may be.

Making the official record of this site with cave paintings; filling in the registration card for the INAH Sonora Center; drafting the floor plan of the two rockshelters that make up the cave painting site with locations where the concentrations of cave paintings (panels) are found (Figure 5); and starting a photographic record, in general with chalkboard and metric scale as well as recording some of the paintings individually and with scale; are only the first steps in documenting this site.

Upon learning of the existence of this site with cave paintings so close to the sea, we had expected to find representations of marine fauna, as in several places that we visited in Baja California, and also because the site is in the former territory of the Comcáac, who are hunter-gatherers and fishermen. But in the Red Rock Shelter site the schematic anthropomorphic figures predominate, as they do in known places with cave paintings in the surroundings of the city of Hermosillo and in the Sierra Libre in the municipalities of Hermosillo and Guaymas. No ceramics were observed on the surface, nor any projectile points or diagnostic archaeological material that can help us know the possible chronology. The failure to find archaeological material on the surface is common in sites with rock art on the Central Coast of Sonora.

Acknowledgments. To Mr. Mario Miler Encinas, owner of the land, for reporting the existence of the paintings, allowing us access to his property, and accompanying us on our first visit, and to Mr. Francisco Antonio Escobar Archeta, also for reporting the site and accompanying us on the visit. To Dai Elihu Blanquel García and Pablo Javier Martínez García, for helping me in the registration and realization of the site plan. To Tomás Pérez Reyes, for the comments and suggestions for this paper.

References Cited.

Bowen, Thomas
   1965 A Survey of Archaeological Sites near Guaymas, Sonora, The Kiva 31(1).
   1976 Seri Prehistory. The Archaeology of the Central Coast of Sonora, Mexico. Anthropological Papers of the University of Arizona 27. The University of Arizona Press, Tucson.

Grant, Campbell
   1967 Rock Art of the American Indian. Thomas Y. Crowell, New York.

Harman, Jon
   2008 Using Decorrelation Stretch to Enhance Rock Art Images. Electronic document, http://dstretch.com/AlgorithmDescription.html, accessed January 8, 2020.

Quijada López, César Armando
   2005 Pintura Rupestre y Petroglifos en Sonora. In Arte rupestre en México: Ensayos 1990-2004, edited by María del Pilar Casado López and Lorena Mirambell Silva, pp. 189–218. Instituto Nacional de Antropología e Historia, México City.
   2016 Visita de Inspección a un sitio con pinturas rupestres al Norte de Bahía Kino, Municipio de Hermosillo, Sonora. Informe de Protección Técnica y Legal de Zonas Arqueológicas en el Estado de Sonora. Archivo de la Sección de Arqueología del Centro INAH Sonora, Hermosillo, Sonora, México.

Villalpando Canchola, María Elisa
   1989 Los que Viven en las Montañas: Correlación Arqueológico-Etnográfica en Isla San Esteban, Sonora, México. Noroeste de México 8:9–95. Revista del Centro Regional Sonora, INAH, Hermosillo, Sonora. México.

Las pinturas rupestres del Abrigo Roca Roja: Un ejemplo de la gráfica rupestre de la Costa Central de Sonora

César A. Quijada

En el territorio de la Costa Central de Sonora, México, que comprende desde la bahía de Puerto Libertad al norte hasta la bahía de Guaymas en el sur, en los municipios de Pitiquito, Hermosillo y Guaymas. En las dos últimas décadas, se han ido conociendo y registrando cada vez más sitios con grabados y pinturas rupestres, que en los cien años anteriores. Aunque ya se sabía de la existencia de sitios con Gráfica Rupestre al este de las poblaciones Comcáac de Punta Chueca y El Desemboque, en 2016 se reportó un sitio con pinturas rupestres al norte de poblado pesquero y turístico de Bahía Kino. Se presentan aquí los primeros resultados de su estudio.

La tradición arqueológica de la Costa Central de Sonora, se ubica en la parte centro-oeste del Estado de Sonora, en el noroeste de México. El concepto fue manejado inicialmente por Thomas Bowen (1965:14), comprende un territorio desde la bahía de Guaymas hasta el poblado de Puerto Libertad, al noroeste de la desembocadura del río San Ignacio cercana a la comunidad del Desemboque de los Seris y un centenar de kilómetros, tierra adentro, en su parte más ancha (Figura 1). La extensión de esta región se ha ido definiendo por la distribución del mismo tipo de vestigios arqueológicos como fogones para la preparación de alimentos y siendo la cerámica Tiburón Lisa (conocida en inglés como Tiburon Plain), uno de los más diagnósticos (Villalpando 1989:13). En La Costa Central es donde viven aún los Comcáac, también conocidos como Seris, pero en la actualidad, en un territorio muy reducido, anteriormente se dedicaron a la caza-recolección y pesca como forma de subsistencia, aprovechando los recursos que les ofrece la naturaleza, apoyados en una economía de apropiación.

Una de las primeras referencias de la presencia de sitios arqueológicos con gráfica rupestre en la Tradición Arqueológica de la Costa Central, es la de Thomas Bowen (1976:51-52), cuando menciona que hay cuevas con pinturas conocidas por los seris. Una de ellas, en los cerros al este de Desemboque, fue registrada por Richard White, que la describe como dos cámaras conectadas por un pasadizo. En superficie se halló un pequeño número de tiestos Tiburón Lisa y Seri Histórico, junto con algunas lascas y conchas. Dispersos en el talud bajo el sitio se observaron un gran número de tiestos, probablemente pertenecientes a una sola vasija. Hay siete paneles de pinturas, todos salvo dos de ellos localizados en la cámara más pequeña. La mayor parte de las figuras están realizadas en rojo, siendo el amarillo-naranja, azul-negro y el blanco usados en una menor medida (citando comunicación personal de White, fecha no especificada).

Se sabía de la existencia de un sitio con pinturas rupestre al norte de Bahía Kino, desde tiempo atrás, cuando menciona que en el municipio de Hermosillo se encuentran algunos sitios cercanos al estero de Tastiota, así como en el cerro Chichi Chora, al norte de Bahía de Kino, y en los cerros cercanos al asentamiento Comcáac de Punta Chueca" (Quijada 2005:207). Durante 2016, se localizó y registro el sitio Abrigo Roca Roja, unos 10 kilómetros en línea recta la noroeste de Bahía de Kino, dentro del territorio tradicional Comcáac, en el municipio de Hermosillo (Figura 2).

La vegetación que se puede apreciar en los alrededores del sitio con pinturas rupestres consiste en mezquite (*Prosopis juliflora*), ocotillo (*Fouquieria splendens*), sahuaro (*Carnegiea gigantea*), palo verde (*Parkinsonia aculeata*), nopales (*Opuntia spp.*), palo fierro (*Olneya tésota*), más una variedad de arbustos espinosos

(Figura 3). La orientación del cerro es de sur a norte, característico de los cerros de la región. Se sabe de la existencia de sitios arqueológicos conocidos como "concheros", son campamentos de cazadores, recolectores y pescadores, a más de cuatro kilómetros al suroeste, nueve y veinte kilómetros al sureste, estos últimos en la margen oriental del estero Santa Cruz. La distancia al mar del sitio con pinturas, en línea recta, es de un poco más de cuatro kilómetros. Para llegar al sitio, se empieza el ascenso por el cauce de un arroyo, a mitad de la ladera, se observa un abrigo rocoso (Figura 4).

Este sitio consta de varios paneles, donde existen figuras antropomorfas y geométricas (Figura 5). En el abrigo más grande, existe un grupo de pinturas en su pared norte (Figura 6), el cual denominamos panel norte. Unos metros más al norte existe un segundo abrigo rocoso, pero cuyo piso se encuentra un nivel más bajo, en relación al suelo de la falda del cerro, en esta oquedad (Figura 7), se aprecia tres áreas donde hay pinturas rupestres, también en color rojo.

El panel principal del primer abrigo, tiene 3 metros de largo de este a oeste y una altura menor a los 2 metros. Es un conjunto de más de 20 pinturas, donde hay figuras antropomorfas, antropomorfas parciales y geométricas, de diversos tamaños, que varían entre los 10 y 30 centímetros de altura (Figura 8a). Las representaciones fueron hechas en un mismo período de tiempo, se ve la misma tonalidad en la pintura. A simple vista no se ven sobre posiciones, para estar seguros se utilizó DStretch (Figura 8b), apoyando nuestra opinión.

Las pinturas antropomorfas del panel principal, son de diferentes tamaños, pero todas esquemáticas y en color rojo, por ejemplo en el centro del panel hay una figura antropomorfa cuyo tamaño de los brazos es desproporcionado, una proporción de 2 a 1 con respecto a las piernas (Figura 8 y 9a), hay dos figuras antropomorfas, una debajo de la otra, la de la parte superior tiene un tórax muy largo, igual que las piernas (Figura 9b), la figura de abajo, el tamaño de los brazos, el tórax y las piernas son proporcionales (Figura 9c). Pero todas son representaciones antropomorfas son esquemáticas y en color rojo.

En este panel también hay figuras antropomorfas que tienen la cabeza, los brazos, el tórax, pero no tiene las piernas, (Figura 10a), se utilizó DStrecht en búsqueda de algún resto de pintura, para saber si antiguamente estaban completas (Figura 10b), al no ser así, llamamos a estas pinturas representaciones antropomorfas parciales. También en el panel hay un grupo de ocho figuras geométricas a base de líneas paralelas (Quijada 2016:5), el largo es de diferentes medidas, pero el ancho es más o menos homogéneo, de unos dos centímetros, por lo cual, se propone que fueron hechas utilizando varios dedos a la vez (Figura 11).

Se encontró en el extremo suroeste del primer abrigo, que existe un túnel natural (Figura 12), en la parte superior existen pinturas geométricas a base de líneas inclinadas y verticales paralelas (Figura 13). Este túnel conduce a donde hay una especie de embudo (ver Figura 5), que no se pudo explorar en su totalidad, es refugio de murciélagos y en toda la oquedad hay mucho guano, donde se reproduce un hongo, que, si llega a los pulmones y estos se infectan, puede ser causa de una peligrosa enfermedad conocida como histoplasmosis, por lo cual, hace peligrosa una estancia prolongada ahí. Así que solamente se limitó a señalar la existencia de la oquedad, sin definir donde termina.

Cercanas a la entrada del túnel, hay otro grupo de pinturas, son líneas rectas, pero sobre sale una figura antropomorfa estilizada, con una altura de 80 centímetros, la representación de la cabeza, los brazos y las piernas son pequeñas en proporción a lo largo del tórax (Figura 14a). Usando DStretch se aprecian otras pinturas en la parte superior derecha de la figura grande, como dos líneas curvas y una en zigzag (Figura 14b).

El segundo abrigo rocoso, está unos metros al norte, con un desnivel de un metro, en relación al suelo de la ladera del cerro. La estrada mide tres metros de suroeste a noreste y en su parte central la profundidad es de unos cuatro metros. Al revisar las paredes del segundo abrigo, se encontró que el número de pinturas rupestres es menos, siguen siendo en su mayoría antropomorfas esquemáticas, hechas con los dedos de la mano, debido al ancho de las líneas. En la pared del lado norte, sobresalen dos figuras antropomorfas esquemáticas, una casi sobre la otra (figura 15a), que tienen dos puntos abajo de los brazos, dando a la impresión de ser un rostro (Quijada 2016:5). Pero al utilizar DStretch (Figura 15b) se puede ver que solamente se trata de una sobre posición de las dos figuras antropomorfas, no sabemos porque están así, parecen que son contemporáneas y hay aun espacio en la roca, donde poder pintar.

En esta misma pared del abrigo, un poco más al fondo, hay don líneas compuestas, cada una representa la mitad de una figura humana, (Figura 16a), pero que ya no se ve la representación de la cabeza. Se utilizó DStretch LSD en búsqueda de si estuvo pintada la cabeza, pero no hubo éxito (Figura 16b).

En la pared sur de este segundo abrigo, hay otro grupo de pinturas, en su mayoría son líneas, las cuales están en varias posiciones, verticales, horizontales, inclinadas. Y en el fondo del abrigo, del lado sur, pero ya difícil de apreciar, existieron más pinturas (Quijada 2016:5).

Comentarios finales.

Al seguir investigando en la bibliografía del tema, se encontró que Thomas Bowen (1976:52) nos dice que Campbell Grant (1967:128-129) registró varios sitios pictográficos en la Costa Central, incluidos algunos en Isla Tiburón. Aparentemente reconoce dos estilos, uno que consiste en figuras de "animales de caza y humanos estilizados en rojo," y otro de "animales y figuras humanas triangulares sin piernas" en blanco y negro (Grant 1967:129). Todos se caracterizan por ser muy simples y sencillos. También Bowen menciona que en una cueva que está en los cerros al este de Desemboque, así como en otras más, donde existen pinturas, son consideradas por los Comcáac como el lugar donde se pueden buscar visiones. Los Comcáac creen que las pinturas son representaciones de espíritus o formas que muestran la visión buscada por los espíritus (E. y M. Moser: comunicación personal a Bowen, fecha no especificada).

El sitio de Abrigo Roca roja consta de varios paneles, donde existen figuras geométricas, pero predominan las representaciones antropomorfas estilizadas y en color rojo como mencionan tanto Grant como Bowen. Pensamos que estas pinturas son un ejemplo de la gráfica rupestre de la Costa Central, pero por el momento no se cuenta con elementos, que nos indiquen, que tan antiguas puedan ser.

Hacer el registro oficial de este sitio con pinturas rupestre, llenado de la cédula de registro de sitio del Centro INAH Sonora, hacer el dibujo de planta de los dos abrigos rocosos que conforman el sitio con pinturas rupestres, ubicando donde se encuentran las concentraciones de las pinturas rupestres (paneles), empezar un registro fotográfico, tanto de manera general con pizarrón y escala métrica, como de algunas de las pinturas de forma individual y con escala, son solo los primeros pasos para documentar este sitio.

Al saber de la existencia de este sitio pinturas rupestres, tan cercano al mar, se tenía la expectativa de encontrar representada fauna marina, como varios lugares que se han visitado en la Península de Baja California. Además, por encontrarse en el antiguo territorio del grupo Comcáac (cazadores-recolectores y pescadores). Pero en el sitio Red Rock Shelter, predominan las figuras antropomórficas esquemáticas, como lo hacen en sitios con pinturas rupestres que se conocen en los alrededores de la ciudad de Hermosillo y en la Sierra Libre en los municipios de Hermosillo y Guaymas. No hay en superficie cerámica, puntas de proyectil o cualquier material arqueológico diagnóstico que nos pueda ayudar a saber su posible cronología. El no encontrar material arqueológico en superficie, es común en los sitios con gráfica rupestre en la Costa Central de Sonora.

Agradecimientos. Al señor Mario Miler Encinas, dueño del terreno, por reportar la existencia de las pinturas, permitirnos el acceso a su propiedad y acompañarnos en la primera vista, al señor Francisco Antonio Escobar Archeta, también por reportar el sitio y acompañarnos en la visita. A los arqueólogos Dai Elihu Blanquel García y Pablo Javier Martínez García, por ayudarme en el registro y la realización del plano del sitio. Al arqueólogo Tomás Pérez Reyes, por los comentarios y sugerencias a esta ponencia.

Bibliografía

Bowen, Thomas
  1965 A Survey of Archaeological Sites near Guaymas, Sonora, The Kiva 31(1).
  1976 Seri Prehistory. The Archaeology of the Central Coast of Sonora, Mexico. Anthropological Papers of the University of Arizona 27. The University of Arizona Press, Tucson.

Grant, Campbell
  1967 Rock Art of the American Indian. Thomas Y. Crowell, New York.

Harman, Jon
  2008 Using Decorrelation Stretch to Enhance Rock Art Images. Electronic document, http://dstretch.com/AlgorithmDescription.html, accessed January 8, 2020.

Quijada López, César Armando
  2005 Pintura Rupestre y Petroglifos en Sonora. In Arte rupestre en México: Ensayos 1990-2004, edited by María del Pilar Casado López and Lorena Mirambell Silva, pp. 189–218. Instituto Nacional de Antropología e Historia, México City.
  2016 Visita de Inspección a un sitio con pinturas rupestres al Norte de Bahía Kino, Municipio de Hermosillo, Sonora. Informe de Protección Técnica y Legal de Zonas Arqueológicas en el Estado de Sonora. Archivo de la Sección de Arqueología del Centro INAH Sonora, Hermosillo, Sonora, México.

Villalpando Canchola, María Elisa
  1989 Los que Viven en las Montañas: Correlación Arqueológico-Etnográfica en Isla San Esteban, Sonora, México. Noroeste de México 8:9–95. Revista del Centro Regional Sonora, INAH, Hermosillo, Sonora. México.

Contextualizing the Pictographs of Southwest Maine

Peter Anick

I revisit two pictograph sites in southwest Maine that were first brought to the attention of archaeologists in the early 1990s. Although they were studied prior to inclusion in a multiple-property listing in the National Registry of Historic Places in 1997, they have received scant attention since then, despite their likely connection to the widely researched pictograph traditions of the Canadian Shield. Taking advantage of new technology for image enhancement and online historical research, as well as progress in the study of Canadian Shield rock art, I reconsider the sites' images with respect to rockface features, landscape, ethnography, and local history.

In 1957, artist and author Selwyn Dewdney embarked on the first systematic study of the pictographs of the Canadian Shield (Dewdney and Kidd 1962). Concentrating primarily on the region north of the Great Lakes in Ontario, Dewdney tracked down and recorded over 100 sites. Most of these were located on vertical cliffs along the shores of boreal lakes and rivers. Individual images were relatively small, usually between 5 and 30 cm, and painted in red ochre using the fingertip as a brush. The subject matter consisted, for the most part, of simple abstract elements (lines, circles, geometric designs), handprints, anthropomorphs, zoomorphs, and canoes with their occupants rendered as short vertical lines. The occasional portrayal of European imports, such as the horse and rifle, demonstrated that the Algonquian-speaking peoples who lived in the northern woodlands for hundreds, and likely thousands, of years were still creating pictographs during the contact period.

Since Dewdney's initial survey, the number of known sites has grown to over 700, with their range extending eastward nearly to the Gulf of St. Lawrence (Arsenault and Zawadzka 2014). Research interests have evolved as well, from a focus on recording sites to understanding them in the context of the traditional Algonkian world view, in which the landscape is alive and populated by powerful spirits (Zawadzka 2016). Through fasting and dreaming, spiritually gifted individuals (often referred to as "shamans") could communicate with these spirits and obtain "medicine," the knowledge, songs, and objects needed for success in healing, hunting, love, or warfare. Travelers, too, relied on the cooperation of local spirits for safe passage along the often hazardous rivers and lakes that made up the aboriginal highway system. Based on oral history and analogues in the mnemonic picture writing found on birchbark "song scrolls," many researchers now link rock art imagery to communication with spirits who reside in the rocks and water (e.g., Conway 1993:83–123; Rajnovich 1994). The positioning of sites along principal travel routes suggests that they may have also played a role in secular communica-

Peter Anick
Brandeis University; New England Antiquities Research Association (Massachusetts state coordinator)

tion among dispersed hunter-gatherers (Norder and Carroll 2013; Zawadzka 2013).

Although Maine's geology places it just outside the Canadian Shield, Maine's geography and indigenous culture have much in common with those of its northern neighbors. Petroglyphs, such as those on Machias Bay in northeast Maine, were documented as early as 1868 (Mallery 1893:82). But it wasn't until 1991 that archaeologist Mark Hedden verified the presence of pictographs at a lakeside site in Lovell (Maine Archaeological Survey site 21.26), in southwest Maine (National Park Service 1997:G:2). Hedden detected variations in style and paint that suggested multiple painting episodes and noted that the figures shared elements "typical of late prehistoric or early historic Canadian Shield pictographs generally" (National Park Service 1997:FII:3). In 1994, he confirmed the presence of at least one painted anthropomorph at a second site (MAS site 12.28) less than fifty miles away (National Park Service 1997:G:2). This was on a rock formation overlooking Sebago Lake, a local landmark with a longstanding reputation for lost or faded Indian images (Allen 2013). In 1997, the two sites were included, along with several petroglyph sites in northeastern Maine, in a multiple property listing on the National Registry of Historic Places (National Park Service 1997).

Other than an unpublished dating study presented at the 1996 meeting of the Eastern States Rock Art Research Association (Patterson-Rudolph 1996:5), these sites have received little further attention, despite their potential significance as the southeasternmost manifestations of the Canadian Shield pictograph tradition. Edward Lenik's 2002 compendium of Northeast Woodland rock art, "Picture Rocks," includes a brief description with several black and white diagrams (Lenik 2002:64–67).

This paper offers a more in-depth survey of the imagery at both sites, taking advantage of DStretch image enhancement technology (Harman 2008) to draw out not only the painted figures themselves but also details of the underlying rock face. I discuss similarities between features of Maine's sites and those reported in the Canadian Shield literature. In the spirit of phenomenological archaeology (Tilley 1994), I share some of my subjective impressions and observations, particularly regarding the landscape. I also turn to local historical records and folklore, when available, to provide additional context for interpretation.

Site 21.26 in Lovell, Maine, is a fragile, archaeologically sensitive site on private property, which should not be visited without permission. For these reasons, precise location information has been withheld. Site 12.28, in Raymond, Maine, is also a fragile site on posted private property. However, its location on a popular tourist lake has been well known for at least two centuries. With the help of binoculars and a telephoto lens, it may be viewed from the water or the ice, depending on the season. The approximate locations of all sites referenced in this paper are shown in Figure 1.

Lovell Site

I visited the Lovell site in May 2011 along with two colleagues and a local guide acquainted with the landowner. Reaching the site involved hiking down a long incline to the edge of a lake and wading through a stretch of knee-deep water to a narrow strip of brush-filled land just below a tall cliff. According to our guide, the lake had been dredged and dammed, so the water

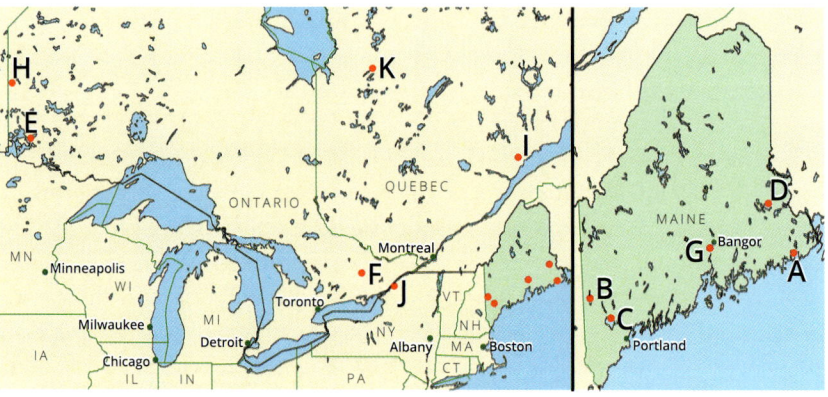

Figure 1. Map showing approximate locations of sites mentioned in this paper:
(A) Machias Bay, petroglyphs.
(B) Lovell Maine, pictographs.
(C) Raymond Maine, pictographs (Frye's Leap).
(D) Grand Lake Stream Maine, petroglyphs.
(E) Picture Rock Island, Lake of the Woods Ontario, pictographs on calcite.
(F) Mazinaw Lake Ontario, pictographs.
(G) Hampden Maine, pictographs (lost).
(H) Artery Lake Ontario, pictographs.
(I) Nisula Lac Cassette Quebec, pictographs.
(J) Black Lake New York, pictographs.
(K) Lac Nemiscau Quebec, pictographs.

was now a few feet deeper than it had been originally. The pre-dam lake level would have left a larger area of sandy land between the cliff and the lake shore, making this a convenient stopping place for canoers entering the lake from a nearby brook. As seen in Figure 2, the pictographs are clustered within a small section of vertical cliff, roughly two meters high and two meters wide, with the uppermost images forming a line about three meters above the current ground level. A sloping ridge of softer, protruding rock along the right side of the cliff base puts the rightmost images within arm's reach (Figure 3). If the pictographs had been painted before the softer base had eroded away and left behind the arched cavity seen in Figure 3, all of the painted images would have been within easy reach of a standing adult.

The granitoid-gneiss face on which the pictographs have been painted bears a number of long, horizontal fractures, which in some places form shallow recesses. The entire surface has suffered considerably from exfoliation, such that the light brown patina of the weathered crust is interrupted nearly everywhere by patches of silvery-gray where the underlying rock has been more recently exposed. The DStretch LDS setting is particularly good at amplifying this distinction and will be used for the majority of the digitally enhanced images presented in this paper. Small traces of ochre on the surviving patinated surfaces suggest that this panel once contained many more images. Like most Canadian Shield pictographs, the figures are relatively small (<20 cm tall) and composed of finger-width lines, no doubt drawn using a fingertip dipped in hematite (iron oxide) paint. Arsenault (2004:345) refers to such finger-width drawings as "digital lines."

The Figures

The most readily identifiable figures on the main panel are three anthropomorphic forms in the upper right, whose proximity and stylistic similarity give the impression of forming a single "scene" (Figure 4). The two larger figures are in identical poses, facing forward with legs apart and arms raised. The figure on the left appears to be wearing a robe, concealing the legs, while the figure on the right has legs fully exposed.

Figure 2. (a) Pictographs on cliff face at the Lovell site; (b) DStretch LDS rendition. The extent of the main panel is outlined by the large box within the DStretch enhanced image. The smaller box is the locus of a single line painted on a protruding piece of black stone, and a possible parallel line below it. In the DStretch rendition patinated surfaces show up as yellow while exfoliated surfaces are blue (photo by Walter van Roggen, 2011).

Part of one leg of the smaller, apparently ithyphallic figure in the middle has spalled off but the phallus and toes give the impression of walking to the right. Three painted lines appear among the group of figures, just out of reach of their outstretched arms.

Figure 3. (a) A view of the pictograph panel relative to the 6'4" tall author standing on the sloping ridge at the base of the cliff; (b) DStretch YRD enhancement. To the left of the sloping ridge, rock has eroded away, leaving a cavity and making all but the rightmost images difficult to reach (photo by Donna Thompson, 2011).

Figure 4. (a) Close-up of possible "scene" including three anthropomorphic figures. (b) The DStretch LDS image brings out differences in hues between elements painted on patinated and unpatinated surfaces (photo by Peter Anick, 2011).

Figure 5. (a) Angular geometric design within a natural recessed rectangular frame at the upper left corner of the main panel; (b) DStretch LDS enhancement. A configuration of splayed lines appears within a patinated fragment in the upper right and part of a curvilinear horseshoe below that (photo by Walter van Roggen, 2011).

To the left of this scene, at the same elevation, are remnants of several undecipherable figures that have nearly completely spalled off (Figure 5). One of these is a group of four rayed lines that appear to emanate from a single (spalled off) point. The next relatively complete motif is an unusual angular design, painted to fit within a distinctive recessed rectangular section of the cliff face. This "framed" image marks the upper left extremity of the panel. Lenik (2002:66) suggests this figure may be the remnant of a stylized anthropomorph with a diamond-shaped body. Historic incised images at Grand Lake Stream, 250 miles northeast, contain diamond-shaped torsos (Lenik 2002:62). However, the other lines do not resemble limbs and, given the lack of space available within the frame above the diamond "torso," it is not clear that a head could have been rendered there. Another relatively complete angular design has survived near the center of the panel, partially framed by a natural semicircular ridge (Figure 6). Several orphaned straight lines can be seen below and to the right on nearby patinated islands. Those below appear to have a darker hue.

Scattered about across the panel are a few instances

Figure 6. (a) Angular geometric design within a natural semicircular frame near the center of the panel; (b) DStretch LDS enhancement (photo by Peter Anick, 2011).

of small, crude curvilinear marks of a different quality from the precise lines comprising the larger geometric designs (Figure 7). In contrast to the relatively consistent coloration of the geometric designs, DStretch LDS reveals a mix of hues, ranging from orange and red to purple.

Variations in Color

The National Registry nomination for the site asserts that

Figure 7. Examples of crude curvilinear marks with different hues on patinated surfaces with DStretch LDS enhancements. Notice how some lines follow the borders of the patinated islands. The bottom figure is vaguely zoomorphic (photos by Peter Anick [upper] and Walter van Roggen [middle and lower], 2011).

magenta torso and arms. Without DStretch, the difference is less obvious, but can be detected as shades of brown and brick red.

Closer scrutiny of the DStretch image shows that the red hue occurs within patinated (yellow) sections, while the magenta hue appears over exfoliated (blue) areas. With one or two possible exceptions, this scene is the only place on the entire panel where paint has been applied over exfoliated surfaces. Thus, the color difference observed here may be the result of a natural interaction of identical paint with different background surfaces. Alternatively, it may reflect the use of different ochres at different points in time, perhaps in an effort to retouch the images after they suffered from spalling.

A Marked Rock

To the left of the main panel, at nearly the same height as the highest row of pictographs, a thick mass of smooth black stone projects sharply from the cliff face (location indicated by the smaller box in Figure 2). As the close-up in Figure 8 shows, this thick block of stone, naturally sculpted in relief, has zoomorphic characteristics, resembling a beaver facing to the right, or a bear facing down. A waterfall-shaped vertical swath cuts across it where water flowing over it has apparently deposited a white mineral coating. Centered within this whitened section, partially covered by the precipitate, is a single slanting line of red ochre. Directly below on the cliff face, where the white discoloration continues, faint traces of what may be a parallel slanted red line peek suggestively through the precipitate.

surfaces were used for more than one episode of painting over an indeterminate period of time by more than one person. Thin overlays of silica containing carbonaceous matter were sampled at site 21.26 by Alan Watchman, a geologist specializing in radiocarbon dating of very small quantities of carbon. Dates of 3000±212 years and 1126±200 years were obtained on 2 distinct layers of silica, the first covering red ochre on the bare rock, and the second overlying a red ochre painting fragment under a middle layer. No stylistic features are visible for either layer [National Park Service 1997:FII:3].

Unfortunately, the details of Watchman's study were never published, making it impossible to correlate our observed differences in paint tints with the dates Watchman obtained by accelerator mass spectrometry. However, a span of 2,000 years would certainly account for the substantial loss of painted crust due to exfoliation.

The DStretch rendition of the anthropomorph "composition" (Figure 4) also reveals a difference in paint color between elements in this group, particularly noticeable in the contrast between the fiery red hue of the outer figures and the magenta hue of the two lines between them. The small anthropomorph in the center has a mix of both hues, with red legs and a

Figure 8. (a) Tilted red line painted within white precipitate on a protruding block of dark stone to the left of the main Lovell panel; (b) DStretch LDS enhancement (photo by Walter van Roggen, 2011).

Visually, the slanted red line within the white cascade reminds me of a canoe descending a rapids or waterfall. Perhaps its minimal imagery was intended to accompany petitions for a safe journey. Zawadzka (2011:19) presents another intriguing possibility:

> Light coloured surfaces were also created by calcite/silica precipitate that has been observed at many rock art sites. For example, at the Picture Rock Island site (Ontario), a heavy and widespread coat of precipitate has been exploited for rock art creation [see Figure 9]. The precipitate is visible at a great distance and is not uniform but ranges from white to grey. From a distance, this characteristic makes it resemble a frozen waterfall issuing from the rock itself. Through their ethnographic research, Conway and Conway (1990:12) were able to obtain seventeen original rock art sites names. The names such as Ka-Gaw-Gee-Wabikong or "Raven Rock White Cliff Beside the Water" alluded to birds of prey, which were a metaphor for Thunderbirds. The White is said to refer to bird excreta, which can be observed below nests. Therefore, the white calcite washes are a metaphor for Thunderbird droppings (Conway and Conway 1990:12–13).

One further feature of the site deserves mention in this context—a long natural gash running up the side of the cliff face just south of the pictographs (Figure 10). It is filled with the same dark stone as the block protruding from the cliff face and bears an uncanny resemblance to the long mark left on a tree that has been struck by lightning. If the site was indeed perceived as the home of a thunderbird, this gash may have been considered another example of the powerful bird's handiwork.

Figure 10. A long natural fissure in the cliff face to the left of the Lovell pictograph panel (photo by Peter Anick, 2011).

Comparison with Canadian Shield Rock Art

Dewdney and Kidd (1962:18) estimated that a good half of all figures appearing on Canadian Shield pictograph panels were "unidentified abstract symbols." These included lines, crosses, circles, U-shapes, and tally marks, as well as more complex designs. The

Figure 9. Pictographs painted within a calcite precipitate at Picture Rock Island, Ontario (photo courtesy of Dagmara Zawadzka, 2011).

remainder were figurative—anthropomorphs, natural and mythological animals, hands, and human-made objects such as canoes.

The surviving painted material at the Lovell site consists of a small subset of these categories: crudely rendered curvilinear marks; well-articulated, linear geometric designs; and stick-figure anthropomorphs. The site's crude marks, such as the short lines and V- and U-shaped elements, have analogues at many other sites. The better articulated angular designs may well be idiosyncratic, although they share some elements with figures elsewhere. For example, a highly decorated stretch of cliff along Mazinaw Lake in eastern Ontario, has a number of motifs constructed of angled lines, in addition to figurative images (Figure 11). A drawing by Dewdney (Dewdney and Kidd 1962:99) from the same area (Figure 12) shows a complex branching design with V-like terminals, which are reminiscent of the V-like limb seen in Figure 5. It is possible that such diagrams encoded topographical information. Given

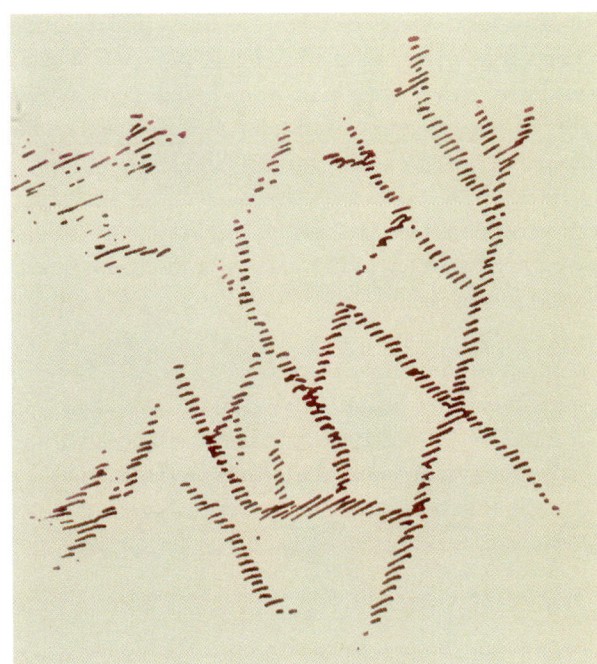

Figure 12. Complex geometric motif recorded by Dewdney from a panel at Mazinaw Lake in eastern Ontario (Dewdney and Kidd 1962:99). Note the diamond-shaped enclosures and v-shaped terminals, similar to features in Figure 5.

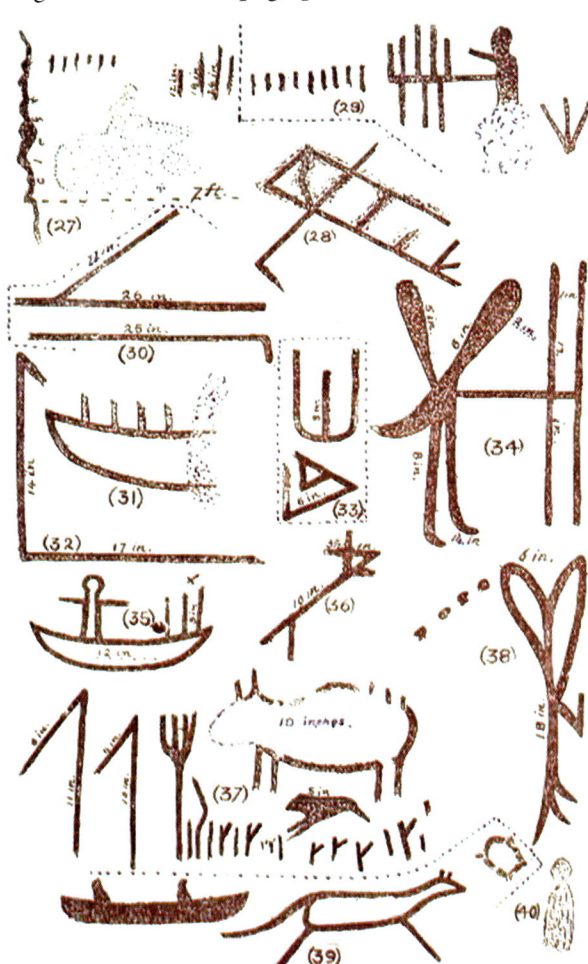

Figure 11. Drawings of abstract and figurative motifs on a cliff at Mazinaw Lake (Boyle 1896:48, Plate IV).

the Lovell site's location near the intersection of a lake and brook, it likely served as a navigational landmark for long distance travelers (Zawadzka 2013).

The anthropomorphic composition bears the most direct resemblance to Canadian Shield imagery. Rajnovich (1994:75) asserts, "the upraised arm figure is arguably the most common figure on the pictographs." Using historic translations of mnemonic images preserved on Ojibway birchbark song scrolls as a guide, she argues that upraised arms represent giving and receiving medicine. Among the traditional dispensers of medicine were the Maymaygwayshiwuk (plural form of Maymaygwayshi). These little men, no more than two or three feet tall, lived inside the rocks by the water, entering the cliffs through cracks and crevices. Mischievous at times, they possessed knowledge, magic, and power objects, which they could be enticed to share. Dewdney writes:

> Specially gifted Ojibwa shamans, I was told, had the power to enter the rock and exchange tobacco for an extremely potent "rock medicine." Many Indians to this day leave tobacco gifts on the ledges or in the water as they pass certain rocks—"for good luck," they usually explain [Dewdney and Kidd 1962:14].

As denizens of the cliffs, the little people were often credited with creating the marks on the rocks themselves, as well as appearing in the imagery. Dewdney reports that a Deer Lake Indian told him that "a rock painting of a man with his arms held like this (and he held his own in a loose 'surrender' position) signified a Maymaygwayshi" (Dewdney and Kidd 1962:14).

Each of the northeast Algonkian tribes had their own version of these little people. Maine folklorist Fannie Hardy Eckstorm (1921:12) wrote about the Abenakis' Mikumwessuk:

> Hampden Narrows was always a place of mystery and awe to the savage. There lived the little dwarfs, Mikumwessuk, who have their homes in the rocks and make beads and little kettles and teapots for the Indians, and who write upon the rocks. Often they would talk with the Indians, these little people only as long as your finger foretelling what was to come, and always they took tally of the canoes passing down the river and wrote it upon the rocks. So that place was called EDALOWEKEK-WARDIMUK, "place where they drew marking or writing", or as Father O'Brien has it WANAGAMESSUK-EDALAWIK-HEDEGIT.

Elsewhere, she described them as "men a finger-length tall, with their narrow faces and slitted eyes and queer little straight noses" (Eckstorm 1917:2).

Several features of the Lovell anthropomorphic scene (Figure 4) suggest it describes an encounter with a Maymaygwayshi. The central figure is small, naked, with a stick figure body and narrow head, in contrast to the larger figures on either side, which have fuller bodies and large round heads. All three have hands up, a pose possibly indicating either offering or receiving medicine. The lines they appear to be reaching for may be schematic representations of medicine bags, indicative of the knowledge or power objects transferred. A medicine bag was an essential accoutrement for the traditional Ojibway shaman. Made of the skin of an animal, such as an otter or muskrat, the bag held the special plants, minerals, stones, and bones that its owner had accumulated to assure success in healing, hunting, or warfare. These power objects and the knowledge of how to use them were typically obtained through fasting and dreaming at power spots, where shamans would communicate with spirits. A more elaborate depiction of a shaman holding a medicine bag appears in a panel at Artery Lake in Ontario (Figure 13).

Another panel thought to portray Maymaygwayshiwuk is found at the Nisula site on Lac Cassette (Figure 14). Located in Innu territory in eastern

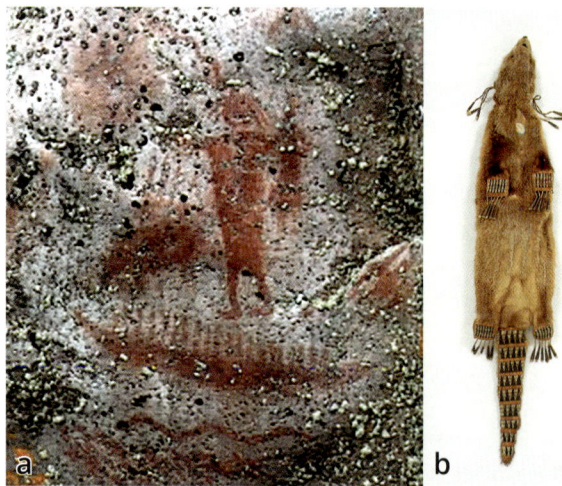

Figure 13. (a) Shaman figure holding a medicine bag, from a panel at Artery Lake, Woodland Caribou Provincial Park, Ontario (photo courtesy of Peter Albinger [Albinger 2014]). (b) Marten skin medicine bag from the Great Lakes region (photo copyright Musee du Quay Branly-Jacques Chirac).

Quebec, this is the easternmost known pictograph site in the Canadian Shield. Clustered within a single large panel are many small stick figures. The leftmost figure has raised arms and a line that may represent a medicine bag, like the central figure in the Lovell scene. Among the other Nisula figures, one has horns, which may signify a shaman. This particular individual seems to be wearing a garment that covers the legs, similar to the leftmost figure in the Lovell trio (Figure 4). Just above the horned figure is an anthropomorph noticeably larger than the stick figures surrounding it. Arsenault and Zawadzka (2014:125) suggest that this large figure is depicted "with big feet pointing towards the right, to indicate the direction the figure is walking, which is toward a crevice." The painter had incorporated the crack in the rock face to indicate that the large anthropomorph was about to cross through a portal between the upper and lower worlds.

Arsenault and Zawadzka (2014:125) describe other ways in which painters appear to have exploited features of the underlying rock face (such as mineral veins and silica deposits) to enhance the story told by the figures. Perhaps the layout of elements on the Lovell panel also made symbolic use of surface features, in this case the adjacent areas of patination and exfoliation. The small (presumed) Maymaygwayshi, painted half on and half off the patinated surface, may be positioned there to show him in the process of crossing through the stone, while the lines, representing offerings or medicine, are either in one world or the other. Given the parallelism in both angle and pose of the two outer figures, they

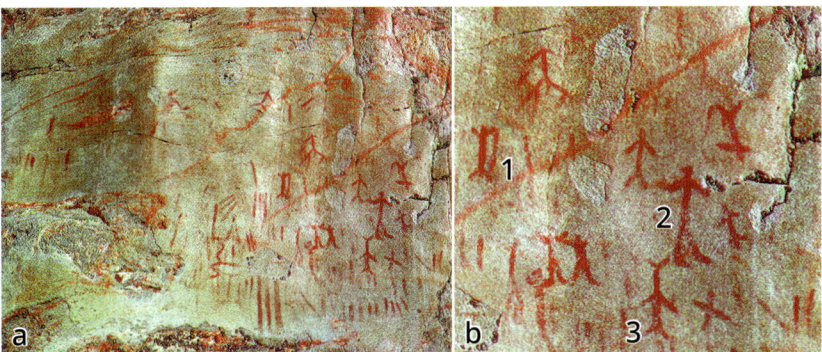

Figure 14. (a) Anthropomorphs and "tally" lines on Nisula panel on Lac Cassette, Quebec, enhanced with DStretch YRD. (b) Close-up includes (1) a figure on the left with raised arms and a line which may represent a medicine bag, (2) a large central figure with feet aimed to the right towards a crack and arm appearing to reach into a crack, (3) a horned figure apparently wearing a garment partially covering the legs (photo courtesy of Dagmara Zawadzka).

may represent a single person in different states: in shaman's garb on the left and in the form of an (anthropomorphic bear or feline?) spirit animal on the right.

Relative dating

The range of stylistic variation, rarity of superimpositioning of images, and lack of archaeological or ethnographic contexts for many sites have thwarted most attempts at dating Canadian Shield pictographs (Colson 2007). In a few cases, oral history ascribes specific pictographs to historic shamans recording their dreams or acknowledging the help of spirits in the rocks (Rajnovich 1994:41–44). Dewdney and Kidd (1962:9–11) suggests using clues from erosion and exfoliation for relative dating of images. The Lovell site, with its small number of distinct styles and several propitious weathering features, may be a candidate for exploiting such clues. As noted earlier, softer stone at the base of the cliff has eroded away, leaving a concavity and reducing the ground level by about a meter (Figure 2). Although we do not know the time scale, it is reasonable to assume that the upper row of the panel was within arm's reach at the time that the upper left images were produced. Similarly, it is likely that much of the exfoliation on the cliff face occurred subsequent to the production of the earliest images, since there are traces of paint across the entire panel. We have noted that, apart from several elements of the anthropomorphic composition, painters avoided painting directly over any exfoliated areas. With these considerations in mind, I propose the following chronology:

The earliest painters, provided with a relatively clean canvas and a high ground level at the base of the cliff, added the single red line onto the (then reachable) black protruding stone. They also selected the naturally framed portions of the cliff face to paint first, recognizing that the frames would help shield the paintings from the elements. One of these locations was the rectangular frame on the upper left that is now far out of reach. Another was the semicircular frame in the center. Taking advantage of the relatively unweathered crust, they created the large linear designs. As storms eroded away the base and exfoliation degraded the canvas, the amount of accessible and usable real estate was diminished. One section on the upper right, within which several large patinated spaces survived, remained within reach thanks to the sloped ridge below it. This region was selected for the large anthropomorphic composition. The painter(s) incorporated exfoliated sections in a creative, possibly symbolic way. As exfoliation continued, only smaller patinated islands remained for subsequent painters to use. These were crudely marked, with the paint often hugging the outlines of the disappearing crust.

While this chronology is based on a number of assumptions, the 2,000-year time span indicated by Alan Watchman's AMS dating is consistent with a multiphase history of usage with plenty of time for weathering between episodes.

Raymond Site

Roughly 50 miles southeast of Lovell is Sebago Lake (Figure 15). Maine's second largest lake was a major corridor for prehistoric travel between Canada and the Atlantic Coast. Many archaeological sites along its shoreline attest to its suitability for sustaining hunter-gatherers over the last 9,000 years (Geraghty 2012). Contact-period Abenaki cherished its fish resources and fought (unsuccessfully) to prevent the colonists' dams from blocking the rich annual runs of anadromous fish (Allen 2013). During the 1820s, the teen-aged Nathanial Hawthorne summered there. Another notable visitor was the poet Henry Wadsworth Longfellow, who drew inspiration from the local folklore and incorporated it into his poetry (Ward 1968:192).

Postcards from the early 1900s show a massive granite outcrop decorated with romanticized scenes of Indian life (Figure 16). These modern renditions were said to be replacements for faded images left by Indians,

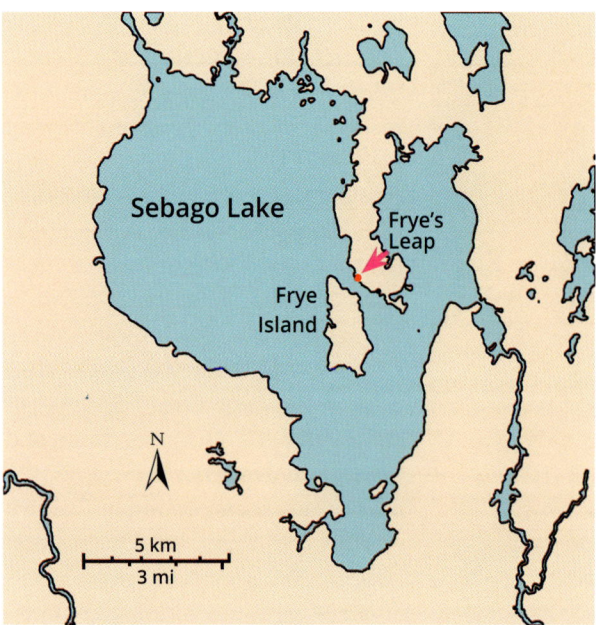

Figure 15. Map showing the location of Frye's Leap on Raymond Cape, just opposite Frye Island. Travelers on water routes heading northwest or southeast would pass close to the site within the narrow "Notch."

tographs. As we approached the rugged outcrop from the southeast, a large mass of faded red ochre came into view alongside a natural recess in the irregular cliff face (Figure 17). Pulling up closer, we could make out two distinct painted sections (Figure 18). A partially exfoliated red ochre wash of varying intensity filled a meter-wide square area directly below a pronounced horizontal fissure. Within the wash, certain vertical lines retained a thicker application of paint, as if they once formed a figure. A somewhat similar faded image at Obabika Lake in northeastern Ontario has been described as a thunderbird (MacDonald 2015:108). One could imagine body, wings, and tail, even a bit of a "head" above the crevice here, but the putative likeness could be no more than the eroded remnants of a nonfigurative, rectangular ochre wash, such as those reported at Black Lake, New York (Parker 1922) (Figure 19).

who, according to one old advertising brochure, "used the rocky face of this escarpment as a picture gallery before the coming of the whites" (Lenik 2002:67). The 80-foot cliff, once named "The Images," is now known as "Frye's Leap." Located near the southern tip of a long cape jutting into the lake, it was purportedly the spot where Indian hunter Captain Frye leaped into the frozen, snow-covered basin and fled to a nearby island (Frye Island) to escape capture by Indians. Turn-of-the-century steamboat excursions on Sebago Lake would stop by the cliff to allow passengers a view of the "Indian Images" while a rifle-toting actor dressed as an Indian fired a shot and shouted war whoops (Allen 2013).

In September 2018, a friend and I paddled along the shoreline in a canoe to seek out traces of the pic-

Figure 17. Approaching Frye's Leap from the southeast (photo by Peter Anick, 2018).

Above and to the right of this nebulous "wash" stood the figure that had greeted us from afar. From this vantage point, the approximately 2-meter tall image gave the appearance of a broad-shouldered, armless torso, topped by a rounded head. With what may be a "leg" on the left extending onto the boulder below and another possible "leg" extending onto the boulder comprising the rear of the niche, the red outline appeared to be stepping into the rectangular stone portico formed by the arrangement of boulders. "No trespassing" signs discouraged climbing the cliff face for a closer look, but blowing up DStretched photos later revealed that the curved outline of the ochre "torso" conformed to the edges of exfoliation around the perimeter of the boulder. Thus, while it is possible that a painter worked the edges of the boulder to match the desired shape, it is likely that the entire boulder was once painted and the

Figure 16. Frye's Leap, on Sebago Lake, as depicted on a postcard from the 1930s.

Figure 18. (a) Ochre stains on Frye's Leap, Sebago Lake. Note the natural "doorway" to the right of the upper ochre-stained area. (b) Close-up enhanced using DStretch YRD (photo by Peter Anick, 2018).

on the underside of the boulder. This section of the cliff also contains many natural light orange stains (Figure 20).

Lenik (2002:67) describes an anthropomorphic figure, 50 centimeters tall, to the left of the lower square wash. We located it, now partially hidden by vegetation, close to the floor of a relatively flat natural platform set between two taller, sloping sections of stone (Figure 21). The outline of this painted image vaguely

Figure 19. Pictograph panel with large rectangular ochre washes on a bluff rising from Black Lake in New York state (Parker 1922:301, plate 214).

Figure 20. Another view of the large ochre wash on Frye's Leap resembling a head and torso (DStretch LDS) (photo by Peter Anick, 2018).

current torso shape is a fortuitous result of natural deterioration. The same is probably true of the rounded "head" above it (Figure 20).

Rajnovich (1994:66) reports that many pictograph sites in the Canadian Shield consist entirely of ochre wash and no other figures. One informant told her that the wash denotes "the special spirituality of the site." It is the mountain or cliff itself that is sacred, not the rock art. This is likely the case here as well, especially as the natural stone "portal" adjacent to the painted area may have been viewed as a door used by a spirit of the cliff to enter the lower world. Within this large rectangular niche, a thin, horizontal line of a different hue stretches across the back wall, just beneath the roof stone. Some reddish patches are observable on the ceiling but it is difficult to tell whether they are natural, given the dimmer lighting

resembles a robed figure with an arm extending to the right. Scattered vestiges of paint appear below it. Considering the layout of the surrounding cliff face, the flat platform, just below the stone "portal," would have been a convenient place to conduct rituals or leave offerings for the spirit being(s) who dwelt here.

Figure 21. (a) Location of anthropomorphic figure on Frye's Leap; (b) DStretch LDS close-up (photos by Peter Anick, 2018).

We continued paddling to the north face of the outcrop, the view portrayed in the antique post card with the romanticized modern paintings of Indian life. No trace of these images remained. Nor were there any remnants of earlier Indian ochre paintings that might have inspired the modern replicas. Paddling past the end of the outcrop, we discovered a narrow, natural stone tunnel several feet high and of indeterminate length and depth (Figure 22). A tight fit, we resisted the urge to squeeze our canoe inside.

Figure 22. A natural cave on the shoreline of Sebago Lake, just north of Frye's Leap (photo by Peter Anick, 2018).

Lenik (2002:67) had reported another locus of pictographs "on the south side of the granite ledge in a sheltered cove." It took us several passes along the shore south of the ledge to locate them through the trees. As shown in Figure 23, an angled slab of bedrock (on the left) shelters a pair of small, smooth boulders decorated with thick, red vertical lines. The tapered ends of some of the strokes (e.g., the three long lines on the right side of the cluster) suggest the use of a brush, rather than fingers or hands, to apply the paint. The DStretch close-up (Figure 24) shows that most of these lines were painted on top of patinated portions of the weathered surface. However, several of the broad strokes run across both patinated and exfoliated surfaces, providing an answer to our earlier question regarding the influence of surface type on the hues of paint. Here, the ochre appears reddish-brown when applied to a patinated surface and a darker brick red when applied to the underlying rock, which translates into red and magenta hues when applying DStretch LDS, similar to what we observed at the Lovell site (Figure 4). The absence of traces of paint on most of the small remaining islands of patinated surface on the right side of the larger boulder suggests that the stones

Figure 23. (a) Pictograph panel under a sloping "rockshelter" on the southeast side of Frye's Leap; (b) DStretch LDS enhancement (photos by Peter Anick, 2018).

Figure 24. Close-up of panel on southeast side of Frye's Leap (DStretch LDS), showing lines of paint applied over both patinated and exfoliated surfaces (photo by Peter Anick, 2018).

had been decorated after much of the exfoliation had already taken place. Three short, finger-width lines of paint appear on the right side on the boulder (Figure 23). These were all placed so as to fit within the bounds of the remaining patinated regions. This is reminiscent of the way the crude marks on the Lovell panel (Figure 7) were placed to fit within the confines of small patinated islands. The varying color tints suggest at least two different paints were used here.

This cluster of bold, broad strokes deviates from the typical pattern of finger-width lines found at the Lovell site and many Canadian sites. Beyond their greater length and width, their arrangement is also unusual, containing several idiosyncratic configurations that Lenik (2002:67) suggests might be schematized thunderbirds or anthropomorphs. The trident-shaped figure on the smaller boulder bears some resemblance to a motif that appears at the Kaapehpeshapischinikanuuch site EiGf-2 on Lake Nemiscau, Quebec (Figure 25). Vaillancourt (2008:115) considers a range of possible interpretations for the shape, including a stylized thunderbird, a bird or Maymaygwayshi footprint, and an anthropomorphic spirit in transit between worlds, its legs invisible within the rock itself.

Figure 25. Trident-shaped motif at Kaapehpeshapischinikanuuch site EiGf-2 on Lake Nemiscau, Quebec (photo courtesy of Pascale Vaillancourt).

On the inclined bedrock immediately to the left of the painted boulders are two extremely faint motifs (Figure 26). One is the only finger-width "digital line" figure I observed at the site. The motif resembles a cross, although the left arm is cut short. The wall on which they are painted is part of the eastern base of the massive Frye's Leap outcrop. A narrow path runs south along the wall, on which several other blurry patches of ochre can be made out behind dark lichen. In a review of Lenik's *Picture Rocks*, Mark Hedden (2002:6–7) alludes to these patches, asserting that "lichen growths in the shallow rock shelters that still show traces of red ochre have largely obscured two elongated anthropomorphic forms which Lenik apparently did not see." Without the aid of DStretch, Hedden may have been mistaken in his assessment, but the lichen has indeed rendered at least one long ochre form nearly invisible except for some red dots. Another, shown in Figure 27, may be Hedden's "anthropomorph." With an "arm" pointing to the left, the long triangular form could be a mirror image of the one-armed anthropomorph we saw earlier by the southern platform (Figure 21). The

Figure 26. (a) Very faint ochre designs on the sloped wall of the "rockshelter" on the southeast side of Frye's Leap; (b) DStretch LDS enhancement (photo by Peter Anick, 2018).

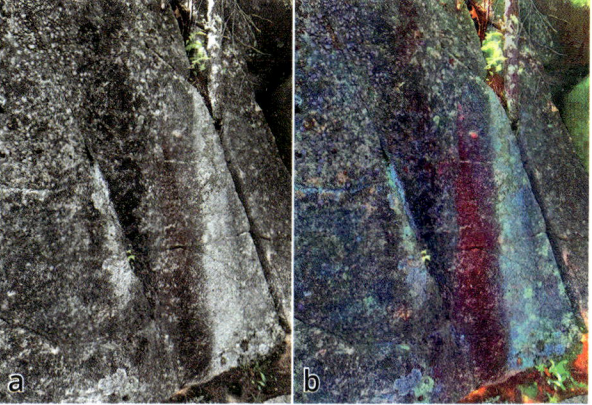

Figure 27. (a) Faint vertical ochre image along southeast base of Frye's Leap; (b) DStretch LDS enhancement (photo by Peter Anick, 2018).

short ascending trail terminates at the southern corner of Frye's Leap, just around the bend from the "ochre wash" panels.

Historical Research

Having completed a cursory site inspection, I was keen to learn more about the history of the famous Raymond landmark. Has any Indian folklore about the area survived? What was the water level prior to manipulation of the landscape by settlers? When were the modern images painted on Frye's Rock? Had they really been inspired by Indian pictographs, and if so, do any historic descriptions of their precursors exist?

An online report from the Maine Geological Survey (Johnston 1999) answered my question regarding water levels. Construction of the Eel Weir Dam, begun in the 1820s, had raised the water level approximately twelve feet to its current "full pond" level of 266 feet. This means that the base of Frye's Leap would have been a good ten feet lower than it was when I canoed around it. The platform area beside the ochre wash, rather than being directly accessible by canoe, would likely have been reachable only by land, probably by following the ochre-marked path along the eastern side of the bluff. Furthermore, any pictographs painted at prehistoric water levels would have been submerged by the late 1820s.

Seeking early historic mentions of the lake, I came across a story in the 1910 Portland Board of Trade Journal (Portland Board of Trade 1910:129) describing a steamship ride through the "Notch," the narrow neck of water separating Raymond Cape from Frye's Island:

The northern "outpost" of the Notch, and which the steamer is allowed to drift slowly by, is the "Images" from whose beetling heights a simulated Indian gives the dread war-whoop and fires his rifle, to the great delectations of the small boy.... It is so called by reason of sundry characteristic "images" having been painted thereon by the Indians, and whose faded "art studies" have been in a way reproduced by modern pale faces. Of especial sentimental interest is "Hawthorne's Cave" a lateral opening in the precipice, about four feet wide, twenty feet below and six feet above the water-line. Into this natural grotto—from which one can in fancy hear a Delphic oracle from the shade of America's great romancer—"Nat" Hawthorne when a lad, was wont to sail his little boat a distance of twenty-five feet, whence he could clamber through a short passage to the outer world. Tradition has it that Capt. Frye, closely pressed by hostile Indians, leaped from this cliff and swam to the island now bearing his name, thus saving his life.

Notwithstanding the alternative account of Captain Frye's escape (by water rather than over a frozen lake), it was reassuring to find an allusion to Indian images, albeit a rather vague one. The shallow cave we had encountered just north of the Leap was surely Hawthorne's Cave. The amount of headroom must have been significantly greater during Hawthorne's youth, a decade before the construction of the Eel Weir Dam. Checking Hawthorne's diary (Pickard 1897:49), I found a mention of a boat ride he took to "the Images," indicating that the name was already in use in the early 1800s. Disappointingly, he does not describe them.

I also came across a 1906 magazine article about Longfellow's vacations in Maine, which, to my surprise, revealed some of the Indian folklore regarding the site (Lombard 1906:26):

Yonder are the "Images," the presiding genii of the lake.

As one confronts this great granite cliff rising sheer to a height of seventy feet above the water, he cannot wonder at the superstitious awe with which the Indians regarded it.

From where these rocks are seen towers the humid blue of the distant mountains. There was the dwelling place of Manitou, the Mighty, whose voice they heard in the crashing thunder, whose weapon was the terrible lightning, and whose precincts it were profanation to invade.

A long, long time ago when the deep snow covered all the hills, and the ice never thawed from the streams, Manitou, the Mighty One, sent his son from the cloud-capped summits of the Wonderful Hills to the earth below. The land grew warmer under his breath and mists arose till he could no longer see his native place. Then, of a sudden, he felt himself falling through the air to a place beside the waters of a lake. Before the mists cleared away so that he could once more see his former home, he became enamored of a beautiful maiden, the spirit of the lake.

For that deed of disobedience, he was changed to an unshapely mass of stone.

Bound to earth, it was the Indian belief that he still held converse with the Great Spirit, and guarded the lake from intrusion.

In some places, the granite strata is seamed, in others, worn smooth and stained by the action of the weather, but the antiquarian whose chief delight it is to search out the heart of old myths regards these so-called weather stains as Indian marks. Rock tracings were the Indians' only substitute for local and national records.

Once again, the author is vague concerning Indian marks, likening them to "weather stains." However, his romanticized tale of the guardian of the rock rings true in many respects. The Algonkians throughout the northeast attributed unusual landscape features to the escapades of powerful beings (e.g., Speck 1935; Zawadzka 2016) and it would be unlikely that this impressive outcrop was not associated with a creation legend. "The cloud-capped summits of the Wonderful Hills" is a reference to Mt. Washington, visible in clear weather from Sebago Lake. It was sometimes called Agiochook, or Agiocochook, meaning "the place of the Great Spirit" or "the place of the Concealed One" (Piotrowski 2002:182). The mountain's mercurial and notoriously extreme weather made it a logical home for the Indians' most powerful spirit, personified as "Manitou."

A similar folk tale is recounted about a guardian spirit assigned to protect a stone talisman on Mount Washington (English 1906:112):

> It was safely guarded by an evil spirit, a wicked Indian who had climbed the mountain top in defiance of the Manitou and who, as a punishment, had been killed, and his spirit stationed as a guard to perpetually watch over the stone. In his hand he held a fiery spear; and the human being who approached was bound to be enveloped in a haze of mist and smoke.

If Frye's Leap was the home of such a guardian spirit, then the large ochre panels painted next to the stone "portal" may well have served as a public reminder of his presence. The red billboards would have been difficult to miss, located as they were at a narrow bottleneck on a busy Indian thoroughfare. The wary traveler would be wise to make him an offering to guarantee safe passage.

Buoyed by these finds, I continued my quest for a more definitive description of the elusive Indian "images." I turned next to the *Bridgton Weekly News*, whose online searchable archive goes back to its first issue in 1870.

The earliest mention of the Images appears in an 1871 account of a trip on the Sebago Lake route of the little steamer Oriental (C. O. S. 1871):

> We are now in the narrowest part of the "Notch," which here is but 84 rods wide, and five miles from the Lake Station. The Captain causes the engine to be stopped, and the boat is steered close to the celebrated Images, past which we leisurely drift.... We perceive in two places on the smooth precipice the famous "blood stains," which certainly are bloody-looking enough and about which there is much speculation and mystery. On the top of the cliff are the names and initials of visitors who have carved them in the thin dry moss.

This passage is intriguing. In the phrase "celebrated Images," the capitalized term refers to the name of the cliff itself. But there is no mention of any Indian paintings, ancient or modern. Instead, the author comments on two mysterious "blood stains," which sound suspiciously like the pair of ochre wash panels that still drip from the southern end of the outcrop.

In an 1892 article about a local farmer and artifact collector named Luther Longley (of Raymond), interviewer James Mead (1892) brings up the topic of the Images, which is obviously still a subject of local curiosity. He quotes Longley as saying:

> You know they have been reproduced but not according to the correct letter of history, for now we gaze at bear fights, braves and squaws on the face of the cliff while the old paintings appeared on the inside of the cave and not in sight of the passer-by at all.
>
> As near as I have been able to inform myself, the facts are these: About the time Poland was killed, a raiding band of Indians was pursued by a party of white men from down Windham way. The red skins finding themselves so hard pressed, took refuge in the cave and amid the rocks on the cape, and from their concealment saw the pursuing party in five boats pass by.
>
> In order to give information to the balance of their war party who were to follow them, they painted on the walls of the cave five canoes filled with white men heading towards Songo and also in the rear a canoe containing a single white man supposed to refer to Captain Frye's relative, whom they probably saw leave the island. Such I believe to have been the true history of the images though I have met men who asserted they could remember the paintings on the face of the cliff; but the only signs of paint ever pointed out to me there were washings of something resembling iron rust which had run out of crevices in the ledge.

The plot thickens! We learn that the modern images had been painted some time before 1892. We also get a narrative about canoes painted not on the cliff but within the adjacent (Hawthorne's) cave. If accurate, it suggests that during the contact period, Indians were conveying time-sensitive messages using painted images at established locations. This same practice might account for the canoe tallies mentioned by Eckstorm (1921:12), as well as the many canoe paintings (and tally marks) decorating the cliffs around the Great Lakes. During the seventeenth century, when the Ojibway were fending off encroachment from Iroquois invaders, they may have found it expedient to post intelligence regarding the movements of the Iroquois at existing pictograph sites along well-traveled routes.

Longley's assertions about paintings "on the face of the cliff" (Mead 1892) are also informative. He again notes the rust-colored washings, which he attributes to natural mineral stains from crevices. Mead estimates Longley's age at 50 years. If so, he would have been born after the Eel Weir dam had raised the water level, submerging any Indian cliffside images. But he could well have met folks old enough to remember the site before the dam was built.

A very similar account of canoe images in the cave turns up in an 1885 article (C. M. S. 1885:1), in which the author describes the remnants of a large Indian encampment that "must at some time have consisted of more than one hundred lodges." He writes:

> The locality was well chosen, the view up the lake being especially fine. Raymond Cape however shuts off a portion of the great basin but Jordan's Bay, Fry's, and Indian Islands are plainly visible, as is always a portion of the Images, which the guide book of the celebrated Sebago Lake route says were named from a fancied resemblance to something or other. I don't know what. The facts are these. During the French and Indian wars, from 1675 to 1748, the early settlers extending from the Saco river to ancient Falmouth, and inland to New Gloucester, were at constant warfare with the savages, men went armed to their fields or shut themselves up in the block houses, fearing that every dark nook and recess in the forest might contain an ambush. It was during these times that a party of whites had started up the lake to rescue if possible, a captive which the Indians had taken the night before from the settlement at Windham, and were carrying to Canada, the remainder of the family having been murdered. The rescue party consisted of some eight or ten men who were in two boats and well they knew the route of the Indians would be up the lake, on through Songo river, Brandy and Long ponds, at the head of which began the Piqwakett trail leading to Fryeburg, and so on to Canada.
>
> Now it has always been supposed that a part of the Indians were there in the caves of the Images with their captives and that the remainder were still behind their pursuers, having doubtless been raiding the settlements in some other locality, for when they reached the Images the savages had gone, but on the upper side wall of the water cave (as it is called, being unable to enter it without a boat) they found painted two boats containing white men facing up the lake, the number of men corresponding with their own party. These Images as they were called could be seen when near the cave without entering and it was supposed by the whites that they intended to give warning to their friends behind, indicating to them the number of the boats, the number of men in each boat, and the direction they were following.
>
> Time has long since obliterated all traces of the boats and their occupants and nothing now remains in the cavern to indicate the presence of the Indians. However, the figures remained a long time and there is yet living in Raymond one who has set upon his father's knees and heard him say that while quite a small boy the two images could be quite plainly seen.

This account suggests that the name "Images" may well have been inspired by images at the mouth of the cave, rather than any paintings on the cliff itself. It seems unlikely that their memory would have faded so quickly.

Finally, an article from 1886 rewards us with a date for the creation of the modern images (Bridgton News 1886a):

> Now the captain of the Sebago is a most enterprising gentleman, and a few weeks ago he engaged an artist to do an ingenious job for him. He put him ashore at the "Images" with instruction to "image" them. The young man camped there three or four days, and the work he did is extremely effective and is worth going miles to see. On the lowest boulder above the water's edge is painted the canoe with its Indian pointing up the lake; on the uppermost rock, labelled "Frye's Leap" is represented the hardy captain; in another place you see a faggot-fire burning; in another a tent; again there is an Indian tomahawking a white man, while another poor victim is being burned at the stake; on the opposite side is a squaw carrying a papoose on her back. The effect of these pictures upon this great rock-mass on the shore of the wide, lonely lake is indescribably weird. The painting is done in crude colors and is just barbarous enough in style to make it appear that the natives had done it themselves to remind us forever of their cruel sway in days gone by.

Ironically, it may have been the painting of the modern images that precipitated the changing of the name of the cliff from "The Images" to "Frye's Leap." Not only were the words "Frye's Leap" emblazoned in bold lettering across the top of the cliff, but reenactments of the leap became yet another tourist draw for steamer passengers. The August 20, 1886, paper (Bridgton News 1886b) reads:

> The painting of the Images on the Sebago Lake Route is completed and a big Indian has been engaged to appear on the high cliffs, dressed in full Indian costume, and fire a salute with cannon and fun as the steamer passes on her trips. Mr. Gibbs says he is perfecting arrangements whereby Capt. Frye shall daily make his great leap for life!

Over time, the real story behind "The Images" was lost and the name faded along with the modern paint. Meanwhile, local youths took to imitating Frye's "daring leap" themselves, despite the occasional fatal result.

Conclusions

Maine's two known pictograph sites share a number of features with those of the Canadian Shield. Both sites consist of red ochre images decorating prominent lakeside cliff faces along native travel routes. Given their proximity, both were likely visited by many of the same aboriginal travelers, shamans, warriors, and supplicants. And yet, from a pictorial perspective, there is little overlap. The Lovell site features finger-width "digital line" images, while the Raymond site favors broad strokes, bold washes, and ill-defined stains. Perhaps this was a reflection on the spirits that dwelt there. A powerful guardian turned to stone, little people sharing medicine, a thunderbird's nest—each would inspire its own pictorial response. Furthermore, historical references to painted canoes, now lost, reinforce the notion that not all images at a sacred venue were spiritual in nature. Maine's sites have suffered from considerable natural weathering and erosion, as well as human manipulation of water levels. However, their remnants provide valuable clues concerning the southeastern expression of a widespread pictograph tradition about which there is still much to learn.

References Cited

Albinger, Peter
   2014 Anishinaabe Pictographs On The Bloodvein: The Artery Lake Site. Electronic document, https://albinger.me/2014/08/24/anishinaabe-pictographs-on-the-bloodvein-the-artery-lake-site/, accessed August 2019.

Allen, Ned
   2013 *The Sebago Lakes Region: A Brief History*. The History Press, Charleston, South Carolina.

Arsenault, Daniel
   2004 Analyzing and Dating the Nisula Site, Quebec. In *The Rock-Art of Eastern North America: Capturing Images and Insight*, edited by Carol Diaz-Granados and James R. Duncan, pp. 344–360. The University of Alabama Press, Tuscaloosa, Alabama.

Arsenault, Daniel, and Dagmara Zawadzka
   2014 Spiritual Places: Canadian Shield Rock Art Within Its Sacred Landscape. In *Rock Art and Sacred Landscapes*, edited by Donna L. Gillette, Mavis Greer, Michele Helene Hayward, and William Breen Murray, pp. 117–137. One World Archaeology, Springer, New York.

Boyle, David
   1896 Archaeological Report 1894–95: Appendix to *Report of the Minister of Education Ontario*. Warwick Bros. & Rutter, Toronto.

Bridgton News
   1886a The Sebago Lake "Images." *The Bridgton News* 15(50):1, July 30, 1886. H. A. Shorey & Son, Bridgton, Maine. Electronic document, accessible via search at http://bridgton.advantage-preservation.com/, accessed September 21, 2019.

   1886b <Untitled clip>. The *Bridgton News* 17(1):2, August 20, 1886. H. A. Shorey & Son, Bridgton, Maine. Electronic document, accessible via search at http://bridgton.advantage-preservation.com/, accessed September 21, 2019.

C. M. S.
   1885 Old Indian Camping Ground at Sebago Lake. *The Bridgton News* 15(44):1, June 19, 1885. H. A. Shorey & Son, Bridgton, Maine. Electronic document, accessible via search at http://bridgton.advantage-preservation.com/, accessed September 21, 2019.

Colson, Alicia J. M.
   2007 What Do these Symbols Mean? A Critical Review of the Images Found on the Rocks of the Canadian Shield with Specific Reference to the Pictographs of the Lake of the Woods. In *Revista de Arqueología Americana, No. 25, Manifestaciones Simbolicas En Meso y Norte America*, pp. 101–185.

Conway, Thor
   1993 *Painted Dreams*. Northwood Press, Minocqua, Wisconsin.

Conway, Thor, and Julie Conway
   1990 *Spirits on Stone: the Agawa Pictographs*. Heritage Discoveries Books, San Luis Obispo, California.

C. O. S.
   1871 An account of a trip on the Sebago Lake Route on the little steamer Oriental. *Bridgton Weekly News* 1(41):2, June 23, 1871. H. A. Shorey & Son, Bridgton, Maine. Electronic document, accessible via search at http://bridgton.advantage-preservation.com/, accessed September 21, 2019.

Dewdney, Selwyn, and Kenneth E. Kidd
   1962 *Indian Rock Paintings of the Great Lakes*. University of Toronto Press, Toronto.

Eckstorm, Fannie Hardy
   1917 Maine Indian Legends. In Fannie Hardy Eckstorm Papers, University of Maine. Electronic document, https://digitalcommons.library.umaine.edu/eckstorm_papers/34/, accessed August, 2019.

   1921 Local Indian Place names, University of Maine. Electronic document, https://digitalcommons.library.umaine.edu/eckstorm_papers/ 37/, accessed August, 2019.

English, J. S.
    1906 White Mountain Legends. *New England Magazine* 35:97–112. America Company, Boston.

Geraghty, Gail
    2012 Protecting Prehistoric Sites in the Lakes Region. *The Bridgton News* (online), July 6, 2012, Bridgton, Maine. Electronic document, http://www.bridgton.com/protecting-prehistoric-sites-in-the-lakes-region/, accessed September 21, 2019.

Harman, Jon
    2008 Using Decorrelation Stretch to Enhance Rock Art Images. Electronic document, http://www.dstretch.com/AlgorithmDescription.html, accessed August, 2019.

Hedden, Mark
    2002 Review of Lenik's *Picture Rocks*. *E.S.R.A.R.A. Newsletter* 7(4):6–7.

Johnston, Robert A.
    1999 Why is Sebago Lake So Deep? Maine Geological Survey, Department of Agriculture, Conservation, & Forestry. Electronic document, https://digitalmaine.com/cgi/viewcontent.cgi?article=1315&context=mgs_publications, accessed July 2019.

Lenik, Edward J.
    2002 *Picture Rocks: American Indian Rock Art in the Northeast Woodlands*. University Press of New England, Hanover and London.

Lombard, Lucina Haynes
    1906 Longfellow's Vacations at Gorham. *Pine Tree Magazine* 7(1). Sale Publishing Company, Portland, Maine.

MacDonald, Brandi Lee
    2015 *Methodological Developments for the Geochemical Analysis of Ochre from Archaeological Contexts: Case Studies from British Columbia and Ontario, Canada*. Ph.D. Thesis, McMaster University, Hamilton, Ontario.

Mallery, Garrick
    1893 *Picture-Writing of the American Indians*. Tenth Annual Report of the Bureau of Ethnology 1888–'89, pp. 1–822. Smithsonian Institution, Washington, D.C. Facsimile reprint 1972, Dover Publications, New York.

Mead, James C.
    1892 Interesting Collection of Indian Relics. *The Bridgton News* 22(22):1, January 8, 1892. H. A. Shorey & Son, Bridgton, Maine. Electronic document, accessible via search at http://bridgton.advantage-preservation.com/, accessed September 21, 2019.

National Park Service
    1997 Native American Petroglyphs and Pictographs in Maine. National Registry of Historic Places Multiple Property Documentation Form. Electronic document, https://npgallery.nps.gov/NRHP/GetAsset/NRHP/64500267_text, accessed August 2019.

Norder, John W., and Jon W. Carroll
    2013 Applied Geospatial Perspectives on the Rock Art of the Lake of the Woods Region of Ontario, Canada. In *Emerging Methods and Multidisciplinary Applications in Geospatial Research*, edited by Donald P. Albert and C. Rebecca Dobbs, pp. 77–93. IGI Global, Hershey, Pennsylvania.

Parker, Arthur C.
    1922 *The Archaeological History of New York*. The University of the State of New York, Albany.

Patterson-Rudolph, Carol
    1996 Radiocarbon Dates for Pictographs. *E.S.R.A.R.A. Newsletter* 1(2):5.

Pickard, Samuel T.
    1897 *Hawthorne's First Diary with an Account of its Discovery and Loss*. Houghton, Mifflin and Company, Boston.

Piotrowski, Thaddeus
    2002 Indian Names in New Hampshire. In *The Indian Heritage of New Hampshire and Northern New England*, edited by Thaddeus Piotrowski, pp. 178–192. McFarland and Company, Jefferson, North Carolina.

Portland Board of Trade
    1910 The Songo River and Sebago Lake Region. *Board of Trade Journal* 23(1), May 1910. Portland, Maine.

Rajnovich, Grace
    1994 *Reading Rock Art: Interpreting the Indian Rock Paintings of the Canadian Shield*. National Heritage Books, Toronto, Canada.

Speck, Frank G.
    1935 Penobscot Tales and Religious Beliefs. *The Journal of American Folklore* 48(187):1–107.

Tilley, Christopher
    1994 *A Phenomenology of Landscape: Places, Paths and Monuments*. Berg, Oxford.

Vaillancourt, Pascale
    2008 The Kaapehpeshapischinikanuuch (EiGf-2) Site: Results of a Multidisciplinary Analysis of a Unique Rock-Art Site in the Nemiscau Lake Region. *Recherches amérindiennes au Québec* 38(2–3):109–125.

Ward, Robert Stafford
    1968 Longfellow's Roots in Yankee Soil. *The New England Quarterly* 41(2). MIT Press, Cambridge, Massachusetts.

Zawadzka, Dagmara
    2011 Spectacles to Behold: Colours in Algonquin Landscapes. *Totem: The University of Western Ontario Journal of Anthropology* 19(1):6–37.

    2013 Beyond the Sacred: Temagami Area Rock Art and Indigenous Routes. *Ontario Archaeology* (93):159–199.

    2016 *Cultivating Relations in the Landscape: Animism and Agency in the Rock Art of Temagami Region, Northeastern Ontario*. Ph.D. Thesis, Université du Québec à Montréal.

Samsal: A Bison-form Petroglyph Boulder Near the Sweet Grass Hills, Montana

Cynthia Sturm and James D. Keyser

The Samsal petroglyph boulder, located on the west flank of the Sweet Grass Hills in northern Montana, has both Hoofprint and Biographic tradition rock art. The boulder's shape, mimicking that of a reclining bison, is the reason the initial artists carved hoofprints, faces, cupules, and humans for ritual purposes. Lines, cupules, and a shaman are carved to emphasize the boulder's bison shape. A later artist, recognizing the boulder as sacred space, added his own war honor—a combat scene involving three warriors. This Biographic tradition scene is unique for Northern Plains petroglyph boulders, but like many scenes at nearby Writing-on-Stone, in Alberta.

Petroglyph boulders—also known as "buffalo stones," "ribstones," or "medicine rocks"—are widely scattered across the Northern Plains. They range from the Middle Missouri region of South Dakota north through western North Dakota and into Saskatchewan. Westward they are found across Montana north of the Missouri River and throughout southern Alberta to as far north as Edmonton (Figure 1). Most of these are glacial erratics, often of non-local material transported hundreds of kilometers by continental glaciation during the Pleistocene period, though some Montana erratics, including the Samsal boulder, are sandstone from local sources moved only short distances.

Often these boulders are smoothed and rounded by glacial transport and a few of them have naturally acquired the general shape of a reclining bison. These latter examples are often enhanced in various ways with added ribs, horns, facial features, and a dorsal spine to accentuate their resemblance to a bison. In addition, such stones often served as "scratching posts" for bison who frequently could be observed rubbing up against them to rid their hides of dirt, winter hair, and parasites. Such petroglyph boulders are widely reported in the ethnographic literature to have been venerated by local tribes who are reported to have left a wide variety of offerings at such sites (Grinnell 1908:162–163; Kroeber 1908:281).

The Samsal petroglyph boulder (24TL959), first reported in the literature by Brumley and Johnson (2012), is the farthest west example of this site type in Montana. In their article, Brumley and Johnson (2012) published what is primarily a photographic survey of the petroglyphs they recognized on the Samsal boulder. Several of their photographs show some of the images in sharp detail. As such that article is a "must-read" for anyone serious about comparing the Samsal boulder to others. However, the reader will quickly discern that our findings and interpretations differ in a few significant ways from those offered by Brumley and Johnson. While some of this is merely a matter of individual interpretation (e.g., whether one identifies an image as a snake or

Cynthia Sturm
*Oregon Archaeological Society,
Portland, Oregon*

James D. Keyser
*Oregon Archaeological Society,
Portland, Oregon*

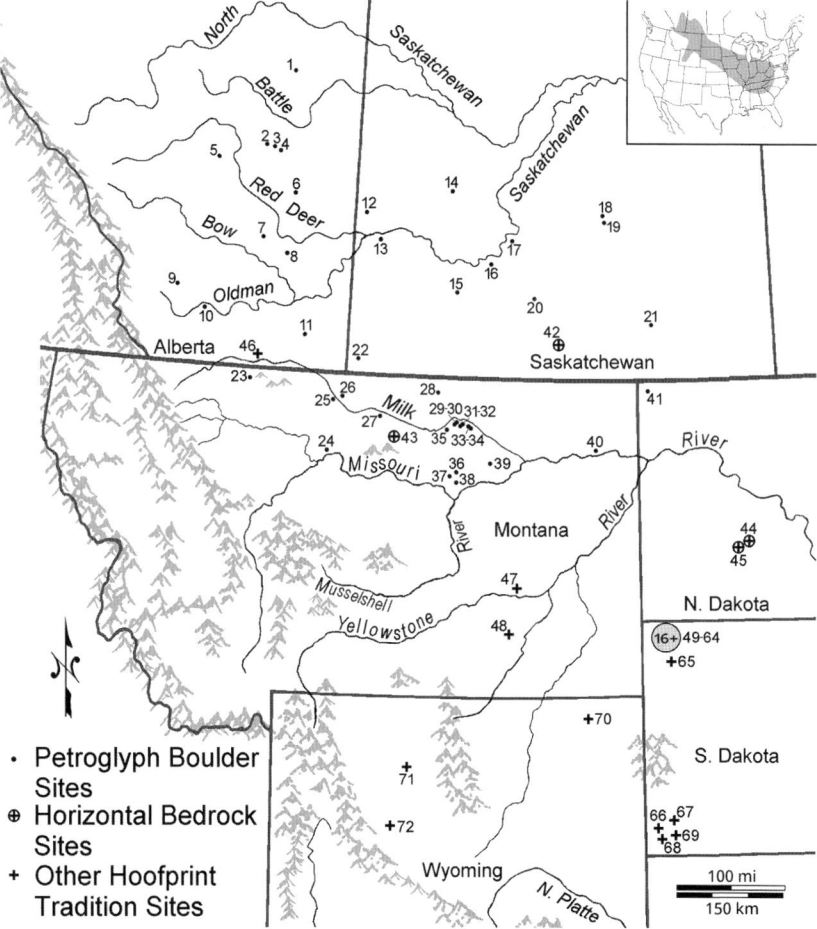

Figure 1. Petroglyph boulders and other Hoofprint tradition sites across the Northern Plains. Note: the gray circle in far northwestern South Dakota represents a cluster of 16 Hoofprint tradition sites in the North Cave Hills. Site numbers correspond to those on Tables 2 and 3. Inset shows distribution of Hoofprint rock art across North America.

the Samsal family and obtained permission. Then, during September of 2018, a small field crew from the Oregon Archaeological Society (OAS) visited the site with McCormick and several members of the Samsal family. The family participated with us in making a detailed recording of the images that had been reported to be pecked on the boulder, and Mrs. Randi Samsal even found a small endscraper in a rodent backdirt pile just north of the boulder.

The Site and Its Setting

The Samsal boulder sits a short distance below the crest of a low ridge just 10 km (6 mi) west of West Butte, the westernmost of the three Sweet Grass Hills. Because the boulder sits below the ridge crest on its west side, West Butte—even though it rises slightly more than 275 meters (900 ft) above the surrounding prairie—is not visible from the site. However, an observer can see the boulder from more than a kilometer away when approaching it from the north or northwest. The general site location is typical Northern Plains shortgrass prairie. Other major rock art sites and site complexes are found at Writing-on-Stone on the Milk River, just 15 km (10 mi) to the north; the Kevin Rim, 25 km (15 mi) west; and the lower Cut Bank Creek area, about 65 km (40 mi) to the southwest (Figure 2). A major Foothills Abstract tradition site in the Sweet Grass Hills is Mask Cave on Middle Butte, less than 30 km (19 mi) southeast. The nearest currently known petroglyph boulders are in the Havre and Big Sandy, Montana, areas, 120 km (75 mi) to the east.

The boulder itself is a large, slightly curved slab of local sandstone, transported only a few kilometers at most by the action of continental glaciers. This transport roughly rounded off the corners of the otherwise rectangular slab and left it sitting upright to form a shape that resembles a reclining bison (Figure 3). A large piece of the slab has begun to detach along a weakness between sedimentary layers in the piece but sits essentially parallel with the larger slab on its south side.

instead just a curved line—see discussion of the images, below), other issues are important and merit detailed discussion. This occurs primarily in the sections on the boulder's resemblance to a reclining bison.

After reading the original article (Brumley and Johnson 2012), we desired to see the Samsal boulder because the human face and combat scene carved[1] on it held particular interest. The face is unique for this area, but similar to others at several Hoofprint tradition sites to the east, and the combat scene is unique for a petroglyph boulder site, though it has many counterparts on vertical faces at Writing-on-Stone and other sites throughout Montana. Likewise, the presence of two shield-bearing warriors in a scene like this is uncommon in Northern Plains art (Keyser and Poetschat 2014). Thus, we asked Tom McCormick, our local partner in the Cut Bank petroglyph project (Keyser 2017), if he could contact the Samsal family and obtain permission to visit the site. In early 2018 Tom contacted

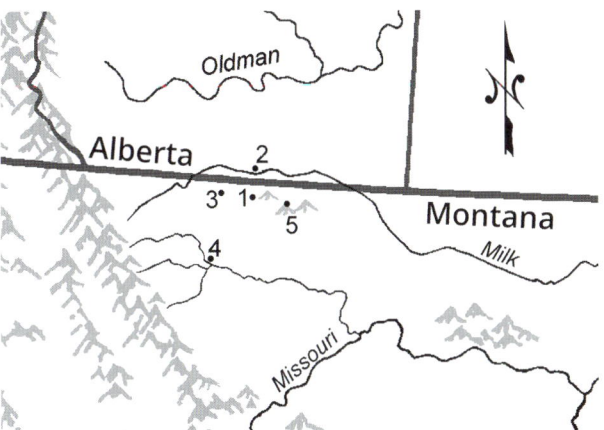

Figure 2. Rock art sites in the area of the Samsal boulder. 1, Samsal boulder; 2, Writing-on-Stone; 3, Kevin Rim pictograph; 4, Cut Bank Creek sites; 5, Mask Cave.

Figure 3. Profile view of the Samsal boulder (top) compared to the profile of a reclining bison (bottom). Photograph by David Minick.

Outcrops of similar sandstone in the immediate vicinity suggest that the boulder has been moved only a short distance, a fact consistent with its fragility, relatively angular shape, and minimal geologically caused rounding. Had the boulder been transported any great distance it would likely have been destroyed. The boulder measures 2.8 m long and rises about 150 cm above the relatively level ground surface. As with many such boulders, there is a slight depression surrounding it, caused by the trampling of bison who typically rub up against stones like this when using them as "scratching posts."

Despite the report by Brumley and Johnson (2012:45) that "there are no smoothed and/or polished areas on this boulder's surface indicating that buffalo or…cattle have ever rubbed upon it," we believe that there is extensive indication of such animal modification. The boulder's shape shows smoothing along the rear two-thirds of the dorsal "spine," the "head" end, and the north face, all of which is smoothing or rounding unlike most of the back side of the boulder. All of these places are low enough that they could have been rubbed by a bison using its head, neck, the side of its body, or even its underbelly to abrade and round off the angular edges of the stone. In addition, the only parts of the rest of the boulder to show such rounding are the slightly smoothed top of the primary slab and the most forward part of the secondary slab behind it. Both of these are relatively high places on the slab(s) where a bison-sized animal, having put his head over the stone while standing on its north side and then turning his head to the left, could have rubbed his upper throat and jaw against them. The presence of so much smoothed area on the front (north) side of the boulder versus almost none on the rear (south) side is easily explained by the position of this second, lower slab, which parallels the larger, higher one but precludes an animal's easy access to the slightly incurving surface of the larger one, which also leans to the north (Figure 4). This would have effectively precluded a bison-sized animal closely approaching the rear of the stone to rub against it.

The evidence indicates that such rubbing occurred both before and during the time the boulder was modified by the carving of images. The north side was obviously smoothed before most of the extant images were carved, though we cannot determine if there were earlier images completely rubbed away. The occurrence of one very shallow hoofprint suggests there might have been earlier carvings. We can demonstrate that some of the abrasion was during precontact times based on the much greater rounding of the pecked lines in the Indian imagery when com-

Figure 4. This end-on view of the Samsal boulder shows it is a relatively thin slab of sandstone that could have been transported only a short distance by continental glaciation. The concave shape of the slab's back side would have precluded animals rubbing against it to smooth that surface. All petroglyphs are along the boulder's dorsal spine and on its front (right) side, which shows extensive smoothing from animal rubbing. Photograph by David Minick.

pared to those in the 1894 graffito. However, the slight erosion of the lines in the graffito indicates there has almost certainly been some minimal cattle rubbing against the stone, possibly up until quite recently, since the barbed-wire animal enclosure currently surrounding the boulder is not present in the 2010 photographs (Brumley and Johnson 2012:41–43).

Site Recording Methods

The photographic recording of the Samsal boulder by Brumley and Johnson (2012) was enough to establish there were both Hoofprint and Biographic tradition art carved on the boulder. However, no detailed tracings of images were provided in that report. Thus, on September 16, 2018, the authors and five other field crew members visited the site to make a rubbing of the boulder's carved surfaces and to make direct tracings of some of the images. Site owners Randi Samsal and her son Jason observed the recording project. The rubbing was done using graphite and green vegetation in order to expose a negative copy of the images carved on the boulder (Figure 5). We used this rubbing technique because it was obvious that the boulder had been seriously abraded along its top ridge and on its north face by bison and possibly cattle rubbing up against it. A rubbing done in this manner does no harm to the bedrock but often brings out very faint, highly eroded images that would be difficult—if not impossible—to recognize any other way (Keyser and Poetschat 2012:12–13). We also made direct tracings of several of the more deeply pecked images on the boulder using Sharpie® pens on clear plastic.

Objects Left at the Site as Offerings

During our visit to the Samsal petroglyph boulder, we found two artifacts that appear to have been left at the site as offerings. The first is a small endscraper found by Mrs. Randi Samsal, owner of the property on which the boulder is located. The Samsal family currently has this scraper in their possession. The second was a small modern tobacco bundle made of ribbon, which we found at the site, then examined and photographed, and left in place.

The small endscraper, made on a flake of translucent, dark caramel-colored chert (Figure 6), was found within two meters of the boulder atop a backdirt pile at the entrance to a ground squirrel burrow within the fenced area enclosing the Samsal boulder. Although somewhat resembling Knife River Flint, this chert did not fluoresce when subjected to ultraviolet light, as Knife River Flint is known to do (Evilsizer 2016:62-64). Thus, it must

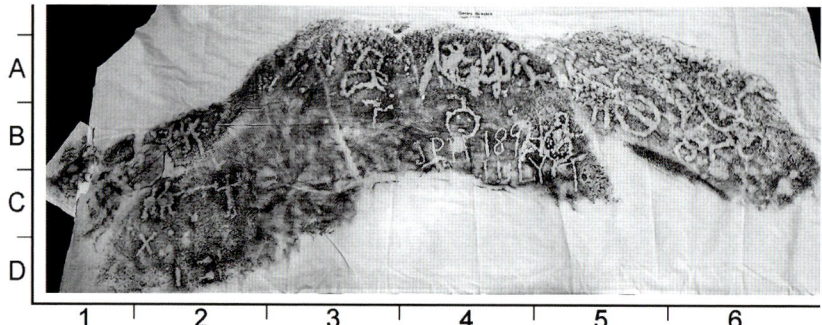

Figure 5. Our rubbing of the petroglyphs on the Samsal boulder. Grid to aid in location of various motifs. Photograph by David Kaiser.

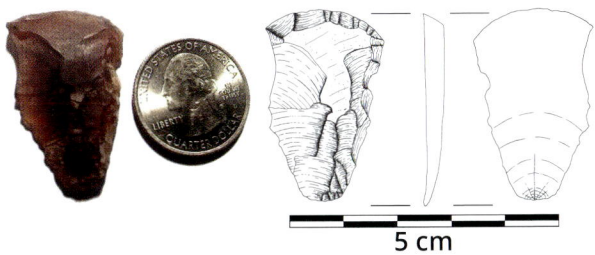

Figure 6. This endscraper, found in a rodent backdirt pile near the Samsal boulder, probably represents a votive offering. Photograph by Randi Samsal, drawing by Keyser.

be one of the many other Northwestern Plains lithic raw materials of similar caramel color. The small flake scraper shows minimal wear on its working end and was clearly discarded at the site before it had exhausted its potential use-life. Cursory examination revealed no other prehistoric artifacts or lithic debitage in the site area.

The absence of any other indication of occupation in the area of the boulder strongly suggests this was an offering left here because of the petroglyphs. Similar archaeological offerings have been found at other Hoofprint tradition petroglyph boulders (Park 1990:46), and even today perishable offerings of tobacco, red cloth, and ribbons are occasionally found at such sites. One such offering was noted at the Samsal boulder during our visit.

A brightly colored "holiday" ribbon, folded into a small packet and tied with white cotton string, was found on the ground just in front of the Samsal boulder (Figure 7). The wired ribbon, decorated with appliqued gold and silver glitter in a curvilinear pattern, is hemmed with a red plastic border that contains a small-gauge wire, permitting the ribbon to be folded into the small bundle shape that was then tied and left at the site. The bundle itself measures nine centimeters in maximum dimension. Erosion and discoloration of the material, which has removed the glitter in some places, indicates that the packet has lain at the site for several years. In a few small places—especially where the material was in contact with the soil—the hem has separated from the fabric and it is possible to see inside the bundle and observe flakes of a brown leafy material that is almost certainly tobacco. Modern offerings of this sort involving colored cloth, ribbons, and tobacco are frequently found at Northern Plains rock art sites, and they are especially common at petroglyph boulders (Fig-

Figure 7. This small bundle of tobacco is a modern votive offering left at the Samsal boulder. The packet is made of a holiday ribbon folded around a few shreds of leaf tobacco and tied with a string. Photograph by David Kaiser.

ure 8). Such offerings are known to be placed at these sites by members of nearly all Plains Indian tribes.

We did not observe the alignment of small stones (apparently cobbles from glacial till) photographed by Brumley and Johnson (2012:42–43) at the base of the boulder in front of the face on which most of the petroglyphs are carved. They note that this alignment appeared at the time of their visit to be relatively recent, based on how little the individual stones were "sodded in" (Brumley and Johnson 2012:42). All we noted in the area of this alignment were a few cobbles (that might be some of those in the photographs) laying scattered in front of the boulder. Given the demonstrated use of the site in recent times by native people we suspect that if this stone alignment was intentional, it was placed

Figure 8. Votive offerings at other sites. (a) Indian Lake Petroglyph boulder (site 38); (b) Thunderbird Cave, Writing-on-Stone (site 46). Photographs courtesy of Mavis and John Greer (a) and David Kaiser (b).

there relatively recently, like the tobacco bundle. Possibly it was done for similar reasons, but whether it was put there by American Indian visitors or others cannot be determined.

The Petroglyphs

Rock art at the Samsal boulder consists solely of pecked petroglyphs found on the north-facing side and the ridgetop of the sandstone boulder. Classification of the imagery pecked on the boulder identified more than 40 separate elements that includes anthropomorphs, zoomorphs, items of material culture, and various geometric images (Table 1). Although most of these images are scattered across the surface of the boulder without any apparent order, two groups are arranged in recognizable compositions. One of these is a combat scene between three humans that also has a large X-shape associated with it, and the other is the boulder itself, whose natural form has been modified with cupules to accentuate its resemblance to a reclining bison. There is also one Historic graffito pecked onto the north face of the boulder.

Anthropomorphs

Six anthropomorphs are pecked on the Samsal boulder. Three of these are warriors engaged in a combat scene (Figures 5C/2 and 9), two are faces (Figures 5D/2, B/4, 10 and 11), and the other is an upside-down human (Figures 5B/6 and 12) carved on what would be the top of the head of the reclining bison form. Two of the three humans in the combat

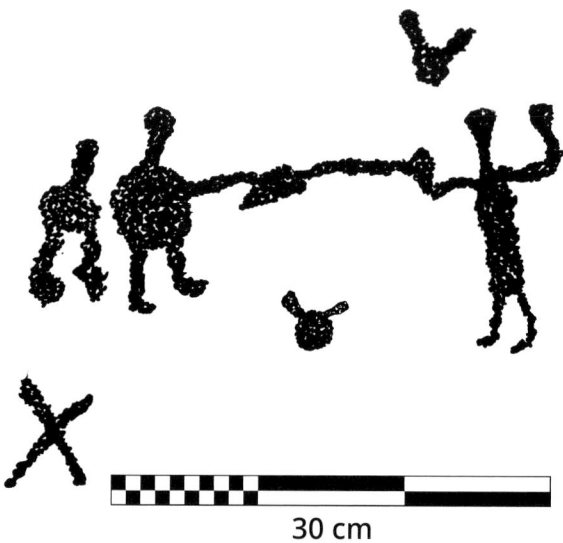

Figure 9. Direct tracing of the Biographic tradition combat scene on Samsal boulder. Note small shield size, outsized triangular spear point, and X at lower left. Two "eared" cupules are also juxtaposed with the scene.

scene are shield-bearing warriors who carry relatively small shields. Both have two legs, plantigrade feet, and a long neck topped by a relatively small round head. The lead warrior of these two has a short club, which extends outward at about the 3 o'clock position on the

Table 1. Motifs on the Samsal Boulder

Anthropomorphs
- Shield-bearing warriors — 2
- Rectangular-body humans — 2
- Faces — 2

Zoomorphs
- Hoofprint — 1
- Bear Paw — 1

Bison composition (entire stone)
- Nose (two nostrils/cupules) — 1
- Modified spine — 1

Composition
- Battle Scene — 1

Material Culture
- Shield — 2
- Spear — 1
- Club — 1
- Headdress/Hairstyle — 2
- Rattle — 1
- Feather Fan — 1

Geometric Images
- Freestanding "line and dot" — 1
- Bisected Oval — 1
- "X" — 1
- Abstracts — 6
- Cupules — 14
- Eared cupules — 2

Graffiti
- Date and initials "J.P.H. 1894 July 7" — 1

Total — 45

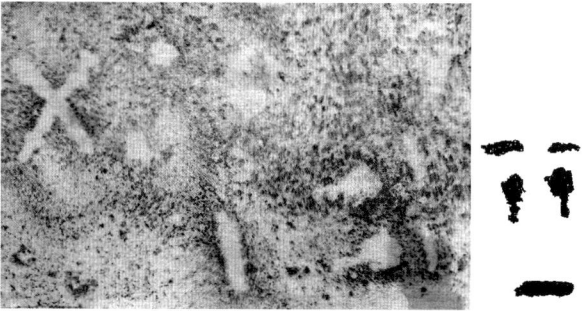

Figure 10. Rubbing and "flood-fill" photo-tracing of simpler face on Samsal boulder. Note eyebrows and tear streaks. Horizontal position is accurate placement. Photo-tracing (at right) rotated for ease of recognition.

Figure 11. Direct tracing of more complex face, graffito, and associated images. Initial "H" has impacted the neck of the face.

Figure 12. This human, wearing a bison-horn headdress and holding objects in each hand, is pecked on the forehead area of the reclining bison shape of the Samsal boulder. On the boulder, the human is in an inverted position (see Figure 5B/6). Phototracing done with flood-fill technique.

shield's circumference. This warrior appears to use his club to defend against the much larger spear of the attacking warrior.

Using the measurement system designed by Keyser (2010:90–94) these men's shields are both just more than 27 inches (70 cm) in diameter, which places them directly within the range of equestrian shields from either the Protohistoric or Historic periods. Such a date, between about A.D. 1700 and 1800, is consistent with the weaponry—a long spear tipped with an outsized triangular point—which is thrust at the shield bearers by what appears to be the victorious warrior. Both of these shield bearers, with their long necks, small heads, and characteristic weapons including relatively small shields fit comfortably in the Blackfoot style of shield-bearing warriors (Keyser and Poetschat 2014:58–64).

Two rectangular-body humans are carved on the boulder. One is a tall, solidly pecked human in the combat scene. He has short legs, plantigrade feet, a small round head atop a long neck, and two arms that extend straight out to his sides and bend up at the elbows to end in round blobs for hands. With the left hand[2] he thrusts a long spear, tipped with an outsized triangular point, at the lead shield-bearing warrior, who parries this thrust with a club.

The second rectangular-body human (Figures 5B/6) is positioned upside-down at what would be the crown of the reclining bison's head. When viewed in a rightside-up position (Figure 12) the human has a round head surmounted with distinctly curved bison horns representing a bison-horn headdress, somewhat hunched shoulders, arms extending out to each side of the body, and at least one leg that curves out and up from the bottom of the body. The leg on the right side of the body is lost in a large pecked geometric abstract image. At the end of the right arm is a large globular shape that appears to represent a rattle and at the end of the left arm is a more fan-shaped item that we identify as a feather fan. Both are typical objects used in Plains ceremonies. There is a triangular pecked area in the center of this human's chest in the approximate position of the heart. The positioning of the figure—with its explicitly curved bison horns—on the crown of the reclining bison's head is almost certainly not coincidental.

The two other human figures are faces. One is a simple, horizontally oriented face. If we view this face in the natural upright position, it shows two eyes with eyebrows above, positioned just above a straight-line mouth. Each eye has a short, straight tear streak extending downward from its bottom center. The second face is a circular head atop a solidly pecked short neck. The head has two short stubby ears, two eyes, and a small oval mouth. A short scalplock, formed of a single pecked line extends upward and bends to the left. The neck region is heavily impacted by the letter "H" in the initials graffito that was carved on the panel in 1894.

Zoomorphs

In addition to the reclining bison formed by the entirety of the boulder as elaborated by pecked elements (see Compositions, below), there are two zoomorphs represented on the boulder by a cloven hoofprint and a bear paw print. The bear paw (Figures 5A/3 and 13) shows a long crudely rectangular pad

Figure 13. Bear paw with associated rectangle (above) and short line (below). Photo-tracing done with flood-fill technique.

with three long curved claws extending out and down from the right end. One short stubby appendage below these three probably represents a fourth claw. This paw print is conflated with a second rectangular form, which appears to be superimposed on the paw print, but erosion of the boulder surface and lichen growing in the pecked grooves precluded us from determining the superimposition sequence with certainty.

The second zoomorph is a cloven ungulate hoofprint that was revealed when we made the rubbing of the boulder's highly abraded surface (Figures 5C/2–3 and 14). This rubbing technique enables

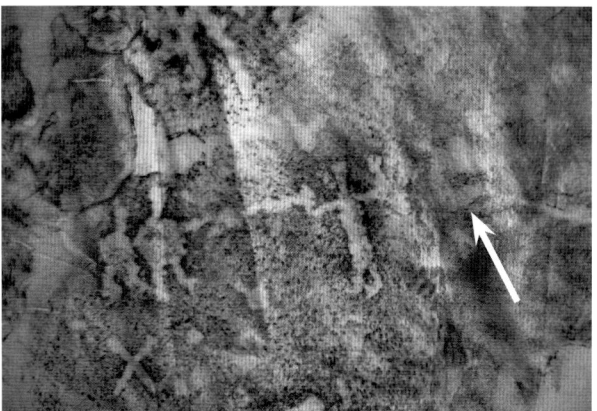

Figure 14. The arrow indicates the very eroded hoofprint revealed by our rubbing technique to be just to the right of the combat scene.

the recorder to identify very eroded lines (Keyser and Poetschat 2012:21), which is what happened in this instance. After we made the rubbing, we were able to feel the slight indentation for the hoofprint, confirming its existence. The hoofprint itself is a cloven hoof showing two horizontally oriented, teardrop-shaped toes separated by an unpecked central ridge. No dewclaws could be located. This is a typical deer or bison track in Hoofprint tradition rock art (Keyser 1984:13, 41–45).

Material Culture Items

Half of the eight material culture items depicted on the boulder occur in the biographic scene involving three warriors (Figure 9). In this battle scene there are two shields, each partially covering the torso of the two warriors on the left. Based on measurements relative to their body size (Keyser 2010:90–94), both are equestrian-period shields. Two combatants carry weapons, the larger warrior on the right in the scene thrusts a long spear with an outsized triangular point toward the two shield-bearing warriors on the left. The forwardmost shield bearer uses a much shorter club as if to parry his opponent's spear thrust.

Three additional items of material culture are worn or held by a human pecked on what would be the bison's head. This human (Figure 12) wears a bison horn headdress, represented by long, emphatically curved horns at each side of the top of his head. Such headdresses were common in all Plains Indian groups. In his right hand he holds a large round, bulbous "instrument," which we identify as a rattle. In his left hand he holds a more fan-shaped instrument, which we identify as a feather fan. Both the rattle and fan are typical items used by shamans in religious ceremonies.

The other item of dress is the hairstyle worn by the face pecked on the smoothed surface of the boulder. Drawn as a single line, it almost certainly represents a scalplock—a single braid arising from the rear center of the head and typically hanging down the person's back. It was a common hairstyle in many Plains tribes.

Geometric Images

Various geometric images pecked on the Samsal boulder include two very simple "characters" and six more complex abstract designs. The characters are a clearly depicted bisected oval on the crest of the boulder at its west (head) end (Figure 5B/5) and a large X on the opposite end of the boulder on the smooth north face, below the biographic scene of fighting warriors (Figure 5D/2). The X may represent a "coup mark" and is discussed in greater detail in the context of the "Combat Scene." The bisected oval (Figures 15 and 16) is a typical Hoofprint tradition image found at several other petroglyph boulders and other sites of the Hoofprint tradition (Tables 2, 3). In its various guises it has been interpreted as either a vulvaform or a hoofprint; in fact, this example could be either.

We recorded seven geometric abstracts. A rectilinear "box" is conflated with the bear paw image, but

Figure 15. At the top of the forehead of the reclining bison's profile prehistoric artists carved a bisected oval and a rectangular geometric form (indicated by arrow). The rectangular form has been heavily abraded by animals leaning across the top of the boulder to use the dorsal spine as a scratching post. Although the human with bison-horn headdress is upside down below the bisected oval in this photograph (cf. Figure 5B/6), it is difficult to see due to the heavy lichen growth. Photograph by David Minick.

Figure 16. Flood-fill photo-tracing of the bisected oval and rectilinear geometric on the Samsal boulder.

does not appear obviously related to it, and the erosion is such that it is not clear which image is superimposed on the other. A second very simple abstract is a pair of short line segments associated with two dots pecked just below the bear paw. This pair of lines and dots are discussed in more detail below. Five other areas of more complex line clusters appear to be abstract compositions or images that are either too eroded or too enigmatic to identify with any certainty. The simplest of these is a group of four or five straight lines that intersect to form a crude letter-like image along the boulder's spine just above the combat scene. We suspect this is part of the modification of the crest of the boulder done as part of the effort to recognize its bison effigy shape. Four more complex curvilinear scrawls occur higher on the boulder from near its crest and at the top of the smooth north face to the area of the human with horned headdress. Just to the right of the human face and superimposed by the graffito (Figures 5B/5 and 11) is a somewhat pear-shaped image that has a reasonably good resemblance to a Shmoo—a cartoon character named by the cartoonist Al Capp. A circular head-shape sits "atop" the oval, pear-shaped "body" and there are two lines somewhat suggestive of appendages. However, the image (like the nearby face) is heavily eroded by animal rubbing in some places, and the graffito "Y" overlaps the area where a second leg might have been. While the rounded form is suggestive of an anthropomorphic figure, there are simply not enough attributes to actually identify it as such. Finally, just to the left of the bisected oval is a rectilinear pecked area with short appendages that is discussed below.

Two petroglyphs in our "Geometric" category have been previously identified (Brumley and Johnson 2012:42) as biological forms. The first of these is a short, curved line with a bulbous upper end, which is situated just below the bear paw (Figures 13 and 17). Brumley and Johnson identify this as a snake. In fact, this very short line segment has only one bend to the right, and it is part of a pair of short lines. The bulbous end is part of a pair of small cupules. While it is possible this petroglyph does represent a snake, snakes in Plains rock art typically show a longer, more zigzag body and usually have rattles distinctly depicted. While this image appears to have a series of dints at its lower end that could be interpreted as rattles (Figure 17, arrow), the rubbing (Figure 13) shows these individual dints are, in fact, in a shallow, pecked groove, which is now heavily eroded by animals rubbing against this surface and can be identified only by this rubbing technique. This calls into question whether the appearance of these "rattles" is a product of erosion, or an intentional design element. In any case this image is much shorter than would be typical for a snake representation, and it is part of a group of pecked lines and dots (Figure 13), so we include it here as a geometric.

Brumley and Johnson (2012:42) also tentatively identified the image just "above" the bisected oval as a stylized human handprint (Figures 15 and 16). We were far less convinced of this identification, noting that parts of the image are heavily abraded and that

Table 2. Petroglyph Boulder Sites on the Northern Plains

Map Number	State/Province Site	Buffalo Form	Ribs Indicated	Facial Features	Hoofprint	Vulvaform	Bear Paw	Bird Track	Bird	Bison Head	Turtle	Snake	Quadruped	Human	Hand Print	Foot Print	Face	Tear Streaks	Bisected Oval	Circle	Cross	Cross in Circle	Zigzag	Line	Cupules	Abstract	Pit & Groove
	Alberta																										
1	Viking (group)	ISK/RST	✓																						✓	✓	✓
2	Byemoor	RB		✓	✓													✓								✓	✓
3	Endiang (group)	RST	✓																						✓	✓	✓
4	Scapa	RB																							✓	✓	
5	Trochu				✓	✓											✓								✓	✓	✓
6	Sunnynook	RB											✓												✓	✓	
7	Kekip																								✓	✓	✓
8	Millicent															✓										✓	✓
9	EbPk-18	RB	✓																		✓					✓	
10	Monarch													✓							✓	✓				✓		
11	Foremost/Stevens														✓						✓					✓	✓	
	Saskatchewan																										
12	Cabri Lake																				✓		✓		✓			
13	Leader																								✓			
14	Herschel (group)															✓	✓				✓	✓			✓		✓	✓
15	Swiftcurrent				Xx									✓							✓	✓	✓		✓			
16	Gouldtown														✓						✓							
17	Riverhurst																		✓									
18	Swanston															✓	✓											
19	Last Mountain															✓	✓											
20	Wood River															✓												
21	Weyburn															✓	✓											
22	Vidora				x	✓							✓															
	Montana																										
23	Samsal	RB	✓	✓	x	?	✓			?			✓							✓	✓			✓		✓	✓
24	CM Russell								✓		✓															✓	✓	
25	24HL91																									✓	✓	
26	24HL635				x									✓														
27	Wahkpa Chu'gn				x																							
28	Lyman Corney	RST	✓																									
29	Buffalo Plunge (grp)				XX					✓				✓		✓		✓								✓		
30	Cree Crossing				XX	✓															✓							
31	LaFond				x		✓													✓	✓	✓			✓		✓	
32	Buster Aiken				x		✓																				✓	
33	Sleeping Buffalo	RB	✓	✓																								
34	Monument				XX	✓									✓	✓					✓				✓			
35	Simanton (group)				XX	✓			✓												✓	✓	✓	✓				
36	Tank Coulee				Xx			✓					✓	✓							✓						✓	
37	Second Creek (grp)				x																✓						✓	
38	Indian Lake				XX	✓															✓	✓	✓					
39	24VL224				Xx	✓									✓	✓												
40	24RV1026				XX																					✓		
	North Dakota																										
41	Writing Rock (grp)					✓															✓					✓	✓	✓

RST = Ribstone   RB = Reclining Bison Form   ISK = Iniskim Form
x = 1- 5 hoofprints   Xx = 6 - 10 hoofprints   XX = 11 or more hoofprints   ? = Probable Occurrence

most handprints on other petroglyph boulders are more realistic than this image. However, during the last stage of editing, Ken Hedges remarked that this design of a bisected oval and the juxtaposed geometric previously identified as a stylized human handprint could easily be interpreted as a vulva capture scene (see Kaiser and Keyser 2020:34). We had not previously noted this striking correspondence, and are grateful to Ken for pointing it out. Such a composition would be well within the function of rock art imagery in both the Hoofprint and Biographic traditions and further work at the site might clarify whether this is, in fact, an example of vulva capture.

Cupules

Multiple cupules are pecked on the Samsal boulder; we count 18 in total. Many of these appear on the upper dorsal crest of the boulder (Figure 18b) and may have had some ritual purpose—possibly to emphasize its effigy bison shape—in addition to being a design feature. Cupules on the boulder's "head" end appear placed to represent eyes or nostrils and those on the tail end are where kidneys and the tail root are often indicated on other bison effigy boulders (cf. Figures 18b and 19). Large natural depressions at the top of the "hump" might well have served as an offertory receptacle, similar to a pecked depression on the Sleeping Buffalo boulder found near Malta, Montana (Figure 19).

Two cupules, located just above and below the combat scene, have small "ears" creating a peculiar V-shaped profile for the small marks (Figure 9). These are obviously intentional in both cases, but we cannot imagine any reason for them or determine with any veracity whether they were meant as part of the combat scene.

Graffito

A single graffito—J.P.H. 1894 JULY 7—mars the abraded-smooth vertical north face of the Samsal boulder. The initials and date are pecked over the very obvious face and the Shmoo-like figure in a finer and less weathered script than the underlying petroglyphs (Figures 11, 17). Local lore has this graffito being carved by a North West Mounted Policeman (a "Mountie") traveling here from the nearby Mounted Police Outpost at Writing-on-Stone (only 15 km distant). There is even rumor of a second inscription with the same initials somewhere in the nearby Sweet Grass Hills. Despite our best efforts and those of the Samsal family we were unable to get more specific information about this local legend.

Searching the archives of the Royal Canadian Mounted Police (the organization descended from the North West Mounted Police), we were able to identify only a single Mountie, James Perley Hicks, with those initials during that time period. Hicks was posted at Medicine Hat and Maple Creek outposts between 1882 and 1898. He was employed principally as a teamster, and re-enlisted for a second tour of duty in 1894.

Table 3. Other Hoofprint Tradition Sites on the Northern Plains

Map Number	State/Province Site	Hoofprint	Horse Hoofprint	Vulvaform	Animals						Humans				Geometrics					
					Bear Paw	Bird Track	Other Track	Elk	Bison Head	Turtle	Quadruped	Human	Hand Print	Foot Print	Face	Bisected Oval	Circle	Cross	Zigzag	Line	Abstract	Cupules
HORIZONTAL SURFACES																						
	Saskatchewan																					
42	St. Victor	XXX		✓*	✓				✓			✓	✓	✓	✓						✓	✓
	Montana																					
43	Snake Butte	Xx		✓*									✓		✓							
	North Dakota																					
44	32GT129	XX			✓	✓			✓													
45	Pretty Rock Butte	x																				
VERTICAL CLIFF SURFACES																						
	Alberta																					
46	Thunderbird Cave	x																				
	Montana																					
47	Porcupine Lookout	XX		✓																		
48	Recognition Rock	XX		✓	✓		✓						✓								✓	
	South Dakota																					
49	39HN1	x		✓	✓									✓								
50	39HN17	XX		✓		✓						✓	✓								✓	
51	39HN54	x		✓													✓					
52	39HN120	x																				
53	39HN121	x		✓																		
54	39HN159	XX						✓														
55	39HN160	x		✓				✓			✓											
56	39HN171	XX	✓	✓																	✓	
57	39HN205	XX																				
58	39HN209	x	✓																			
59	39HN210	XX	✓	✓								✓	✓									
60	39HN227	XX	✓	✓	✓							✓	✓		✓							
61	39HN228	x																				
62	39HN232	x	✓					✓														
63	39HN234	Xx		✓																		
64	39HN487	Xx																				
65	39HN433	x			✓	✓		✓														
66	39FA7	Xx		✓	✓							✓	✓	✓	✓							
67	39FA58	x		✓	✓																	
68	39FA79	x										✓	✓									
69	39FA277	XX																				
	Wyoming																					
70	Medicine Crk Cave	XX		✓	✓		✓															
71	No Water	XX		✓		✓						✓									✓	
72	Red Canyon	XX													✓							

✓* = with penisform in copulation scene
x = 1- 5 hoofprints Xx = 6 - 10 hoofprints XX= 11 or more hoofprints XXX= 100 + hoofprints

Both Medicine Hat and Maple Creek are 125–160 km (80 and 100 miles) to north and northeast of Writing-on-Stone, but as a teamster it seems quite possible that Hicks might well have made trips to the Writing-on-Stone outpost and from there gone to visit the Samsal boulder. We know that many different Mounties at the Writing-on-Stone outpost were fascinated with the rock art there and carved their names or initials and dates on many of those sites.

Compositions

There are two compositions evident on the Samsal boulder. One of these is the combat scene pecked into the north-facing side of the boulder, which involves three warriors and their weapons. It may also include a large X pecked just below the fight scene. The second composition is more holistic in that it involves several groups of petroglyphs that are positioned on the boulder to highlight its shape, which resembles a reclining bison. These images are placed in their respective locations to help the boulder itself correspond to generalized Plains cosmological principles.

Reclining Bison

We view the Samsal boulder as representing a reclining bison, based on its overall profile (Figure 3) and the position of various petroglyphs carved upon it. However, our view differs significantly from what appears at first glance to be a very similar interpretation offered by Brumley and Johnson (2012:39, 42). Basically, we believe Brumley and Johnson err in identifying the "bison's" silhouette as having its head pointing to the east. They do this in three places, once saying it directly ("the head end [points] to the east") and in two other descriptive statements referring to cupules and lines being placed on the "forehead" and "bridge of the nose" areas. Taking them at their word, this indicates they see the boulder's highest point as the top of a bison's head with a long down-sloping "forehead" and a relatively long, flat nose extending out to the east. However, this is not the profile of a bison's head (or skull) let alone that of a reclining bison (cf. Figures 3, 19, 20). The only animals with a head shape like this are elk and horse, but Brumley and Johnson clearly state they see this as a bison. In addition, it is highly unlikely that this was originally seen as a horse's head by local Indians, since most of the art on the boulder almost certainly predates the Plains Indians' acquisition of that animal.

Our interpretation of the boulder's profile is almost the exact opposite (Figures 3, 18). We see the highest part of it at its west end (the right end when looking at the boulder facing the carved surface) as representing the bison's hump, which then creates a

Figure 17. The north face of the Samsal boulder, smoothed by large animals rubbing against it, was chosen as the "canvas" for most petroglyphs. Arrow shows location of dints at the end of the curved line. Photograph by David Minick.

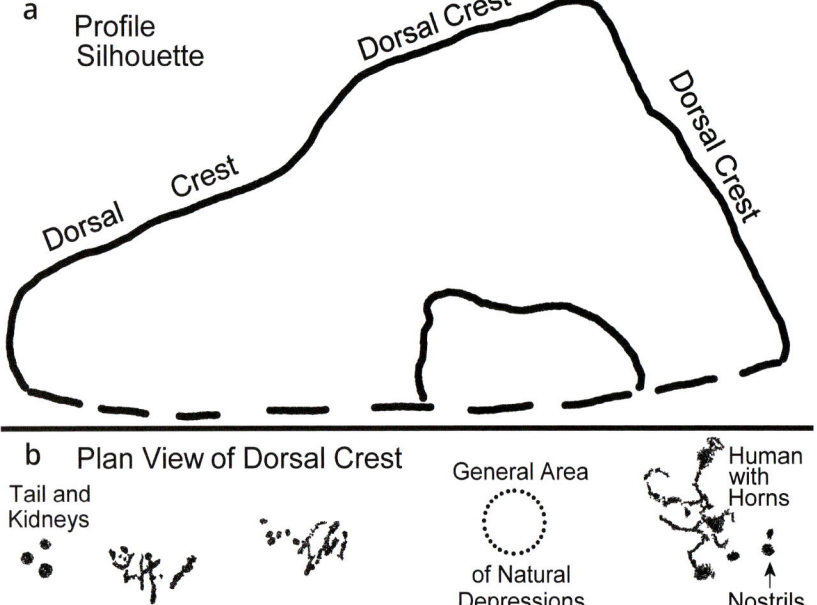

Figure 18. Profile drawing of the Samsal boulder with schematic, plan-view arrangement of petroglyphs along the dorsal crest. Note the approximately correct anatomical position for various organs. The lines and cupules between the "tail and kidneys" were apparently done to emphasize the backbone. The natural depression at the boulder's highest point may have served as an offertory receptacle.

more or less realistic cervico-dorsal profile of a reclining bison without a head (or one can imagine a head turned away from the viewer). In comparing this silhouette (Figure 18a) to other bison silhouettes drawn by prehistoric artists (Figures 21, 22), the results seem straightforward to us. This west-facing profile is consistent with bison portrayed in rock art both realistically and in more stylized drawings, including many of the latter from the Plains (Figure 21a–c). It also better fits Dobrez's (2017:141; Dobrez and Dobrez 2013) arguments about how humans innately identify canonical forms as a means of rapid identification when first seeing an animal. That is, humans perceive the salient features of an animal's profile—especially the cervico-dorsal line and horns—as a survival from deep time when quick recognition was necessary in order to immediately assess the potential threat posed by an animal. Therefore, we argue that the Samsal boulder was seen—at least by the original artists—as a bison lying down with its head pointed to the west toward the Kevin Rim and the Rocky Mountains beyond.

With an orientation putting the hump and head to the west, this places several of the carved images in anatomically (and cosmologically) appropriate positions to fit the perceived shape. Thus, instead of having the several cupules and two groups of lines, which are carved across (or almost across) the top of the boulder positioned on the "bridge of the nose" and "lower forehead" (as per Brumley and Johnson 2012:42) where they have neither anatomical nor cosmological rationale, they instead extend up the dorsal spine, from the tail to the base of the hump. In this position large cupules at the very east (or rump) end of the boulder (apparently not recognized by previous investigators) can be seen to represent the base of the tail and kidneys (Figure 18b). These and the next two groups of lines and cupules then demarcate the animal's dorsal spine, and natural depressions at the top of the boulder take the place of a carved depression often placed there (cf. Figure 19). Then the human with a bison horn headdress is positioned where the animal's "head" (and horns) would be. And finally, two prominent cupules at the very west end of the boulder

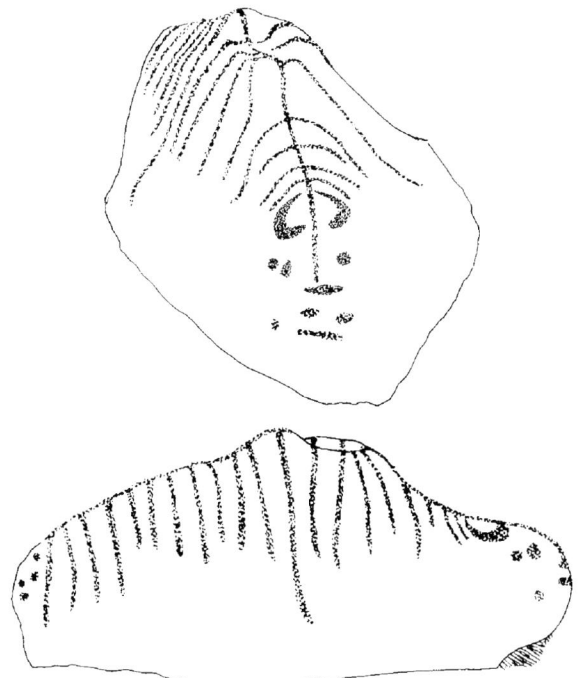

Figure 19. The Sleeping Buffalo petroglyph boulder, found near Malta, Montana, has ribs and other anatomical features to emphasize its bison shape. Some of these features, such as kidneys, nostrils, and horns, are placed similarly to those on the Samsal boulder. Note the depression at the top of the hump, which is, even today, often used as an offertory receptacle.

are in a position where they would represent nostrils (Figure 18b).

If we position these cupules, lines, natural depression, and the human with bison horn headdress in a scaled schematic arrangement as if looking from directly above (Figure 18b), the resultant pattern is similar to that of the Sleeping Buffalo boulder (Figure 19) and has appropriate anatomical parts in correct positions, although—especially for the horns—not at the correct scale. This arrangement, particularly considering the kidneys and nostrils, also corresponds very well to a general Plains belief system that designates kidneys and a bison's breath as loci of supernatural power. Therefore, we do identify the Samsal boulder as a reclining bison, but we suggest it faces west rather than east.

Combat Scene

The combat scene (Figures 9, 14) is a typical Biographic tradition fight scene like many found elsewhere on the Northern Plains. In this scene all three warriors stand on an implied

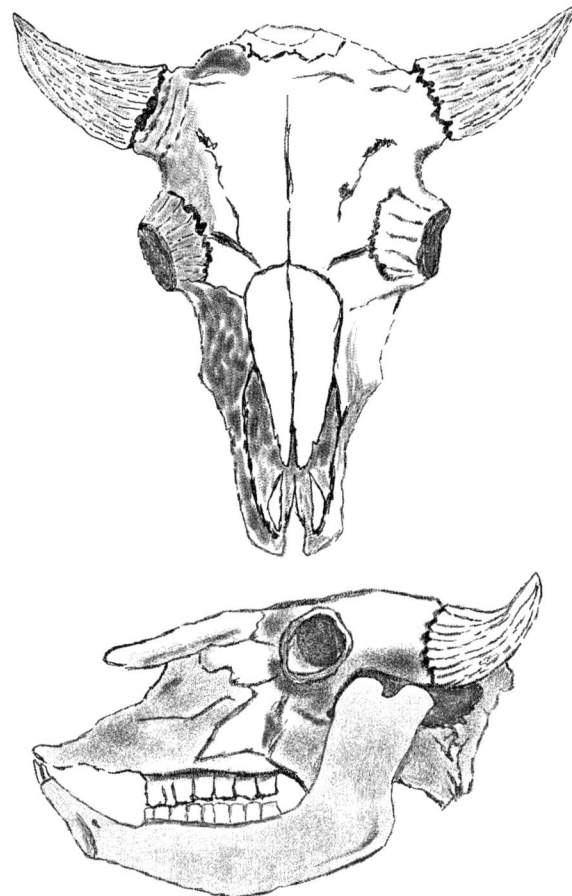

Figure 20. This illustration of a bison skull shows that the Samsal boulder does not have a profile of a bison's head, but rather has the profile of a reclining animal.

ground line with the two shield bearers on the left facing toward the larger, more actively posed rectangular-body style human at the right. This rectangular-body human is apparently the victor, since he thrusts a long spear tipped with an outsized triangular point at the larger of two shield-bearing warriors. The size of the projectile point and its distinctively triangular shape

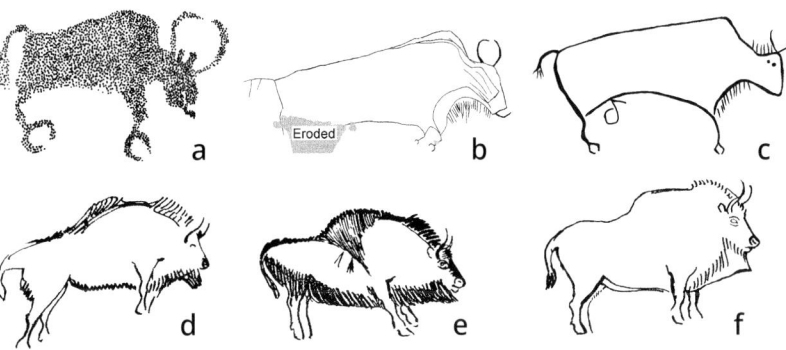

Figure 21. Bison drawn in rock art on the Plains (a–c) and in European caves (d–f) all show a characteristic, high-humped profile like that of the Samsal boulder.

Figure 22. These two bison silhouettes from French cave art show how prehistoric artists often viewed bison with an exaggeratedly high hump, low hindquarters, and an almost imperceptible head.

implies that it was a metal point. The lead shield bearer appears to attempt to parry his adversary's thrust with a short, stout club. Using a club in this way to defend oneself, or even to disarm an opponent, was typical of Historic period close-quarter warfare (Denig 2000:161; Ewers 1955:202).

Juxtaposed with the combat scene are a few smaller geometric images. Two are very eroded cupules, which appear to predate the scene, but others are a pair of cupules with "ear-like" projections and a large X-shape that appear to be roughly of the same age as the scene itself. We know of no analogous images to the "eared" cupules in any Biographic tradition rock art, but the X resembles a coup mark used by several tribes to indicate different war honors. Among the Crow, Hidatsa, and Mandan a freestanding X like this signified the first blow struck on an enemy in a fight, and among the Blackfoot it represented a stolen horse (Keyser and Klassen 2001:267, 2003:11; Wissler 1911). Whether this X represents such a coup mark in this context is conjectural, especially since simple geometric images are common in Hoofprint tradition art. However, the size of the shields in this scene and the probable metal spear point date the images to the Historic period, when such coup marks were commonly in use.

Interpretations

Two rock art traditions are represented by the petroglyphs pecked on the Samsal boulder. Most of the petroglyphs can be assigned to the Hoofprint tradition, some expressions of which are named the Vulva-Track-Groove rock art style by Sundstrom (2004:83–90).

The Hoofprint tradition is one of the most widespread rock art traditions in North America (Keyser 1984:25, 51, 2004:56; Keyser and Klassen 2001:176; Sundstrom 2004:91), found from Georgia to the Northern Plains (Figure 1). Hoofprint tradition art is found in large quantities on the Northern Plains from the Jeffers petroglyphs in southwestern Minnesota, westward through Medicine Rock, North Dakota, the Black Hills and Cave Hills of South Dakota, to Medicine Creek Cave in Northeastern Wyoming, and then across Wyoming to No Water, Red Canyon, and White Mountain in the Bighorn, Wind, and Green river basins (Buckles 1964; Keyser 1984:51; Keyser and Poetschat 2009; Lothson 1976; Porsche and Loendorf 1987; Sundstrom 2004). In Montana, Porcupine Lookout and Recognition Rock in the middle Yellowstone River drainage also have large numbers of hoofprints and bear paws (Eichhorn 1958; Fredlund 1993), but the most common Hoofprint tradition sites north of the Yellowstone River are petroglyph boulders (some of which are called "Buffalo Stones") and a few sites on horizontal bedrock outcrops, which are found from Dickinson, North Dakota, westward to the Samsal boulder (Conner 1962; Darroch 1976; Hoy 1969; Johnson 1975; Jones and Jones 2012; Park 1990). A site at Cranbrook, British Columbia (Cornford and Cassidy 1980), is the furthest west extension of the Hoofprint tradition.

Hoofprint tradition art is composed primarily of very clearly depicted ungulate hoofprints, simple grooves (which, when parallel, are interpreted as representing the bison's ribs), bearpaws, human faces, cupules, bisected ovals, and vulvaforms of various shapes and sizes. It also contains a few other human and animal figures, including bison and bison heads, outsized elk, and occasional complete human representations. Some boulders have primarily geometric imagery composed as cupules and meandering lines.

Several of the glacial erratic "Buffalo Stones," common to the Glaciated Plains landscape north of the Missouri River, bear a fanciful resemblance to a reclining bison, and these are often further modified by the addition of "ribs," cupules along the "spine" and "hump," or various features such as horns, eyes, mouth, and nostrils demarcating the "head." The most famous of these is the Sleeping Buffalo petroglyph boulder, which was originally found on the Milk River northeast of Malta, Montana (Figure 19), but several other petroglyph boulders (including the Samsal boulder) have a general "reclining bison" shape (Table 2). The smaller of the two Viking Ribstone boulders in central

Alberta is even shaped somewhat like an extremely oversized *"iniskim"* buffalo stone. Many *Iniskim* stones were fossil ammonite shell segments (Peck 2002), which were used by the Blackfoot tribes to lure bison into kill sites, so having a petroglyph boulder shaped like an *insikim* but elaborated with pecked spine, ribs, and a few cupules is consistent with the idea that these boulders were thought to be bison. Finally, much simpler ribstones are found throughout the area and merely show a series of rib-like grooves pecked into any shaped boulder or slab (Hoy 1969:60–61).

Throughout its range, Hoofprint tradition art is intimately tied into typical Plains Indian beliefs about bison. In several ways the images appear to have functioned in a broadly construed fertility context intended to ensure the propagation of the bison and the continuation of the human groups so dependent on these animals. Among some Siouan-speaking groups the typical Hoofprint tradition motifs are carved at the mouths of caves or crevices believed to be the underground home of the bison, from where they originally emerged to populate the world and where they retreat in the winter (Albers 2003; Sundstrom 2006). Among some of these societies the bison is revered as the progenitor of the entire group, and women typically make Hoofprint tradition art as part of their vision quest ritual designed to acquire the powers of Double Woman (Sundstrom 2002a:104–111).

For other groups Hoofprint tradition art serves as a connection to the bison because the very boulders on which the images are carved are those used by the animals as scratching posts. Still other hoofprint boulders, such as those at Wahkpa Chu'gn (Greer and Greer 2000:3) and on Saddle Butte (24HL635), are placed at or very near bison kills as if to serve—like the *iniskim*—to lure the animals into a trap.

The Samsal boulder fits very comfortably into the petroglyph boulder subset of Hoofprint tradition sites. Initially, the boulder's shape closely mimics that of a reclining bison, even including a large crack highlighting the position the animal's front leg would occupy as it lies down. In fact, there are only two "lying-down bison form" petroglyph boulders that are slightly more realistic among the more than five Northern Plains examples. Those are the "Sleeping Buffalo" near Malta, Montana (Figure 19), and the Pine Coulee Ribstone found just east of Stavely, Alberta, which resembles a reclining bison with its head turned back licking its flank (Fedirchuk and McCullough 1991).

As with its shape, the fact the Samsal boulder was used as a bison scratching post certainly was noted by prehistoric inhabitants of this area, who may have witnessed the activity as it was ongoing. In the minds of Northern Plains people, this provided another link between the animal and the boulder and verified that it was indeed a stone buffalo. Cupules along the boulder's "spine" and in the extreme front, where they could have been thought of as eyes or nostrils, are further support for prehistoric people viewing this as a bison turned to stone.

Although a few designs carved on the Samsal boulder are generic shapes and meandering lines (Figure 11), the recognizable motifs—other than the Biographic tradition combat scene—are further testament to this belief system linking bison and petroglyph boulders, since they are all typical of the Hoofprint tradition. Faces, both those with a neck and those with tear streaks, are a common component of Hoofprint tradition art (Table 2), especially on boulders and horizontal outcrop sites north of the Missouri River (Jones and Jones 2012:48–49, 58; Keyser and Klassen 2001:181–183; Schneider 2003:144, 155, 159–164). Likewise, the bisected U-shape and single hoofprint are typical Hoofprint tradition elements found on such boulders across the region (Table 2). Finally, a human figure carved on what a prehistoric artist could have inferred to be the reclining bison's forehead wears an outsized bison horn headdress and has what could be interpreted as a rattle and a feather fan held at the ends of his outstretched arms. Such implements are known to have functioned in dances and other ritual activity centered on calling or hunting bison (Catlin 1844:1:163–164, Plate 67; Schultz 1923:219–221).

Exactly how the Samsal petroglyphs functioned within the Hoofprint tradition is a matter of conjecture. Elsewhere, Sundstrom (1993, 2002a, 2002b, 2004, 2006) has made a very convincing case that Hoofprint tradition rock art marked women's vision quests. The conflation of hoofprints themselves with vulvaforms and the attendant symbolism, coupled with the numbers of tool grooves, which are assumed to have resulted from sharpening women's typical tools (e.g., awls, cannon bone fleshers) makes a convincing argument that Hoofprint tradition petroglyphs were made as part of women acquiring their spirit helper (Keyser and Poetschat 2009:55–58, 78–81; Sundstrom 2002a:107–109). However, the sites Sundstrom studied are not primarily petroglyph boulders, but rather Hoofprint tradition sites found on vertical cliff faces. Petroglyph boulders typically lack the tool grooves and large numbers of vulvaforms that are characteristic of Sundstrom's Hoofprint tradition sites.

Such is the case here, at Samsal boulder, where the indications of female associations seem more subtle. There are no tool grooves like those characteristic of the sites Sundstrom studied, and there is only a single small (probably deer's) hoofprint and one bisected U-shape, which could be interpreted as either a vulvaform or a bison hoofprint. If the bisected oval is a vulvaform, as similar designs have been identified (Greer and Greer 2000:5), it is not as convincing as are other rock art examples at the sites Sundstrom documents (Figure 23). Furthermore, there is no overt sexual symbolism like the juxtaposed vulvaforms and penisforms pecked at Snake Butte (Figure 24). Likewise, there is only a single incontrovertible hoofprint preserved on the boulder. Since this hoofprint was nearly lost due to animals' rubbing on the boulder's vertical face, one could suggest there were others originally on the boulder, but now completely lost to animal-caused erosion. However, we have no way to demonstrate this and our recording technique—making a graphite/vegetation rubbing on a thin muslin sheet—should have yielded evidence of others, even if they were heavily eroded.

The suggestion that the Hoofprint tradition petroglyphs functioned in bison "calling" rituals is equally difficult to verify. Certainly, the boulder's shape suggests a reclining bison and interpreting the bison-horn-bonnet-wearing man on the boulder's "forehead" region as a shaman or bundle owner conducting some ritual activity is reasonable, but it lacks specific corroboration. Therefore, with only this limited suite of imagery, such a suggestion remains speculative.

In fact, we suggest that both these explanations may be partly correct, and the Hoofprint tradition art on the Samsal boulder did commemorate the linkage between fertility (a woman's realm), women's visions, and the bison as an economic and cultural mainstay. As a reasonable supposition, this fits very well with the art on the Saddle Butte boulder (located about 125 km [80 mi] to the east), which shows a stick-figure woman superimposed on a bison hoofprint (Figure 25a). Although the Greers (2000:6) state this human's gender is not obvious, pendant labia drawn in this manner are a typical Plains art convention for "woman." Such a depiction seems especially appropriate in Hoofprint tradition art, since the illustrated labia at 24HL635 mimic the shape of a cloven hoof; and, in fact, a female figure at another site with multiple hoofprints has an indisputable hoofprint in place of a vulvaform (Figure 25b). In addition to the conflation of a woman and bison tracks at Saddle Butte, the boulder's location is directly across the Milk River from a series of ten major bison kill sites spanning the last 2,000 years (Keyser 1979). Its butte-top location just across the river from these sites suggests it may well have served a buffalo-calling function. The petroglyph boulder at Wahkpa Chu'gn and the Pine Coulee ribstone are in similar settings.

The Samsal boulder may have also served to help call the buffalo. The Samsal family knows of a relatively large bison kill in the vicinity of the boulder, but this site is privately owned and has never been professionally investigated. In any case, it is not unreasonable to think that shamans tasked with calling bison to a nearby kill site might have been responsible for some of the images carved on the Samsal boulder. This seems particularly relevant for the modification of the boulder's "bison" shape and the presence of the horned human holding ritual items pecked on its "forehead" area.

Finally, there is evidence that women among the Blackfoot, one of the tribes who would have inhabited this area in the last centuries of the Late Prehistoric period, did undertake vision quests. According to a well-known and often recounted Blackfoot mythic story, the most notable woman's vision resulted in a starving woman finding the first *iniskim* (Schultz 1923:169–202; Wissler and Duvall 1908:85–87). As part of her vision the *iniskim* provided the woman instructions for calling the buffalo and when she taught the men of the camp the song and ritual associated with it, she was able to bring a herd near the village so the men could kill enough animals to survive the starvation winter (Schultz 1923:169–202). Given this report of women's

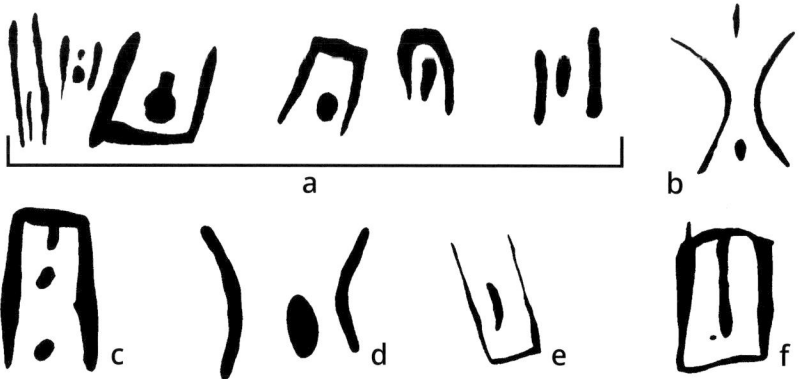

Figure 23. Vulvaforms are a common component of Hoofprint tradition rock art. These are found at sites in the North Cave Hills. The six examples in (a) are a natural grouping.

port for the site's use by women, since such scrapers are one of a woman's primary hide-working tools.

In summary, it seems to us that a reasonable case can be made for attributing the Hoofprint tradition rock art on the Samsal boulder to both women and male shamans who may have sought visions at the site, left offerings there, and solicited the help of the supernatural in bringing bison to a nearby kill site.

The occurrence of a Biographic tradition scene on the Samsal boulder is atypical for this type of site, but we do know of one scene involving three bison and a series of dots that might represent a human's path on the Tank Coulee petroglyph boulder near Malta, Montana (Hoy 1969:59). The Samsal boulder example represents a typical Biographic tradition combat scene, structurally like many at Writing-on-Stone less than 15 km (10 miles) to the north (Keyser 1977). Drawing such a scene on the Samsal boulder might well reflect the fact that its pre-existing Hoofprint tradition art had marked it as a sacred site. The authorship of this scene might well be Blackfoot, given the style of the warriors, but the site lies right in the path of a documented war trail from the confluence of the Yellowstone and Missouri rivers to Blackfoot country, which was drawn by an Assiniboine warrior in 1853 (Denig 2000:Plate 77). As drawn, this war trail passes up the Milk River and directly around the northwest side of the Sweet Grass Hills. Such a war trail could well have been used by Mandan and Hidatsa warriors, both of whom used the X as an indicator of counting coup (Keyser and Klassen 2001:267).

Discussion of Offerings

Items left as "offerings" at the Samsal boulder are fairly typical of such objects found both archaeologically and as current votive items left at such sites as expressions of a wish or vow. Archaeological excavation at the Simanton petroglyph boulder site (24PH2072) recovered a small amount of red ochre and a tubular pipe made of catlinite (Park 1990:46), and a similar pipe along with a small pottery vessel were recovered from a burial linked to the St. Victor petroglyphs in southwestern Saskatchewan only about 170 km (110 mi) northeast of Simanton (Jones and Jones 2012:12). These artifacts are diagnostic of the Devils Lake-Sourisford burial complex, which dates between A.D. 900 and 1400 (Jones and Jones 2012:122; Syms 1979:304). At other petroglyph boulders bits of bison bone and arrowpoints have been found where they were left as votive offerings. The endscraper found at the Samsal boulder was an isolated find and there was no other

Figure 24. This head-and-neck face and vulvaforms paired with penis forms (above) are found at Snake Butte south of Harlem, Montana (site 43). Photograph courtesy of Stu Conner.

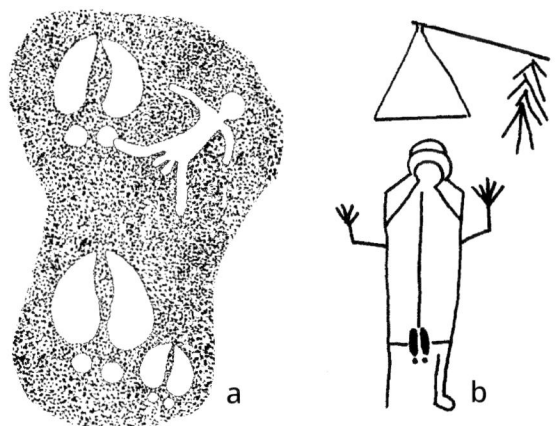

Figure 25. Women in Hoofprint tradition art sometimes have genitalia shown as a hoofprint. (a) Saddle Butte (24HL635) at Fresno Reservoir (site 26); (b) White Mountain, Wyoming. Weapon floating overhead is a Missouri War Axe in the act of counting coup.

visions related to calling the buffalo, it seems likely that the Samsal "buffalo stone" may well have been a place for women's vision questing. The finding of an endscraper left as an offering at the site provides some limited sup-

lithic debitage found in the area, nor are there tipi rings in close proximity. This strongly implies that the scraper was a votive offering, probably left at the site by a woman.

The tobacco "bundle" left at the site is a modern offering, like many others found at petroglyph boulders and other types of rock art sites across the Northern Plains. Such modern votives are simply continuations of the prehistoric practice and include the same sorts of things, only as modern versions. Documented modern offerings include various sorts of colored ribbon, pieces of cloth (from small scraps to entire bolts), tobacco, cigarettes and other smoking materials, coins, candles, and even utilitarian objects as commonplace as tire chains (Gillette and Greer 2014:265; Greer and Greer 2000:2, 2016:159). Ribbon and cloth offerings are often red, a sacred color. This is true of the brightly colored ribbon at Samsal boulder, which has red plastic edging and red and silver glitter glued on in decorative swirls.

Obviously, votive offerings are limited to certain classes of objects, which suggest they are part of prayers directed to the petroglyphs and even the boulders themselves in some instances. Early ethnographers reported such offerings as part of prayers for desired outcomes or general good fortune. As Greer and Greer (2016:159) note,

> Individuals…made such offerings because they considered the [petroglyph] boulders to be spiritually significant, capable of interceding with the supernatural on behalf of themselves or their group for a desired outcome…It appears that the act of leaving an offering is an important part of the prayer ritual, and the kinds of offerings are limited in scope both in the past and today.

Dating the Samsal Boulder Petroglyphs

We currently have no way of directly dating the Samsal boulder petroglyphs, but the motifs carved thereon provide some general dating clues. Initially, the graffito J.P.H. 1894 JULY 7 superimposes one of the faces and a nearby ovoid geometric, indicating that these images at least predate that year. The fact that this graffito is significantly less weathered than any of the other carvings, coupled with the extensive lichen growth restricted to most of the other earlier motifs, indicates that the American Indian petroglyphs are likely significantly older than the 1890s.

The faces, one with a neck and scalplock and the other with tear streaks, suggest that the Hoofprint tradition art is of the Late Prehistoric period, since those same motifs are found at St Victor, 39FA7, and the Weyburn Glyph Stone, all of which are sites assigned to the Late Prehistoric period based on other criteria (Jones and Jones 2012; Sundstrom 2004). Two sites, including St. Victor and Simonton, have directly associated artifacts diagnostic of the Devils Lake-Sourisford burial complex, which dates between A.D. 900 and 1400. And, in fact, Mask Cave (24TL238) in the nearby Sweet Grass Hills has red-painted walls and cultural deposits that contained two cached Mississippian-style shell masks, which are associated with Late Prehistoric period Old Women's Phase side-notched projectile points (Beery 1998:69; Greer and Greer 1996:46; Jaynes 1997). Such masks are also diagnostic artifacts of the Devils Lake-Sourisford burial complex (Syms 1979:304), although new research suggests that the masks may indicate a date as late as A.D. 1650 for the complex (Beery 1998:43). Despite no direct linkage between Mask Cave and the Samsal boulder, this additional spatial association between these specific rock art face motifs and masks characteristic of the Devils Lake-Sourisford complex is suggestive.

Finally, petroglyph boulders at two other sites, Wahkpa Chu'gn and 24VL224 (Darroch 1976:22–23), are directly associated with other artifacts of the Old Women's Phase, which spans the period from about A.D. 700 to 1700. Evaluating a broad range of chronological clues from these sites and many other Hoofprint tradition sites, Keyser and Klassen (2001:183–184) concluded that the Hoofprint tradition began about A.D. 500 and lasted at a few sites to about A.D. 1800. Given the totality of evidence at Samsal boulder, we propose that the Hoofprint tradition art at the site dates within the latter half of that time period, ca. A.D. 1200–1700.

The Biographic tradition combat scene appears to date sometime between A.D. 1700 and 1800, based on the relatively small diameter of the warriors' shields and the probable metal spear point. There is no obvious superimposition of this scene on any Hoofprint tradition image, but the only actual hoofprint noted on the boulder is just to the right of this scene and it is nearly eroded away, suggesting that it may be considerably earlier. However, there are often different degrees of erosion due to animal rubbing on adjacent images. For instance, the head, neck, and upper half of the shield of the rear shield-bearing warrior in the combat scene are far more eroded than any part of either of the other two warriors or their weapons.

In sum, it appears that the petroglyphs on the Samsal boulder were made in both the Late Prehistoric period (possibly as much as 1000 to 1500 years ago for some of them) and the Historic period (at least the combat scene).

Conclusion

The Samsal boulder is part of the Hoofprint tradition, one of the most widespread rock art traditions in North America. On the Northern Plains, Hoofprint tradition rock art can be found on other boulders, horizontal outcrops, and vertical cliff surfaces from the Black Hills and Cave Hills of South Dakota north to southwestern Saskatchewan and west throughout the Montana plains and northern Wyoming. The primary site users were people who carved Hoofprint tradition art, but if the images span the Late Prehistoric period this could easily include several groups in addition to the local Blackfoot tribes.

The Hoofprint tradition art on the Samsal boulder appears to have functioned in a belief system that conflated women and bison, much like that described by Sundstrom for sites in South Dakota and northeastern Wyoming but lacking the emphasis on tool sharpening grooves. This disparity may be due to a slightly different set of beliefs lacking the concept of Double Woman as a female spirit toward whom visions were directed, but instead focusing on the bison. This lack of tool grooves is consistent with most other petroglyph boulders in the region. And the natural shape of this boulder and modifications of it with cupules are equally consistent with the treatment typical of many Northern Plains boulders. Whether the Hoofprint tradition images were carved by men or women cannot be determined, but it seems likely that the endscraper left as an offering represents a woman's use of the site.

In any case, a warrior visited the site some time in the relatively early Historic period and carved a coup count scene on its face. The distinctive style of shield bearing warriors he carved suggests this artist was a Blackfoot man, although if so, the large X apparently associated with the scene cannot be readily explained. Possibly this X represents a stolen horse coup, as similar marks do in Blackfoot robe art and rock art (Keyser and Klassen 2003:11). However, this symbol was also used by other Plains groups (Mandan, Hidatsa, and Crow) to indicate a counted coup—exactly what is being shown in the scene. Unfortunately, the only rock art shield-bearing warriors that can be reasonably inferred as the product of Mandan or Hidatsa artists based on their occurrence in sites in central North Dakota and the North Cave Hills of South Dakota (Keyser 1984:32; Over 1941:43) share only very general similarities with these. Likewise, of those drawn in Crow country only two examples are even vaguely like this style (Keyser and Poetschat 2014:184, 206), and either or both of them could be drawn by a non-Crow artist. All other Historic period shield-bearing warriors associated with diagnostic Crow imagery are very different from these figures (cf. Keyser and Poetschat 2014:165–168, 174–176, 184; Kyte 2001). Thus, it is clear this is a coup count scene, most likely drawn by a Blackfoot warrior, but possibly by an artist from another group. It is also possible that a second artist from a group different than the one who carved the warriors juxtaposed the X next to the scene to indicate his counting of a coup.

Notes

1. Throughout the manuscript we use the more generic verb "carve" to subsume several methods of rock art production (pecking, abrading, and incising). This is done for simplicity because many of the images show a combination of these techniques and we often refer to multiple images, which demonstrate two or all three techniques.

2. In all descriptions of the imagery, right and left are indicated from the perspective of the viewer with the image in correct anatomical position. Thus, this man in the combat scene is actually thrusting his spear with "his" right hand, but for descriptive purposes it is the left hand from the viewer's perspective. The same is true of the shaman figure holding the rattle and feather fan.

Acknowledgments. We thank Tom McCormick for initially contacting the Samsal family to obtain permission to visit the site. We thank the Samsal family for permission to visit and record the site. Their stewardship of the site and their desire to learn more about it is a model for private landowners everywhere. Mrs. Randi Samsal did the UV light test on the scraper to determine that it was not Knife River Flint. David Kaiser, David Minick, Becky Steed, Julia Cleary, Sueann Jansen, and Mary Doak all assisted with laboratory work and classification efforts for the recording project. Kaiser, Minick, Randi Samsal, and Mavis and John Greer provided photographs we use in this report. We also thank an anonymous AIRA reviewer for alerting us to the Albers reference and the UV light testing method used to determine whether the scraper was made of Knife River Flint.

References Cited

Albers, Patricia C.
  2003 *The Home of the Bison: An Ethnographic and Ethnohistorical Study of Traditional Cultural Affiliations to Wind Cave National Park.* 2 Volumes. Report Submitted to the U.S. National Park Service, Wind Cave National Park, South Dakota. Electronic document http://npshistory.com/publications/wica/home-of-the-bison-v1.pdf, accessed November 12, 2019.

Beery, Derek Stetler
  1998 *Montana Masks: The Implications of Shell Mask Gorgets to Trade Between the Plains and Southeast.* Master's Thesis, University of Montana. Graduate Student Theses, Dissertations, & Professional Papers 3011. Electronic document, https://scholarworks.umt.edu/etd/3011/, accessed March 22, 2019.

Brumley, John H., and Ann M. Johnson
  2012 Samsal Ranch Petroglyph Boulder and Adjacent Sites in Toole County. *Archaeology in Montana* 53(2):39–50.

Buckles, William G.
  1964 *An Analysis of Primitive Rock Art at Medicine Creek Cave, Wyoming, and its Cultural and Chronological Relationships to the Prehistory of the Plains.* Master's Thesis, University of Colorado, Boulder.

Catlin, George
  1844 *Letters and Notes on the Manners, Customs, and Conditions of the North American Indians.* Third edition. Two Volumes. Wiley and Putnam, New York. Facsimile reprint 1973 with an introduction by Marjorie Halpin and photographs of the original paintings, Dover Publications, Inc., New York.

Conner, Stuart W.
  1962 *A Preliminary Survey of Prehistoric Picture Writing on Rock Surfaces in Central and South Central Montana.* Billings Archaeological Society Paper 2. Billings, Montana.

Cornford, Jackie, and Steve Cassidy
  1980 Cranbrook Petroglyphs. *Datum: B.C. Heritage Conservation Branch Newsletter* 5(2):7–9.

Darroch, John I.
  1976 A Hoof, Hand, and Footprint Petroglyph Boulder Recovery from Valley County. *Archaeology in Montana* 17:19–28.

Denig, Edwin
  2000 *The Assiniboine.* University of Oklahoma Press, Norman. Reprint edition, original publication 1930 as *Indian Tribes of the Upper Missouri*, Forty-Sixth Annual Report of the Bureau of American Ethnology, Smithsonian Institution, Washington, D.C.

Dobrez, Livio
  2017 A Universalist Taxonomy for Pictures. In *American Indian Rock Art, Volume 43*, edited by Ken Hedges and Mark A. Calamia, pp. 139–148. American Rock Art Research Association, San Jose, California.

Dobrez, Livio, and Patricia Dobrez
  2013 Canonical Form and The Identification of Rock Art Figures. In *American Indian Rock Art, Volume 39*, edited by William D. Hyder, pp. 115–129. American Rock Art Research Association, Glendale, Arizona.

Eichhorn, Gary
  1958 Petroglyphs at Porcupine Lookout, a Site in Rosebud County. *Archaeology In Montana* 1(1):3–5.

Evilsizer, Laura Jean
  2016 *Knife River Flint Distribution and Identification in Montana.* Master's Thesis, University of Montana. Electronic document, https://scholarworks.umt.edu/etd/10670, accessed February 25, 2020.

Ewers, John C.
  1955 *The Horse In Blackfoot Indian Culture.* Bureau of American Ethnology Bulletin 159. Smithsonian Institution, Washington, D.C.

Fedirchuk, Gloria, and Edward J. McCullough
  1991 Prehistoric Art and Spiritualism: A Perspective from Pine Coulee, Alberta. *Alberta Archaeological Review* 22:11–19.

Fredlund, Lynn
  1993 *Archaeological Investigations and Rock Art Recordation at Recognition Rock (24RB165), Rosebud County, Montana.* GCM Services Inc., Butte, Montana.

Gillette, Donna L., and Mavis Greer
  2014 Spirituality in Rock Art Yesterday and Today: Reflections from the Northern Plains and Far Western United States. In *Rock Art and Sacred Landscapes*, edited by Donna L. Gillette, Mavis Greer, M. Helene Hayward, and William Breen Murray, pp. 253–273. One World Archaeology, Volume 8. Springer-Verlag, New York.

Greer, Mavis, and John Greer
  1996 Central Montana Rock Art. *Archaeology in Montana* 37(2):43–56.

  2000 Boulder Rock Art of Montana. Paper Presented at the 58th Annual Meeting of the Plains Anthropological Society, St. Paul, Minnesota. Electronic document, https://www.greerservices.com/Assets/publications_pdfs/2000_Greer_Plains_NE_MT_BoulderRA.pdf, accessed July 30, 2019.

  2016 Indian Lake Medicine Boulder and Fertility on the American Northwestern Plains at EuroAmerican Contact. In *Native American Landscapes: An Engendered Perspective*, edited by Cheryl Claassen, pp. 151–176. The University of Tennessee Press, Knoxville.

Grinnell, George Bird
  1908 *Blackfoot Lodge Tales: The Story of a Prairie People.* Charles Scribner's Sons, New York.

Hoy, Judy
  1969 Petroglyph Boulders in Phillips County, Montana. *Archaeology in Montana* 10(3):45–65.

Jaynes, Stanley
  1997 Marine Shell Mask Gorgets in Montana. *Central Plains Archaeology* 5(1):99–103.

Johnson, Ann M.
  1975 Hoofprint Boulder (24RV1026). *Archaeology in Montana* 16(1):43–47.

Jones, Tim E. H., and Louise Jones
  2012 *St. Victor Petroglyphs: The Place of the Living Stone.* Houghton Boston, Saskatoon, Saskatchewan.

Kaiser, David A., and James D. Keyser
  2020 Hoofprints and Footprints—The Grammar of Biographic Rock Art. In *American Indian Rock Art, Volume 46*, edited by Richard A. Rogers, Evelyn Billo, and Robert Mark, pp. 23–45. American Rock Art Research Association, Cupertino, California.

Keyser, James D.
1977 Writing-On-Stone: Rock Art on the Northwestern Plains. *Canadian Journal of Archaeology* 1:15–80.

1979 Late Prehistoric Period Bison Procurement on the Milk River in North-Central Montana. *Archaeology in Montana* 20(1):1–221.

1984 Rock Art of the North Cave Hills. In *Rock Art of Western South Dakota: the North Cave Hills and the Southern Black Hills*, edited by L. Adrien Hannus, pp. 1–51. Special Publication 9. South Dakota Archaeological Society, Sioux Falls.

2004 *Art of the Warriors: Rock Art of the American Plains.* University of Utah Press, Salt Lake City.

2010 Size Really Does Matter: Dating Plains Rock Art Shields. In *American Indian Rock Art, Volume 36*, edited by Ken Hedges, pp. 85–102. American Rock Art Research Association, Glendale, Arizona.

2017 The Cut Bank Creek Survey: New Sites in Central Montana (USA). *INORA The International Newsletter on Rock Art* 78:13–20.

Keyser, James D., and Michael A. Klassen
2001 *Plains Indian Rock Art.* University of Washington and UBC Press, Seattle and Vancouver.

2003 Every Detail Counts: More Additions to the Plains Biographic Rock Art Lexicon. *Plains Anthropologist* 48:7–20.

Keyser, James D., and George Poetschat
2009 *Crow Rock Art in the Bighorn Basin: Petroglyphs at No Water Wyoming.* Oregon Archaeological Society Press, Publication 20. Portland, Oregon.

2012 *Clan Crests and Shamans' Masks: Petroglyphs in Southeast Alaska.* Indigenous Cultures Preservation Society, Portland, Oregon.

2014 *Northern Plains Shield Bearing Warriors: A Five Century Rock Art Record of Indian Warfare.* Oregon Archaeological Society Press, Publication 22. Portland, Oregon.

Kroeber, A. L.
1908 *Ethnology of the Gros Ventre.* Anthropological Papers of the American Museum of Natural History, Volume I, Part IV.

Kyte, Michael
2001 Site on the Musselshell River. Illustrated Letter Report dated May 21, 2001, on file with James D. Keyser.

Lothson, Gordon Allan
1976 *The Jeffers Petroglyphs Site: A Survey and Analysis of the Carvings.* Minnesota Historical Society, St. Paul.

Over, W. H.
1941 *Indian Picture Writing in South Dakota.* Archaeological Studies, Circular 4. University of South Dakota Museum, Vermillion.

Park, John A.
1990 The Simanton Petroglyph Hill Site (24PH2072): A Ceremonial Complex in Northern Montana. *Archaeology in Montana* 31(2):41-19.

Peck, Trevor R.
2002 Archaeologically Recovered Ammonites: Evidence for Long-Term Continuity in Nitsitapii Ritual. *Plains Anthropologist* 47(181):147-164.

Porsche, Audrey, and Lawrence L. Loendorf
1987 The Dual Function of Rock Art on the Northern Plains. *Archaeology In Montana* 28(2):57–60.

Schneider, Erinn Dayle
2003 *Rock Art in Southern Saskatchewan.* Master's Thesis, Department of Archaeology, University of Saskatchewan, Saskatoon.

Schultz, James Willard
1923 *Friends of My Life as an Indian.* Houghton Mifflin Company, Boston and New York.

Sundstrom, Linea
1993 *Fragile Heritage: Prehistoric Rock Art of South Dakota.* South Dakota Historical Preservation Center, Vermillion.

2002a Steel Awls for Stone Age Plainswomen: Rock Art, Women's Religion, and the Hide Trade on the Northern Plains. *Plains Anthropologist* 47:99–119.

2002b Prayers In Stone: Hoofprint-Vulva-Groove Rock Art in the Context of Northern Plains Indian Religion. In *Rock Art and Cultural Processes*, edited by Solveig Turpin, pp. 1–26. Special Publication 3. Rock Art Foundation, San Antonio, Texas.

2004 *Storied Stone: Indian Rock Art of the Black Hills Country.* University of Oklahoma Press, Norman.

2006 Reading Between the Lines: Ethnographic Sources and Rock Art Interpretation Approaches to Ethnography and Rock Art. In *Talking With The Past: The Ethnography of Rock Art*, edited by James D. Keyser, George Poetschat, and Michael W. Taylor, pp. 49–72. Oregon Archaeological Society Publication 16, Portland.

Syms, Leigh
1979 The Devil's Lake-Sourisford Burial Complex on the Northeastern Plains. *Plains Anthropologist* 24:283–308.

Wissler, Clark
1911 *The Social Life of the Blackfoot Indians.* Anthropological Papers of the American Museum of Natural History, Volume 7, Part 1.

Wissler, Clark, and D. C. Duval
1908 *Mythology of the Blackfoot Indians.* Anthropological Papers of the American Museum of Natural History, Volume 2, Part 1, pp. 1–163.

A Cryptic Carved Stone Head in the Santa Cruz Mountains: Implications of ICP-MS Results

Chester R. Liwosz

In the mountains of Santa Cruz County, California, a larger-than-life carved sandstone head overlooks towering redwoods, breathtaking peaks, and a steep river valley below. Traces of red pigment on the lips and mouth of this enigmatic sculpture seem to speak of its origins. Surrounding outcrops feature a long and mixed sequence of material culture, from Precontact bedrock mortars, to American Period mining and logging features, to modern graffiti and debris. In order to better estimate the appropriate origin period and significance of this sculpture, a small sample of the pigment was tested in a controlled experiment using inductively coupled plasma mass spectrometry (ICP-MS) to ascertain its chemical composition. These results are discussed in terms of available pigments in the area and commercially available control samples. In addition to the pigments, a 3-D virtual model of the rock carving enables a nuanced investigation of its surface and the likely carving techniques employed.

In the middle of 2017, an unexpected opportunity arose to investigate a rather unique carved sandstone monument in the mountains north of Santa Cruz, California. At the time, the monumental head resided on undeveloped forested private land (Figure 1). The parcel containing this sandstone head was in the process of changing hands into the stewardship of the California Department of Parks and Recreation (DPR, or California State Parks). State Park's primary interest in the land was not as much the archaeological or historical materials that might be present (which at the time were not entirely systematically documented), but rather several species of endemic endangered flora, most notably the Santa Cruz Cypress (*Cupressus abramsiana*). In the process of consulting with DPR and the indigenous Amah Mutsun Tribal Band of Ohlone about the land transfer, the landowner chose to reach out to the Anthropology Department of the University of California Santa Cruz to engage an archaeologist to examine the monumental head and other nearby stone carvings.

Geography

The geographic setting provides the conditions and substrate for making such a carving as this colossal head. It is located in the Santa Cruz Mountains of California's Central Coast (Figure 2). This range of terraced sand hills and low mountaintops emerges out of the Monterey Bay and Pacific Ocean. Here, the collision of the Pacific and North American plates has uplifted bedded marine layers of sandstone and limestone to over one kilometer above sea level at the highest peaks. These relatively soft marine deposits provide a substrate easy to mark or carve with a modest investment of time and labor.

Defining the margins of the aforementioned tectonic plates is the well-known San Andreas Fault, which runs south from the San Francisco peninsula

Chester R. Liwosz
Mesa Prieta Petroglyph Project,
Velarde, New Mexico

Figure 1. Overview of immediate area, with inset of the stone head.

Figure 2. Regional map and location of carving.

through the heart of the Santa Cruz Mountains. Often the culprit behind many California earthquakes, the San Andreas is presently sliding as a strike-slip fault through the Santa Cruz section. Most infamously, the fault's sudden slipping in this area produced the devastating 1989 quake. Named for its epicenter near the highest peak in the Santa Cruz Mountains, the Loma Prieta quake badly damaged the city of Santa Cruz and caused bridges and overpasses to collapse in the San Francisco Bay Area. The peak of Loma Prieta, and the epicenter, are roughly 25 km southeast of the carved stone head.

Background

The large stone head sits in a unique geographical and cultural nexus, such that several cultural traditions should be considered as candidates for its possible origin. Interviews with landholders revealed a common belief that the images were attributable to the local Amah Mutsun Band of Ohlone Native Americans. The historical complexity of the area, however, demands that this presumption not be taken unequivocally, so developing strategies for addressing attribution became a prime research goal.

Demographics

The greater Monterey Bay area in recent centuries has become home to people of diverse ethno-linguistic backgrounds. At the time of contact, the area was occupied by ancestors of peoples who have become known collectively as Ohlone, formerly chronicled as Coastanoans (Jones 2015:10). At the time of contact, Ohlone territory stretched from Big Sur (South of Monterey) northward through much of the San Francisco Bay to the south shore of the Carquinez Straits;

this territory bordered Miwok lands to the north, and Yokuts to the east. Each semi-sendentary Ohlone community expressed a localized group identity through language and ritual. In the Monterey Bay, Ohlone from the southern end around Monterey spoke Rumsen, those along the center of the bay including modern-day Watsonville and Castroville spoke Mustun, and from Santa Cruz north into the mountains, Awaswas (Levy 1978). Early Penutian speakers ancestral to the modern day Ohlone are believed by some to have mixed with or displaced Hokan speakers living in the area some time after 4000 B.P. (Parkman 1986:247).

Leading into the historic times of sustained contact, in-migration of overseas groups from both Europe and East Asia rapidly shifted the demographics of the Monterey and San Francisco Bays. Beginning with the Mission (ca. 1770–1833) and Rancho (1833–1848) Periods, Spanish-speaking Euro-Americans colonized the area and forcibly relocated Native Californians into new communities, largely to be laborers for Catholic missions. Later secularization fostered another reorganization into private farming ventures (Peelo 2010). After the 1846–1848 Mexican-American War, Anglo-Americans rapidly moved into Alta California. The logging industry in the redwoods of the Santa Cruz mountains attracted Scottish settlers during the latter half of the nineteenth century. On the coast, Chinese and Japanese immigrants joined the workforce, largely as laborers who suffered from ethnic tensions with Euro-Americans (cf. Rouse 2003:226, 229). Each of these groups uniquely contributed distinctive cultural traditions to the history of the area, and twentieth century multicultural exchange (exemplified in the "Hippie" movement) significantly inspires the visual culture of a still thriving local folk-art tradition.

Rock Art Traditions

Indigenous Ohlone groups were known to carve petroglyphs into the sandstone and other substrates, as well as less commonly to paint pictographs. An excellent type site of traditional Ohlone rock art designs is CA-SCL-35 (Jones 2015:7, 9). Now largely protected as a California State Park, SCL-35 contains a myriad of complex abstract geometric carvings mixed among many bedrock mortars. Despite SCL-35 largely dating to later in the Precontact Period, its rock art is remarkably similar to older traditions established in the Early Holocene, with the hallmark traits of California shamanic religious expressions (see Whitley 2000). Early images, consistent with Whitley's (2000:47–50) Pit-and-Groove tradition, are by some (e.g. Baumhoff 1980) believed to originate from Hokan-speaking peoples, hypothetical predecessors to Penutian-Speaking Ohlone (Parkman 1986:247). In addition to indigenous traditions, settler groups have also developed a folk tradition of carving images into the soft sandstone and limestone substrate. This Post-contact folk art tradition is well known among local residents and continues to be practiced in the areas of Bonny Doon and Boulder Creek.

Methods

Goals

As mentioned, testing for consistency with the suggested cultural attribution of the head to an indigenous Ohlone group was one of the primary research objectives. Indirect means of supporting or refuting this and alternative hypotheses includes the examination of manufacturing technique, and the determination of a time period for its creation. Indirect dating results came from two lines of evidence: lichenometry and method of manufacture, the latter of which is addressed independently below.

Dating

Given the soft sandstone substrate and lack of obvious organic objects that might be associated with the head's creation, radiometric dating methods were not considered viable for this study. The small amount of red pigment present on it was anticipated to be of a mineral source rather than organic, and all collected samples of it (amounting to <1 ml) were destroyed during compositional analysis, which will be addressed momentarily. Lichenometry, the use of lichen growth rates to estimate the minimum amount of time a rocky surface has been exposed, is at best a contentious dating method. Despite a few high profile researchers enthusiastically adopting this technique (e.g. Bednarik 2002), it does not typically see widespread use in archaeology and rock art studies, especially when other methods are available. It relies on an established set of baseline data for the types of colonies measured calibrated to the area where those measurements are taken, and on assumptions including the expectation that colonies grow at a steady rate (McCarthy 2002). Along California's Central Coast and especially the Monterey Bay, a nearly perpetually humid climate complicates these measures by fostering rapid and possibly uneven rates of lichen growth. To compensate, I used lichenometry only in its most rudimentary form to estimate relative dates. Specifically, I calibrated my measures against a cluster of engraved graffiti tags in the same substrate approximately 100 meters to the southwest. Many of these tags included dates, all after 1965 up to 2012. In addition, undated historic features were noted in between the head and the graffiti, including a shed or cellar cut into the rock. While these are consistent with American Period practices of the nineteenth and early twentieth century, their absence of clear dates eliminated them as potential points of comparison for lichenometry.

Pigment Sourcing

The head being studied, with its partially painted features, presented an opportunity to test for consistency with the informal oral tradition surrounding it. Traces of red pigment were evident in areas of the head best protected from weathering, namely in the mouth and nostrils. Pigment samples were collected as scrapings into sterile, non-reactive test tubes for trace element analysis using inductively coupled plasma mass spectrometry (ICP-MP). Prior to testing, samples needed to be processed in order to extract chemical constituents into a solution that could be properly atomized into the ICP-MS machinery. Two leading hypothetical pigment sources were based on heavy metals: mercury (Hg) in cinnabar for a hypothetical pre-industrial mineral source, and lead (Pb) for a hypothetical commercially produced paint. Because of these possible heavy metal sources, samples were first digested in a 2% nitric acid (HNO_3) solution. Samples were then tested against a blank solution of only 2% nitric acid and a modern commercially available control.

Manufacturing Technique(s)

Finally, the method of manufacture was considered important for making a probable determination of the cultural origins of the large stone head. Most obviously, any indications of the sort of tool used to carve the head could provide strong leads in discerning between Precontact and Historic/Modern Periods. Secondarily, evidence of tailings from the carving process could provide supporting evidence. Since at the time, the head was located on private property with restricted access and no developed trails, field time was limited. To maximize time efficiency without compromising data, I decided to address the manufacturing evidence after the fact from 3-D digital models in the lab. Photogrammetry was the most expedient and most prudent means of building models with sufficient detail in the time allotted. I used a Panasonic Lumix DSLR camera to capture frames of the large stone head from as many angles as possible, and post-processed the data through Agisoft's updated photogrammetry program MetaShape, which replaces Photoscan as their flagship product. The resulting model (see Results below) approaches millimeter accuracy, save for holes in the top rear of the model of the head; overhanging tree limbs prevented me from photographing the head from this angle, and as this was not a critical area to record in such detail I decided that protecting the ecology of this future preserve took precedence over the complete modeling of a non-critical area of the head. The 3-D model did, however, also include a tailings pile at the base of the neck of the sculpture, providing further evidence for later analysis.

Results

ICP-MS

Inductively coupled plasma mass-spectrometry works on a principle of exciting electrons in sample atoms with plasma, and measuring electromagnetic emission lines as these atoms release photons to return electrons to lower energy orbits. Emission lines are distinctive to particular atomic weights, and so are used to deduce the mass of atoms and thus the number of protons and neutrons in each atomic nucleus. Although a "destructive" process, this method works with extremely high precision and requires remarkably little material for confident results. ICP-MS can be used to simultaneously measure the percentages of essentially every known element present in a sample; however, it does not provide a molecular chemical composition. For the purposes of this study, lead (Pb) and mercury (Hg) were the key elements being tested for reasons described earlier. Summary results for these two heavy metals, measured in parts per billion (ppb), are reported in Table 1.

Notice that the modern commercial paint (surprisingly) tested extremely high for lead, suggesting it was not manufactured in the United States and providing an excellent Pb level against which to make a determination of whether the pigments are lead-based, which they are not. The pigments also did not contain any significant levels of mercury. Additionally, both the pigment samples and the modern commercial (red) paint unsurprisingly tested high in iron (^{56}Fe), between 20,000,000 and 65,000,000 ppb. Interestingly, the pigment samples are distinguished from the modern commercial paint by having twenty times or more higher levels of all lanthanides (rare earth metals). The implications of the lanthanide levels and results for all other elements have yet to be ascertained.

Table 1. ICP-MS results for mercury (Hg) and lead (Pb), reported in parts per billion (ppb).

Sample	^{200}Hg	^{201}Hg	^{202}Hg	^{208}Pb
2% Nitric Acid Blank	129.631	0.000	66.667	7,309.369
Modern Commercial Paint	55.556	0.000	166.670	4,462,258.400
Pigment Sample 1 (Mouth)	144.446	33.334	33.334	114,324.800
Pigment Sample 2 (Nose)	111.113	33.334	83.334	45,604.136

Lichenometry

Because of the moist coastal air, lichen growth rates in the area are fast and thus provide diminishing resolution further back in time. Instead of estimating an express time frame, analysis of lichen development was constrained to ascertaining whether the head was made in Precontact, Historic, or Modern times. This was achieved, as described above, by comparing lichen colonization to dated graffiti engravings. Of those graffiti nothing was expressly dated prior to 1965, although more weathered sets of initials were present. Lichen colonies on the head vary by exposure and aspect with the most robust colonies on its north side. It should be noted that some of this surface cannot be definitively determined to be modified, and natural forms predating carving might have been integrated into the finished work. Consequently, only measurements of colonies on the face, an area known to be carved, are used. The colonies are consistently more developed than those on most of the 1960s engraving, and more developed than all carvings from the 1970s and later. Evidence strongly (although not conclusively) suggests the head is therefore at least of historic age (1969 or earlier as of the writing of this paper).

Tool Marks

To further tease out evidence of its cultural origins, and to distinguish between Historic and Precontact Periods, close examination of high-resolution 3-D models developed directly from field data was undertaken (see Figure 3). This process was complicated by the encroachment of potentially protected foliage, and thus a portion of the rear and north sides of the head could not be sufficiently photographed for modeling. The most striking features are on the front of the face, and the model is complete in this area. Of interest, a series of curving grooves form the eyes, eyelids, and brow lines. These were inspected for signs of tool marks. Each of these grooves was weathered, but close inspection of the details shows evidence of slightly V-shaped grooves, strongly in the eyes and moderately so in some of the brow lines. This attribute suggests carving with a metal tool, thus indicating that carving took place post-contact.

A still-visible tailings pile provides a modest amount of additional information. This is located at the base of

Figure 3. Screenshots of 3-D model of the stone head, from the front (upper) and in profile (lower).

the head, below the face (east side) and the north side. Due to its softness, the sandstone in the area has a tendency to liquefy when sufficiently water logged. Once dried it re-solidifies, sometimes fusing loose pieces into single masses. This process has evidently occurred at the head, as the material at its base was neither loose stone nor gravel. The tailings pile however did show an exceptional "lumpiness" compared with weather-smoothed bedrock of the surroundings, suggesting this process of liquefaction had not yet obliterated the last signs of the tailings. Combined with apparent significant weathering on the forehead, this evidence suggests a moderate age, neither recent nor of substantial antiquity.

Discussion

To summarize, evidence from tool marks, weathering, and pigment composition begin to narrow the possible origins of the cryptic carved head. Trace-element analysis eliminated the possibility of a cinnabar-based paint, and thus the folklore surrounding the head is not consistent with the data. The results are also not consistent with a pre-1970s lead-based commercial paint. Given the reasonably high iron levels, this leaves two possibilities: either the pigment is modern paint, or it is from a natural mineral source such as ochre. Lichenometry strongly suggests the head was carved before the 1970s; however, tool marks indicate a post-contact date. All of this is consistent with statements by Amah Mutsun that the head was probably not of Ohlone origin, and instead dates to the Historic (Mission, Rancho, or American) Period. In all, the evidence best supports the hypothesis that the big stone head is an expression of the area's folk art tradition, making it diagnostic of this peculiar art movement and the product of a skilled artist. Further diagnostic data may yet be located in the re-solidified tailings pile or on the surrounding landscape, and the implications of the full elemental results have yet to be explored, meaning that the potential remains for important scientific and historical data. Considering these findings, the cryptic carved head is likely eligible for both state and federal protection, namely through the California Environmental Quality Act and the National Historic Preservation Act.

Acknowledgments. I would like to extend special thanks to the University of California Santa Cruz for providing access to equipment, and especially to Professor Rob Franks of the UCSC Chemistry Department. I would also like to thank the UCSC Anthropology Department for referring the case of the stone head to me.

References Cited

Baumhoff, Martin A.
  1980 The Evolution of Pomo Society. *Journal of California and Great Basin Anthropology* 2(2):175–185.

Bednarik, Robert G.
  2002 The Dating of Rock Art: a Critique. *Journal of Archaeological Science* 29(11):1213–1233.

Jones, Doug
  2015 *Ritual and Religion in the Ohlone Cultural Area of Central California*. Master's Thesis, San Jose State University.

Levy, Richard
  1978 Costanoan. In *Handbook of North American Indians, Volume 8: California*, edited by Robert Heizer, pp. 485–495. Smithsonian Institute, Washington, D.C.

McCarthy, Daniel P.
  2002 Lichenometry. In *Monitoring with Lichens—Monitoring Lichens*, edited by Pier Luigi Nimis, Christoph Scheidegger, and Patricia A. Wolseley, pp. 379–383. Springer, Dordrecht, Netherlands.

Parkman, E. Breck
  1986 Cupule Petroglyphs in the Diablo Range, California. *Journal of California and Great Basin Anthropology* 8(2):246–259.

Peelo, Sarah Ginn
  2010 The Creation of a Carmeleño Identity: Marriage Practices in the Indian Village at Mission San Carlos Borromeo del Río Carmel. *Journal of California and Great Basin Anthropology* 30(2):117–339.

Rouse, Wendy L.
  2003 "What We Didn't Understand...": Chinese-American Death Ritual in 19th-Century California. *Proceedings of the Society for California Archaeology* 13:226–232.

Whitley, David S.
  2000 *The Art of the Shaman: Rock Art of California*. University of Utah Press, Salt Lake City.

Tool Grooves and Drill Holes at the Robert's Indian Caves Site, New Mexico

Lawrence Loendorf and Mark Willis

The rock art at the Robert's Indian Caves site (LA14288) was recorded as part of New Mexico's Permian Basin cooperative agreement where oil companies, the Bureau of Land Management, and the New Mexico State Historic Preservation Office have created a system to complete problem-oriented archaeological research. Tool grooves and small holes drilled into the rock surface at the Robert's site were recorded and suggested to represent the making of arrow and atlatl foreshafts. Additional research is needed to find and record similar holes at other sites for comparison to the Robert's site.

Hundreds of small holes drilled into the sandstone, in tight concentrations, were discovered while recording Robert's Indian Caves (LA14288), a large multicomponent site in southeastern New Mexico. During additional research into the meaning of the holes, we learned they are found at other regional sites, in the same kind of concentrations, along the Pecos River into Texas. They are typically found with vertical tool grooves. We think the grooves and the holes are a product of making arrow, and possibly dart, shafts, although this hypothesis requires additional research. As explained below, there are competing ideas about the origin of the holes and grooves.

Robert's Indian Caves

The site is located northwest of Carlsbad, New Mexico, along Sacahuiste Draw and Old Ranch Canyon where it extends up the western edge and onto the ridge above these drainages. The western flank of Sacahuiste Draw is a 15 to 20 m cliff or canyon wall that is composed of interbedded sandstone and limestone (Figure 1). Massive ring middens are the major features at the site with one that is 20 m by 15 m across and nearly 2 m high. Other features include a rock alignment, rock rings, and rock shrines.

Robert's Indian Caves has a long history in the archaeology of southeastern New Mexico. Early interest in the site involves a series of human burials in the talus below the canyon wall which were being looted by pothunters when Susan Riches Applegarth (1976) undertook controlled archaeological work at the site. She recovered dozens of stone tools and hundreds of ceramic sherds. According to Riches Applegarth, the tools include Middle Archaic Almagre points and Late Archaic San Pedro points, but most were Formative period points like Livermore, Hayes, Bonham, Harrell, Perdiz, Fresno, and Scallorn types. The projectile points were recently reclassified into essentially the same types (Miller et al. 2019). Ceramics include Jornada Brown, Jornada Brown red wash, El Paso Brown, Roswell Brown, El Paso Polychrome, Chupadero Black on White, and several other types that fit well within a time frame

Lawrence Loendorf
*Sacred Sites Research, Inc.,
Albuquerque, New Mexico*

Mark Willis
*Sacred Sites Research, Inc.,
Albuquerque, New Mexico*

Figure 1. Overview of the Robert's Indian Caves site. One of the rockshelters is easily seen while the other is along the canyon wall. Five panels of rock art are found in a shelter with an additional 26 panels along the canyon wall. Note the proximity of the water.

of A.D. 200–1400. Riches Applegarth also exposed a hearth feature in the excavation that had a radiocarbon age of 1075 ± 50 B.P. (WIS 579; charcoal; δ13C = -21.6‰), cal A.D. 880 to 1030. A small test unit in front of the same rockshelter, excavated in 2017, produced charcoal that had a conventional radiocarbon age estimate of 1080 ± 30 B.P. (cal A.D. 895–1020), a calibrated age range that closely matches the date obtained by Riches Applegarth in 1971 (Miller et al. 2019:185). It is clear the site has been utilized from Archaic times with heavy use in the Formative period.

There are two rockshelters at the site, one with and one without rock art. There are also 26 panels of rock art along the canyon wall where the rockshelters are found. The rockshelter with the rock art measures 4.60 m wide, 1.65 m high, and 2.85 m deep (Figure 2). It contains five panels of rock art. Four of the five panels in the rockshelter exhibit tool grooves and drill holes.

Panel 1 is on the left margin of the rockshelter where it faces almost directly west at 260°. The vertical surface contains drill holes and tool grooves within an area that measures about 90 cm high by 1 m wide (Figure 3). The figures are between 176 cm and 265 cm above the rockshelter floor.

The rock surface color is pink (7.5YR7/4). The grooves are the same color. Some holes are a dark grey (7.5YR8/4). Colors herein are specified in the Munsell Color System (see Munsell n.d.).

There is a group of eroded red lines in the upper left of the panel that appear to have been part of a geometric form. Other painted areas include a set of intersecting lines that are eroded but appear to have once been part of a geometric design. There are about 30 tool grooves that are, for the most part, oriented vertically across protuberances of the rock surface and there are about 75 small holes drilled into the rock in association with the tool grooves.

Panel 2 is to the right of and adjacent to Panel 1, inside the shelter on a vertical surface that continues the curve coming down from the ceiling. It faces south at 180°. The panel is 1.9 m wide by 1.3 m high with the figures between 20 cm and 1 m above the rockshelter floor.

The rock color is pale brown (10YR 6/3) near the pictograph and light grey (10YR 7/2) in the area of the drill holes. The painting is red (10R4/6) with the outline of yellow (2.5Y8/8). The yellow is a natural fungus.[1]

The paintings include four or five undulating or zigzag lines, arranged horizontally, with two meeting at a point. They appear to be part of an eroded geometric design. There are also other short wavy lines that are part of the eroded forms. They are all in red paint.

Some 30 to 40 vertically oriented tool grooves are found on the panel. Some are slightly angled and most

Figure 2. View of the rockshelters containing paintings, drill holes, and tool grooves.

Figure 3. Panel 1 in the rockshelter. The tool grooves are more prominent on the protruding rock surfaces. The holes are typical of others at the site.

cross over ridges or protuberances of the rock face. There are also about 300 holes drilled into the rock face in association with the grooves. There is additional discussion about the size and shape of the holes below. Several holes have been occupied by an insect that leaves a web of cotton-like material (Figure 4). It is unclear if this nesting plays a role in enlarging the holes.

Panel 3 is adjacent to Panel 2 where it encompasses an area about 1.3 m in height and 2.1 m in width. The panel on the ceiling and down the vertical wall faces west at 245°. The lowest painting is 52 cm above the rockshelter floor and the highest is 1 m, where it continues a short distance onto the ceiling.

Figure 4. Panel 2 in the rockshelter. The density of the holes is apparent with some that have an insect living in them. The tool grooves are less obvious, but they are visible across the top and to the upper left of the panel. The paintings, abstract red forms, are on the wall above the holes.

The rock is pale brown (10YR6/3) near the paintings. The paintings are dusky red (10R3/4). The yellow outlining the paintings is suspected to be a fungus that may survive, in part, from the organic matter in the paint.

The paintings include sets of parallel zigzag lines that emanate from the ceiling and trail down the wall (Figure 5). One group is three zigzag lines separated into single motifs with associated dots of red paint. One form is a complicated set of intersecting lines, some straight while others intersect them at right angles. The overall form has a rectilinear shape. Other red lines are arranged at an angle across the surface. One has a right-angle corner and others are in parallel sets. A set of undulating or wavy lines arranged in a parallel group appears to come from a crack in the rock. Other line groups include two lines that intersect at a right angle, parallel wavy lines, and a row of four vertical parallel lines made as dash marks and dots in a row.

There are eleven drill holes at the left base of the panel and a single drill hole set apart to the right from the others. No tool grooves are found among these holes.

Panel 4, located on a vertical area of the back wall of the rockshelter, faces west at 262° and measures 15 cm to 18 cm high by a meter across. It is in two sections with figures between 60 cm and 73 cm above the shelter floor.

The wall color is reddish gray (10R1/5) and the paintings are weak red (10R4/3). Yellow figures (2.5Y7/8) appear to be dry pigment, but may be a lichen-like fungus.

The paintings include a set of three vertical, parallel lines about 10 cm in height with two that have branches curving off to the right (Figure 6). There are also sets of curving vertical yellow lines, with some that are on top of the red painted figures. One bold set of red angled lines is oriented parallel to one another and near an oval-shaped form with a tail on the bottom and a split v-shape on the top. It is superimposed by the thin, meandering yellow lines. The yellow lines are confusing. They ap-

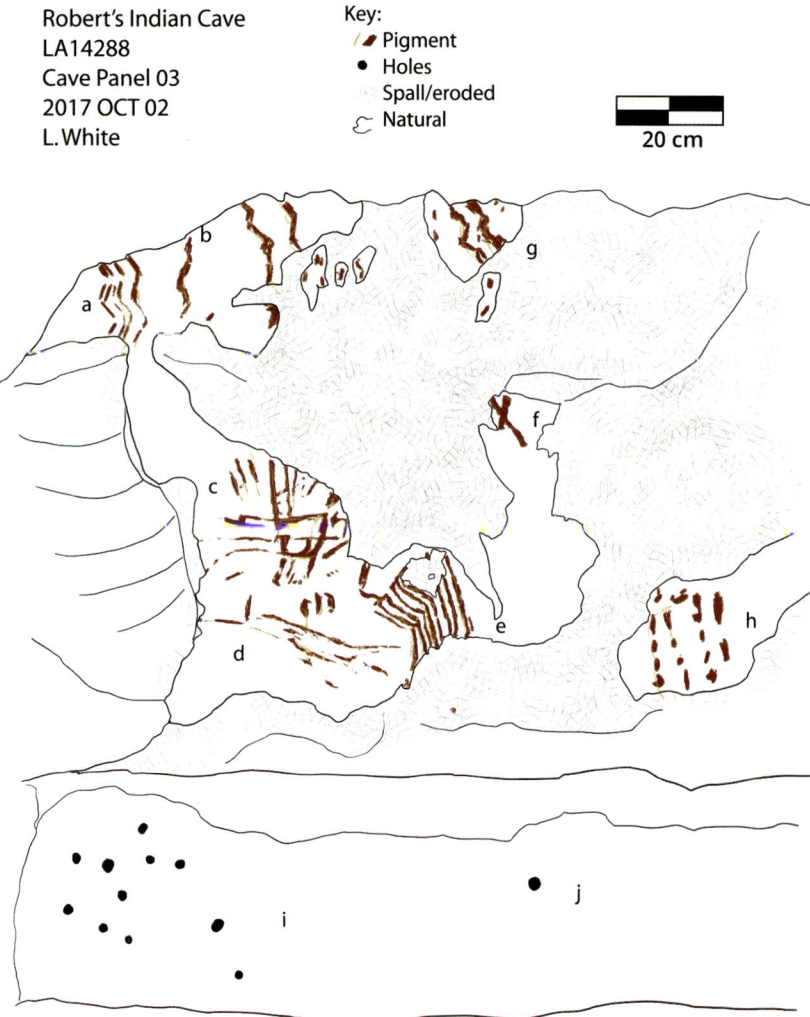

Figure 5. Drawing of Panel 3 in the rockshelter. Letters assigned for identfication in the original site report.

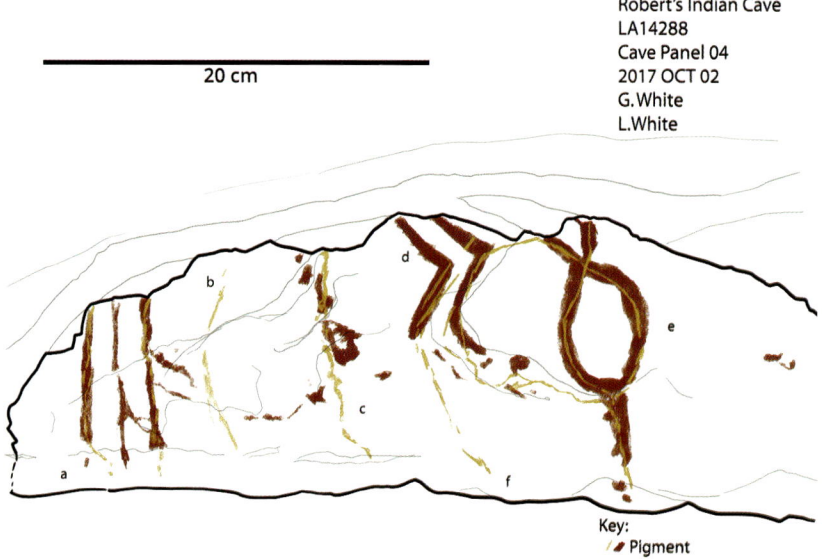

Figure 6. Drawing of Panel 4 in the rockshelter.

pear to be like the lichen-like lines on other panels, but they do not outline areas of red paint on this panel.

Panel 5 (Figure 7) is on the right side of the rockshelter, where it faces north at 360°. About 25 drill holes are found on the panel with some that are slightly larger than others. There are no grooves or paint remnants. The surface rock and the drill holes are pink in color (7.5YR7/4). They are found in an area that measures 40 cm high by 75 cm wide. The holes are between 60 cm and 80 cm above the shelter floor.

Tool grooves with associated drill holes are also found at one of the cliff side rock art panels. They are in a recessed area of the canyon wall, on a vertical surface that faces northwest at 342°. The area is small, measuring about 32 cm high by 50 cm wide. Like the panels in the rockshelter, the grooves tend to be oriented vertically and over humps or protrusions in the rock face. The parent rock is also grainy with bits of sandstone that would have worked well for smoothing antler, bone, or wood.

It may be significant that these grooves and drill holes are closely associated with a group of red paintings that include a double row of short finger lines (almost dots) that are oriented, one above the other, in horizontal patterns across the cliff face; a set of abstract lines with some that intersect at acute angles; a red circle; a grid-like pattern of red dots, 10 to 12 across and 3 to 8 high; and a row of black and red vertical, parallel lines.

Establishing an Age for Robert's Indian Caves

The large numbers of arrow-size projectile points and the ceramics indicate the site had significant use in the Formative time period. This age is supported by the radiocarbon date of 1075 ± 50 B.P. as reported above.

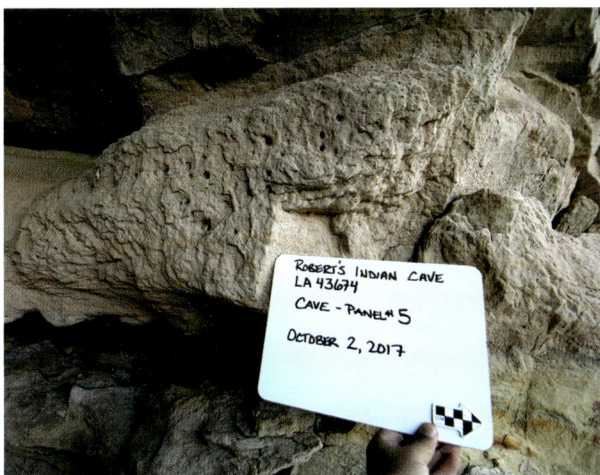

Figure 7. Panel 5 in the rockshelter. The panel has only drill holes on it.

Excavated and surface-collected projectile points indicate the site had an earlier use in the Late Archaic period. Direct dating of two painted wavy-line motifs found in the rockshelter support the Archaic age of the site.

The paintings were dated by Karen Steelman, who sampled while wearing sterilized gloves and using a clean scalpel to scrape a tiny amount of paint into the foil envelope (Figure 8). Steelman processed the samples, along with a sample of the background rock, through a plasma oxidation system at the Shumla laboratory. She learned the samples contain enough organic matter for dates and determined that the background was sufficiently clean to submit the samples for dating.

Figure 8. Dr. Karen Steelman removing a tiny sample of the paint for a radiocarbon date.

The two figures dated are on Panel 3. They are part of a group of parallel wavy lines, in red pigment, that adorn the rockshelter's back wall where the motifs continue to the ceiling (Elements a and b in Figure 5).

They were purposefully collected from similar figures in proximity to test the accuracy of the dating method. The two dates are 2350 ±100 and 2560 ± 80 B.P. The two dates are very close with an average age of 2480 ±63 B.P. Before discussing the implications of the dates, we discuss the tool grooves and the drill holes.

Tool Grooves

Tool grooves are a recognizable feature as they are found at archaeological sites across western North America. There has been debate about their origin with some researchers claiming they represent a symbolic system of communication with an especially vocal group of individuals who considered them to be "Ogam," an ancient Celtic language (McGlone et al. 1994). While individuals still argue that the grooves are a system of communication, there is strong evidence to suggest they served in shaping and sharpening tools.

Tool grooves are made by an abrading action. They are often in parallel rows, but occasionally a groove is cross-cutting a parallel group. This adds to the notion that they are signs or symbols in a communication system. In fact, individuals who have undertaken experiments in making tool grooves indicate that a groove wears out, like any sandpaper, and a new one is needed for proper abrasion (Feyhl 1980). Grooves that cut across others serve to enhance the grinding, as the tool being shaped encounters the edges of the former groove. This means that the cross-cutting grooves in grid patterns or one-pole ladder patterns serve to enhance the shaping or sharpening of the tools. It may also be that the individuals making the grooves made patterns simply to make them more attractive in a practice not unlike doodling.

There is little question, however, that the grooves were used for shaping tools as demonstrated by Kenneth Feyhl, who undertook experimental research to make bone and antler tools that were shaped on sandstone surfaces. Feyhl wrote to geologists he knew working around the world to ask about rock grooves and learned that not only are these linear grooves found across much of the western United States, but that very similar features occur in such diverse places as Brazil, the Solomon Islands, Egypt, and Ghana (Feyhl 1980:15–19). Especially interesting was the fact that some sites in Brazil were still used by native peoples for shaping and sharpening stone axes.

Ethnographic evidence supports this same conclusion. In the journals of Peter Fidler, the chief surveyor and mapmaker for the Hudson's Bay

Company in the 1790s, there is a reference to the use of stone surfaces in tool manufacture by Kutenai Indians of western Montana. Fidler reported that the Kutenai made wedges and chisels by rubbing the antlers of red deer back and forth across a rock surface (Feyhl 1980:26, citing MacGregor 1966:78). Fidler's red deer, also called elk or wapiti, is the cervid whose massive antlers were used for making a variety of tools, among them digging sticks, scrapers, and knife handles.

Feyhl took the additional step of making three experimental tools: a scraper handle from an elk antler, and two bone perforators, one from a deer cannon bone and the other from a deer antler. The perforators were patterned after archaeological examples found at sites in Montana and the scraper handle was like ones used by Plains Indian groups. After a relatively short period of time, Feyhl was able to replicate historic and archaeologically recovered artifacts and, of particular interest to rock art researchers, in the process he created exact replicas of the tool grooves found on rock surfaces across North America (Feyhl 1980:20–26).

Many abraded rock grooves were made in tool manufacture with bone tools, like those Feyhl replicated. It is also clear that abrading or shaping wood artifacts would leave grooves on rock surfaces. It should be clear from the foregoing discussion that there are many different sizes and shapes of tool marks on rock surfaces. It is our contention that the ones at the Robert's site have the size and shape of grooves used to manufacture compound arrows and possibly reduce the ends of atlatl dart hardwood shafts to fit into reed foreshafts.

Drill Holes

Unlike tool grooves, drill holes are not commonly reported at sites across western North America, but they do occur at a dozen or so sites along the Pecos River and its tributaries south into Texas. They may also be found at other sites north of Carlsbad and go unreported because they are thought to be formed from natural causes. In fact, a newly identified species of bee (*Anthophora pueblo*) drills holes into sandstone surfaces for a protective home (Orr et al. 2016). The holes made by these bees differ from the Robert's holes as they often have interior passageways or tunnels that interconnect the drill holes. Tool grooves that are invariably found with holes like those at the Robert's site and other regional sites are not associated with the holes made by *Anthophora pueblo* bees.[2]

There are insects living in the holes at the Robert's Indian Cave site. They could be mud daubers that are taking advantage of existing holes, but their identification has not been verified by an entomologist.

The reason the holes were drilled into the rock is uncertain, but they are not an anomaly as they have been reported at other regional sites. A. T. Jackson describes the holes at several sites in Texas. Site #190 in his numbering system is in Loving County along the Pecos River to the south of Carlsbad. Willis tried to relocate this site for comparison purposes, but it has either been destroyed by oil field activity or it is under water in Red Bluff Reservoir, on the Pecos River between Pecos, Texas, and Carlsbad, New Mexico. The site certainly appears from Jackson's photographs and description to have the same features:

> In addition to the petroglyphs, there are many abrading marks and small conical holes probably formed by utilitarian use. Some of the petroglyphs probably started as abrading marks, formed by sharpening bone awls, etc., and later were added to for the purpose of forming definite designs. Apparently others were shaped originally as intentional designs [Jackson 1938:137].

Although Jackson's research is out of date, he examined similar holes at another site where, based on the presence of ceramics, he concluded the holes were likely made in the time frame from A.D. 1300 to A.D. 1600. We agree, although the ceramics and radiocarbon ages of A.D. 880 to 1030 suggest the age may be somewhat recent for the Robert's site.

This age means that bows and arrows were part of the cultural assemblage and it seems possible that the holes were used for manufacturing arrows. Arrows in the Jornada region are found as two basic types—solid shaft or compound shaft. Solid shaft arrows are commonly made from greasewood, chokecherry, willow, and rose stems. The main shafts of compound arrows are made from these same woods with common reed grass (*Phragmites* sp.) connected at either the proximal or distal end (Figure 9).

Many arrows did not have stone tips but were instead sharpened wooden tips that were sometimes fire hardened (Waguespack et al. 2009). The drill holes may have functioned as a place to work on wooden arrow tips, perhaps to make them into bunts, or the holes represent work on the end of an arrow to reduce it to a smaller diameter to fit into the reed portion of a compound arrow.

Cornelius Burton Cosgrove (1947), who worked extensively in the Jornada Mogollon region, found 19 complete arrows, 22 reed foreshafts, and more than

Figure 9. Schematic drawing showing a compound arrow. In the example the hardwood foreshaft is fitted into the reed main shaft, but this can reverse with the reed being the foreshaft and the hardwood the main shaft. The drawing is done to show how the hardwood piece needs to be ground down to fit into the reed component. The drawing also shows one kind of decoration that was found on arrows found in regional caves. Terry Moody drawing.

2,000 arrow fragments at sites in the Upper Gila and Hueco areas of New Mexico and Texas. He describes the ends of arrows, seated in reed shafts, as made in three ways, "first, with a straight tapered tang; second, with a slightly concave tapered tang; and third, with a straight tapered tang and with a shoulder which fits against the end of the reed" (Cosgrove 1947:62). These different techniques for attaching the wooden arrow to the reed portion suggest the effort was important and the holes may have been used in arrow making for reasons other than simply sharpening a wooden end (Figure 10).

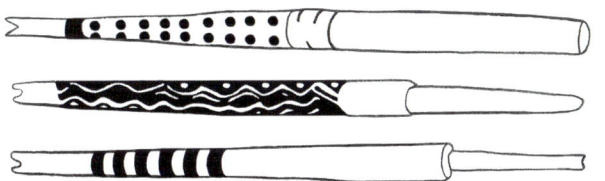

Figure 10. Drawings of arrow shafts from Jornada regional caves. Note the types of preparation to make the inserts for the shafts into reeds and the decoration on the arrows. Terry Moody drawings.

Cosgrove (1947:56) notes that arrows he measured had diameters ranging from ¼ inch (.64 cm) to ⅜ inch (.95 cm). We originally assumed that atlatl foreshafts would have larger diameters but Cosgrove (1947:54) also measured atlatl dart wooden foreshafts and found the butt or proximal ends were 5/16 inch (.79 cm) to ⅜ inch (.96 cm), or not much larger than arrow shafts.

To learn if the Robert's drill holes were of the correct size to be associated with the making of arrows, 105 holes were measured at the site. The diameters ranged from .6 cm to 1.9 cm with a mean size of 1.09 cm and a median of 1.1 cm. The mean size of 1.09 cm is slightly larger than the diameter of arrows and dart ends, as would be expected if the arrows or darts were shaped in the holes.

Because no holes had been measured on the panels with the radiocarbon dated paintings, we returned to the site and measured the diameters of an additional 30 holes on Panel 3 and Panel 5. The holes are the same size, or a bit smaller, than the ones on other panels.

They range from .05 cm to 2.5 cm in diameter with a mean size of 1.07 cm and a median size of 1 cm.[3] While these hole sizes are small, it is important to recognize that many of the drill holes at Robert's Indian Caves could have been used to shape atlatl dart ends, and the Archaic age for the zigzag paintings is within the time frame of the atlatl dart manufacturing period.

We also categorized the holes as having a bowl-shape, funnel-shape, cone-shape, or straight sided-shape. About 68 percent of the holes have bowl-shaped bottoms with another 30 percent that have straight sides and bottoms. A very few have cone- or funnel-shaped sides and bottoms. Their depths measure between .02 cm and 2 cm with median of 1 cm and a mean depth of 1.09 cm. The straight-sided types are slightly deeper, with a mean depth of 1.2 cm, than the bowl-shaped, which have an average depth of .95 cm. It is not clear if this is significant.

Another fact that may be important regarding the use of the holes for arrow or dart making is the location of the sites. All the known sites are found near water where willow, rosewood, and chokecherry bushes are likely to grow. Further, these are areas where *Phragmites*, the cane reed used in compound arrows and atlatl darts, is also found (Whitehead and Flynn 2017:31). We noted *Phragmites* at the Robert's Indian Caves site, where the plants were growing along the wet arroyo bottom adjacent to the cliff with the rock art.

A final consideration is the rock paintings associated with the groove and hole panels. There is a possibility that some of them represent the designs painted on the arrows or atlatl dart shafts (Figure 11). Cosgrove (1947) identified several repetitive patterns that were painted on arrow shafts. Some of them were quite intricate with sawtooth motifs arranged in triangular groups, but more common examples were bands of dots or parallel zigzags. These same patterns occur in the rock paint-

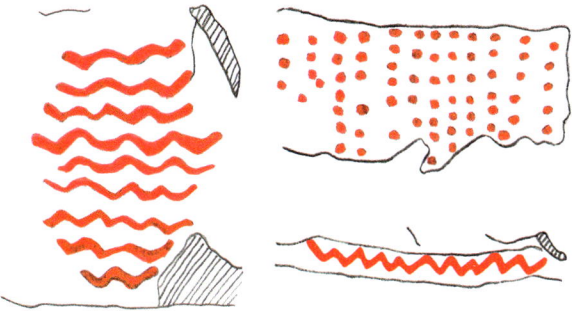

Figure 11. Selected motifs from the Robert's Indian Cave pictographs that resemble the markings on arrows. Terry Moody drawings.

ings on the panels with the tool grooves and drill holes, which leads to the speculation that the paintings are shaft markers for ownership of the arrow or dart.

It is often reported that Indians put ownership or property marks on arrows. A recognized authority on American Indian technology, Otis T. Mason (1894:48), identified the marks on arrows as ribands and noted they are generally around the arrow shaft. He suggests they represent individuals and clan symbols.

Garrick Mallery (1893:441) notes that many decorated arrows are housed at the United States National Museum (Smithsonian Institution) but he thinks they are not useful in trying to understand picture writing: "They are not valuable unless they can be connected with the makers or owners by concurrence of the devices with the signs adopted by persons or by classes, the evidence of which can not now except in rare instances be procured." In other words, the arrows' owners would need to be connected to the arrows to make sense of the designs. The individuals who made the designs is not relevant to discussion of whether the painted images near arrow making holes might represent the same motifs as on the arrows.

With so little research, it is not certain the arrow designs represent ownership marks. Cosgrove (1947:65) suggests the decoration might have been done for ceremonial reasons with painted arrows left in caves as offerings. Arrows carried and left in caves, shot into caves, and shot at rock art images and into rock crevices are practices that occurred among Native groups across the whole western United States.[4] It might make more sense that paintings on the walls at Robert's Indian Caves are ceremonial marks that were left because they were used to decorate arrows for offerings. Whether there is a correlation between the painted designs and arrow designs is a topic for additional research.

Future Research

It is important to recognize there are different kinds of drilled holes in sandstone surfaces and they may have been made for different reasons. Holes on vertical surfaces, identified as cupules, are found at sites across the west (Van Hoek 2007:105). These features, however, are much larger with diameters of 10 cm. The drill holes described in this paper are about 1 cm in diameter and 1 cm in depth. They are made in rows across the rock surface with no apparent patterns. There are sites, however, where holes of many sizes were drilled into rocks as parts of decorative designs.

There are several areas for continued research into drill holes. One is to locate and record more sites. The known sites along the Pecos River in Texas (e.g., Figure 12) need to be systematically recorded with panel drawings of associated painted and incised designs. This might help researchers understand if there is a relationship between painted designs and arrow markings.

Figure 12. Drill holes at site 41CX2 along the Pecos River in Texas.

Another important project would be to measure the diameter of more arrow inserts to learn if they correspond to the size of the drill holes. Arrows have been recovered from several regional sites like Arrow Grotto at Feather Cave, which is located about one hundred kilometers northwest of the Robert's site (Ellis and Hammack 1968). Measurements of atlatl darts from Tularosa Cave in west-central New Mexico could also offer information on diameter size (Martin et al. 1952).

We also hope that by publishing this article we will get some leads to additional sites with drill holes and grooves in other locations across the Desert West. If the hypothesis that the holes are the product of arrow or dart making is correct, they should be found in areas where compound arrows were popular. For example, Malotki and Dissanayake (2018:77) illustrate a site with drilled holes. The caption indicates the site is in Arizona, but there are no other details about the site setting.

After we presented a paper on the Robert's drill holes at the 2019 ARARA conference, Elaine Holmes and Anne McConnell arranged to take Loendorf to a site with drill holes on the Muddy River near Logandale, Nevada. The site, known locally as Punctate Shelter, has not been officially recorded. It is a small sheltered area in a sandstone outcrop with surrounding dense stands of willow, invasive tamarisk, and cottonwoods. The banks of the river support cattails and cane, although the latter are introduced species that have competed with native *Phragmites*.

The site consists of a single panel that is about 7 m to 8 m wide by 1.5 m high. It contains hundreds of holes of varying sizes, some less than .3 cm in diameter and others that are 5 cm or more across. There are also many grooves with some straight and others in circular patterns which have not been found at sites in Texas and New Mexico. An important difference at the Nevada site is some of the holes were made in the grooves. This produces decorative patterns especially in the rounded grooves with equally spaced holes around the circle forms (Figure 13).

The site setting, next to a river with willows and reeds to make arrows, is reminiscent of the Robert's site and the sites on the Pecos River in Texas. But the number of variable size holes at Punctate Shelter and the way they are obviously part of a decorative scheme in some of the figures is quite different from Robert's and other known sites. Punctate Shelter needs to be intensively recorded before reaching any conclusions, but the site may have started as an arrow making area that morphed into a decorative site though time.

More research at other drill hole sites is needed before reaching any definitive conclusions. At this point, though, it seems reasonable to hypothesize that one function of the sites was related to manufacturing arrows and possibly reducing the ends of atlatl darts.

Acknowledgments. We appreciate the support of Martin Stein and the Carlsbad Bureau of Land Management. Myles Miller, Versar, Inc., directed the project; Laurie White and Greg White did the final panel drawings. David Kaiser and Terry Moody assisted with fieldwork (and Terry with report illustrations). Tim Graves completed the overall analysis of the site's features and artifacts. Arden Comanche, James Kutnisis, and Jacob Daukei (Mescalero Apache), and Joel Nicholas (Hopi) consulted on the project. We are fortunate to work with such a great team of people.

Notes

1. The yellow lines that outline and superimpose the red paintings were examined by Karen Steelman and others at the site. The yellow does not represent paint as it appears to be a natural lichen-like fungus on the rock. It has not been analyzed but we suspect it might be living on the organic binder in the paint, which seems to be a reasonable explanation for most of the yellow lines. There are some examples, however, that are across the rock surface, not in association with any paintings. The yellow lines need additional research, but we do not believe they represent yellow paint.

2. An entomologist at New Mexico State University was consulted regarding holes in rock surfaces that are made by bees or other insects. Bees can drill holes in the rock, but they are usually several centimeters deep where cells are cut. There is the possibility that the holes could be from ancient bees and preserved as fossils, but again they would be expected to be deeper in the rock. Perhaps a good way to differentiate bee holes from cultural holes is by their depth.

Figure 13. A portion of Punctate Shelter, Nevada. It appears that some of the holes are arranged in decorative patterns, especially those that are within the grooves.

One fact is abundantly clear: the holes at the Robert's site are not commonly found at regional sites. Over the past decade Sacred Sites Research has intensively recorded more than 50 rock art sites in southern New Mexico and west Texas and visited many more. In addition to the examples presented in this article, we have only found small numbers of drilled holes at two other sites which are on the Pecos River or tributaries to the river.

3. Future research into the size of these holes should develop a method for eliminating holes with surface erosion because a small hole might represent the tapered area near the bottom of the hole and not reflect the true diameter of the original hole.

4. There are multiple ethnographic accounts that describe arrows that were shot at rock art sites. Although less common, there are also examples of arrows shot directly into caves or directly at crevices in the rock. Arrow Rock in Montana, for example, is a site where the practice was so common that the adjacent stream was called Shot Stone River by early fur trappers (Wood and Thiessen 1985:190). In this case Crow Indians shot arrows into the rock to placate the Little People who resided there.

References Cited

Cosgrove, Cornelius Burton
    1947 *Caves of the Upper Gila and Hueco Areas in New Mexico and Texas.* Papers of the Peabody Museum of American Archaeology and Ethnology Volume 24, No. 2. Harvard University, Cambridge.

Ellis, Florence H., and Laurens Hammack
    1968 The Inner Sanctum of Feather Cave, A Mogollon Sun and Earth Shrine Linking Mexico and the Southwest. *American Antiquity* 33(1):25–44.

Feyhl, Kenneth
    1980 Tool Grooves: A Challenge. *Archaeology in Montana* 21(1):10–31.

Jackson, A. T.
    1938 *Picture-Writing of Texas Indians.* Anthropological Publications Volume 2. University of Texas Press, Austin.

MacGregor, James Grierson
    1966 *Peter Fidler: Canada's Forgotten Surveyor, 1769–1822.* McClelland and Stewart, Toronto.

Mallery, Garrick
    1893 Picture-writing of the American Indians. Tenth Annual Report of the Bureau of Ethnology 1888–'89, pp. 1–822. Smithsonian Institution, Washington, D.C. Facsimile reprint 1972 (in two volumes), Dover Publications, New York.

Malotki, Ekkehart, and Ellen Dissanayake
    2018 *Early Rock Art of the American West: The Geometric Enigma.* University of Washington Press, Seattle.

Martin, Paul S., John B. Rinaldo, Elaine Bluhm, Hugh C. Cutler, and Roger Grange, Jr.
    1952 *Mogollon Cultural Continuity and Change: The Stratigraphic Analysis of Tularosa and Cordova Caves.* Fieldiana: Anthropology, Volume 40. Chicago Natural History Museum, Chicago.

Mason, Otis T.
    1894 *North American Bows, Arrows and Quivers.* Annual Report of the Smithsonian Institution for 1893, pp. 631–679. Smithsonian Institution, Washington, D.C.

McGlone, Bill, Ted Barker, and Phil Leonard
    1994 *Petroglyphs of Southeast Colorado and the Oklahoma Panhandle.* Mithras, Inc., Kamas, Utah.

Miller, Myles R., Lawrence L. Loendorf, Tim B. Graves, and Mark Willis, with a contribution by Karen Steelman
    2019 *Landscapes of Stone and Paint: Documentation and Analysis of 21 Rock Art Sites in Southeastern New Mexico.* Report prepared for Bureau of Land Management, Carlsbad Field Office, Permian Basin Programmatic Agreement, BPA Project No. 6. Versar Cultural Resources Report No. 863(a)EP, NMCRIS No. 139465. Versar, Inc., El Paso, Texas.

Munsell
    n.d. What is "Munsell Color." In *Is There a List of Munsell Colors by Name?* FAQ, Munsell.com. Electronic document, https://munsell.com/faqs/list-of-colors-by-notation-name/, accessed January 24, 2020.

Orr, Michael C., Terry Griswold, James P. Pitts, and Frank D. Parker
    2016 A New Bee Species That Excavates Sandstone Nests. *Current Biology* 26:R779–R793. Electronic document, https://www.cell.com/current-biology/fulltext/S0960-9822(16)30902-2, accessed July 31, 2019.

Riches Applegarth, Susan M.
    1976 *Prehistoric Utilization of the Environment of the Eastern Slopes of the Guadalupe Mountains, Southeastern New Mexico.* Ph.D. Dissertation, University of Wisconsin-Madison.

Van Hoek, Maarten
    2007 Atypical cupules at Two Rock Art Sites in Southeastern Utah. In *American Indian Rock Art Volume 33,* edited by Don D. Christensen and Peggy Whitehead, pp. 105–122. American Rock Art Research Association, Phoenix, Arizona.

Waguespack, Nicole, Todd Surovell, Allen Denoyer, Alice Dallow, Adam Savage, Jamie Hyneman, and Dan Tapster
    2009 Making a Point: Wood- *versus* Stone-tipped Projectiles. *Antiquity* 83:786–800.

Whitehead, William, and Conor Flynn
    2017 *Plant Utilization in Southeastern New Mexico: Botany, Ethnobotany and Archaeology.* Report prepared for Bureau of Land Management–Carlsbad Field Office. SWCA Environmental Consultants, Phoenix.

Wood, W. Raymond, and Thomas D. Thiessen
    1985 *Early Fur Trade on the Northern Plains: Canadian Traders among the Mandan and Hidatsa Indians, 1738–1818.* University of Oklahoma Press, Norman.

"Your Guess is as Good as Any":
Rock Art, Public Interpretation, and Ownership

Richard A. Rogers

Interpretive signs at rock art sites, pamphlets available at trailheads, and displays in visitor centers and museums have substantial potential to shape people's understandings of rock art and indigenous peoples. The U.S. rock art literature, however, offers little in the way of systematic analysis or guidelines for "best practices" in the public interpretation of rock art. Interpretive materials are developed and operate amidst multiple and at times competing exigencies and constraints, including educational, institutional, ethical, political, cultural, and epistemological factors. The public wants to know, above all, what it means. However, sometimes that knowledge does not exist, sometimes the public dissemination of that knowledge is constrained, sometimes meanings may be fundamentally contested, and sometimes "meaning" is not the only or most relevant information to share. The public interpretation of rock art involves issues of representation, ownership, and authority that complicate any simple sense of interpretation as "Here's what we know. How can we best communicate that to the public?" Insofar as the public interpretation of rock art contributes to common understandings of indigenous peoples past and present, it is unavoidably political and ethical. The tensions involved in developing interpretive materials are shaped by available knowledge about rock art, the role of affiliated indigenous communities, ownership claims, institutional and regulatory practices, and the informational desires of visitors. By examining examples of public interpretation, common problems and some central tensions are identified, hopefully serving as a foundation for future discussions of "best" and "worst" practices in the public interpretation of rock art.

Interpretation is, of course, a central issue in rock art studies: shamanism versus sympathetic magic versus archaeoastronomy versus territorial markers versus—the list is long. But this paper is not about the different interpretive models and hypotheses proposed and debated at conferences like ARARA, in the pages of *American Indian Rock Art*, and in anthropological and archaeological journals. Instead my focus is one that is rarely seen in print, and even less frequently discussed in any substantial depth: the interpretive materials made available to the public, taking the form of interpretive signs at rock art sites, pamphlets, kiosks, displays at nearby museums or interpretive centers, and the scripts of tour guides. My focus is not which interpretations of the meaning and function of indigenous marks on rock are correct—that is, the common focus of much rock art scholarship—but instead on how marks on rock are interpreted for those members of the general public who visit a rock art site or an interpretive center with a substantive focus on petroglyphs and/or pictographs.

The Importance of Public Interpretation

The interpretation of rock art may be a primary concern and a central point of debate for members of the rock art community, but the place where the rubber meets the road—or perhaps I should say where the hammerstone or the yucca brush meets the rock surface—is in the public interpretation of rock art, a question that is less in the realm of traditional archaeology and

Richard A. Rogers
Professor of Communication,
Northern Arizona University
Flagstaff, Arizona

anthropology and more in the province of Cultural Resource Management (CRM) or, as I prefer to call it along with many outside of the U.S., Cultural Heritage Management (CHM).

The U.S. rock art literature is appropriately occupied by many works of relevance to CHM, addressing topics such as preservation: natural and human threats to rock art sites, including topics ranging from lichen to graffiti removal, from rock climbing and spelunking to New Age shrines and rituals (e.g., ARARA 1995; Childress 2004; Dandridge and Meen 2003; King 2002). Site recording, significance assessments, and site monitoring programs such as the Arizona Site Stewards fall within CHM, as do decisions related to publicizing site locations and the development of sites (e.g., trails, parking lots, and barriers). And, of course, decisions relating to site development include interpretation: whether to provide interpretive materials of some kind and, if so, what those interpretive materials should say.

Debates within the rock art community about how to interpret rock art are important, but articles in academic journals and *American Indian Rock Art* are not the primary means by which most people's understandings of rock art are formed. This is critical because people's understanding of rock art is implicated, quite directly, in how they view the cultures who made the rock art, their relationship to those cultures, and their relationship to the rock art. Setting aside whatever relevant concepts, stereotypes, and ideologies are residing in a visitor's mind before they arrive at a site, I argue that it is the pamphlet available at a trailhead, the sign or signs at the site itself, or the display at a museum or visitors' center that has the most potential to shape people's—*many* people's—understanding of rock art, of its producers, and of visitors' relationship with both the rock art and its producers.

Public Interpretation in the U.S. Rock Art Literature

Based on a survey of the table of contents, not a single article in *American Indian Rock Art* has focused on how rock art is or should be interpreted to the public, and this is typical of the broader U.S. rock art literature. With relatively few exceptions, U.S. rock art researchers have not published works focused on questions such as the following: How is rock art being interpreted for the public? What are the constraints present in efforts to interpret rock art for the public? What are the criteria or guidelines for how rock art should be interpreted for the public? What are "best" and "worst" practices in the public interpretation of rock art? There is very little on public interpretation in the U.S. rock art literature at least, but this is a key form of discourse by which the insights of rock art scholars and consultants can shape the larger (and largely non-Native) public's understanding of rock art, the indigenous cultures that produced it, and the living Native peoples whose cultural heritage it is a part of.

Critically, when interpretive materials at rock art sites and educational efforts in schools are addressed in the literature, these discussions are often singularly focused: Information and education are not an end in themselves, but are only a means to another end—the reduction of vandalism and unintentional damage at rock art sites.

In 1992, Sanger issued a plea in *American Indian Rock Art* (and presumably at that year's ARARA conference) for a focus on public education by members of the rock art community generally and ARARA specifically, but that call was based solely on the role of education in reducing vandalism. Reducing vandalism is a laudable goal, but as I hope to make clear, there are many other issues with educational and interpretive materials other than their potential to reduce vandalism and unintentional damage.

In Whitley's (2011:187–188) chapter on management and conservation in *Introduction to Rock Art Research*, for example, there are two relevant paragraphs. The first, echoing Sanger (1992), is solely focused on the need to educate people in order to reduce vandalism and unintentional damage. The second points to guide books that already provide good information. There is nothing about content or the complex issues involved in how to develop the content of interpretive materials.

Loubser's (2001:100) chapter on management planning in the *Handbook of Rock Art Research* similarly posits that vandalism and unintentional damage by visitors are caused by "a lack of knowledge about the range of significance values represented by such places." Interpretation and education are instrumental actions to address conservation issues: "The goal of interpretation should be to surprise visitors with new information and so positively change their attitudes and behaviors" (Loubser 2001:103). Guidelines for the content of interpretive materials are typically thin: Interpretation ought to be "balanced" versus "one sided" and grounded in "thorough research" (Loubser 2001:103–104).

Lee's (1991) *Rock Art and Cultural Resource Management* does address interpretive materials such as signs, pamphlets, and kiosks. While much of Lee's discussion is focused on practical concerns like the fading of outdoor signs and their cost, the discussion includes about five pages on the suggested content of interpretive materials. However, the guidelines are very general and, frankly, out of date in terms of (1) the implications of NAGPRA and the role of affiliated indigenous communities in managing rock art sites, and (2) critical approaches to CHM.

Sundstrom and Hays-Gilpin's (2011) chapter "Rock Art as Cultural Resource" addresses interpretation in detail and with nuance to its complexities, but with more focus on interpretive research as opposed to pubic interpretation. Unlike previous work, they make reference to the need to "rein in" the "spurious and fantastic interpretations" that images on rock generate (Sundstrom and Hays-Gilpin 2011:352). In terms of the content of interpretive programming, they echo previous writers in linking the reduction of vandalism to "interpretive materials explaining the historic and cultural significance of rock art" (Sundstrom and Hays-Gilpin 2011:357). Significantly, however, Sundstrom and Hays-Gilpin (2011:357) also emphasize that "such information must be sensitive to the views of descendent and native people who embrace the rock art as their cultural heritage." In highlighting the role of descendant communities, Sundstrom and Hays-Gilpin's (2011) discussion of the management of rock art sites points toward a critical approach to cultural heritage management.

Critical Approaches to Cultural Heritage Management

Despite its characterization as "simply the technical processes concerned with the management and use of material culture perceived by sectors of the community as significant" (Smith 2004:6), a range of analyses demonstrate that CHM is an institutional practice guided by ideologies. In enacting those ideologies, CHM makes them materially consequential. Specifically, scholars have demonstrated not only CHM's relationship to archaeological theory and practice, but its social consequences, political affiliations, and implications in structures of power (e.g., Smith 2004, 2010; Tainter and Bagley 2005; and other essays in Mathers et al. 2005).

CHM reframes how we think about rock art: not archaeologically, with an almost exclusive focus on the past, but critically, with an emphasis on the roles that petroglyphs and pictographs made in the distant past play in the present. As Taçon and Brady (2016:4–5) write in the introduction to their groundbreaking volume on the roles of rock art from the past in the present-day,

> For all the attention devoted to interrogating the past function and symbolism of rock art, a major challenge facing researchers today is how to approach and engage with rock art as a contemporary phenomenon.... More specifically, how can researchers develop a greater awareness and understanding of the present-day significance, meaning, and relevance of rock art to both indigenous and non-indigenous communities?

The interpretation of rock art in the context of CHM brings the focus onto the present and onto the relationships between rock art, its (largely non-Native) viewers, and contemporary indigenous communities. Taçon and Brady (2016:5) argue that we need "to shift the focus of rock art discourse from one that is primarily archaeologically driven to one that considers how rock art, as a distinctive symbolic marker surviving in the modern world, is used to negotiate contemporary relationships between people, places, and identity." An example of this approach in a North American context is Norder and Zawadzka's (2016) case studies of managed rock art sites in the midcontinent in both the U.S. and Canada.

In addition to shifting our focus to the contemporary implications of the management and interpretation of rock art, CHM also pushes us to adopt a critical perspective, one that highlights the role of power, especially relations of unequal power. The ways that archaeological sites are valued, managed, conserved, and interpreted are all implicated in systems and structures of power, not only in terms of state authority, but also, and importantly, in terms of the relationships between Native and non-Native communities, control over the heritage of one's own culture, control over the heritage of others' cultures, and control over how cultures are portrayed in public forums. A critical approach to CHM, in other words, highlights the ethical and political dimensions of the management of rock art sites, including interpretation.

The Interpretation of Rock Art for the General Public

Based on the critique of interpretive materials about rock art sites in the Western U.S. developed previously (Rogers 2018), for the purposes of practical application I have identified two initial issues. The first is the primitive and primitivism, which place the rock art in a colonialist frame. The second is the theme of the unknown nature of the meanings of rock art, which leads to the invitation to guess as to its meanings, ultimately alienating indigenous peoples from their cultural heritage and shifting authority and ownership to the visitors and their culture. My purpose here is not to just rehearse existing critiques, but to use those critiques to begin to think about criteria for "best" and "worst" interpretive practices.

The Primitive and Primitivism

Issues related to the category of the *primitive* and the ideology of *primitivism* have been discussed in the rock art literature, but in the U.S. these discussions have been primarily focused around critiques of the shamanic hypothesis (Bury 1999; Kehoe 2002; see also Hays-Gilpin 2004 for broader implications for rock art studies). In the context of South Africa, however, critiques of the pubic presentation of rock art imagery have been grounded in a concern over deployment of the Western view of "primitive" peoples (Dowson 1999; Smith 2016) as well as primitivism (Lewis-Williams 1995). Dowson (1999), for example, points out that hunting scenes are frequently selected for public reproduction, far out of proportion to their occurrence in the overall corpus of South African rock art, reflecting and reinforcing the dominant Western image of the "primitive."

The "primitive" is a category in Western thought that stands in dualistic opposition to "civilized"—the frame in operation here is "the West and the rest" (see, e.g., Dilworth 1996; Hall 1992; Said 1978). "Primitive" connotes both inferiority and opposition to the "civilized": less developed socially and technologically, superstitious rather than scientific, nature-worshipping instead of Christian, immoral or at least amoral, static rather than dynamic, violent, overly emotional, childlike, and so forth. The dualism of "primitive" versus "civilized" is, of course, at the root of colonialism as well as cultural and even racial genocide. In the case of interpretive materials at rock art sites, blatant invocations of a primitive frame for understanding indigenous peoples and their rock art are less common than they once were, although the fact that many interpretive signs have a life cycle measured in decades means that one can still encounter examples, such as a Bureau of Land Management sign at Sand Island along the San Juan River just outside of Bluff, Utah, that I last saw in 2006 (Figure 1). Describing the long cliff face filled with hundreds of petroglyphs, the sign stated, "This primitive bulletin board contains the dreams, ambitions, and fears of people who had no written language." The word

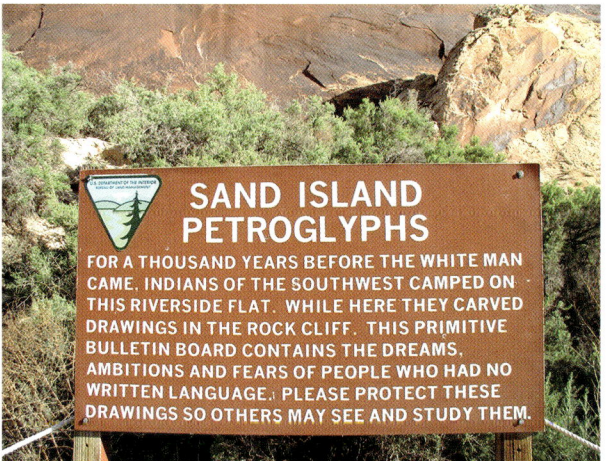

Figure 1. Bureau of Land Management interpretive sign, Sand Island, San Juan River, San Juan County, Utah (last observed in 2006, no longer present in 2018).

"primitive" alone is not what makes this sign problematic. Although this sign did humanize the indigenous inhabitants of Sand Island (they have "dreams, ambitions, and fears"), it defined them in negative terms, by what they lack in comparison to "civilized" peoples ("people who had no written language").

On my last visit to Sand Island, during the 2018 Utah Rock Art Research Association conference, I noted—happily—that this sign has been replaced. The new sign contains more "factual" content and less loaded language, including a basic definition of petroglyphs, their probable age range, and the site's listing on the National Register of Historic Places (Figure 2). It also states that Sand Island "is a place of ancestral importance to Native Americans," which is a more positive way of asserting the site's value than describing it as a

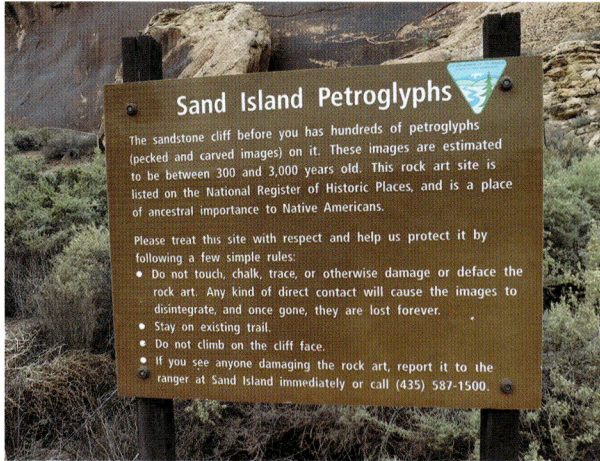

Figure 2. Bureau of Land Management interpretive sign, Sand Island, San Juan River, San Juan County, Utah (last observed in 2018).

"primitive bulletin board" made by "people who had no written language."

While invocations of the *primitive* are increasingly likely to be seen as problematic, *primitivism* is alive and well. Primitivism is not merely a category, but an ideology based on the primitive/civilized dualism. In primitivism, the category of the primitive and its opposition to civilization remain, but the valuations are flipped. Primitivism is an ideology driven by "civilized" people's dissatisfaction with civilization, specifically many contemporary Westerners' unease with industrialization, urbanization, materialism, individualism, the desacralization of the natural world, and the dominance of rationality over spirituality or emotion (Dilworth 1996:4–5; Kadish 2004). In primitivism, "primitive" cultures are idealized as "authentic" in contrast to the "spurious" nature of contemporary Western culture (Dilworth 1996; see also Kadish 2004 and Sapir 1924). These cultures' supposedly "simpler"—and, far more importantly, harmonious, egalitarian, communal, spiritual, sustainable—ways of life are idealized, manifesting a deep nostalgia for a more meaningful existence, a nostalgia placed onto the past and onto "less developed" cultures in the present. This is what Rosaldo (1989:68–88) terms "imperialist nostalgia": a nostalgia created by and for the colonizers, manifesting a longing for the very forms of life they intentionally altered or destroyed. Primitivism, in other words, is not a rejection but a continuation of colonialism, although now it is the *culture* of the colonized, as opposed to the natural resources and cheap labor, that is the resource of interest. Primitivism utilizes a fantasy about the lifeways of indigenous peoples in order to assuage Western anxieties about Western cultures, not to mention the guilt over the colonialist oppressions of the past.

For example, an interpretive sign present in Capitol Reef National Park in 2006 begins by suggesting that "these petroglyphs might have been part of a ceremony to ensure good hunting." Having advanced the hunting magic hypothesis, it then questions that interpretation by saying that "the human shapes seem to be more than everyday hunters." It offers the possibility that "supernatural creatures or a shaman" may have been needed to entice bighorn sheep to return. After making this shift from subsistence to spirituality, the sign concludes, "By etching their imaginations on canyon walls, the Fremonts have communed with the earth, with the spirit world, and with people who came after." This invocation of the widespread trope of Native Americans as both deeply spiritual and spiritually in tune with the natural world clearly articulates the ideology of primitivism, turning the Fremont into a mirror onto which Westerners project their deepest fantasies—fantasies that likely reveal a lot more about contemporary Westerners than the Fremont culture of a thousand years ago. Primitivist interpretations of indigenous rock art are particularly hard to address, in part because primitivism is not as widely recognized as racist and colonialist as the category of the primitive; because it reverses the negative evaluation of indigenous peoples, it is a belief system that is often closely articulated to the identity of being anti-racist and anti-colonialist.

Unknown Meanings and the Invitation to Guess

A somewhat less noticeable issue is present in many rock art sites I have visited across the western U.S. The common pattern unfolds like this: Rock art could mean X, Y, or Z, but we really don't know, so what do you think it means? The most blatant and problematic example of this type of interpretive sign is at Klare Spring along the Titus Canyon Road in Death Valley National Park (Figure 3). I first observed this sign in the late 1990s, and I suspect it might have been erected a decade or more before that. On my last visit in 2017 it was clear the sign had been repositioned after being moved by a flash flood and had been carefully repainted as well. The sign reads, "Indian rock carvings are found throughout the western hemisphere. Indians living today deny any knowledge of their meaning. Are they family symbols, doodlings, or ceremonial markings? Your guess is as good as any. Do not deface—they cannot be replaced."

Several things about this sign are notable. First, the claim that "Indians living today deny any knowledge of

Figure 3. National Park Service interpretive sign, Klare Spring, Death Valley National Park, California (last observed in 2017).

their meaning" is demonstrably false and likely originates from Julian Steward's 1929 *Petroglyphs of California and Adjoining States* (Whitley and Clottes 2005). Second, not only the invitation to guess, but the sign's establishment of anyone's guess as equally authoritative to anyone else's—including rock art scholars, archaeologists, anthropologists, and of course the Native peoples of the region—is astonishing. When confronted with a set of marks on rock whose meaning is uncertain, the move made here is to establish an interpretive democracy, but a democracy founded on the exclusion of one set of voices—indigenous voices, those with, arguably, the strongest claim to the petroglyphs. The sign, in short, represents an authoritative institution usurping an important part of indigenous people's cultural heritage. This type of interpretive statement is quite common at sites across the western U.S. even if it is often less extreme.

The interpretive sign at Newspaper Rock just outside of Canyonlands National Park follows the same basic pattern: "We do not know if the figures represent story telling, doodling, hunting magic, clan symbols, ancient graffiti or something else. Without a true understanding of the petroglyphs, much is left for individual admiration and interpretation" (Figure 4). Similarly, the kiosk sign at Grimes Point (last visited in 2018) highlights the question "What were they saying?" and provides this simple answer: "Nobody knows for sure." Explaining that "the meaning of rock art is still debated by scholars"—Native knowledge is not even mentioned—the sign concludes with another invitation to guess: "What stories do you see etched on the rock?"

Figure 4. Bureau of Land Management interpretive Sign, Newspaper Rock State Historic Monument, San Juan County, Utah (last observed in 2005).

This theme of "we don't know, so what do you think?" seems innocent enough on a couple of levels. First, often "we" really do not know, and so it is in many ways better to present hypotheses with the qualification "but we're not sure." Second, from an educational and interpretation standpoint, these questions and invitations are a way to get visitors actively involved in their experience of rock art rather than just reading an authoritative sign that presents "the facts." But innocence is an all-too-common disguise for colonialist appropriations. The bottom-line effect of these signs is to shift the authority to interpret rock art away from not just archaeologists and anthropologists, but, far more importantly, indigenous peoples themselves. By presenting either direct claims that Native peoples lack relevant knowledge or indirect claims to the same effect by saying "no one knows what it means," interpretive authority is granted to everyone, creating the implication that since no one really "owns" the rock art (knows it meaning), then I (the visitor) "own" it as much as anyone else.

This shift in the ownership of rock art sites is often reinforced by the "site etiquette" signs present at the sites as well. These signs often include statements that rock art and other archaeological resources are part of "our American heritage" that needs to be protected "for the benefit of all Americans." While statements such as "please do your part in preserving our prehistoric heritage" makes the rock art part of the heritage of *all* visitors, one sign even encourages visitors to "help protect your rock art." The intent here may be to frame rock art as "ours" in order to decrease the likelihood of vandalism. However, in the context of these kinds of statements, the invitation to guess functions to perpetuate the idea that Native Americans have no higher of a claim to authority or ownership of rock art than "anyone else." It is "ours," after all.

An important shift in some interpretive signs is the inclusion of explicit statements recognizing not only that the rock art is part of the heritage of Native American communities, but also the importance of the rock art to living Native peoples. An older sign at the registration book outside the Cave Valley site in Zion National Park (last visited in 2006), for example, follows its statement that "Rock art is an irreplaceable part of the cultural heritage of all Americans" with "and many modern American Indian groups greatly value rock art as a means to teach their youth about their culture." A more recent sign at White Tank Mountain Regional Park outside of Phoenix states, "To our present day Na-